SOUTHWEST WISCONSIN LIBRARY SYSTEM
W9-ADG-955

The Cinema of

George Lucas

The Cinema of

George Lucas

Written by

Marcus Hearn

Foreword by

Ron Howard

Harry N. Abrams, Inc., Publishers

$28.75
Jun '05

Library of Congress Cataloging-in-Publication Data

Hearn, Marcus.
The cinema of George Lucas / Marcus Hearn ;
foreword by Ron Howard.
p. cm.
Includes bibliographical references and index.
ISBN 0-8109-4968-7 (alk. paper)
1. Lucas, George, 1944– I. Title.

PN1998.3.L835H43 2005
791.4302'33'092—dc22
2004020411

Published in 2005 by Harry N. Abrams,
Incorporated, New York

Printed and bound in Singapore

Harry N. Abrams, Inc.
100 Fifth Avenue
New York, N.Y. 10011
www.abramsbooks.com

Abrams is a subsidiary of

www.starwars.com

Front End Paper - *On location in 1976 for* Star Wars. *Lucas and crew prepare to shoot a scene on the Lars family homestead. Cameraman Ronnie Taylor has sunglasses on head; director of photography Gilbert Taylor is behind him with hat and sunglasses.*

Back End Paper - *During the Tunisia shoot for* Star Wars, *Lucas speaks with two stormtroopers.*

Contents

Foreword

In 1972, word was out that George Lucas was casting for a "musical." I'd heard about George's exploits even then—particularly the award-winning short he'd made while at USC. I was about to major in film at USC, too, and like every high-school graduate, I had the summer off. Consequently, with some trepidation, I decided to audition for George's low-budget song-and-dance movie—which the public would soon come to know as *American Graffiti.*

During the interview, George and I talked for a few minutes, and then I had to be honest: "George, I have to admit one thing," I said. "I know I was in *The Music Man*, but I think they cast me because I couldn't sing—because I really can't. And I certainly can't dance. In fact, I can just barely carry a tune."

"Oh, don't worry about it," George said.

"Yeah, but I heard it was a musical."

"Yeah, but you wouldn't have to sing."

"Does anyone sing?"

"Well, no one really sings. But it is a musical," he explained.

And that was it. Eventually, I was cast as Steve; but during preproduction, I didn't bring it up again, because I'd read the script and it didn't say much about the music. After I'd gotten to know George a little better during filming, I asked him, "What was all that about calling this a 'musical'?"

"Well, it is a musical," he said. "The rock-n-roll songs from that era are going to help tell the story the way songs do in musicals."

I still didn't entirely get it, though I finally did, later, while watching *Graffiti* in a theater. Each scene was made lyrical and amplified by great melodies from the Beach Boys, Buddy Holly, Chuck Berry, and others. The audience just went nuts.

This was my introduction to how George often thinks "outside the box." Throughout our friendship, I've often marveled at how George applies to his projects a kind of hyper common sense, which for him is self-evident but which for others is often obscure. The concept of *Star Wars* confused studios when he first tried to explain it to them. But the same mind that defined *Graffiti* as a "musical" took traditional genres, along with an outside-the-box attitude toward history and mythology, and then truly energized them through film.

This sort of approach also makes George a really interesting problem solver. How many people think the solution to gaining quality control, improving fiscal responsibility, and stimulating technological innovation is to start their own special-effects company? But that's what he did—and it was exciting to visit Industrial Light & Magic in its infancy, to see the motion-control camera or get a quick lesson on the latest breakthroughs. In fact, while I was there during postproduction on *Cocoon*, George first spoke to me about my directing *Willow.* We began discussing the possibilities, George explained his ideas, and I accepted the assignment.

Willow's screenwriter, Bob Dolman, was the next to be pleasantly surprised by the quality of George's mind. As he and I would drive home after story conferences at Skywalker Ranch, we'd talk about George's uncanny ability to create interesting story solutions. Indeed, by the time postproduction on *Willow* wrapped, I felt I'd completed my doctoral work in movies, particularly in the areas of visual effects, intuition, and the type of storytelling rhythms that go beyond good actors executing well-written material. One key lesson came as we watched the whole movie cut together for the first time. George would choose a moment and say, "For this kind of story, we need to visually open things up here, so let's go back and do some matte paintings and pick-up shots to give it some scope and scale." By causing the film to drop back from time to time, George ultimately enabled audiences to experience fully the movie's fantasy world. It was the kind of visual sensitivity that silent filmmakers understood.

During the years after *Willow*, I was always prodding George to return to directing. Then there came a time when he would call me and say something like, "With digital effects, I can finally do the next installment of *Star Wars* and come a lot closer to my ambitions than ever before—interested in directing it?"

"You direct it, George. You do it," I'd always respond.

Of course, he eventually took on the assignment. Ten years of nonstop directing—and there are things he doesn't like about that job: the expeditionary aspect, communication glitches, location work, the physicality. All of that is fun for me; not so much fun for George. He's happiest conceptualizing and editing. Nevertheless, George is a total filmmaker, and he's still pushing the cinematic envelope. Digital filmmaking is a perfectly logical step—for George—and I think everyone else will soon embrace that logic.

I've known George for so long and we talk all the time, so I've come to understand that his many innovations and endeavors are all borne out of a personal sense of what's right and what's wrong, both in the film industry and the world. When people ask me what George Lucas is like, I say he is truly the most honorable person I've ever met; his word is his bond. That's been my experience. Ultimately, George's pioneering spirit comes from a very developed sense of integrity, which also makes him a great friend—the kind of friend everyone hopes for in a lifetime.

Ron Howard

Hollywood, California, 2004

Opposite - *Director George Lucas (right) and actor Ron Howard (Steve) discuss a scene during one of the many night shoots on* American Graffiti *(1973). Charles Martin Smith (Terry) is on the far right.*

USC

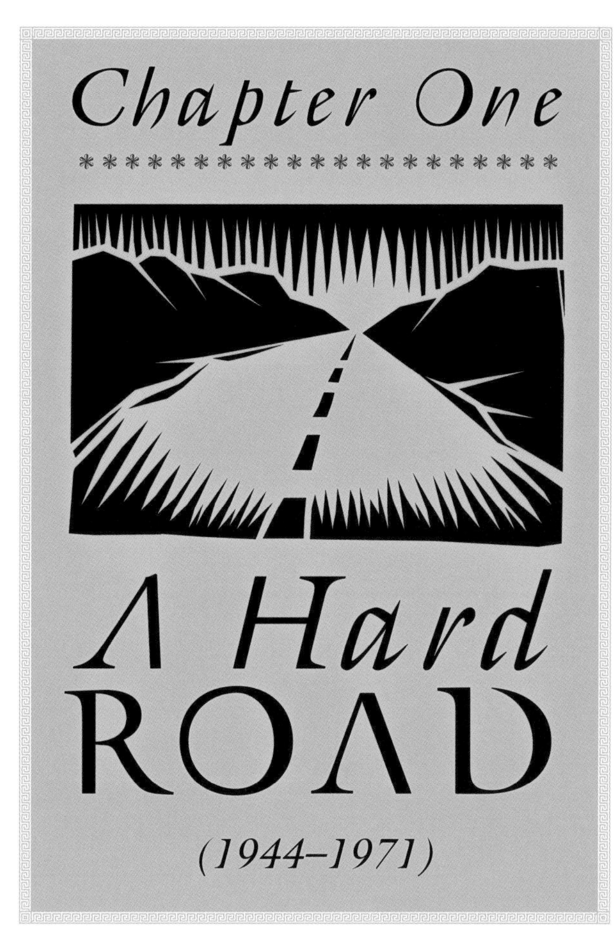
Chapter One
A Hard
ROAD
(1944–1971)

odesto is a quiet city that lies at the northern end of the San Joaquin Valley in California. The area's rich and fertile soil has formed the basis of a thriving farming and fruit-growing community, which includes the nearby Gallo winery.

The centerpiece of the town is a twenty-five-foot-high arch that spans 9th and I Streets. The arch was constructed in 1912 and bears the slogan: "Modesto: Water, Wealth, Contentment, Health." In keeping with the town's name, which is Spanish for "modesty," there are few other landmarks of note. One of the most recent, however, is a bronze statue in the "five points" area, where

Downey, 17th Street, McHenry Avenue, J Street, and Needham Avenue meet. The statue shows two teenagers from the early 1960s in relaxed pose. The girl is sitting on the hood of a '57 Chevy, and the boy is leaning against its side. The scene celebrates the cruising culture beloved of teenagers of the era, and more specifically honors the work of a local man whose fictionalized account of Modesto cruising earned international acclaim. A nearby plaque outlines the achievements of Modesto's most famous son—filmmaker George Lucas, whose 1973 movie, *American Graffiti*, was inspired by his memories of his hometown.

George Walton Lucas Jr. was born on May 14, 1944, the son of Dorothy and George Sr. In the 1940s, Modesto had a population of less than 20,000 and had preserved its secluded, small-town feel. Lucas's father owned the L. M. Morris stationery store on I Street, and his son would make deliveries for him after school. George had three sisters—two older, one younger—and his father confidently expected him to inherit the business.

The Lucas family lived on Ramona Avenue, and George has fond memories of close-knit communities, tree-lined suburban streets, and neighborhood schools. "I had a lot of friends on my block," he recalls. "I put on a lot of carnivals, built a lot of soapbox racers, built forts and funhouses, and put on circuses. It was very old-fashioned." There was little to spoil Lucas's childhood, except the drudgery of school and the ill health of his mother. Dorothy spent frequent and protracted spells in the hospital, leaving her husband most of the responsibility for their family. George Sr. was firm but fair with his children, doing his best to instill in them the conservative work ethic that had served him so well.

eorge Jr. had a vivid imagination, and from an early age devoured novels such as *Treasure Island*, *Robinson Crusoe*, and the adventures of Tom Sawyer and Huckleberry Finn. He amassed a collection of comic books and, while not a particularly outstanding student, developed a keen interest in history, studying biographies of General Custer and Thomas Edison.

Perhaps unsurprisingly, Lucas became entranced by radio, creating thrilling pictures in his mind to accompany the melodramatic serials. "I've always been fascinated by the fantasy of radio," he says,

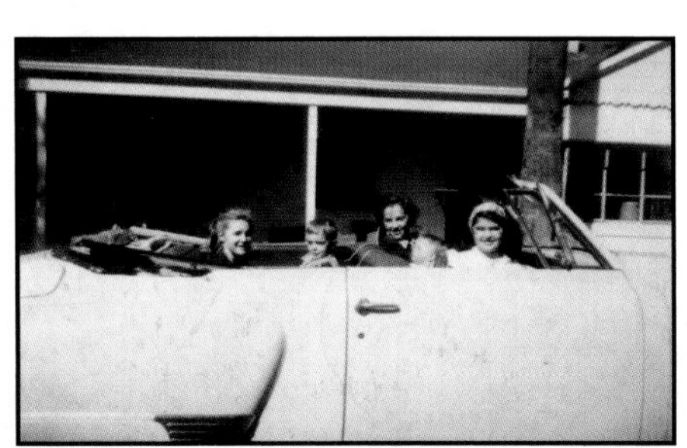

Previous *- Lucas with his friend and early mentor Francis Ford Coppola on the set of* THX 1138 *(1971), American Zoetrope's first feature film.*

Above left *- Lucas with his two sisters and father, George Sr.*

Above right *- Lucas in the yard of his family's Modesto home in 1944.*

Far left *- Lucas with his cat.*

Left *- Lucas, age four, in a car with his sister and other teenagers.*

reflecting on the beginning of a lifelong interest. "I loved to listen and imagine what the images would look like." When Lucas was ten years old, his father bought the family a television set, and there was a new rival for his son's attention. Among Lucas's favorite shows was *Adventure Theater*, which reran the Saturday matinee serials that had been a staple of American cinemas for nearly forty years. The best-known of the serials were those adapted from comic strips. Universal had produced the first, *Tailspin Tommy*, in 1934, and subsequently unleashed *Flash Gordon* in 1936. Flash Gordon starred Olympic freestyle swimming champion Larry "Buster" Crabbe in the title role, alongside Jean Rogers as Dale Arden, Priscilla Lawson as Princess Aura, and scenery-chewing Charles Middleton as the evil Emperor Ming. Buster Crabbe returned to the role in *Flash Gordon's Trip to Mars* (1938) and *Flash Gordon Conquers the Universe* (1940). In 1939, Crabbe took the title role in *Buck Rogers*, another science-fiction serial based on a comic-strip hero. *Buck Rogers* ran to twelve episodes, the last eleven of which would recap the story so far in the form of a brief synopsis that scrolled from the bottom of the screen toward a distant vanishing point.

When Disneyland opened in Anaheim in 1955, the Lucas family headed for Orange County and stayed in the new theme park for a week. The 160-acre site was segregated into such delights as Main Street USA, Adventureland, Fantasyland, Frontierland, and Tomorrowland. The Lucases enjoyed themselves so much that they would make numerous return visits for their annual vacations.

In the late 1950s, George Sr. moved his family from Ramona Avenue to an outlying ranch-style house set on thirteen acres of walnut trees. Lucas had difficulty adjusting to their new home on

Above - *A statue honoring Lucas and his film* American Graffiti *(1973) was erected on Modesto's George Lucas Plaza in 1997.*

Right and far right - *Class photos.*

Middle - *George Lucas at six weeks, with his father, two sisters, and mother, Dorothy.*

Sylvan Road, and his academic career continued to disappoint his parents. "I daydreamed a lot," he remembers. "I was never described as not a bright student. I was always described as somebody who could be doing a lot better than I was doing, not working up to potential. I was so bored."

Since the eighth grade, Lucas had developed a keen interest in woodworking, but adolescence would bring less constructive distractions. "Motorcycles kicked in when I was thirteen or fourteen, on the ranch," he says. "When I was fifteen, cars kicked in. I started hanging out at a garage, doodling with cars and working on engines.

I started driving at fifteen, just around the ranch. But once I was sixteen, I got my license and I could really drive around, out on the streets, and I kind of got lost in cruising from that point on—cars were all consuming to me."

Lucas and his friends drove up and down 10th and 11th Streets from dusk until the early hours of the morning, listening to rock-and-roll and trying to pick up girls. Music became an obsession and homework was rarely a priority. Indeed, as he neared the end of his time at Thomas Downey High School, his borderline grades threatened his chances of graduation.

On Tuesday, June 12, 1962, three days before his graduation, Lucas decided to visit the city library in his Fiat Bianchina. The small car was hardly the hot rod of his dreams, but he had made some special modifications, adding a roll bar and a heavy-duty racer's seat belt. Lucas headed home in the early evening, as the light was beginning to fade. As he made a left turn onto the road leading up to his house, he suddenly became aware of another car behind him. It was his classmate Frank Ferreira, gaining fast in his

Above *- George Lucas in his yellow Fiat Bianchina.*

Far left *- Lucas was a member of the Central Valley Esquire AWOL Racing Club, whose patch he wears on his arm.*

Left *- To customize his Bianchina, Lucas added a roll bar and racing seat belt, fine-tuned its engine, and painted it. With other members of his racing club, he engaged in autocrosses—or closed-circuit races against the clock.*

Chevy Impala. "He was doing eighty or ninety miles an hour, showing off and trying to pass me," says Lucas. "I never saw him. He hit me broadside just as I was turning into our drive. The car turned over seven or eight times and ended up wrapped around one of our own walnut trees."

The Fiat hit the tree with such tremendous force that the tree was wrenched from its roots. Lucas would probably have been killed in the impact were it not for the fact that his seat belt snapped and he was thrown from the car moments before the collision. Ferreira was unhurt, but Lucas was found unconscious, with no trace of a pulse. His lungs were crushed, and he had several broken ribs and bones. He was rushed to Modesto City Hospital, where he spent the next forty-eight hours in a coma and the next two weeks in intensive care. Lucas graduated from high school without leaving his hospital bed.

The long period of convalescence and contemplation had a life-changing effect on the eighteen-year-old Lucas. "I realized that it probably wouldn't be smart for me to be a race driver—especially after this accident," he said in 1981. "Before that first accident, you are very oblivious to the danger because you don't realize how close to the edge you are. But once you've gone over the edge and you realize what's on the other side, it changes your perspective. I was in a club with a lot of guys who were race drivers—one of them went on and drove at Le Mans—and he eventually quit, too, because of the same thing. You see what the future is there, and you realize that you'll probably end up being dead. And I just decided that maybe that wasn't for me. I decided I'd settle down and go to school."

THE MODESTO BEE

McClatchy Newspapers Service

MODESTO, CALIFORNIA, WEDNESDAY, JUNE 13, 1962 PAGE D

Youth Survives Crash

Just what part in saving his life the roll bar, arrow, and a safety belt played is not known but George W. Lucas, Jr., survived this crash yesterday. The highway patrol said the safety belt snapped and Lucas was thrown from the car, which was slammed into the tree by another vehicle in the collision.

Once he had fully recovered, Lucas enrolled in Modesto Junior College to study psychology, anthropology, and philosophy. "For the first time, I was into something I really cared about and my whole grade situation just turned around," he says. "I had thought I was a terrible student, and then suddenly I was a great student."

Lucas never lost his passion for cars, but channelled his enthusiasm toward photographing them rather than racing them. His father had encouraged his interest in photography, buying him a 35mm camera and allowing him to develop his pictures in his own dark room at home, but he saw his son's interest as nothing more than a hobby. When Lucas was eighteen, his father told him that he expected him to one day take over the family business. "I knew immediately that that wasn't what I wanted," says Lucas. "He had built it up for me to take it over, and he was pretty much devastated when I refused to get involved in it. I got really mad at him and told him, 'I'll never work in a job where I have to do the same thing over and over again every day.' And he just didn't want to hear that. He had worked very hard to be able to give this to me, and so for me to refuse it was a big deal. He thought that I would go off and starve to death as some kind of artist, living in a garret."

Above - Front page of local newspaper The Modesto Bee *with a graphic photo of the wreckage of Lucas's car following the accident that almost ended his life. Indeed, because he missed his high-school graduation the next day, for years afterward, former classmates would greet him with the comment, "Oh, I thought you were dead."*

Right - Lucas poses with his Fiat.

For all his protestations, Lucas was unable to tell his father exactly what he did want to do with his life, although he felt sure it would have something to do with cars. Over the following months, Lucas toyed with an old ambition to become an architect, and eventually decided he would pursue a career as an illustrator. His ambition to enroll in Pasadena's Art Center College of Design was stymied, however, when his father refused to pay the tuition fees. He told his son that he was free to get a job and cover the costs himself, but Lucas knew he would never be able to save enough and so quietly dropped the idea. He remained determined not to compromise his future happiness, however, and opted to pursue his favorite academic subject into higher education.

He decided to enroll at San Francisco State University and major in anthropology. Lucas was accepted, but then discovered something that made him reconsider. "My best friend was going down to USC to go to the business school and he wanted me to go and take the test with him. But I said, 'What am I going to do down there?' He said, 'Well, if you go down there, they have a school of cinematography, which is like photography, and I know you like photography.' I thought this seemed close enough to art school, and I really wanted to go to art school. So we drove to Stockton and took the test—the entrance exams. And I applied. I didn't think I'd get in because even though my grades had come up considerably in college, I didn't think they were good enough."

Lucas's father was sufficiently impressed by the University of Southern California's reputation to not raise any objections. For the remainder of the summer of 1964, Lucas continued to work at a local garage, attending races to photograph the cars. It was at one such competition that he met cinematographer Haskell Wexler. "I met George in the race-car pits," says Wexler. "I got to know him through our mutual interest in automobiles. My friend, the mechanic, came up to me and said, 'Is there anything you can do to help? He's bugging the hell out of me!' George wanted to get into USC."

Wexler offered to help Lucas with his application, and the two agreed to stay in touch. A few months later Lucas was accepted, and so the twenty-year-old packed his bags and left Modesto behind, confident that he had finally found a direction in life. At USC, however, his ambitions would change once again.

Above *- Allen Grant and George Lucas in car no. 96. The newspaper caption reads: "Allen Grant waves from the wheel of the racer he will drive in the Pacific Grand Prix this weekend on the Laguna Seca course. With him is George Lucas of Modesto, head of Grant's pit crew."*

Left *- The house that Lucas shared with roommate Randal Kleiser while attending the University of Southern California (USC) in 1966. The car is Lucas's.*

Right *- A 1967 photo of Lucas at USC, on location during the shooting of his student film* THX 1138 4EB.

George Lucas arrived at the University of Southern California as a cinema major, hoping to pursue his interest in art and still photography. As a teenager, his visits to the cinema were usually motivated by the desire to "chase girls and hang out," but there were exceptions. "We had a couple of theaters in Modesto," recalls Lucas. "They'd show *The Blob* and *Lawrence of Arabia* and things like that, but no foreign films came there. Once I started driving, I'd go to San Francisco on the weekends and occasionally see a foreign film or other kinds of films. There was a group called Canyon Cinema, which did avant-garde, underground movies. There were a few little theaters where they'd hang a sheet on a wall and project a 16mm movie onto it. I liked the more avant-garde films, the ones that were more abstract in nature."

Lucas's early experiences at USC would come as a revelation—he soon discovered a passion and aptitude for filmmaking that took him, and those around him, by surprise. "I discovered the school of cinema was really about making movies," Lucas recalls. "I thought this was insane. I didn't know that you could go to college to learn how to make movies. But once I got there, I fell in love with it and just decided this was it for me. It combined my interest in social issues with my interest in art and drawing and photography, and it was a whole new medium that I didn't know anything about. So I really fell into it by accident."

USC's film school was more formally known as the Division of Cinema at the School of Performing Arts. The Division of Cinema was America's first film school, and was already thirty-five years old by the time George Lucas enrolled in the fall of 1964. It would be a mistake, however, to assume that age had conferred any respectability on the establishment. USC was located in Los Angeles, the heart of the American film industry, but few of its graduates had yet to make much of an impression on that industry.

Thanks to a little financial assistance from his father and a letter of recommendation from Haskell Wexler, who was friends with certain faculty members, Lucas studied English, astronomy, and history at USC. His two film classes covered the history of film and animation. "I had to take my film writing classes, but I suffered through them. I had to go into the drama department and do drama and stage work, but I hated getting up and acting. I really wanted to be in a real situation with a camera on my shoulder following the action. That was exciting to me."

Lucas spent his first undergraduate semester living on campus. Film students were an insular, tightly knit group, and Lucas formed close, enduring friendships with many of them. Robert Dalva has fond memories of his years at the university: "USC was a good school, but it needed people. So we all got in. The way USC was organized at the time was that if you had the drive to make a film, then you got to make a film. Of the eighty or so people who took the classes and made the department function, there were eight or ten of us who ended up making movies while we were there. It was an incredible group."

Lucas's other undergraduate and graduate contemporaries included Hal Barwood, Caleb Deschanel, Willard Huyck, Howard Kazanjian, Randal Kleiser, Christopher Lewis, Charles Lippincott, John Milius, Basil Poledouris, and Walter Murch. All of them would go on to become some of the earliest exceptions to the rule that film-school students did not make professional films. "Even though I was going to go into completely abstract filmmaking, I got involved in all kinds of filmmaking," Lucas recalls. "And the great thing about being in that film school was that there were filmmakers that were interested in comic books, there were filmmakers that were interested in [Jean-Luc] Godard, there were filmmakers that were interested in John Ford, and there were filmmakers that were interested in commercials and surfing movies. And we all got along together."

One of the students' greatest inspirations was the renowned Serbian montagist Slavko Vorkapich, who was the dean of the cinema school from 1949 to 1951. Vorkapich's former colleague Sergei Eisenstein had pioneered the art of film editing in the 1920s. Put simply, the montagists aimed to provoke their audiences through the juxtaposition of sometimes unrelated images using a variety of editing techniques.

"Vorkapich's influence was everywhere at the school," remembers Lucas. "We focused a lot on filmic expression, filmic grammar. I was not into storytelling. I was into trying to create emotions through pure cinematic techniques. All the films I made during

Left *- The USC campus as it appeared when Lucas was a student during the mid-1960s. Founded in 1929 by the Academy of Motion Picture Arts and Sciences, the Division of Cinema was based around a Quonset hut on the edge of campus, between the main school and the girls' dormitory. "We would sit on the grass and try to hustle the girls as they went by," remembers Lucas's fellow student John Milius.*

FELLOW ALUMNI

* *

The University of Southern California is justifiably proud of the fact that since 1965, when George Lucas completed his first year of undergraduate studies, only two years have passed in which at least one USC graduate has not been nominated for an Academy Award.

Lucas's contemporaries were a remarkably talented group, many of whom would maintain their close working and personal relationships with him over the subsequent decades. Hal Barwood, Willard Huyck, John Milius, and Matthew Robbins would become screenwriters and directors, while Caleb Deschanel would receive four Academy Award nominations for his cinematography. Walter Murch would coin the term *sound designer*, and win Academy Awards for his sound and film editing. Robert Dalva would become a film editor, working on diverse productions such as *The Black Stallion* (1979) and *Jurassic Park III* (2001).

Howard Kazanjian and Charles Lippincott would work with George Lucas during the 1970s and 1980s, but would both also produce movies outside Lucasfilm. Donald Glut and Christopher Lewis would be active in the field of exploitation cinema, while Basil Poledouris would become a prolific composer of film music, notably scoring John Milius's 1982 movie, *Conan the Barbarian*. Randal Kleiser's career as a director includes *Grease* (1978) and *The Blue Lagoon* (1980), and although he hasn't worked with Lucas since *Freiheit*, in 1965, the two remain friends.

Top - The USC campus.

Above - One of USC's Divison of Cinema editing rooms, where film students competed for time on scarce equipment. The walls were covered with graffiti written by students present and past.

Left - Making a student film on campus.

that time center on conveying emotions through a cinematic experience, not necessarily through the narrative. Throughout my career, I've remained a cinema enthusiast; even though I went on to make films with a more conventional narrative, I've always tried to convey emotions through essentially cinematic experiences."

In 1965, Lucas's clearly defined ambition to be a documentary filmmaker converged with his interest in animation and montage when he created his first student film, *Look at Life.* Lucas's animation tutor Herb Kosower gave him one minute's worth of 16mm black-and-white film, and Lucas did not waste a single frame of it.

Look at Life is a montage of striking images from the pages of *Life* magazine. Tranquil guitar music accompanies an image of what seems to be a young victim of war, peering through a gap in a broken fence. This is a haunting prelude to loud conga rhythms and a rapid-cut barrage of seemingly disparate images. Repeated viewings reveal a clear progression to the piece: following images of violence, politicians, political oppression, and human suffering, the film pauses briefly as the word "LOVE" is spelled out in large letters. We then see objects of affection in various forms. The film ends with three captions: "ANYONE FOR SURVIVAL," followed by "END" and finally "?"

"I didn't know anything about movies before I started film school," says Lucas, "but as soon as I made my first film, I thought, 'Hey, I'm good at this. I know how to do this.' From then on I've never questioned it. Everything I've done since then I've felt very confident about—even when I don't pull it off!" Kosower had instructed his students to make silent films, but Lucas took the initiative of adding sound to *Look at Life.* The film made a big impression on Kosower and won awards at a number of film festivals.

Lucas moved out of the dorms and into a rented house on Portola Drive. He sublet one of the rooms to fellow student Randal Kleiser, and the two have been friends ever since. "George spent most of his time upstairs in his part of the house, at his drawing board," he remembers. Lucas and Kleiser became friendly with fellow student Christopher Lewis, who was the son of actress Loretta Young. "It was exciting for us to meet a real star, and Loretta couldn't have been friendlier," says Kleiser. "Chris, George, and I formed a filmmaking partnership called Sunrise Productions, with offices on Sunset Boulevard."

Sunrise's first and last production was a short film called *Five, Four, Three* (a reference to the last three visible digits at the beginning of film leaders). *Five, Four, Three* was a satire depicting the making of a teen beach movie, *Orgy Beach Party*, the footage for which was shot by Lucas. Kleiser starred as the beach boy who rescued his bikini-clad girlfriend from the clutches of a monster. The soundtrack featured the voices of studio executives commenting on the film.

Above top and above middle *- The beginning and end frames from Lucas's first student film, the fast-paced montage* Look at Life *(1965). "When I finally decided that I was going to be a filmmaker, all my friends thought I was crazy," remembered Lucas in 1974.*

Above bottom *- The "boy" (Randal Kleiser) makes a desperate sprint for freedom across a symbolic no-man's land in* Freibeit *(1965), Lucas's second student film.*

Left *- Lucas, Randal Kleiser, and Nancy Yates on location for* Five, Four, Three *(1965). "As a joke, I made up snappier stage names for George and me," Kleiser recalls, "I was 'Randal Jon' and he was 'Lucas Beaumont.'"*

Lucas's next student film, *Freiheit* (German for "freedom"), would be a broader expression of his technical abilities and a specific political statement. The first half of *Look at Life* had been dominated by images showing the escalating violence that accompanied America's increased occupation of Vietnam in 1965. In *Freiheit*, Lucas would depict a desperate bid for freedom across the no-man's land that had separated East and West Germany since 1961.

Freiheit *begins with a forbidding illustration of an observation post, of the sort that punctuated the area along the Berlin Wall. A young man, wearing white socks, short sleeves, and a tie, tears through forest undergrowth, clearly fearful of his unseen pursuers.*

The sound of twittering birdsong gives way to discordant noise—and then the sound of machine-gun fire—as the young man is cut down within sight of his destination. "Freedom is definitely worth dying for," an interviewee says in a voice-over. "It's the only thing worth dying for."

The final comment is: "Of course freedom's worth dying for. Because without freedom, we're dead."

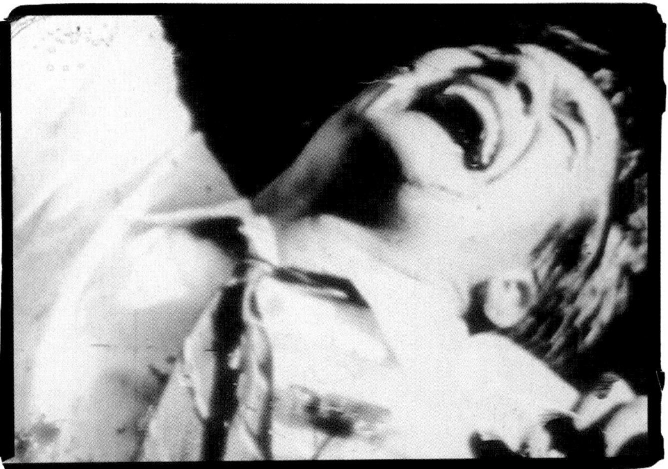

The doomed young student was portrayed by Kleiser, and his briefly glimpsed assailant was played by Lewis. *Freiheit* runs less than three minutes, but its blue-tinted monochrome imagery successfully transports us from sunny Malibu Canyon to Lucas's nightmarish land, despite the fact that he is working with only two actors, an empty field, and a sign planted in the distance.

The passing years may have diminished *Freiheit*'s angry polemic, but the film remains significant as the first expression of a theme that Lucas would go on to explore: the individual's struggle to gain freedom.

Lucas's third student film, *Herbie*, comprised shots of nighttime traffic reflected in the polished bodywork of cars. The end credits read: "These moments of reflection have been brought to you by Paul Golding and George Lucas." The film's title had nothing to do with the Volkswagen Beetle that would be featured three years later in Disney's *The Love Bug* (1969) but rather referred to up-and-coming jazz pianist Herbie Hancock, whose music plays throughout.

Matthew Robbins, who arrived at USC in 1965, remembers: "George had already started his meteoric rise as a superstar film student. I was just amazed by his work; we all were. He could take almost anything and make a movie out of it. And he was very resourceful. He always would find a way to get what he needed in terms of equipment and bodies to put together a crew. He was highly regarded by all the students and a source of puzzlement to much of the faculty."

Lucas's final undergraduate film was his first in 16mm color, and the first that allowed him to indulge his two greatest passions:

Above left - *"Without freedom, we're dead." The "boy" (Kleiser) meets his bullet-ridden demise.*

Above right - *The representative of an oppressive government (Christopher Lewis) and his victim (Kleiser) in the closing moments of* Freiheit.

Right - Herbie *(1966) was Lucas's third student film. It featured reflections in polished chrome and a keen attention to music, two characteristics that would continue in his work.*

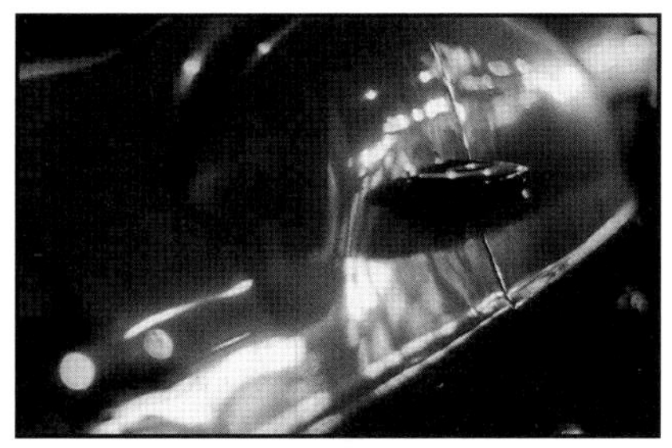

motor racing and documentary filmmaking. "I thought I was going to be a documentary filmmaker," he says. "I came at it from a visual side. The first thing I did was in animation. I started out as a cameraman, and then became fascinated by editing. *Cinéma vérité* was just coming in at that point, and the school was very influenced by the French unit of the Canadian Film Board, so we studied that a lot."

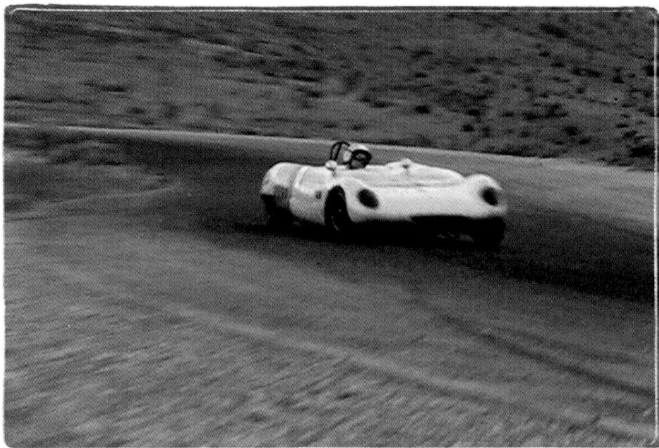

1:42.08 runs just under seven-and-a-half minutes and stars acclaimed racing driver Pete Brock.

We follow the meticulous preparations to test Brock's yellow Lotus-23 racing car on the Willow Springs Raceway in Rosamond, California. The engine splutters to life and Brock begins his circuit. There are rapid cutaways of dashboard instruments, Brock's hand on the gear stick, and the view in the rear-view mirror. Brock loses control, and the engine stalls on a bend. Thanks to some deft film and sound editing by Lucas, Brock's snarl of frustration coincides with the roar of the engine turning over.

Brock resumes his testing, and we see shots filmed from a car that is following him, and point-of-view shots from an on-board camera. At the end of the test an adjudicator's stopwatch is halted with an exaggerated click.

"It's a visual tone poem," says Lucas of *1:42.08*. "They gave us a choice of shooting in color or black-and-white. If we shot it in color, we'd have half the amount of film than if we shot it in black-and-white. They discouraged us from shooting color, because it takes so long to get it developed. We only had ten weeks to make the film, from the point that you start the script to the point where you actually have to have a print. For students, that's quite an achievement. You were supposed to shoot it within three hundred yards of the School of Cinema, but we went about fifty miles out on location."

In the absence of narration or dialogue, the film might seem little more than a highly accomplished technical exercise. But, like *Freiheit* before it, *1:42.08* marks the debut of omnipresent themes in Lucas's work: a fascination about our relationship with machines, and an overriding interest in pure cinema.

By his own admission, Lucas's influences and heroes from this period are too numerous to mention, but of the films released in 1964 he highlights Stanley Kubrick's *Dr. Strangelove* and Richard Lester's *A Hard Day's Night*. In the years before home video, USC afforded what was then a rare opportunity to watch older films. "I loved [Akira] Kurosawa films," says Lucas. "Among the American directors I was interested in were John Ford and William Wyler. Godard and [Federico] Fellini were very big in the States in those days, and they were great influences."

Lecturer Arthur Knight interviewed many celebrity filmmakers at his "Thursday Knight at the Movies" classes, including George Cukor, John Ford, Alfred Hitchcock, David Lean, Sydney Pollack, King Vidor, and Robert Wise. As much as Lucas may have admired many of these directors, their positions of respect within the studio system must have seemed far out of reach. And Lucas's ambitions were not so lofty anyway—he graduated from USC in

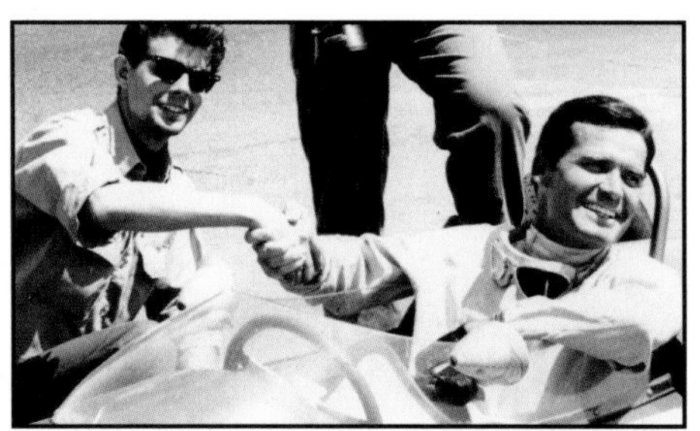

Above left *- A close-up of Peter Brock as his car stalls on a bend in the track.*

Above right *- Brock tests his car at the Willow Springs Raceway in Rosamond, California, in* 1:42.08 *(1966), Lucas's fourth student film—his first in color and his first to feature a fast-moving yellow vehicle.*

Far left *-* 1:42.08 *follows the careful preparations made to test Brock's Lotus 23.*

Left *- While at USC, Lucas is caught on camera with actor James Garner during the training sessions for the latter's 1966 film* Grand Prix.

Opposite *- The first page of Matthew L. Robbins's treatment for what would become Lucas's* THX 1138 4EB, *titled "Breakout" and dated October 4, 1966. "One of the reasons George fell in love with 'THX' was because of the symmetrical nature of the lettering,' says Robbins. 'The letters T, H, and X are all symmetrical."*

August 1966, convinced that if he had any place within the industry it was as a documentary director or cameraman.

After he left USC, Lucas fully expected to be drafted for service in Vietnam, but his Army medical examination revealed that he was suffering from mild diabetes and therefore ineligible. Once he recovered from the shock of the discovery, Lucas took his first step into the world of professional filmmaking when he found employment as a cameraman for Saul Bass. The legendary graphic designer had long been feted for his contributions as a visual consultant to Alfred Hitchcock. By the mid-1960s Bass was working on his own movies. Lucas assisted him on one—*Why Man Creates* (1968), which went on to win an Academy Award for Best Live-Action Short

<u>Breakout</u>

MAN INT.

A man, about 30, in simple, tailored green costume, is running down a long, brightly lit corridor in an unnamed underground city. No other individuals are seen. He comes to a junction, turns, and heads down another empty corridor. Panting, he stops at a flight of stairs leading upward. He glances overhead.

MAN

At the top landing of the stairs is a small TV camera, pointing at the man. Man gradually recedes OUT OF FRAME as camera slowly ZOOMS toward TV camera. Sound of CLICKING computer faintly heard, getting louder as we come in tight on lens of TV camera.

POLICE STATION

ZOOM continues toward TV screen in police station. CLICKING now at full volume. Screen is mounted on a wall, surrounded by computers and other, similar screens. Tape decks and lights are seen everywhere. Four policemen, in dark blue costumes, are watching the screen which shows, as we move in, the image of the man at the foot of the stairs. He is on the verge of panic; as we watch, he turns and runs off in a new direction.

MAN

The man runs through large doorway into new corridor, lined with doors; he suddenly slows down and forces himself to walk slowly past, glancing nervously to right and left. At end of hallway he opens a door and steps into an enclosed stairwell. A spiral stairway leads upward.

TV CAMERA

In one corner of the stairwell, unseen by the man, it points directly at him.

MAN

He is climbing stairs. At top landing he cautiously pushes open another door and steps out into a hallway bathed in red light. Walking as fast as he can, he heads for other end. Suddenly a large number "1" is SUPERIMPOSED over the scene; a second later it clicks to "2", then "3".

POLICE STATION

The four policemen are standing around the screen. CLICKING continues, emanating from computers. One of the policemen, who is seated, glances up at another. He reaches out for a phone, dials a number and leans back.

MAN

He is now on a catwalk in an all-yellow room (shot through yellow filter). Trotting along, he sees another TV camera, but ignores it, running fast and heading for another flight of stairs. Irregular BUZZES are heard.

POLICE STATION #2

A phone rings; a policeman picks up the receiver. A sound, which might be a voice, possibly a language of numbers, is heard. The policeman puts down the phone, turns, and heads for a door.

AKIRA KUROSAWA
∗∗∗∗∗∗∗∗∗∗∗ AND ∗∗∗∗∗∗∗∗∗∗∗
THE HIDDEN FORTRESS

John Milius introduced Lucas to the work of Akira Kurosawa when he urged him to see *Schichinin no samurai* (*Seven Samurai*, 1954) at a USC screening. The film remains Lucas's favorite by the Japanese director, who would become one of the major influences on his outlook and style.

Kurosawa's first film as director, *Sugata Sanshiro* (*Judo Saga*, 1943), was a *jidai-geki* (period drama) that introduced a motif crucial to his subsequent work—the master-disciple relationship. His earliest movies saw him develop trademark elements of his style, such as horizontal optical wipes and fast editing. As well as *jidai-geki*, Kurosawa also won acclaim for his *chambara*, or entertainment, pictures. *Kakushi Toride No San-Akunin* (*The Hidden Fortress*, 1958) would be a combination of both approaches. The lighthearted adventure threw together a distinguished general (Toshiro Mifune), a disenfranchised princess (Misa Uehara), a pair of bickering farmers (Minoru Chiaki and Kamatari Fujiwara), and a cargo of gold bars on a dangerous journey across medieval Japan.

"His visual style is so strong and unique," said Lucas of Kurosawa in 2001. "The graphics, the framing, and the quality of the images goes a long way to telling the story and setting the mood."

A Japanese poster for Akira Kurosawa's *Hidden Fortress* (1958, starring Toshiro Mifune and Misa Uehara), one of Lucas's favorite films and an acknowledged influence on some of his later work.

Subject—and also helped Bass on one of his day jobs, the exhilarating title sequence to John Frankenheimer's *Grand Prix* (1966).

Lucas applied for a job at the Hanna-Barbera animation studio but was turned down. He was eventually hired by editor Verna Fields to help her cut *Journey to the Pacific*, a documentary about President Johnson's tour of Asia she was compiling for the United States Information Agency.

Lucas began developing the ideas he had first explored in *Freiheit*, and he shared his thoughts with Matthew Robbins at a party. "We were in the kitchen just talking about movies," says Robbins. "I think he said he wanted to make a movie about someone escaping from the police, from an all-pervasive Big Brother eye-in-the-sky. I got very excited, and we agreed that I would write it for him."

Robbins worked alongside Walter Murch on a two-page treatment, which was subsequently developed as a short screenplay. The first draft, dated October 4, 1966, was entitled *Breakout*. It begins with an evocative description of a man, approximately thirty years of age, wearing a simple green costume and running down a brightly lit corridor in an unnamed underground city.

On the final page, the man finally escapes the city and emerges from a trap door to the desert surface of an unnamed environment: "As he emerges he is silhouetted against a huge setting sun. Leaving the door open, he runs toward the horizon yelling for joy. The yells echo eerily over a landscape as the man recedes, getting smaller and smaller in frame. A hand reaches out of the underground room, finds the handle on the trap door and slowly closes it."

In January 1967, Lucas returned to USC as a teaching assistant to Gene Petersen, who ran the cinematography class. Petersen's camera department had a contract with the Navy to teach some of its experienced personnel, and certain Air Force representatives, a more relaxed style of filmmaking. "These veteran Navy cameramen had been taught to shoot film by the book," says Lucas. "The Navy wanted to get them to loosen up a bit, so they decided to send them back to school. This class obviously had a lot of film and a lot of cameras because it was sponsored by the Navy. I had to train the Navy guys to shoot using available light, to think about composition, and to try to get them to make a movie in a different way. It was always a struggle to get a film made, to acquire cameras and the film itself. One of the benefits of working with these Navy guys was that I got to make a movie with fifteen minutes of color film, which at the time was a big deal."

As classmate Willard Huyck remembers, "They sent these military guys to join all of us who had shaggy hair and who were protesting and marching. And we would have nothing to do with the

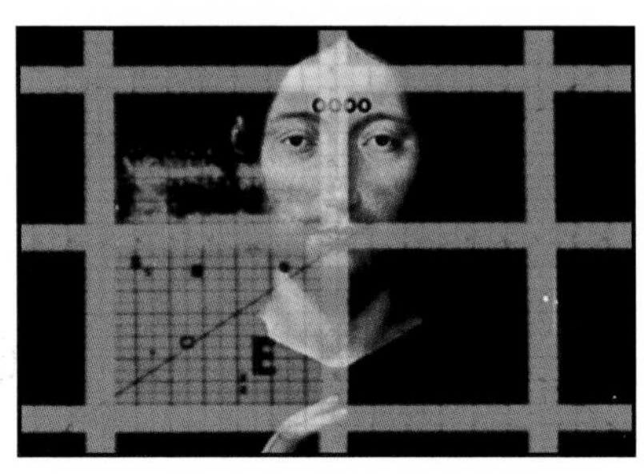

Above right - 8805 orders: "This is authority. You will stop where you are," but THX 1138 (Dan Natchsheim, who also doubled as the film's editor) flees an oppressive subterranean society in THX 1138 4EB *(1967), Lucas's fifth student film.*

Above left - In a startling move, THX manages to obliterate the authority figure who had been trying to prevent his escape.

Far left - Behind the scenes on THX 1138 4EB.

Left - The Christlike deity 0000.

military guys. But George was shrewd. He understood Hollywood immediately the same way. He got to film school, and about two weeks [later], he said, 'Oh, I see how it works.'"

Lucas persuaded Petersen to let him effectively recruit half of the Navy student class as his crew (while the other half worked on their own film), and used *Breakout* as the basis of a script for them to shoot. "I liked the idea of doing something futuristic," says Lucas. "I wanted to do something extremely visual that had no dialogue and no characters—a cross between a theatrical and a nontheatrical experience. Something a little experimental."

Lucas wrote a new screenplay named after the story's persecuted hero: *THX 1138 4EB*. The avant-garde, long-haired postgraduates stood cheek-by-jowl with their highly disciplined Navy crew, and the filming was completed in just three days.

> THX 1138 4EB *is set on May 15, 2187 and begins at 2.53 p.m. A dehumanized society condemns citizen THX 1138 4EB (Don Natchsheim) of the crime designated "sexacte." THX's mate, YYO 7117 (Joy Carmichael), is interrogated, but denies she was ever in love with him. A disembodied voice intones, "I know. I know."*
>
> *THX attempts to escape his punishment, running down seemingly endless corridors in a labyrinthine city. Emotionless personnel monitor multiple images relayed from featureless corridors and walkways. We see a sepia-toned still of the society's deity, a bearded man with "0000" on his forehead.*
>
> *THX enters an elevator, and we hear a shrill electronic sound as he falls to his knees, clutching his ears in agony. As he runs along a huge concrete expanse, an apparently half-cyborg security officer, designated PERFECTBOD 2180, is waiting for him. THX is cornered. He activates a weapon and there is a blinding flash. The security officer falls to the ground.*
>
> *THX jimmies open a door and is bathed in natural light. As he climbs to the surface and runs toward the rising sun, we hear the news being broken to YYO 7117: "I regret to inform you that your mate, THX 1138, destroyed himself at 4.52.39. All possible efforts were made by the authority to prevent this tragedy. I am truly sorry."*

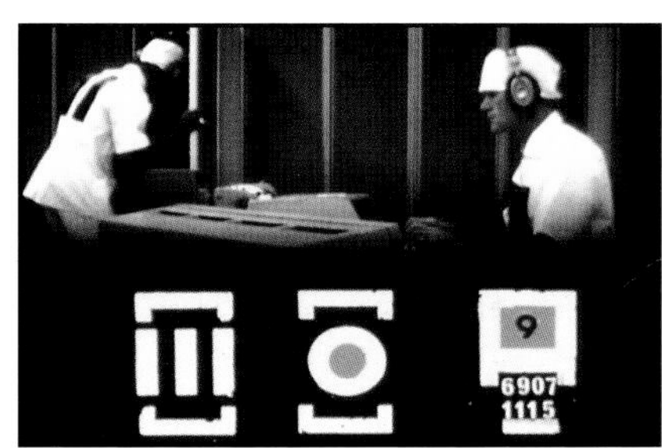

Right *- A frame from* THX 1138 4EB, *exhibiting Lucas's interest in the graphic qualities and possibilities of film.*

Far right *- Lucas supervises filming with some of his class of Navy cameramen.*

THX 1138 4EB is clearly a sophisticated successor to *Freiheit* (albeit with a happy ending). Although markedly superior to any of Lucas's undergraduate work, *THX 1138 4EB* is clearly informed by the *vérité* and montage techniques he came to adopt while at USC, and these help make the film a paradoxically alienating yet compelling experience. The radical sound design, which mixes elements of Bach with air-traffic-control chatter, is as abstract and effective as many of the images on the screen.

Lucas continued to work on the postproduction for *THX* while resuming his academic career. His first postgraduate course project was filmed between February 8 and 20. *anyone lived in a pretty [how] town*, an ambitious fantasy filmed in color and Cinemascope (a 35mm anamorphic process), ran just under six minutes. The screenplay, by Lucas and his *Herbie* collaborator Paul Golding, was nominally based on e. e. cummings's 1940 poem *anyone lived in a pretty how town*.

Like much of cummings's work, *anyone lived in a pretty how town* strives for the same effect as that aimed for by the montagists. In keeping with the experimental nature of the poet's work, Lucas's impressionistic film presents a surreal narrative.

> *In a park, a man awakes beneath a tree. He gets up, smells a flower, and observes a rabbit. Elsewhere, laborers hammer in a factory and a woman works at a sewing machine. A man appears from nowhere with an old-fashioned camera and a tripod. He photographs people who then blink out of existence. He carefully stores his preferred pictures in an album. The ones he doesn't like, he tears up.*
>
> *The man in the park meets a pretty girl and they share a picnic. As they dance in the sun, the photographer appears. He takes a picture of the man, who promptly blinks out of existence. The girl starts crying, and the photographer examines the photograph of the man's shocked expression. He tears it up.*
>
> *Rain begins to fall over the park, and daisies grow from the discarded pieces of the photograph. A small boy smells the flowers and skips away.*

Using the poem as a launching point, Lucas poses a quandary familiar to documentary makers: is it possible to capture accurately the essence of any event on film? Are the subjects of our interest somehow diminished by the process of capturing their likeness?

"On this one, we weren't even allowed to shoot in color," says Lucas. "It was a five-week project, and they said we couldn't possibly do color in five weeks because it took almost a week just to get the dailies back. But we did it anyway, and did it in widescreen, on location, with lots of cast and costumes. We got in trouble, but we were one of the only crews to finish."

Above top - *In* anyone lived in a pretty [how] town *(1967), Lucas's sixth student film, Lance Larson tears up one of the images taken by his camera, hence removing the subject of that image from existence.*

Middle - *Lucas and John Strawbridge on location.*

Left - *A child picks a daisy at the end of* anyone lived in a pretty [how] town.

Less than a month after shooting *anyone lived in a pretty [how] town*, Lucas embarked on an ambitious documentary entitled *The Emperor.* Shot in 16mm black-and-white from March 11 to April 20, the film is an informative, quirky, and poignant examination of a radio disc jockey and his relationship with his audience.

The Emperor is a documentary about a day in the life of Bob Hudson, the breakfast show host at Burbank's Radio KBLA. In 1966, Hudson was enjoying a growing reputation as one of southern California's most successful DJs. Hudson nicknamed himself "Beautiful Bob" and "The Emperor," and interspersed Top 40 tunes with his surreal jingles and sardonic wit. He was middle-aged when Lucas shot *The Emperor* and, one would imagine, old enough to be a father to many of his listeners. The disparity between the young audience's view of Hudson and the reality of his slightly jaded demeanor was clearly a source of interest to Lucas, but *The Emperor* also serves as a valuable—if tongue-in-cheek—document of California youth culture just prior to the Summer of Love.

"The movie is about the relationship between the fantasy of radio and the reality of radio," says Lucas. "People develop this relationship with people on the radio; they think of them as one way and they create a sort of ambiance about themselves. People get very close to the people on the radio except, of course, they're not close at all."

The Emperor *begins with the caption, "Radio is a fantasy...," a quote from Hudson. We see Hudson chauffeured to the radio station in a Rolls-Royce, accompanied by two bodyguards (one of whom is an uncredited Lucas in a goatee, shades, and a military uniform). Once Bob begins DJing, Lucas shows us visual representations of every aspect of the program. The adoring, breathy voices of the jingles are brought to life as voluptuous girls who lip-synch the dialogue. As "Beautiful Bob" spins discs, we hear from fans and detractors on the streets of Los Angeles. "He's out of sight. Psychedelic," says one. "He's a big, fat old man, I think," says another.*

Bob explains radio's appeal to lonely people and is then heard telling a joke. He is about to reveal the punch line when Lucas stops the film and runs the closing credits, which appear eleven minutes into a film that runs almost twenty-five minutes.

Bob makes a rare personal appearance at the end of the film. He claims to dislike meeting the public, preferring his fans to form their own impressions. "My approach to radio is fantasy," he says as he takes off his headphones and vanishes from his seat.

"With the documentary films, I got used to shooting a ton of material and making a movie out of it in the editing room," says Lucas. "It wouldn't be challenging for me to conceptualize something and then have to follow through on it. I'd be bored to death."

Above left and middle *- In his seventh student film, Lucas (right) makes an unusual cameo appearance as a bodyguard to Bob "The Emperor" Hudson, who follows. (Walter Murch is also credited as one of the "performers.")*

Above right *- Hudson plays on the KBLA breakfast show. The film's soundtrack includes extracts from disparate classics such as Love's "Que Vida!" and Donovan's "Season of the Witch."*

Right *- The first frame of* The Emperor *(1967). "The Emperor had a really great quality about it," says Lucas's USC friend Caleb Deschanel of the twenty-four-minute film. "George was the wunderkind of the department because he was always making films that looked like real movies. A lot of the students' movies looked like student movies, but George's movies always had a patina, a finish, that seemed very professional."*

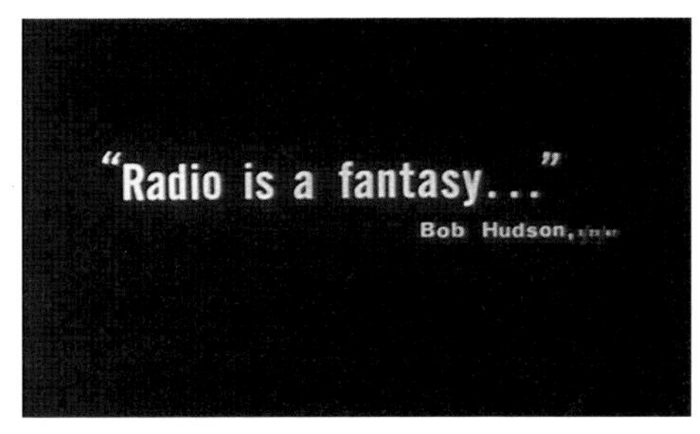
"Radio is a fantasy..."
Bob Hudson,

In spring 1967, Columbia Pictures and producer Carl Foreman approached USC with an offer to sponsor two student films that would examine the production of their forthcoming Western, *Mackenna's Gold*, to be directed by J. Lee Thompson. A similar offer was made to UCLA.

USC nominated Lucas's friends Charles Braverman and Charles Lippincott as student directors, but when Lippincott dropped out, he suggested that Lucas take his place. As filming progressed across Arizona and Utah, Lucas became appalled at what he considered to be the decadent working practices on the production and increasingly uninterested in the process of shooting a big-budget film. After more than three months, he'd had enough. "It takes about a week of watching for you to get bored," he said in 1981. "Watching does not teach you anything."

Perhaps because Lucas felt emotionally distant from the making of *Mackenna's Gold*, his film takes a detached view of its production. He finished filming on June 18, 1967, and gave this date to the title of the largely silent tone poem he compiled from the footage. *6.18.67* is a four-and-a-half-minute film in 16mm color.

> *The film opens as the sun rises over the desert. Grass sways in the breeze, animals graze, and cogs rotate in a huge wind generator. We see an actor on a horse—possibly leading man Gregory Peck—but the image is so distant that it is impossible to tell. As the camera approaches the film crew, sheltered from the sun beneath umbrellas, the word "cut" can be heard in almost a whisper. Time-lapse photography of rolling clouds then heralds a rainbow, fork lightning, and a flash flood.*
>
> *The sun sets, and the cycle of nature continues, oblivious to the activities of the antlike filmmakers in the valley.*

On his return from Arizona, Lucas learned that USC had short-listed him and Walter Murch as potential recipients of the Samuel Warner Memorial Scholarship. The sponsorship offered one student a six-month placement at Warner Bros. studios, working in a department of his or her choice with pay of $80 a week. "It was a big deal," says Lucas. "One student who'd

***Above** - On location in Ogallala, Nebraska, Lucas takes a break from shooting his documentary* filmmaker.

***Left** - Three images from Lucas's elegant tone poem* 6.18.67 *(1967), the documentary he made based on the filming of Carl Foreman's* Mackenna's Gold. *Directed by J. Lee Thompson,* Gold *would not be released until 1969.*

gone into the story department wrote a screenplay and actually sold it."

Lucas nervously waited to hear whether he had been chosen by the selection committee of professors. "Walter and I were sitting in the patio area of the cinema department, waiting to hear which one of us had won the place. Walter was trying get rid of some kittens that his cat had had, so I said to him, 'Look, this is the deal. If I win the scholarship, I'll take a kitten off your hands.' As it turned out I did get the scholarship, so I got the kitten. We were good friends throughout my time at the department, and I was able to help him out later. In those days everybody was helping each other."

Lucas arrived at the Burbank studios of the newly named Warner Bros.-Seven Arts to discover that the once bustling production facility was now virtually deserted. "Jack Warner had just left," remembers Lucas. "Everything was shut down. There was nobody there. The place was completely deserted—it was like a ghost town."

The only film in production was an adaptation of the 1947 Broadway hit *Finian's Rainbow*, a whimsical musical starring an elderly Fred Astaire. Following a short rehearsal period, director Francis Ford Coppola had begun shooting *Finian's Rainbow* on June 26, shortly before Lucas arrived. Lucas was well aware that Coppola was unique among film-school students insofar as he had actually become a full-fledged director. Coppola, who had left UCLA in 1963 to take a position on the writing staff at Seven Arts, had already directed *Dementia 13* (1963).

"They gave me a tour of the studio," recalls Lucas. "They showed me all the departments, and they were all empty. They said, 'We're going to temporarily assign you to this movie *Finian's Rainbow* because it's the only thing we've got right now.' I wasn't really interested for two reasons—I had just finished one scholarship watching *Mackenna's Gold*, and by this time I had pretty much decided I didn't want to go into the theatrical film business anyway. I wanted to be a documentary cameraman, but I was stuck at Warner Bros. watching another film being made."

Lucas was initially unaware that Coppola was also feeling like a fish out of water, albeit for different reasons. "I was about twenty-eight, and very young to direct a Hollywood film," says Coppola. "I was feeling a little engulfed by the studio personnel and what have you. One day I noticed this skinny kid wearing a college sweater. Someone told me he was a student observer from USC. I went over to him and said, 'See anything interesting?' He shook his head and waved his hand, palm down. 'Nope. Not yet.'"

While hovering on the fringes of the set, Lucas also met two former film school students who had found useful roles on the production: Howard Kazanjian, an old friend from USC, who was second assistant director; and Carroll Ballard, a UCLA graduate. Lucas got so bored waiting for something to do that he sloped off to the studio's front office and asked to be reassigned to the animation department—but that had been closed since 1962. "The only person there was the caretaker," recalls Lucas. "The cameras were still there, however, so I figured I'd find some short pieces of film and spend the six months of my work time there making an animated film. Francis found out about this and said, 'What are you doing? Aren't I entertaining enough for you?' I said, 'It's not that, it's just that I've seen them make movies and I'm not that interested. I'd rather go off and make one on my own.' He said, 'Listen, if you stick around here I'll give you a job, but you'll have to come up with one good idea a day.'"

Above - "I don't need Warner Bros." Director Coppola struggles to keep The Rain People *on the road in an off-guard moment from* filmmaker *(1968), Lucas's "making-of" documentary.*

Right - The shooting of The Rain People*'s decisive fight between Jimmy (James Caan) and Gordon (Robert Duvall), as captured in* filmmaker.

As filming of *Finian's Rainbow* progressed, Lucas followed Coppola around with a Polaroid camera, taking snapshots of potential camera angles. "I helped him in any way I could," says Lucas. "We were both young, we both had beards, and everyone else in the crew seemed to be over fifty."

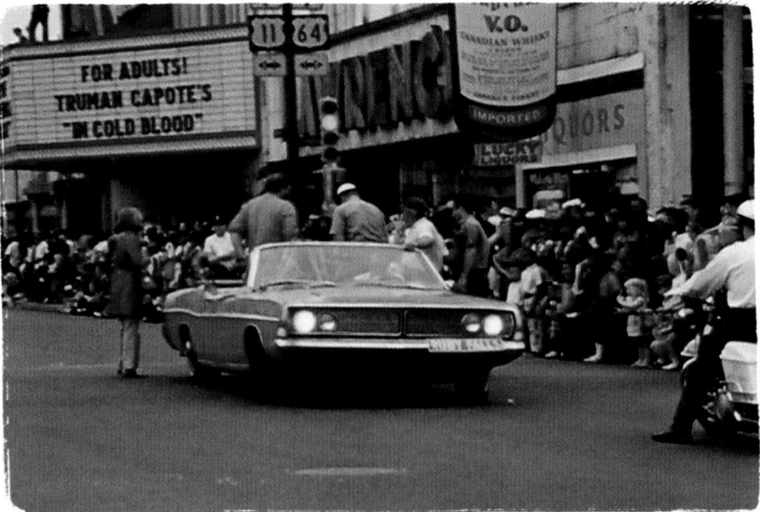

As filming neared its end, Coppola and Lucas had forged a friendship. The director confided in Lucas, sharing his long-cherished ambition to make a road movie based on his short story *Echoes*, for which he had started work on a screenplay. *The Rain People* tells an uncompromising tale of a pregnant woman who deserts her sleeping husband and embarks on an aimless journey with a handsome hitchhiker. Lucas was intrigued. "Francis said, 'I've had it with these big Hollywood movies, I don't want to do this. I've got this plan to do a tiny movie with just a small group of people, a bit like making a student film. I'm going to start in New York, get in a truck and drive across the United States, making a movie as I go. No planning, no nothing—just do it.'"

Coppola asked Lucas to be his assistant on the unfolding adventure, but Lucas was initially reluctant. But Coppola made Lucas an offer he could not refuse—he promised to broker a deal with Warner Bros.-Seven Arts whereby the studio would pay Lucas to write a script for *THX*. That way Lucas could accompany him as his assistant on *The Rain People* and work on *THX* during the journey. Lucas protested that he was not a writer, but Coppola persuaded him that he would never become a good director unless he first made a serious attempt at constructing a screenplay.

By early 1968 Coppola had hustled a $750,000 budget from a wary Warner Bros.-Seven Arts and tailored his script for Shirley Knight. The actress had most recently made an impact in the racial drama *Dutchman* (1966), but her two male costars were less well known. James Caan was cast as footballer Jimmy "Killer" Kilgannon and Robert Duvall played the motorcycle cop, Gordon.

Filming began in March 1968. "George was literally like half of Francis," says Ron Colby, the coproducer of *The Rain People.* "George always wore a white T-shirt, black Levis, and white sneakers. He'd sit around with his hands in his pockets, and he had a beard. Francis had a beard and dressed somewhat similar. There was definitely a joining of the hip there between those two guys. George was very withdrawn, very quiet, very shy. And Francis was quite ebullient and outgoing."

The odyssey from New York to Nebraska was especially grueling for Lucas, who rose at four o'clock every morning to spend two hours working on the script for his *THX* feature before assuming his duties as third assistant director and all-round gofer. In among all this, he somehow found the time to shoot and edit *filmmaker*, a documentary described in its titles as "A diary by George Lucas."

filmmaker *comprises thirteen diary entries, each at a significant stage in the development of* The Rain People. *The first entry is "Los Angeles, September 3, 1968," after shooting is complete. Much like parts of* The Rain People, filmmaker *then goes into flashback to show how its protagonists arrived at this point. At one point, Lucas captures Coppola's persuasive bravado in full flight as he tells someone on the phone, "I feel like I'm on the verge of saying, 'Fellas . . . jump in the lake. I'm gonna make the movie now. Unless you can get the police to come and stop me from shooting . . . because I don't need Warner Bros.'"*

One segment shows Lucas and Coppola clean-shaven. A voice-over from Lucas informs us that once the crew left New

Above *- On the road and behind the scenes during the cross-country shoot of* The Rain People, *Coppola takes advantage of a real-life parade to expand the scope of his film. The marquee advertises Truman Capote's* In Cold Blood *(1967).*

Far left *- Lucas at a symmetrical bifurcation.*

Left *- A clean-shaven Coppola in* filmmaker.

Opposite *- Cast and crew photo of the battle-hardened veterans of* The Rain People*: Lucas (center, standing on truck), Coppola (in dark glasses, holding script); third from left are Robert Duvall, Shirley Knight, and James Caan.*

POLICE

VICTORY ROUNDS

* *

In February 1968, *THX 1138 4EB* was included in a retrospective of USC student films at the Fairfax Theater in Los Angeles. The evening's program comprised films from Lucas's graduating class and included *Marcello I'm So Bored*, an eight-minute piece by John Milius and John Strawbridge. The vibrant satire was scored with the hip sounds of "Taxman" by The Beatles and "Green Onion" by Booker T and the MGs. Lucas had been responsible for the sound editing.

Freiheit was dusted off for the second half of the show, but that film's more sophisticated successor was the star of the evening. In the program notes, *THX 1138 4EB* was portentously described thus: "In the amorphous reality of the non-present, superficial categories dissolve into the all-encompassing world of numbers." The brief description ended with the declaration that *THX* was, "Designed as an exercise in spatial calligraphy."

The two Fairfax evenings were a great success, but another screening of *THX* has assumed a greater historical significance. The film was selected to take part in a festival highlighting the best work by students from USC and UCLA, to be held at the Royce Hall in Los Angeles. A young Steven Spielberg was in the audience.

"I saw a number of really good films," he recalls. "A lot of animation, a lot of stop-motion, some interesting dramas, a few comedies. And then along came this film called *THX 1138*, by a director I'd never heard of. And it absolutely stopped the festival. You could have heard a pin drop in that theater. There was so much virtuosity in the craft, the vision, and the emotion of that story that I couldn't believe it was a student film. I thought some Hollywood genius had slipped something in and that it should be disqualified for its sheer professionalism. I became insanely jealous. Everything I had done before became irrelevant to me."

Spielberg was so impressed by what he saw that at the end of the festival he went backstage, where all the young directors were milling about. Spielberg saw Lucas, who was with Coppola, and took the opportunity to briefly introduce himself.

THX's lengthy lap of honor included winning the drama prize at the 1967–1968 National Student Film Festival in Washington (while *The Emperor* received an honorable mention in the documentary category, and *6.18.67* won an honorable mention in the experimental category).

feb 21·27
FAIRFAX THEATER
Beverly Blvd. at Fairfax Ave.

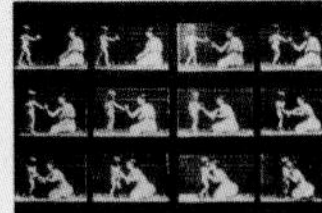

homage to muybridge
2 minutes, black and white.
By: David Hanson.
This film is dedicated to Eadweard Muybridge who devoted his life to studying human and animal locomotion by using still photography.

sensei
13 minutes, color.
By: Matthew Robbins, Walter Murch, Robin Commagere, Basil Poledouris, Fathi Botros.
A graphic examination of the karate Kata emphasizing the development of the spirit through rigorous training.

glut
10 minutes, black and white.
By: Basil Poledouris, John Milius, Randal Kleiser, Chris Lewis, Dorothy Donavan, Fred Rowland.
"Men don't feel grandeur anymore"

baby blue
7 minutes, black and white.
By: Robert Dalva, Robert Steadman, Emmet Alston, Barbara Whitaker, George McQuilkin, Richard Alexander, Don Glut, John Milius.
A young wife, whose husband is fighting in Viet Nam, finds herself in emotional conflict.

marcello - I'm so bored
8 minutes, color, animation.
By: John Milius, John Strawbridge, George Lucas.
An impressionistic happening which tries to mirror the current American social landscape in which a growing lack of sincere human feeling and emotional involvement between people is increasingly evident.

poem of rodia
4 minutes, black and white.
By: Khosrow Haritash, Thomas Maxwell, Richard Rutledge, John Parks, B. Broughton.
Simon Rodia, an Italian immigrant tile mason, devoted his life to the construction of the Towers of Watts which he created out of the discarded junk of four generations.

cycle of entelechy
3½ minutes, color.
By: Jae Carmichael, Robert Dalva, John Bailey, Gary Young, Howard Myrick.
A collage of film and sound utilizing concepts and techniques related to painting in an expression of the conflict between the forces of destruction and those of regeneration.

pulp
By: Bruce Green, Caleb Deschanel, Richard Walter, Dennis Guyitt.
A fast-moving satire on "pulp" magazines and their effect on a leather-jacketed yob, who sees his world from the point of view of their characters.

night shift
7 minutes, color.
By: Matthew Robbins, Caleb Deschanel, Walter Murch, Robin Commagere.
A gas station attendant, at his lonely outpost in the quiet hours of the night, is increasingly unnerved by seemingly sourceless sounds and occurrences.

bird
1 minute, black and white.
Kinestasis.
By: Bruce Green.
Bird, bird, bird.

INTERMISSION

the bug
3 minutes, black and white.
By: David Hanson and Hal Barwood.
This film offers a solution to all of the ills that befall man. (Well . . . almost all)

freiheit
2 minutes, black and white.
By: George Lucas.
A statement about the worth of life and freedom.

dominator
10 minutes, black and white.
By: David Hanson, Jack Graves, Hal Barwood, Dave Pellow.
The relationships between a natural environment, Nature's forces and Man's creations are revealed in this film-poem.

a child's introduction to the cosmos
7 minutes, color, animation.
By: Hal Barwood.
What we believe to be true about the cosmos is not . . . We might just as well forget it, and start from scratch.

down these mean streets
14 minutes, black and white.
By: Willard Huyck, Gary Messenger, Robert Steadman, Jack Craft, Michael Jones, Franz Buerger.
A sentimental satire of life as portrayed in films of the thirties by film-makers of the late sixties.

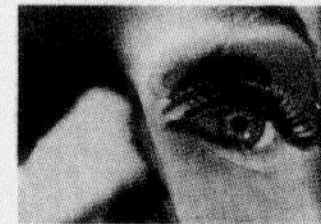

ritual
4 minutes, black and white.
By: Michael Brown.
A visual exploration of the ritual of ocular embellishment and the elaborate paraphenalia involved.

thx - 1138 - 4eb
17 minutes, color.
By: George Lucas, Zip Zimmerman, Charles Johnson, Nelson Harris, Richard Johnson, Dan Nachtsheim, Dan Tueth.
In the amorphous reality of the non-present, superficial categories dissolve into the all-encompassing world of numbers. Designed as an exercise in spatial calligraphy.

wipeout
1 minute, black and white.
By: Paul Golding.
What this film means to you will depend upon your own thoughts and ideas.

Left - Steven Spielberg (in cap) and Lucas, during the shooting of *Jaws* in 1974.

Above - The program from the 1968 student film retrospective at the Fairfax Theater in Los Angeles. Many of Lucas's collaborators, both past and present, are listed, including Walter Murch, Hal Barwood, Matthew Robbins, John Milius, and Caleb Deschanel. Of the films listed, Lucas also receives a credit for *Marcello I'm So Bored*, for which he did the sound editing, and credit for "help" on *Wipeout*.

York, all the men had to cut their hair and shave off any beards in order to present a respectable front to the various towns and cities they were hoping to shoot in.

The documentary ends as Coppola views the first rough cut on October 10, 1968. The credits play over a black-and-white shot of the assembled crew looking like battle-hardened war veterans.

"George was around in a very quiet way," says Ron Colby. "You'd look around and suddenly there'd be George in a corner with his camera. He'd just kind of drift around. But he shot the camera, did his own sound. He was very much a one-man band."

Lucas enjoyed getting back to filmmaking after an absence of nine months, and Coppola enjoyed the experience of making a film away from the Hollywood studio environment. The five weeks of editing and additional shooting that Coppola and Lucas spent in Ogallala, Nebraska, would, in hindsight, take on enormous significance for both men. Coppola had been ruminating on the idea of establishing an independent studio. "We could make movies anywhere in the world," he told Lucas in Nebraska. "We don't have to be in Hollywood."

Coppola had been booked to appear at a convention in San Francisco but suggested to Lucas that he should take his place, primarily because it would give him a chance to meet one of the other attendees, Bay Area filmmaker John Korty. Coppola was aware of Korty's fierce independence and intrigued by his success at running a small but self-sufficient studio at Stinson Beach, a small coastal town north of San Francisco. At the convention, Lucas listened to Korty's stories of how he had recently completed his third independent production—at his own studio. When the panel was over, Lucas immediately called Coppola in Nebraska, urging him to come to San Francisco. Shortly thereafter, Colby accompanied Coppola and Lucas on their visit to Korty Films on July 4.

Heading off Highway 1 and parking their station wagons outside the address they'd been given, in the middle of town, Colby, Coppola, and Lucas approached a large gray barn. "We walked inside, and there was this big open space," remembers Colby. "He had an editing machine and all the toys of a young filmmaker. He seemed like a writer in the country, but with a machine shop at his disposal. It just looked like a wonderful idea. It looked like the perfect way." Coppola was equally impressed, telling Korty, "If you can do it, we can."

Lucas's first draft of *THX 1138*, dated November 1, 1968, is a work in progress that differs from the finished version in a number of intriguing ways. When THX is captured by the authorities, a scientist called DEC tries to rehabilitate him. Acting under the supervision of Robot 999, DEC attempts to discover why THX is not conforming. THX's mate is called LUH now; the name was intended to be suggestive of the word "love," as THX was of "sex." Other new characters included a minor player called SEN and THX's friend SRT, whom he meets in prison. In this version of the story, it is SRT who leads the escape from confinement,

Above - Bay Area filmmaker John Korty in the late 1960s. His Stinson Beach studio served as inspiration for the creation of American Zoetrope.

MADE IN
U.S.A. BY

and THX who follows him. The deity, called 0000 in the student film, has been renamed OMM.

One scene unique to the first draft features a conversation between THX and SRT in which the two men discuss the possible existence of a resilient inner spirit.

THX

I see now that this world we occupy is made of illusion. For a time now I've been struggling to break through the images, just to see. (passionately) If I could see, I could find peace with myself. With LUH I felt something… I'm not sure, but it was something real; an emotion, a feeling, a reality.

SRT

But that is something you can create for yourself.

THX

But there must be something independent; a force, a reality.

SRT

You mean like OMM.

THX

Not OMM as we know him, but the reality behind the illusion of OMM.

SRT

There is a force, OMM if you like, but this force is nothing more than the emotion you felt for LUH. This emotion is what is behind the illusion.

Lucas rented a small house in Marin County's Mill Valley and resumed his efforts to help Coppola establish their new company by looking for business premises in and around the county. Meanwhile, Coppola flew to London with Colby to discuss the British release of *The Rain People.* When their work was finished, Coppola asked Colby if he would like to join him on a visit to Denmark to conduct some research into a small company called Lanterna Films, an independent studio based approximately fifty miles outside Copenhagen.

Left *- Seen against the backdrop of San Francisco in this photo, titled "SHOW" (April 1970), the founders of American Zoetrope, who were tuned into the zeitgeist of many of the more progressive movements of the time. Lucas is in sunglasses and hat; Coppola is holding film can.*

The company's modest output was divided between commercials, soft pornography, and the occasional feature film, all of which originated from a mansion in a tranquil, picturesque setting by a lake. The films were edited and mixed in a nearby barn, which housed Keller and Steenbeck equipment far more advanced and versatile than the Moviolas still being used in America.

This was a European version of the independent filmmaking Coppola had so admired at Korty's studio and an additional inspiration for him to try something similar. Coppola and Colby spent some time inspecting Lanterna's extensive collection of antique projecting devices: lanterns, slides, and examples of nineteenth-century zoetropes. Coppola was happy to accept a gift of a zoetrope as a souvenir of his visit. He next went to the Photokina trade show in Cologne and ordered $80,000 worth of KEM mixing and editing equipment before returning to Los Angeles.

With the equipment on the way from Germany, Coppola's production company needed a home as soon as soon as possible. By May 1969, he had premises at 827 Folsom Street, San Francisco, and a name—American Zoetrope. For Lucas, it was all happening a bit quickly. "Francis came back from Europe and said, 'Guess what, I just bought us a whole mixing studio.' I said, 'Well that's great—now we've got to find somebody to run it!' That's when I called Walter [Murch]. Walter came up and worked in a half-finished room downstairs from where Zoetrope was. . . . Walter worked day and night trying to get *The Rain People* finished in order to present it to Warner Bros. and we finally did it, working in San Francisco, using our own equipment. There were a lot of mechanical breakdowns and a lot of chaos, but it was a lot of fun."

The third floor of a converted warehouse bore little resemblance to the remote country retreats of Korty and Lanterna, but in other respects downtown San Francisco seemed the perfect backdrop to their experiment. From 1966 onward, the city had been the epicenter of American counterculture. A few years later *Rolling Stone* magazine, the subversive manifesto of West Coast psychedelia, moved into offices nearby at 625 Third Street.

"San Francisco was more radical than any other part of the country, which suited us fine, because we wanted that," says Lucas. "I think we felt more secure in that kind of environment because we really wanted to shake up the status quo in terms of the aesthetics of how movies were made and what they were about. We did not want to fall into the corporate reality that was creeping ever more oppressively into the Hollywood mainstream."

Coppola had entrusted Lucas with the role of vice-president of the new company and promised him that *THX 1138* would be its first movie. He had made this promise in the optimistic hope that Warner Bros.-Seven Arts would bankroll the production of the film. However, when Lucas submitted his screenplay in early summer 1969, the studio, under the Eliot Hyman regime, rejected it. Lucas therefore agreed to accompany Coppola to his mountain retreat in southern California for an intensive rewrite. "We sat down and worked on it for two weeks," says Lucas. "My vision was not to do a normal story. I wanted to do something that was abstract, much more like a student film than a [conventional] drama. Obviously, to get it through the studios, it had to be a drama, but by this time *Easy Rider* had come out, so we thought, 'Maybe we can get away with a really wacky, avant-garde film.' I said, 'This is probably the only chance I'll ever get to do something like this,' so Francis finally relented and said, 'Well, you know, I just

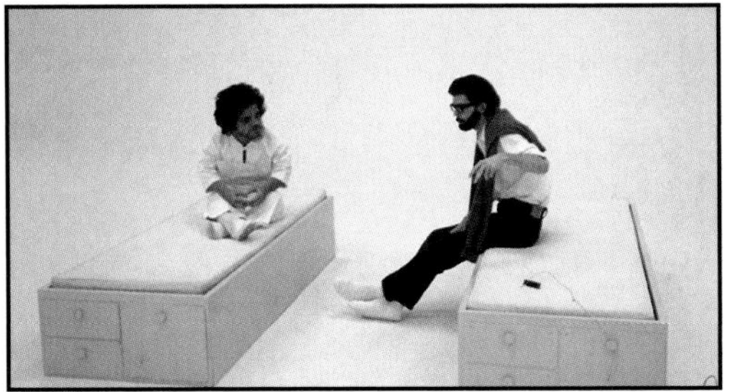

Above - The headquarters of American Zoetrope at 827 Folsom Street, San Francisco, which opened its doors in the summer of 1969.

Far left - Lucas confers with a "shell dweller" (Mark Lawhead) on the "prison" set of his first feature film, THX 1138 *(1971).*

Left - Coppola visiting the set, with Lucas and Don Pedro Colley (SRT) in the background.

Right - An early American Zoetrope brochure vaunts the company's northern California location and its "Executive Staff."

don't understand your vision here, and I've helped you as much as I can on this . . . maybe what we'll do is hire a writer and let him try to do it.'"

At Coppola's behest, the next draft of *THX 1138* was prepared by experienced scriptwriter Oliver Hailey. "I showed him the draft that I had, and the draft that Francis and I had worked on," says Lucas. "He was very talented, but his script wasn't at all what I wanted."

Lucas embarked on a fourth draft with Walter Murch. Their script preserved the stark, almost alienating feel of the original student film. Warner Bros.-Seven Arts rejected this draft as well, but, as Coppola explained to a downhearted Lucas, by this time the opinions of the Hyman regime were academic. In June 1969, the latest slump in cinema attendance prompted Hyman to sell Warner Bros.-Seven Arts to New York-based Kinney National Service Corporation, a company that had previously enjoyed huge success running funeral parlors and parking lots. The head of Kinney, Stephen J. Ross, appointed former talent agent Ted Ashley to run the studio, which soon reverted to its old name, Warner Bros. Coppola told Lucas he would just wait a few weeks, and when the Kinney-appointed executives had moved into their offices, he would submit the script again—without mentioning that it had ever been rejected before.

Lucas was already chairing an open casting call for the film at a San Francisco theater when Coppola interrupted to give him the good news: he had persuaded John Calley, Warner Bros.' new head of production, to back *THX 1138* if it cost less than $1 million. The studio loaned Zoetrope $300,000 to establish its premises and buy equipment, and provided an additional $300,000 toward the script development of *THX* and six other low-budget productions, includ-

American Zoetrope
Corporate and Advertising Film Division

"We're in business to make films. Sure the feature length is our first love. But when you're perched on top of a warehouse full of human energy and talent like we've got here you would have to be crazy not to utilize it for all phases of film production." November 1970

FRANCIS FORD COPPOLA
President—American Zoetrope
Director—"You're A Big Boy Now" Warner Bros. Seven Arts;
"Finian's Rainbow" Warner Bros. Seven Arts.
Producer Director—"The Rain People" Warner Bros. Seven Arts.
Screenplay—"Patton" Twentieth Century Fox
Screenplay and Director—"The Godfather" Paramount

American Zoetrope, a film happening where some of America's best filmmakers have come together . . . situated in San Francisco, the classic film location city, offering the advertising industry and corporate clients a full spectrum of film and video experience. Unquestionably the production and direction of feature films demands the ultimate output from a filmmaker. At Zoetrope we've created an evironment allowing for open expression of film art. We've acquired the best electronic equipment available anywhere. We're equipped to go on location world wide yet are comfortable knowing there's a wealth of varied geography within 200 miles of home. We like what we're into and want to share it with you.

American Zoetrope is an established film production company having produced feature films, TV documentaries, and educational training films and commercials.

Designed to be a self-contained film studio, American Zoetrope has all the facilities required for film production.

The main screening theatre is equipped with both 16 and 35mm interlock projection equipment coupled to KEM dubbers and re-recorders for sound mixing 16, 35, or Super 8 film.

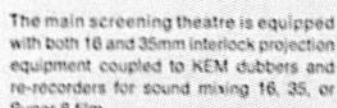

In the same building as the screening room are seven editing rooms equipped with Steenbeck "flat-top" editing machines, and all other necessary tools for editing film. Some of the offices have adjoining sound rooms which can also be treated as recording studios. Another mixing innovation is a video scanner through which film can be run when a projection room set-up is undesirable. American Zoetrope also has production trucks and camera equipment.

The equipment is lightweight and portable designed for mobility and utilizes both the 16 and 35mm Eclair cameras. American Zoetrope is staffed by technicians who are well versed not only in the workings of the equipment but also the specific needs of film producers.

What It's Like Being Within 200 Miles Of Everywhere . . .

A greater diversity of geography, climate, ethnic strains, and architecture exists around the San Francisco Bay Area than anywhere else in the country. Whether you're interested in shooting a television commercial, corporate film, or social environmental piece the location is no more than a day's drive from the studio. Thus considerable economies can be gained by producing within the Bay Area.

A Favorable Union Set-Up

San Francisco unions are cooperative and very enthusiastic. Our contract offers great flexibility resulting in lower film production costs for the client. We work with the I.A.T.S.E., San Francisco, and have the usual contracts with S.A.G. and A.F.T.R.A.

Talent Looks To American Zoetrope

To be cast for a television commercial or corporate film being produced by a feature film company can be magic to an aspiring talent. Consequently we have a select position with the acting profession. Literally hundreds of people stream through the studio weekly. Actors, actresses, some green, others experienced professionals. Plus many filmmakers all in search of an opportunity to come together with people who love what they're doing.

American Zoetrope Executive Staff

GEORGE LUCAS

CHRISTOPHER PEARCE

ROBERT DALVA

GARY SASLAW

BART PATTON

TOM GLASS

EDWARD KESSLER

GEORGE LUCAS
EXECUTIVE VICE-PRESIDENT
Credits:
Director of THX 1138 (Warner Bros. Seven Arts)
"The Filmmaker"—Promotional film for "The Rain People"
Promotional films for "MacKenna's Gold"
National Student Film Festival Grand Prize 1967

CHRISTOPHER PEARCE
GENERAL MANAGER
Credits:
Director Audio-Visual Dept., Robert J. Brady Co. (sub. of Prentice-Hall)
Director of Television & Educational Film Walter Reed Army Medical Center
J. Walter Thompson Advertising (London)

ROBERT DALVA
PRODUCTION DIRECTOR
Credits:
Feature Film Editor—Los Angeles
TV Commercial Editor for Cal Bernstein (Dove Films) and Wakeford/Orloff
Producer-Director: Office of Economic Opportunity
Films: "5 Volunteer Stories" and "Volunteer Training"
Producer: Hour length Educational Films for KQED-TV—"Dying" and "Relating"

BART PATTON
ASSOCIATE DIRECTOR
Credits:
Producer: "The Rain People" Warner Bros. Seven Arts
Producer: "Beachball" Paramount
Producer-Director-Writer: Patton-Weinrib Productions—"Wild, Wild Winter"; Youth Film Samuel Goldwyn Studios; "Out-Of-Sight"—Spy satire filmed for Universal Studios
Production Manager: John Urie & Associates (National Accounts Serviced): Datsun, Lincoln-Mercury, Bigelow Carpets, Honda, Englander Mattress, Metrecal, Procter & Gamble, Shell Oil, Levis', Coronet Tissue

ROBERT A. KULLER
ASSOCIATE DIRECTOR
Credits:
Agency Producer: Vansant Dugdale
BF & J Productions: Baltimore, Maryland
Creative Director: Allegany Airlines, Black & Decker Manufacturing, Marriott Food Corp., Esskay Meat Product, Maryland National Bank

GARY SASLAW
ASSOCIATE DIRECTOR
Credits:
Commercials—
Assistant Director: Bhyre On The Rocks (commercial 1966 Winner of a Cannes Film Festival Award)
Producer-Director: Skelly Oil Co., Consumer Oil Co., Cooper Tire Co., Chrysler Corp.: Chrysler Division & Plymouth Division, Roy Rogers Soft Drinks
Corporate Films—
Director: Memorex Corp., Intermedia Group
Television—
Producer-Director: The Joe Creiger Sports Show NBC
Director: The Sportsman NBC

TOM GLASS
ANIMATOR AND MUSICAL DIRECTOR
Credits:
Musical background includes 10 years experience as band direction for avant-garde, jazz and rock groups
Composed and directed music for commercials and films including: "The [illegible] Tower," Rainy Day Special (1969 San Francisco Film Festival), "Tools For Change" (Carnegie Institute Grant), Sears Fashion Promotion Film

EDWARD KESSLER
REPRESENTING AMERICAN ZOETROPE
DIRECTOR—COMMUNICATIONS PLANNING AND DESIGN
Credits:
Director—Business Development: Dancer-Fitzgerald-Sample/San Francisco
Account Supervisor/Executive: Dancer-Fitzgerald-Sample
Account Executive: Clinton E. Frank, Inc., Chicago
Advertising Manager: Kaiser Jeep Int'l Corp., Oakland
Advertising Supervisor: Monsanto Co., St. Louis

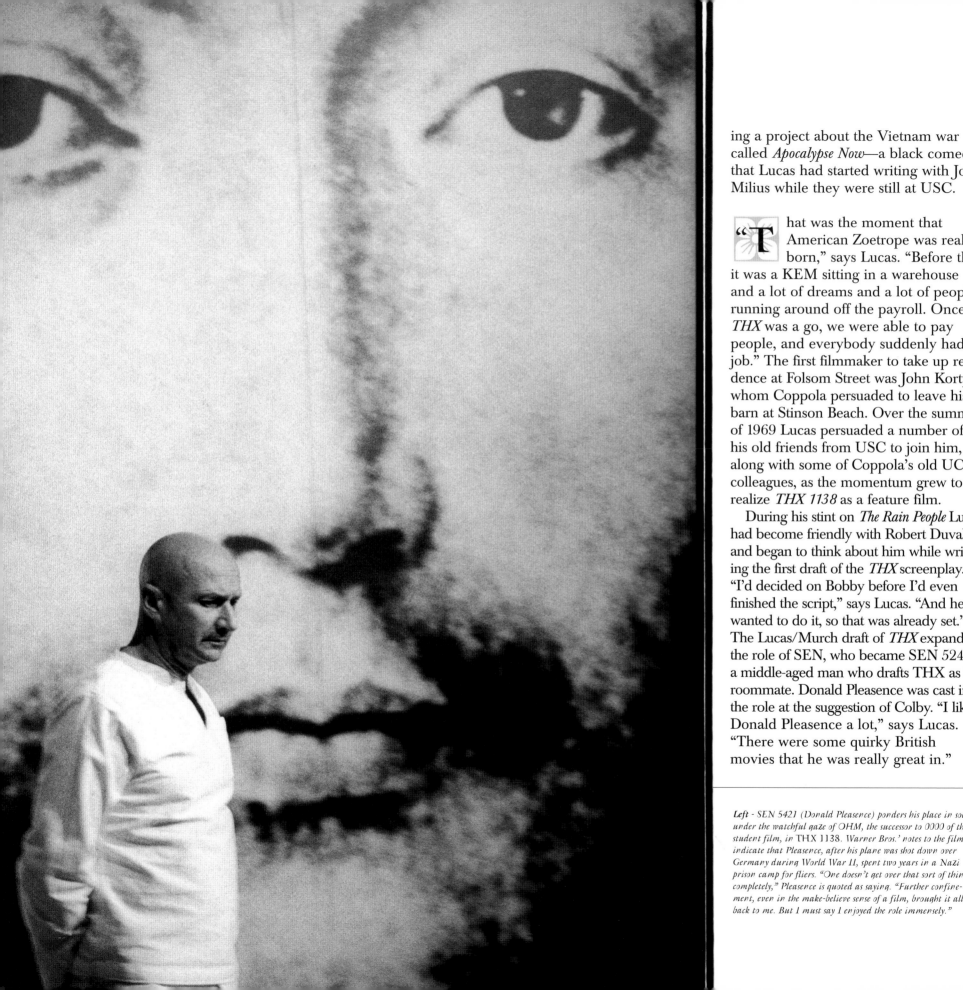

ing a project about the Vietnam war called *Apocalypse Now*—a black comedy that Lucas had started writing with John Milius while they were still at USC.

"That was the moment that American Zoetrope was really born," says Lucas. "Before that, it was a KEM sitting in a warehouse and a lot of dreams and a lot of people running around off the payroll. Once *THX* was a go, we were able to pay people, and everybody suddenly had a job." The first filmmaker to take up residence at Folsom Street was John Korty, whom Coppola persuaded to leave his barn at Stinson Beach. Over the summer of 1969 Lucas persuaded a number of his old friends from USC to join him, along with some of Coppola's old UCLA colleagues, as the momentum grew to realize *THX 1138* as a feature film.

During his stint on *The Rain People* Lucas had become friendly with Robert Duvall and began to think about him while writing the first draft of the *THX* screenplay. "I'd decided on Bobby before I'd even finished the script," says Lucas. "And he wanted to do it, so that was already set." The Lucas/Murch draft of *THX* expanded the role of SEN, who became SEN 5241, a middle-aged man who drafts THX as his roommate. Donald Pleasence was cast in the role at the suggestion of Colby. "I liked Donald Pleasence a lot," says Lucas. "There were some quirky British movies that he was really great in."

Left *- SEN 5421 (Donald Pleasence) ponders his place in society under the watchful gaze of OHM, the successor to 0000 of the student film, in* THX 1138. *Warner Bros.' notes to the film indicate that Pleasence, after his plane was shot down over Germany during World War II, spent two years in a Nazi prison camp for fliers. "One doesn't get over that sort of thing completely," Pleasence is quoted as saying. "Further confinement, even in the make-believe sense of a film, brought it all back to me. But I must say I enjoyed the role immensely."*

THX's female roommate was given a much more prominent role in the feature film. Lucas warned the actresses auditioning for the role of LUH 3417 that everyone in the film—men and women—would have to shave their heads. "I spent a lot of time interviewing on that one," says Lucas. "It was a minimalist role, but it was tough. For an actor, the less you have to do, the harder it is."

Maggie McOmie was a recent drama graduate from San Francisco State College and was just embarking on her career. She was happy to shave her head and was prepared to appear nude in the love scene with Robert Duvall. She remembers she was eating lunch when she discovered she had won the role. "Ron Colby said, 'Quit work—you're in a movie.'" SRT was played by 6′ 4″ actor Don Pedro Colley, who had recently completed a stint as a semi-regular in the fourth and fifth seasons of NBC's *Daniel Boone.* Michael Haller joined the production as art director.

Once Zoetrope received the go-ahead from Warner Bros., Lucas asked Haller to visit Japan to scout potential locations. Coppola was enthusiastic about Lucas's idea to use that country's futuristic architecture to evoke the nightmarish subterranean world of the script. Lucas studied the photographs Haller sent back and then visited Japan himself. He soon realized that getting permission to shoot in nuclear power plants and other industrial facilities was going to be almost impossible, despite the enthusiasm of the officials he met. When Lucas returned to California, Coppola brought his lucky number seven into play—the budget of the film was set at $777,777.77—but there was clearly not enough money for anything as ambitious as a Japanese location shoot.

Shooting began on Monday, September 22, on location in San Francisco's new BART (Bay Area Rapid Transport) system. Throughout the filming, Lucas made a virtue of the fact that the network was still under construction, shooting in eerily deserted tunnels. Shooting would continue, with extra days and extra script pages added as Lucas went along, until Friday, November 21. Throughout the production of *THX 1138*, Lucas aimed for a documentary look (both cameramen—Albert Kihn and David Meyers—were recruited from the world of documentary filmmaking), while striving to create a flawless evocation of an entirely imagined society. Lucas would subsequently define this visual verisimilitude as "immaculate reality," a phrase he borrowed from Kurosawa. The challenge of achieving that look with a shoestring budget would stretch the novice director to the limit.

"I was playing off the fact that it was a documentary, but I wasn't

Above - THX 1138 (Robert Duvall) and LUH 3417 (Maggie McOmie) are allowed a final embrace—for clinical reasons, no doubt. Once shooting for the day had wrapped, McOmie would don a wig.

Far right *- Actors Robert Duvall (left, THX 1138), Maggie McOmie (LUH 3417), and location sound technician Jim Manson prepare to shoot.*

Right *- Lucas and cameraman Albert Kihn.*

doing the shaky camera and all that kind of stuff," says Lucas. "I was doing an extremely stylized look with no camera movement to speak of. The only camera movement occurred if an object moved—I would pan with it. Sometimes I'd shoot people and let them go off camera, or let them get halfway off camera, and I wouldn't adjust the frame."

"It was a film from the future, rather than about the future," says Walter Murch. "We thought of the future as a country like Japan, and Japanese films were interesting to us, because they were made by a culture for itself—and you learned about the culture by looking at that, but it didn't take any time to explain itself to you. And the problem that George and I found with science-fiction films is that they were like American films being made in Japan, which felt that they had to explain these strange rituals to you, whereas a Japanese film would just have the ritual and you'd have to figure it out for yourself. So we thought, 'let's make a film like that: that is, about certain trends that are present in the world today extrapolated into the future.'"

Lucas struggled to implement his ideas on a tight schedule that, at times, forced his crew to adopt guerrilla filmmaking tactics. "We barely got into some of the locations," he remembers. "Sometimes we'd only have about two hours to shoot in a particular place. There were a lot of things that made it feel like a street film—we would get in there, get our shots before the police came, and then run away as fast as we could."

While Lucas and his crew filmed on (and below) the streets of San Francisco, an atmosphere of uncertainty prevailed at Folsom Street. Despite Coppola's agreement with Warner Bros., script supervisor Mona Skager remembers there was a real possibility that Lucas would not be able to complete his first film. "The financing of *THX* was always a little iffy," she says. "We never knew if we were going to be able to shoot the next day, or whether [Warner Bros.] would pull the plug."

In the early mornings and late evenings, Lucas and Murch would debate the evolving nature of the film. Aware they were already expressing a rebellious declaration of independence offscreen, they wondered how experimental they could dare to make the events onscreen. One of the most innovative ideas they developed was to try to give the soundtrack a separate, additional identity from the pictures. "I kept wanting to take it into this abstract world," says Lucas. "Walter and I always like to call [*THX 1138*] a cubist film, because what we tried to do was detach the images; the stories and the themes, and the sound and the images, were all slightly different views of the same thing, seen simultaneously."

While wrestling with these esoteric ideas, Lucas had to deal with more conventional human problems. He was using two-camera setups throughout filming in an effort to get quickly the coverage he'd need for editing. The approach had the added bonus of capturing multiangled footage from the most spontaneous takes. Unfortunately, the technique saved time only if all the actors in the given scene were working to the same pace.

Above - At the Colorvision Studios in Los Angeles, Robert Duvall and Lucas discuss a scene.

Left - Lucas and crew filming the "prison" scenes.

Opposite - Three chrome robot security officers (Johnny Weissmuller Jr.—whose father played Tarzan in many films—Robert Feero, and an uncredited extra) condition THX 1138 (Duvall) to remain in a prison without bars

THX's autojet roars through an express tunnel. Two policemen on sleek, exotic jetbikes round a corner with beautiful precision. Calmly, relentlessly, they pursue THX

FULL ANGLE
The car swerves and scrapes the wall of the tunnel.
. . . The car bobbles as THX has more and more difficulty keeping it under control. A part flies off, causing one of the jetbikes to swerve. The policeman loses control of his bike, tumbles across the roadway and bounces off the wall, parts flying in all directions.

"Bobby Duvall would give his perfect performance on the first rehearsal but Donald Pleasence wouldn't even bother to read his lines until the third take," says Lucas. "So Donald would go for about ten takes, but Bobby would go for one or two and then that would be the end of it. If I had a scene with the two of them, it would be really hard. I hadn't had a lot of experience with that sort of thing, and it was challenging."

The film's only concession to mainstream sensibilities was an expansion of the chase scene in the final act. In the original version, THX escapes the underground metropolis on foot, but in the feature film he steals a car (a refurbished Lola T70) and is pursued by robotic security officers riding motorbikes. Filmed at the end of the schedule, from mid- to late November, this dangerous sequence was designed to follow diagrams that illustrated the projected crash trajectory of each vehicle. Lucas's crew would set up in freezing Bay Area tunnels at 7:30 P.M. and shoot the complex sequence until 4:00 A.M. the following day.

Page 101 of the shooting script contains an evocative description of the action:

"The stunt guy [Duffy Hamilton] took a header and went absolutely flying into the wall," says Skager. "We thought he was absolutely dead. We were at the other end of this tunnel, and all of a sudden we heard this thing go crashing, and we were almost paralytic [with fright]. We ran like crazy down to the other end. Fortunately he survived, but it was really scary."

The difficulty of staging such dangerous action scenes made it more important than ever to establish a multicamera setup, so Lucas asked Haskell Wexler to assist co-cinematographer David Myers. "I did it for free," says Wexler, …"but I got the pleasure of seeing George make his first movie. You can't beat that. I loved *THX* because it was a movie—it was visual, it was different. Here was someone who had a vision. There is a very humanistic base to George's mechanical presentation of the world."

The final shot of the movie, where THX emerges onto the surface and faces a shimmering sunset, was virtually a remake of the same scene in the student film. It was therefore strangely fitting that for that long shot THX was played not by Robert Duvall but by Matthew Robbins, the coauthor of the original story. Robbins laughs when he recalls that the lens used to shoot the scene was "about the length of a Volkswagen."

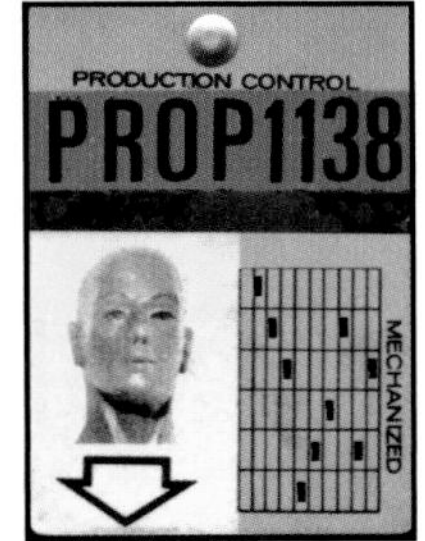

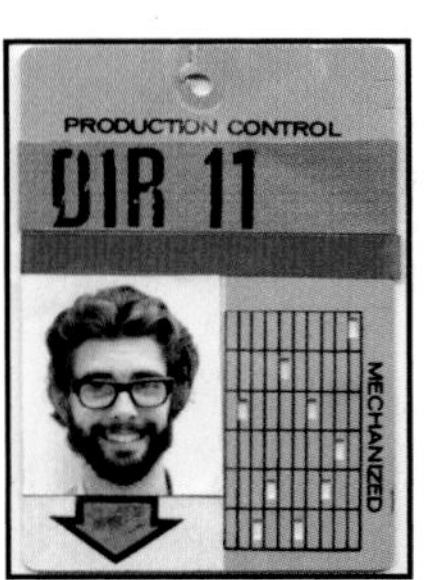

Above *- Seen through a windshield, stuntman Duffy Hamilton goes flying in a controlled motorcycle crash that almost went out of control.*

Left *- Two security badges: Lucas's, and that of a prop for the film.*

Opposite *- The members of American Zoetrope after the completion of its first feature film,* THX 1138*—however, the celebration would not last long.*

(Zoe gk. LIFE + Trope Movement, Turn, REVOLUTION)
HN KORTY
CARROLL BALLARD
TIM HUNTLEY
JOHN MILIUS
BARRY BECKERMAN
LAWRENCE STURHAHN
GEORGE LUCAS
DENNIS JAKOB
ROBERT DALVA
AL LOCATELLI
FRANCIS COPPOLA
STEVE WAX
WALTER MURCH
JIM McBRIDE
SAN FRANCISCO, DECEMBER 12TH: A CELEBRATION of the opening of the AMERICAN ZOETROPE film facility, the completion of photography of its first production, THX 1138, and the beginning of A NEW DECADE.

During the production of *THX* Coppola challenged Lucas to try to write something "warm and fuzzy" for his next project, and Lucas embraced the idea. Searching for inspiration, Lucas thought back to his college days. While studying anthropology, he had come to realize that cruising was a uniquely American mating ritual. "Cruising was gone, and I felt compelled to document the whole experience and what my generation used as a way of meeting girls."

As Lucas developed the story in his mind, he weaved in his fascination with radio DJs (first expressed in *The Emperor*) and his theme of escape. His movie would tell the stories of four groups of teenagers as they spend the night driving up and down the streets of their sleepy home town during a time of momentous social change—traditional rock-and-roll was about to succumb to the beat groups of the British Invasion, and America was stepping up its occupation of Vietnam. The stories would intertwine onscreen, but the teenagers would also be linked by the music of enigmatic DJ Wolfman Jack, whose records would provide an evocative musical backdrop to the entire film. The script identified the small town as Modesto. Lucas called his semi-autobiographical drama *American Graffiti.*

When filming of *THX 1138* was complete, postproduction was carried out in the specially converted attic of Lucas's Mill Valley home. During the day, Lucas edited the film himself. The nightshift was taken by Murch, creating and mixing a unique palette of sounds. "It was really Walter and I making the movie," says Lucas. "We wrote it together; he was around when I was shooting it. And then as soon as we started editing, he'd edit all night; I did it all day. And we would play off each other."

In May 1970, Coppola visited Mill Valley to take his first look at the film he was due to present to Warner Bros. the following day. He was surprised by what he saw, and so he approached his screening of the work print to the studio brass with a degree of trepidation. Coppola suspected they might not understand what they were about to watch.

During and subsequent to the film's projection, the executives at Warner Bros. became upset that Lucas had made a film that was different from the one Coppola had proposed. "Francis pitched it," says John Calley, "but I think George subsequently felt that [the screenplay Coppola pitched] was not necessarily a super accurate blueprint of what he had in mind. I think Francis's presentation of how it was going to work, and George's sense of how it was going to work, perhaps differed in some way. So it came back, and we didn't know what to do with it."

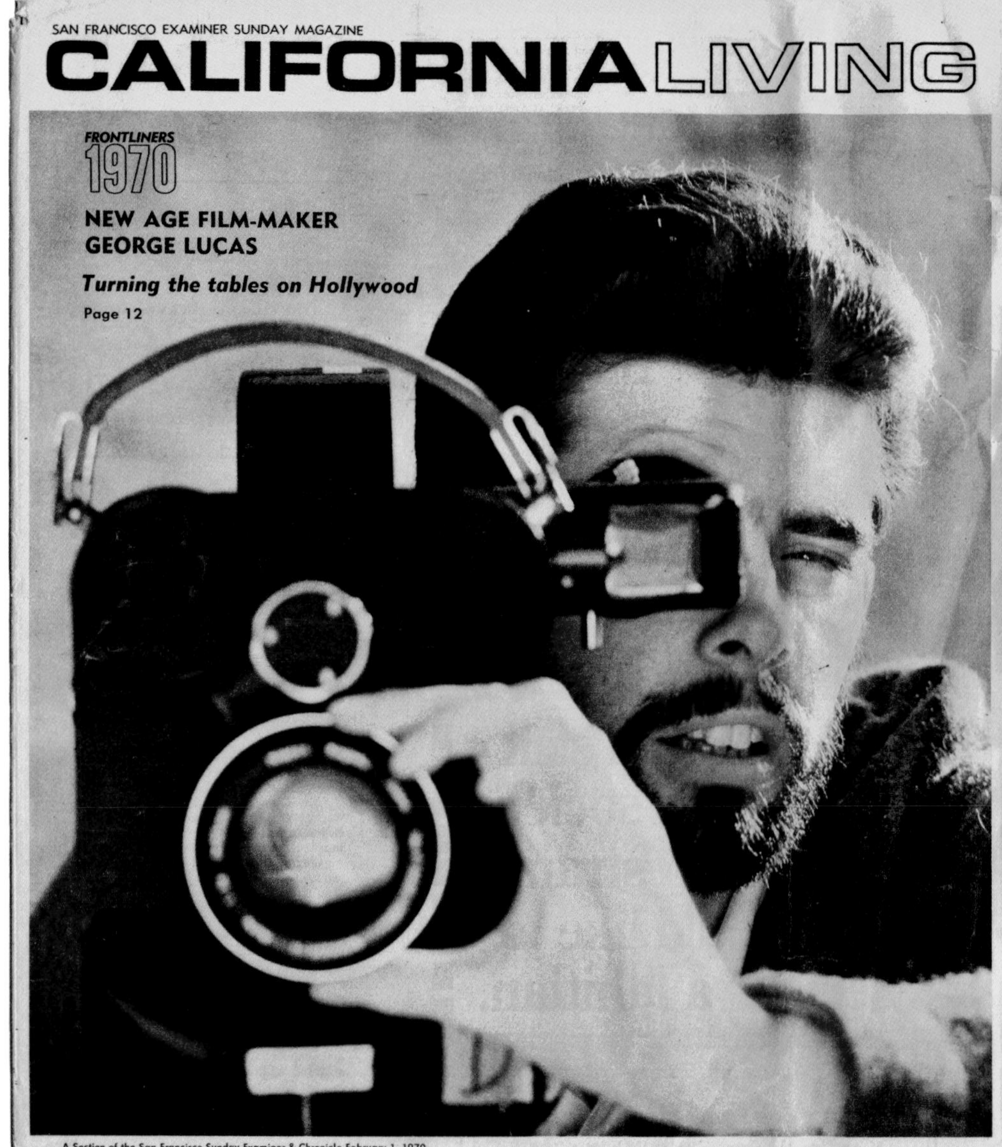
SAN FRANCISCO EXAMINER SUNDAY MAGAZINE

CALIFORNIA LIVING

FRONTLINERS 1970

NEW AGE FILM-MAKER GEORGE LUCAS

Turning the tables on Hollywood

Page 12

A Section of the San Francisco Sunday Examiner & Chronicle February 1, 1970.

Above - Lucas on the cover of the February 1, 1970 San Francisco Examiner Sunday Magazine.

Far left - THX 1138 (Robert Duvall) carries out his duties as a magnum manipulator, constructing chrome robot security officers.

Left - In the world of THX 1138, *sexual physicality is forbidden, but not autoerotic pastimes.*

Ted Ashley appointed Fred Weintraub to oversee a reedit, and Lucas began a dispiriting round of meetings in an effort to find a mutually acceptable compromise. “They said it didn’t have the kind of forward momentum they wanted,” says Lucas, who recalls with horror that one executive told him to “put the freaks up front”—that is, the “shell people,” who appear at the end—and tell the rest of the events in the film as a flashback. “Francis got them away from most of that stuff to just simply taking some of the white limbo scenes out.”

Lucas continued trying to reedit *THX*, but he eventually found it impossible to collaborate any further with Weintraub. The film was consequently taken away from him and edited by Warner Bros. staffer Rudi Fehr, who cut five minutes from the running time of *THX*—and in doing so turned Lucas’s mistrust of corporate Hollywood into resentment. “It didn’t make any sense,” he says. “Whether it’s five minutes shorter or longer, it didn’t change the movie one bit. . . . That’s about the level of intelligence that was going on.”

In late August, Argentinean-born composer Lalo Schifrin began work on the soundtrack for *THX 1138*. Schifrin’s unsettling score recognized and complemented Lucas and Murch’s experimental approach to the film’s sound design, in places even evoking the Japanese influence Lucas had initially hoped to

Above - Sound montagist and cowriter of THX 1138, *Walter Murch is seen here mixing a later American Zoetrope production,* Apocalypse Now *(1979).*

Right - Publicity for the film.

capture by filming there. Schifrin's score was recorded on October 15 and 16, and the final mix was completed soon after. The finished film made for remarkable viewing.

THX (Robert Duvall) is unaware of it, but LUH (Maggie McOmie) is decreasing his drug intake. Free from the influence of sedatives, THX and LUH make love. Shortly thereafter, THX is put on trial for drug evasion and sexual perversion, and is put in detention with other misfits from society, including the ranting SEN. THX declares he is leaving and simply walks away, through a seemingly endless white expanse. SEN follows him.

The two soon meet SRT (Don Pedro Colley), who points

Above - *THX 1138 (Robert Duvall) is subjected to a life of closely supervised drudgery in a subterranean city. The populace is encouraged to purchase hexagons, which are immediately disposed of upon arriving home.*

Left - *This corridor scene was filmed in Frank Lloyd Wright's Civic Center in Marin County, California.*

in the direction of a distant exit. They walk through a door, where they are suddenly swept along by a veritable sea of humanity that separates SEN from THX and SRT. The authorities register that THX and SEN are missing. A capture time is specified and a budget of 14,000 credits is allocated to their recovery.

SEN is talking to a group of schoolchildren when he is finally escorted away by robotic security officers. THX and SRT each steal a car, but SRT drives his straight into a pillar. THX continues his high-speed journey alone, followed by two officers on motorcycles. Shortly after one of the officers crashes his bike, the authorities declare that the primary budget has been exceeded.

THX is accosted by Shell People before he makes his way to Vac Shaft Level One. He begins to scale a ladder attached to the vertical shaft, with an officer close behind. But the attempt to recapture THX is six percent over budget and therefore terminated. THX emerges onto the surface and faces the setting sun.

The simplicity of the production design and the careful choice of locations lend *THX 1138* a timeless quality. The film has neither dated significantly, nor ever been particularly identifiable with the era of its production, with no hairstyles to speak of and only basic costumes. Lucas's vision of the future is presented with the candor of an instinctive documentary filmmaker.

The film's subject matter was informed by prevalent contemporary concerns about the individual's loss of identity in an increasingly mechanized and centralized society. *THX 1138* also takes on the more eternal question of free will. Lucas and Murch tap the prevailing fears while satirizing the West Coast's hippie culture (here is a society where short-haired dropouts are punished for *not* taking drugs) and America's paranoia over communism (on several occasions interrogators echo Senator McCarthy's infamous question, "Are you now or have you ever been . . .").

"Plots are a way of articulating themes," says Lucas, responding to an observation that *THX 1138*—his first "immaculate reality"—is the most conspicuously metaphorical of all his films. "There is a certain hierarchy in the way I put things together. I weave the themes up into the plot, and the plot usually serves the metaphor. The central theme is the strongest one—it's about personal restraints. It's about being trapped in a cage with the door unlocked; it's about being afraid to open that door and go out."

Lucas divides the film into three distinct acts: the first detailing

Above - *Lucas and Walter Murch—together they worked around the clock during postproduction to finish* THX 1138.

Right - *THX 1138 (Duvall), SEN 5241 (Pleasence), and the enigmatic SRT (Don Pedro Colley) test the boundaries of the white void. "I was very risk adverse when I was younger, and it's an extension of THX," says Lucas. "It's an extension of sitting in the white limbo saying, 'Oh, I don't know . . . It's going to be dangerous . . . Something might happen to us.' Francis is very much the THX, going off and saying, 'Come on!' Francis taught me to walk off into the white limbo and not be afraid of it."*

Far right - *The authorities monitor the cost of pursuing THX, until the efforts to capture him go over budget.*

the events before THX is arrested, the second the events that take place while he is under arrest, and the third the events that occur when he tries to escape. "Each act is basically the same story told in a different way. In a sense, it's like a trilogy of three stories, or a three-act play, but, in reality, it's one movie that has the same ideas and themes that move through three different visions. Most of it centers around people's inability to take hold of their situation and move forward."

THX had not been the only casualty of Coppola's disastrous meeting with Ted Ashley's Warner Bros. On Thursday, November 19, 1970, Ashley and his colleagues made it clear that Zoetrope's future was no longer something in which they were interested in participating. To add insult to injury, Warner Bros. demanded the repayment of the $300,000 loan.

After Coppola broke the bad news to Lucas and his other tenants at Folsom Street, one thing was clear to everybody—the party was over. "Francis was in debt to about $400,000," says Korty of the desperate Christmas that followed "Black Thursday." Though Coppola maintained a skeleton staff at Zoetrope, even he felt obliged to look for whatever work he could find to pay back Warner Bros.

Coppola was approached by Paramount to adapt and direct Mario Puzo's 1969 gangster novel, *The Godfather*. Lucas was recutting

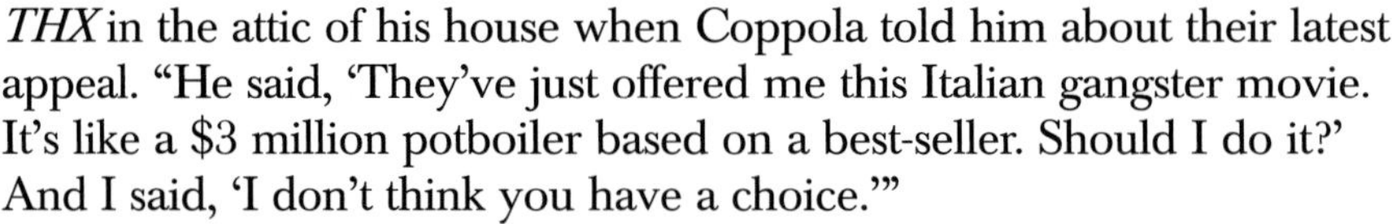

THX in the attic of his house when Coppola told him about their latest appeal. "He said, 'They've just offered me this Italian gangster movie. It's like a $3 million potboiler based on a best-seller. Should I do it?' And I said, 'I don't think you have a choice.'"

Matthew Robbins had introduced Lucas to lawyer Tom Pollock, who recognized immediately that Lucas was scarred from Warner Bros.' treatment of *THX*. Pollock became Lucas's legal advisor and helped him incorporate his own company, Lucasfilm Ltd. Any ambitions to collaborate with John Milius on *Apocalypse Now* had seemingly been dashed by Warner Bros.' dismissal of Zoetrope's forward program, so Lucas returned to *American Graffiti*. Willard Huyck and his wife, Gloria Katz, found time to help Lucas draft a fifteen-page treatment, which Lucas intended to use to attract enough investment to develop a script.

"We were trying to pad it," remembers Huyck, "and we put in a lot of stuff about how cruising was this endless cycle of never getting anywhere, and how these people were desperate to get out of town. George said, 'This is all great for the treatment, but I loved cruising and I love Modesto.' So that was always the pole in the script—whether they were going to stay or whether they were going to go."

Lucas asked producer Gary Kurtz if he would be willing to devote some time to budgeting *American Graffiti*, in the hope that a

Above - *Actually filmed horizontally, THX 1138 (Duvall) seemingly scales a shaft that leads to the surface.*

Far left - *"When I grew up, cars were my life," says Lucas. THX powers his souped-up machine away from oppression.*

Left - *THX 1138 (Robert Duvall) at the wheel of a stolen car, as his final bid for freedom begins.*

studio commission would lead to a salaried role on the production. Kurtz was happy to help. While Lucas and Kurtz pondered ways of funding preproduction on *American Graffiti*, Warner Bros. finally released *THX 1138*.

The film opened quietly on March 11, 1971 to sparse, but generally positive, critical response. Unable to highlight the Shell People, Warner Bros. marketed the film around a close-up image of one of the security officers. The one-sheet poster carried the tagline: "The future is here."

In *Time* magazine, reviewer Stefan Kanfer praised the film's sardonic streak. "The government—a wretched wedding of Mao Tse-tung and the Internal Revenue Service—treats each person as a consumer-producer who lives to enhance the glorious state. In a world of progressive monotony, Lucas flashes some bright signs of humor: when THX (Robert Duvall) watches television, he turns to a channel where a beating proceeds incessantly—the violence and sadism of today's viewing, minus the annoyances of plot."

Steven Spielberg, who had seen Lucas's student short at a UCLA screening and been impressed by it, was initially surprised at the differences between the feature film and the short. "I felt the short was more emotional than the feature film. As I got older and looked at the film fifteen years later, the feature film hit me on an emotional level I was too immature to receive when I first saw it. I hadn't been old enough to appreciate what George had intended. I had to be thirty-five, thirty-eight before I realized that."

In 1971 Lucas reflected on the *THX* experience in a little-seen documentary called *George Lucas: Maker of Films*. The show was produced by Los Angeles PBS channel KCET and presented by author and critic Gene Youngblood. During his conversation with Youngblood, Lucas made little effort to conceal the contempt he felt for Warner Bros. "Making film is an art. Selling film is a business," he said. "The trouble is they don't know how to sell films. As a result, they try to make you make films that people will go to without them having to be sold. This is the real key to the problem. If they can't put a film in a theater and have people rush to the door, they're not interested."

Lucas made no specific reference to *American Graffiti* but hinted that his next project would be very different from *THX*. "I'm moving toward another kind of film," he said. "I learned a lot from Francis's type of theatrical, stage-oriented, drama-oriented filmmaking. I'm learning, I'm growing, trying to see what it's all about."

Above - Lucas's fascination with speed is seen here as the chrome robot police pursue THX through Bay Area tunnels.

Right - Having broken the mental barriers upon leaving the limbo "prison," a motorized THX has to smash through his society's physical barriers before attaining liberty.

Shooting Schedule
THX 1138

as shot

The shooting schedule for THX 1138 dated September 15, 1969, predicts that filming would run from September 22 to October 18. A note on the schedule conceded that additional scenes could be shot "maybe post la shootina"; principal photography would ultimately continue for approximately seven weeks. (The "SPECIAL NOTES" are taken verbatim from the daily production reports; quotation marks signify words taken directly from the script.)

SHOOT DAY 1: Monday, September 22, 1969
Company Called: 8.00am **Time Finished:** 7.00pm
Location: 19th St. Bay Area Rapid Transit [BART] Station; Oakland, California
Set: Debris Receptacle 444: 29-35 [deleted scenes in which THX escapes from garbage room, strangles a beast, continues escape into City Superstructure]
Setups: 22
Pages: 1 6/8
No. of Days [estimated] on Picture Including Today: 40

SHOOT DAY 2: Tuesday, September 23
Company Called: 6.00am **Time Finished:** 3.00pm
Location: Oakland Sports Arena, Hegenberger Road
PG&E Building, 8th and Mission, San Francisco
Market Street Excavation, SF (2nd unit)
Set: Passageway: 17 [LUH and THX speak in corridor], 26 [THX is led away by chrome policeman], 66A [SEN is scared in tram station], 74 [THX discovers LUH is dead], 76, 74A, 76A [Policemen tell them to, "Stay calm," as they try to open the door to the Observation Cell]
Setups: 14
Pages: 1 7/8
Added scene: People running in corridor

SHOOT DAY 3: Wednesday, September 24
Company Called: 2.00pm **Time Finished:** 5.30pm
Location: Lake Merrit BART--8th Street & Oak St., Oakland, Oakland Museum Parking Lot
Set: Corridor, SEN's Apartment: 12, 15 [THX takes air-shower, disposes of hexagon], 17
Setups: 11
Pages: 1 4/8

SHOOT DAY 4: Thursday, September 25
Company Called: 8.30am **Time Finished:** 5.00pm
Location: Lake Merrit BART
Set: Observation Room, Corridor; 16mm: Explosion, Corridor, Operating Room: 7 [view of TV monitors], 76A, 78 [THX and SRT run away and are not affected by the mindlock], 73 [THX and SRT escape from morgue/Plastic Factory], 74
Setups: 16
Pages: 1 1/8
Special Props: Laser tool, bodies, ear-tags

SHOOT DAY 5: Friday, September 26
Company Called: 8.30am **Time Finished:** 5.30pm
Location: Lake Merrit BART (Westinghouse)
Set: Control Center: Pieces of 22, 58, 62, 65, 67, 71, 75, 77, 79, 82, 85 ["Present operation computed to be economically unfeasible"]
Setups: 26
Pages: 6 1/8

SHOOT DAY 6: Monday, September 29
Company Called: 8:30am **Time Finished:** 6:00pm
Location: Lake Merrit BART
Set: Reproduction Center: 59 [deleted scene: THX and SRT wander and talk among jars that contain human embryos–THX: "She put orinase in my sedation... How can I love her?"]
Setups: 25
Pages: 1 5/8

SHOOT DAY 7: Tuesday, September 30
Company Called: 8.30am **Time Finished:** 6.00pm
Location: Berkeley BART, Center St. & Shattuck St.
Set: Plastic Factory: 70 [THX and SRT enter morgue/Plastic Factory], 73
Setups: 24
Pages: 1 7/8

SHOOT DAY 8: Wednesday, October 1
Company Called: 8.30am **Time Finished:** 7.00pm
Location: Berkeley BART
Oakland Sports Arena (re-shoot)
Set: Tunnel/City Shell, Narrow Passage: 86 ["THX is obviously afraid of what lies beyond the door. There is a moment when it looks as if he may turn back. Eventually, he makes a decision and throws the hatch open."]
Setups: 28
Pages: 3/8

SHOOT DAY 9: Thursday, October 2
Company Called: 8.30am **Time Finished:** 5.00pm
Location: Oakland Sports Arena
Studio A, 991 Tennessee St., San Francisco
Set: City Passageway, Narrow Tunnel, Tram Tube: 27A [deleted scene: THX floats down a tube], 68 [deleted scene: THX recovers after fainting in the electronic hallways]
Setups: 7
Pages: 1 7/8
Special Notes: Friday is day off–screening at Northpoint to be announced–COME IF YOU WANT.

SHOOT DAY 10: Saturday, October 4
Company Called: 9.00am **Time Finished:** 4.15pm
Location: Marin County [Civic] Center
Set: Commercial Plaza: 14 [THX purchases hexagon], 7
Setups: 34
Pages: 1 1/8
Atmosphere: 50 extras
Special: 1 autojet, 1 1969 Stingray
Special Notes: Lunch for cast and crew in cafeteria at Marin Center.

SHOOT DAY 11: Monday, October 6
Company Called: 8.30am **Time Finished:** 1.30pm
Location: Studio A
Set: THX Apartment: 1 ["What's wrong?"], 2, 4, 5, 6 [THX and LUH argue, watch TV]
Setups: 32
Pages: 4 4/8

SHOOT DAY 12: Tuesday, October 7
Company Called: 8.30am **Time Finished:** 5.15pm
Location: Studio A
Set: THX Quarters/Mainroom (shot in continuity): 15, 15A [THX arrives and collapses in apartment.]
Setups: 24
Pages: 2 4/8

SHOOT DAY 13: Wednesday, October 8
Company Called: 8:30am **Time Finished:** 6:00pm
Location: Studio A
Set: THX Apartment: 16 [extended THX/LUH scene,

which results in lovemaking]
Setups: 18
Pages: 2 6/8

SHOOT DAY 14: Thursday, October 9
Company Called: 8.30am **Time Finished:** 5.30pm
Location: Studio A
Set: THX Apartment/Kitchen: 18 [extended LUH/THX scene, which begins with them in a hologram cathedral and ends with THX wondering if he can function without drugs], 37 [deleted scene: After he escapes the debris compactor, LUH finds THX in their apartment, bloodied and torn. He collapses and the chrome policemen come and take him away.]
Setups: 21
Pages: 4 1/2

SHOOT DAY 15: Friday, October 10
Company Called: 8.30am **Time Finished:** 5.00pm
Location: Studio A
Set: THX Apartment: 12, 12A [SEN wants THX for his roommate.]
Setups: 13
Pages: 3 3/4

SHOOT DAY 16: Monday, October 13–Nite Shoot
Company Called: 5.30pm **Time Finished:** 1.30am
Location: Lawrence Hall of Science, Berkeley
Set: Rest Plaza/City Mainway/Schedule Office: 9 [LUH tells THX about shift change], 56A, 57 [SRT, SEN, and THX exit white limbo into extremely crowded city mainway]
Setups: 28
Pages: 3
Atmosphere: 80 general (including 30 old people, women for maternity ward); 1 yellow man (trampled trying to receive card); 1 yellow chrome robot

SHOOT DAY 17: Tuesday, October 14–Nite Shoot
Company Called: 4.00pm **Time Finished** 2.00am
Location: Lawrence Hall of Science, Berkeley
Set: Hall + Courtroom: 43 [THX on trial]
Setups: 16
Pages: 3 5/8

SHOOT DAY 18: Wednesday, October 15–Nite Shoot
Company Called: 3.00pm **Time Finished** 9.30pm
Location: Lawrence Hall of Science, Berkeley
Set: Rest Plaza: 10 [deleted scene: THX enters and exits small room filled with benches and old people staring]
Setups: 9
Pages: 2/8

SHOOT DAY 19: Thursday, October 16
Company Called: 8.30am **Time Finished:** 6.00pm
Location: GE Plant–Valesitas Nuclear Center
Set: Operating Cell: 14, 42 [in prison chamber, LUH tells THX she is pregnant]
Setups: 23
Pages: 2

Friday, October 17–Day Off

SHOOT DAY 20: Saturday, October 18
Company Called: 9.00am
Location: Alcoa Building, Clay & Battery St., SF
Set: School Plaza
Pages: 3
Atmosphere: 20 children
[Note: Progress Report missing for this day.]

SHOOT DAY 21: Monday, October 20–Nite Shoot
Company Called: 12 Noon **Time Finished:** 9:30pm
Location: Lake Merrit BART
Set: Tram Int. and Ext.: 66 [SEN exits tram], 27 [deleted scene: THX escapes tram], 28 [deleted scene: chrome policeman calms crowd, which thinks that THX was killed when he exited the moving tram]
Setups: 16
Pages: 1

SHOOT DAY 22: Tuesday, October 21
Company Called: 9.00am **Time Finished:** 7.00pm
Location: Lake Merrit BART, Berkeley BART
Set: Pre-Operating Chamber, Tram Station: 19 [SEN tells THX he's had LUH transferred.], 66A
Setups: 23
Pages: 1 6/8

SHOOT DAY 23: Wednesday, October 22–Nite Shoot
Company Called: 4.00pm **Time Finished:** 12.00am
Location: SF State College, Film and TV Building, 1600 Holloway Avenue
Set: Cathedral: 60 [SEN in cathedral], 63 [SEN attacks monk], 67 [chrome policemen discover slain monk]
Setups: 18
Pages: 1 4/8

SHOOT DAY 24: Thursday, October 23–Nite Shoot
Company Called: 5.00pm **Time Finished:** 5.00am
Location: Pacific Telephone, 430 Bush St, SF; KGO-TV, 277 Golden Gate Ave., SF
Set: Computer Interior, Observation Cell: 61 [THX and SRT run through labyrinth of electronic circuit panels], 64 [SRT places hand on THX, who faints], 7
Setups: 27
Pages: 3 5/8

Friday-Sunday–Days Off

SHOOT DAY 25: Monday, October 27–Nite Shoot
Company Called: 8.30pm **Time Finished:** 6.00am
Location: Los Angeles International Airport, Terminals 6 & 7
Set: Prayer Booth + Passageway: 8 ["Blessings of the state, blessings of the masses..."], 13 [THX vomits in prayer booth], 17 [LUH and THX meet; she knows he slipped on the "cervix transfer"], 43
Setups: 26
Pages: 2 7/8
Special Props: OMH [sic] portrait, Mercicontrol card, white lunch boxes

SHOOT DAY 26: Tuesday, October 28–Nite Shoot
Company Called: 8.00pm **Time Finished:** 5.30am
Location: LA County Hospital, 1200 N. State St. KTLA-TV, LA
Set: Operating Chamber Corridor, Observation Cell: 20 [THX denounces SEN with punch card], 74 [THX sees embryo bottle marked "LUH"], 76 [view of an operation in progress]
Setups: 16
Pages: 3 3/8

SHOOT DAY 27: Wednesday, October 29-Nite Shoot
Company Called: 6.30pm **Time Finished:** 5.15am
Location: Pacific Aero-Motive Corporation, Burbank KTLA-TV, LA
Set: Supervisor's Cell, Observation Cell/Control Center: 21, 30, 32, 34, 71, 28, 22
Setups: 16
Pages: 3 3/8

Thursday, October 30–Move To Colorvision Studios (Set Up Day)

SHOOT DAY 28: Friday, October 31
Company Called: 8.00am **Time Finished:** 6.45pm
Location: Colorvision Studios, 4376 Sunset Drive, LA
Set: Prison Chamber: 44 [THX is led to white limbo], 45, 47 [extended white limbo action and dialogue]
Setups: 34
Pages: 5 3/8

SHOOT DAY 29: Monday, November 3
Company Called: 8.00am **Time Finished:** 6.30pm
Location: Colorvision Studios
Set: Prison Chamber: 48, 49, 50
Setups: 28
Pages: 10 7/8

SHOOT DAY 30: Tuesday, November 4
Company Called: 8.00am **Time Finished:** 7.00pm
Location: Colorvision Studios
Set: Prison Chamber: 51, 52, 53
Setups: 42
Pages: 8 1/2

SHOOT DAY 31: Wednesday, November 5
Company Called: 8:00am **Time Finished:** 7:30pm
Location: Colorvision Studios
Set: Prison Chamber: 51, 52, 53
Setups: 38
Pages: 4 1/8
Special Notes: There will be a party tonight, 11/5/69, on Stage 1 for crew, cast, and hangers on. Happy Guy Fawkes Day!!! Love Peace...

SHOOT DAY 32: Thursday, November 6
Company Called: 8:00am **Time Finished:** 5:35pm
Location: Colorvision Studios
Set: Prison Chamber: 42, 39 [trainee uses THX as a guinea pig]
Setups: 28
Pages: 6

SHOOT DAY 33: Friday, November. 7–Nite Shoot
Shooting Call: 9:00pm
Location: Crocker Plaza Garage, LA
LA Music Center Parking Lot
LA Int'l Airport (Terminal 7)
Set: City Shell (Shell Dwellers), Prayer Booth

[Note: Progress reports unavailable for Shoot Day 33 and the rest of shoot; information taken from call sheets and the revised master shooting schedule. All following shoot days were second unit.]

Monday, November 10–Moving Day
Location: San Francisco
Evening: Location search all tunnels/Richmond Bridge

SHOOT DAY 34: Tuesday, November 11–Nite Shoot
Shooting Call: 7.00pm
Location: San Jose Hospital
Set: Organalysis

SHOOT DAY 35: Wednesday, November 12–Nite Shoot
Shooting Call: 11.00pm
Location: Funston Tunnel, Park Presidio Blvd.
Set: Tunnel Chase (1 scene)

SHOOT DAY 36: Thursday, November 13–Nite Shoot
Location: Broadway Tunnel
Set: Tunnel Chase, Empty Tunnel (16mm Shot for TV Monitor) (3 scenes)

SHOOT DAY 37: Friday, November 14–Nite Shoot
Location: Fort Baker Tunnel, Richmond Bridge
Set: Tunnel Chase–Runbys (1 scene)

SHOOT DAY 38: Monday, November 17–Nite Shoot
Shooting Call: After midnight
Location: Posey Tube (between Oakland & Alameda)
Set: Tunnel (1 scene)

SHOOT DAY 39: Tuesday, November 18–Nite Shoot
Location: Caldecott Tunnel (between Berkeley & Orinda)
Set: Tunnel Chase

SHOOT DAY 40: Wednesday, November 19–Nite Shoot
Location: SF Airport Garage
Set: Module Dispersal Center (1 scene)
Pages: 2

SHOOT DAY 41: Thursday, November 20–Nite Shoot
Location: Caldecott Tunnel
Set: Tunnel–Motorcycle Dump (2 scenes)
Notes: Crashes break down into two sections (car crash at Orinda w/ scaffold–motorcycle dump at Oakland end); two hours necessary to rig tunnels both nights–split call; 3 cameras operate; tunnel is extremely cold!!

SHOOT DAY 42: Friday, November 21–Nite Shoot
Location: Caldecott Tunnel
Set: Tunnel–Car Crash(es) (2 scenes)

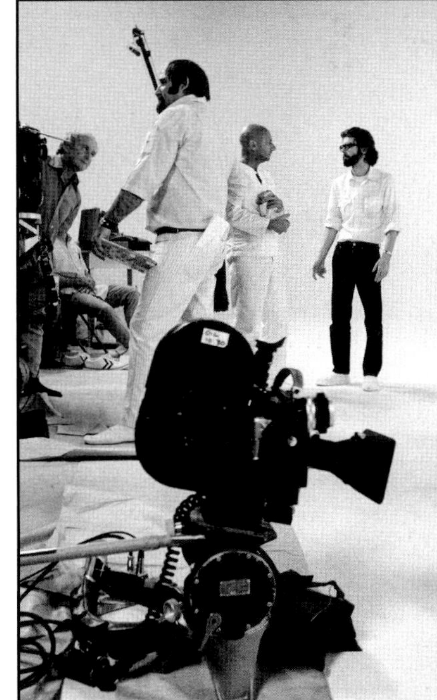

Left - Lucas prepares a shot of Robert Duvall (THX 1138).

Above - Behind the scenes, Lucas talks with Pleasence (SEN 5241).

Mels drive-in
Mel's

Chapter Two

****

Some Enchanted EVENING

(1972–1973)

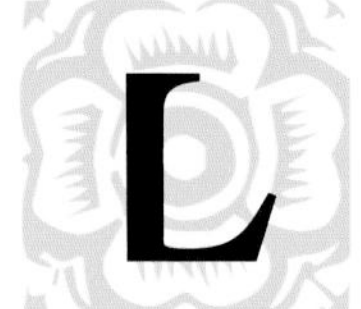

Lucas knew that *American Graffiti* would have to find a home elsewhere than Warner Bros., so he began a long slog around the studios, promoting his ideas with little success. He admits to "literally starving to death" during these years.

One of the few people to recognize Lucas's potential after *THX 1138* was producer Alan Trustman, who offered Lucas the chance to direct *Lady Ice*, a caper movie. The fee was a relatively astronomical $150,000, plus a large percentage of the profits—but Lucas turned down the assignment, determined to pursue his own projects.

By this time, Lucas had more to offer the studios than just the *Graffiti* treatment. His enduring affection for cliffhanger serials (even the titles of *THX 1138* had been preceded by an original trailer for an episode of *Buck Rogers*) had led him to another idea: an epic space opera produced in the style of *Flash Gordon* and *Buck Rogers*. He had originally hoped to direct a new version of *Flash Gordon*, and met with licensors King Features. "They didn't really want to part with the rights," recalled Lucas in 1977. "They wanted Fellini to do *Flash Gordon*."

Lucas wasn't deterred for long, and began formulating an alternative strategy. "I realized that I could make up a character as easily as [*Flash Gordon* creator] Alex Raymond, whose characters were inspired by Edgar Rice Burroughs," he said in 1977. "It's your basic superhero in outer space. I realized that what I really wanted to do was a contemporary action fantasy."

Still unsure whether he'd ever make another movie, Lucas was delighted to discover that *THX* was going to be screened as part of the Director's Fortnight at the Cannes Film Festival in May. Along with his friend and cowriter Walter Murch, he scraped together $2,000 and bought a ticket to France, eschewing the glamorous hotels for a more economical campsite (without a festival pass, Lucas and Murch even had to sneak into the screening of *THX 1138*). While there, Lucas met David Picker, the president of United Artists. UA had been intrigued by *American Graffiti* and the as-yet-untitled science-fantasy project, so Picker promised Lucas $10,000 to develop *Graffiti* as a screenplay.

Lucas wanted to spend another five weeks in Europe and hoped the Huycks would have a screenplay by the time he returned. But they were about to start work on their own film, *The Dead People*, so Lucas had to find someone else to prepare a script. After talking the problem through with Kurtz, he decided to ask Richard Walter, an old friend from USC.

Walter was flattered, but instead tried to pitch a screenplay called *Barry and the Persuasions*, a story of East Coast teenagers in the late 1950s. Lucas held firm—his was a story about West Coast teenagers in the early 1960s. Lucas offered Walter the $10,000 promised by David Picker, and Walter set to work translating the treatment into a script for *American Graffiti.* Lucas was dismayed when he returned and read the result, which he recalls was written in the style of a "Hot Rods to Hell" exploitation flick. Walter redrafted the script, but it soon became clear that his ideas were out of sync with Lucas's intentions.

After paying Walter, Lucas had exhausted his development fund. Because he had spent all of his own money on his trip to Europe, there was no alternative: he would have to write the screenplay himself. Lucas wanted to have something to show Picker as soon as possible and felt that valuable time had been lost. He wrote his first draft in just three weeks, painstakingly guiding the four concurrent narratives toward a point where they converged as the sun rose over Modesto. Drawing upon his large collection of vintage 45-rpm singles, Lucas wrote every scene with a specific musical backdrop in mind. *Graffiti* would be the first film to feature such an

Previous - *Glorious automobiles shimmer at Mel's Drive-in, the focal point in Lucas's 1973 film,* American Graffiti. *John Milner (Paul Le Mat) can be seen next to his yellow hot-rod.*

Above - *Charlie Martin Smith, Lucas, Haskell Wexler, and William Niven prepare to film the scene in which the under-aged Toad attempts to buy a bottle of Old Harper's.*

Right - American Graffiti *was filmed almost entirely at night. In the earliest morning hours of Friday, July 7, 1972, director George Lucas confers with producer Gary Kurtz on Petaluma Boulevard concerning the scene in which Curt sabotages a police car.*

extensive soundtrack of original rock-and-roll recordings.

The cost of licensing the seventy-five songs Lucas wanted, however, may have been a contributory factor in UA's ultimate rejection of the script, which the studio felt was too experimental—"a music montage with no characters." They also passed on the science-fantasy idea, which Lucas temporarily shelved. Lucas spent the rest of 1971 and early 1972 trying to raise interest elsewhere in his script for *Graffiti. THX 1138* had brought him an unwelcome notoriety, and he was instead offered the chance to direct movies based on the Broadway hit *Hair* and The Who's rock opera *Tommy*—"Basically record albums . . . movies that don't have any plots."

When the second draft was finished, Lucas and Kurtz renewed their efforts to sell *American Graffiti* and finally found favor at Universal. "It was the tail end of the dynasties, of the big executives," says Kurtz. "Universal was still being run by Lew Wasserman. He had very eccentric tastes, and he made a lot of very, very commercial movies. . . . They did all this low-budget stuff as well. The low-budget program at Universal was based on this concept that if they liked the script, and the elements were okay with them—the key cast—they in effect wrote you a check and told you to go away and come back with a finished movie. They never bothered you at all. It was a very, very good atmosphere."

The aftershocks of *Easy Rider* were still being felt at Universal. Like Warner Bros.' John Calley, Universal's Ned Tanen was prepared to nurture independent talent on the condition that their projects cost less than $1 million. The studio allocated $775,000 to *American Graffiti*—less than Lucas had received from Warner Bros. for *THX 1138*.

Universal's support of *American Graffiti* came with an additional caveat: Lucas would have to find a well-known name to lend the film marquee value. Lucas knew that the film's limited budget would be diminished by about 10 percent in order to cover the clearance costs of the rock-and-roll tunes he felt were vital: there was nothing in the budget for any major stars, and,

Above *- Lucas and "visual consultant" Haskell Wexler (in cap) during an unusual daytime shoot. Charlie Martin Smith (Toad) is in the pink shirt.*

Far left and left *- Cars on the streets as they participate in what Lucas felt was a fast-disappearing youth ritual of the 1950s and early 1960s: cruising.*

with a cast of characters that were largely teenagers, there was little opportunity to find a place for any. In March 1972, Coppola's *The Godfather* opened in New York and soon went on to become one of the most commercially successful films in history. Lucas had remained close to Coppola, so he asked him if he would lend his name to *Graffiti* in order to reassure Universal. Coppola was happy to come on board as producer.

A production office was established in San Rafael, and production assistant Jim Bloom was put in charge of finding the numerous cars that would be needed. Advertisements for 1962-era custom automobiles were placed in the Marin County newspaper and on local radio stations. Kurtz's assistant (and sister-in-law) Dorothy "Bunny" Alsup took Polaroid photographs of the cars. By the time the process was complete, Bloom had large notebooks containing photographs of more than five hundred vehicles from which Lucas could choose. Between forty and fifty cars were short-listed to take part in the balletic cruising sequences Lucas intended to film on the streets of San Rafael:

> ***TRAVELING G STREET–DUSK–CURT, STEVE, LAURIE–EDSEL***
> *Curt is in the back seat, gazing out the window at the main street of the small farm community. The one-way street is lined with used-car dealers, small shops, and an endless parade of kids in flamed, lowered custom machines rumbling through the seemingly adultless, heat-drugged little town. On the radio, the Wolfman is talking to a teenie bopper on the phone.*

Lucas's choice of background music was crucial to the mood of each scene, but he was realistic about the complexities of copyright clearances and suggested a number of alternative tracks. "In the end we had to make some choices, so George picked two or three possibilities for each scene," says Kurtz. "When I took it to the head of music at Universal Pictures, he practically had a heart attack. He said, 'This has never been done before. How about we just hire an orchestra and we'll rerecord all these songs?' I said, 'We can't do that—we have to use the original records.'" To simplify the process,

Right *- The inner workings of Milner's yellow car, finely tuned to make him the fastest driver in the valley.*

Far right *- Milner (Paul Le Mat) drives up with Steve (Ron Howard), Curt (Richard Dreyfuss), and Toad (Charlie Martin Smith) standing by Steve's Chevy Impala.*

Universal proposed a flat deal that offered every music publisher the same amount of money. This was acceptable to most of the companies representing Lucas's first choices, but not to RCA—with the consequence that Elvis Presley is conspicuous by his absence from the soundtrack.

Finding suitable actors was similarly complex. The film's lengthy casting process was overseen by Fred Roos (one of the casting directors on *The Godfather*) and Mike Fenton. They took the time to host open casting sessions and visited numerous high-school drama groups. "George had great patience for interviewing actors," says Roos. "Tape wasn't prevalent in those days, so we sat for weeks and weeks interviewing everyone. . . . George has an excellent eye for casting and he made the right choices—he was right on."

Curt Henderson, the graduate taking stock of his life during his last night in Modesto, was played by Richard Dreyfuss, who had done most of his work in television. "We went through probably one hundred people for that part, and none of them were really pleasing to George," said Roos in a 1978 television interview. "The reason for that was that the Curt character was pretty much George Lucas. The movie was to some degree autobiographical." As Lucas explained in 1973, "I was Terry the Toad, fumbling with girls. Then I became a drag racer like John [. . .] And finally I became Curt. I got serious and went to college."

Lucas was impressed by Dreyfuss's thoughtful analysis of the role. In a 1978 radio documentary, Dreyfuss recalled he was confident he would be cast as soon as he completed his screen test. "I knew the character and I did the test well," he said. "I looked at that character from the point of view that twenty years later he would remember this night, and that's why he did everything he did."

The actor Roos had in mind for the role of Steve Bolander was a child star he'd encountered when he spent some time as the casting director for the CBS comedy *The Andy Griffith Show.* Griffith played small-town sheriff Andy Taylor, and Ronny Howard played his son, Opie. The series ran from 1960 to 1968, and when it finished Howard went straight into its sequel, *Mayberry RFD*, which ran until 1971. Howard was still only eighteen years old when Roos approached him for the role of Steve in *American Graffiti.* "Ronny Howard had been on the screen for most of his life, but he was in an awkward down period," says Roos. "All his TV series had finished

Clockwise from above left *- Richard Dreyfuss (Curt), Ron Howard (Steve), Mackenzie Phillips (Carol), and Harrison Ford (Bob Falfa).*

Opposite *- Howard and Cindy Williams (Laurie) during a location shoot. All five would go on to become major television and film stars following the release of* American Graffiti. *"Lucas took notes in very small handwriting, using a light pencil you could barely read," recalls casting director Fred Roos. "We had interviews, call-backs, then readings; we picked our best candidates for each role and spent two or three days screen-testing."*

and were running in syndication. He was so much identified with this Opie character he was not considered for major movies. At that time there was a big prejudice against people who were identified with TV series." Howard's performance in Lucas's screen tests was so compelling, however, that Lucas and Roos decided to go with him.

The third narrative concerned anguished tough guy "Big" John Milner, who spends most of his night's cruising saddled with a style-cramping twelve-year-old Carol Morrison. Milner was named after John Milius, although Lucas points out that the character was inspired by the hot-rod enthusiasts he had known in Modesto, rather than by any of his USC friends. The role marked the film debut of nineteen-year-old amateur boxing champion Paul Le Mat.

The fourth story followed the misadventures of misfit Terry "The Toad" Fields. Eighteen-year-old Charlie Martin Smith missed the auditions because he was backpacking in England. Shortly after he returned to California, he was in MGM's Thalberg Building when he was spotted by Lucas. Smith won the role—and the booby prize of the film's least flattering haircut.

Each of the four male protagonists is complemented by a female character. Curt is haunted by glimpses of an enticing beauty who remains frustratingly out of reach. The blonde at the wheel of the white Thunderbird was played by Suzanne Somers. Although her performance amounted to only a few minutes of screen time, her character's role as a metaphor for the siren, enticing him to stay in town, is a key element of the film.

Curt's sister Laurie was played by Cindy Williams, an actress who became best known for her starring role in the long-running sitcom *Laverne and Shirley.* John Milner's traveling companion, Carol, was played by twelve-year-old Laura Mackenzie Phillips. Mackenzie was the daughter of the Mamas & The Papas' John Phillips and step-

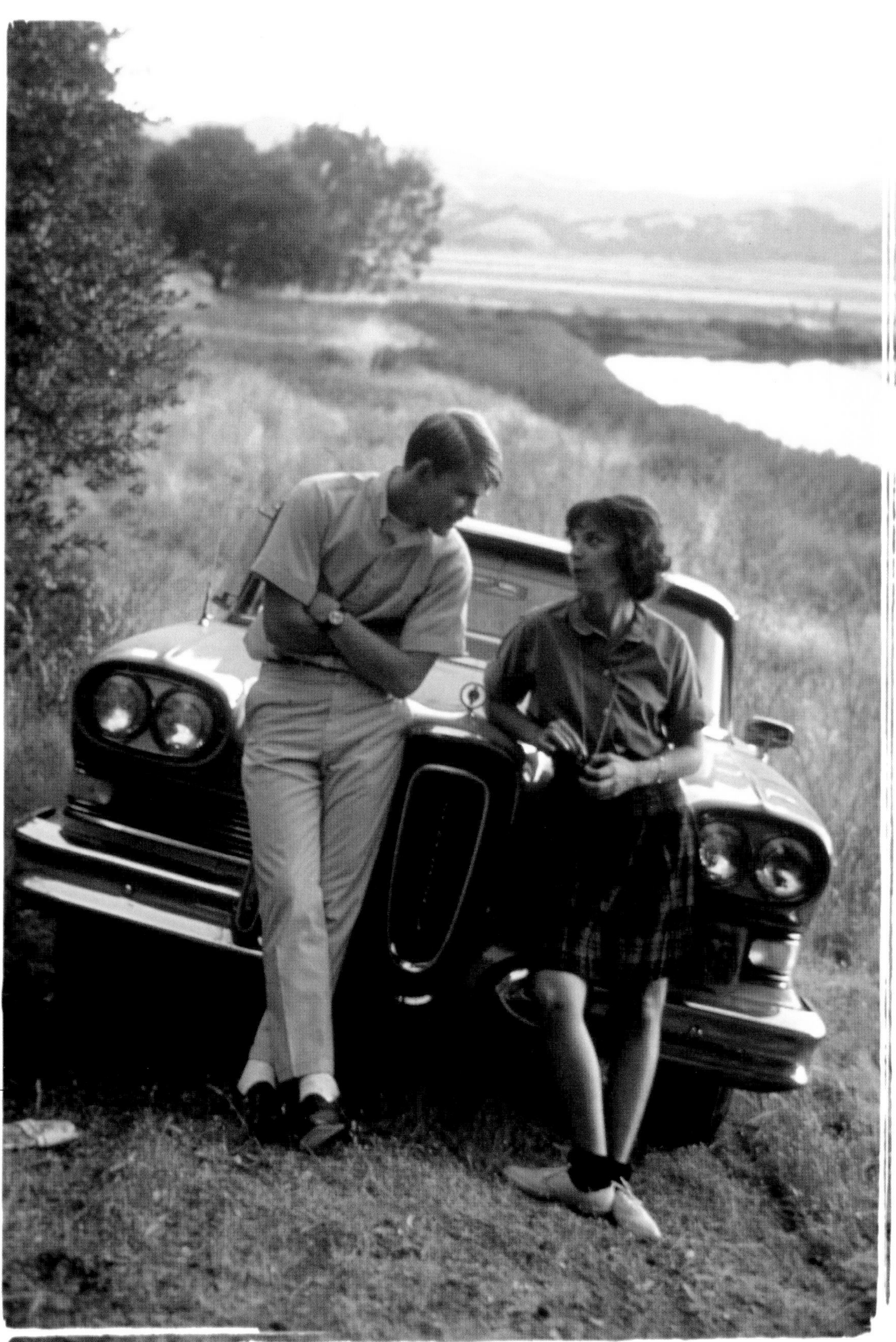

daughter to John's fellow group-member Michelle. Roos had spotted her fronting her own band at a talent night at the Troubador club in Los Angeles and assumed she was older.

Terry picks up Debbie Dunham, a girl he meets on the street and spends the rest of the night trying to impress. Actress Candy Clark had to endure a wig made of yak hair in order to effect her transformation into a flirty blonde bombshell. Her detailed and far-from-stereotypical performance played the comic potential of the character to the hilt.

For the role of the outrageous XERB DJ, Wolfman Jack, Coppola encouraged Lucas to ask the DJ to play himself. The screenplay described the omnipresent character thus:

> *The Wolfman is an unseen companion to all the kids. Witty and knowledgeable about the trivia that counts, he's their best friend, confidant, and guardian angel.*

The Wolfman is heard on car radios throughout the film, but appears only in the atmospheric scene in which Curt summons up the courage to approach his idol at the XERB building. The meeting proves to be a turning point in the teenager's life, and a major influence on his decision to leave town. "He was a legend," says Lucas, "the mythical character that I was dealing with in terms of the fantasy of radio."

"It was played as close as I could to what it really was," said the Wolfman, aka Robert Smith, in 1978. "If anything, it was 98 percent real. George Lucas and I went through thousands of Wolfman Jack phone calls that were taped with the public. The telephone calls [heard on the broadcasts] in the motion picture and on the soundtrack were actual calls with real people."

While Curt encountered Wolfman Jack, Lucas drew together the Steve, John, and Terry stories by gathering the characters on the outskirts of town for the final act. John Milner is challenged to a racing duel at dawn by reckless hot-rodder Bob Falfa (the name clearly inspired by Lucas's USC friend Robert Dalva). This small but crucial role went to little-known Harrison Ford, an actor who had been appearing in films since 1966 but who had made little impact. He was concentrating on an alternative career when Roos brought him to mind. "Harrison was a terrific carpenter and had done a lot of work for me, remodeling my house and building some furniture," says Roos. "We were preparing *American Graffiti* at the American Zoetrope offices at what was then called the Goldwyn Studios. In our suite of offices, we wanted a fancy door with a section of glass and the Zoetrope logo. We got Harrison to put it in." Roos persuaded Ford to take the role, and Ford agreed on the condition that he would not have to cut his hair. A compromise was eventually reached whereby Ford wore a Stetson to cover his hair.

As Lucas continued to work on the script, he encountered difficulties with the Steve and Laurie storyline. Nearly two years on from his original approach, he asked Willard Huyck and Gloria Katz if they would work on the third draft, and specifically on the scenes featuring Steve and Laurie. This time they were free to say yes. "I don't think we ever worked as hard or as fast in our lives," says Katz. "We were under pressure to go, so we would try to write ten pages a day. It was a very new format, and to balance all those characters in one screenplay was tremendous. George was cursed with a twenty-eight-day shooting schedule, and I think we delivered a 160-page script. Everybody said, 'You have to rewrite it, you have to cut it,' so we just typed it very small! George, being George, was never dissuaded." The 114-page draft, signed "George Lucas, Gloria Katz, and Willard Huyck" is dated May 10, 1972, and bears the title and introduction "rock radio is AMERICAN GRAFFITI (saga of the low riders)."

Left - Lucas and Mackenzie Phillips (Carol) share a joke in John Milner's car.

Opposite - Like the Emperor of Lucas's student film, Wolfman Jack (Robert Smith) is an inspirational DJ who rules the airwaves from a tiny radio station on the outskirts of town. He and Lucas recorded an entire radio show, which was then used as part of the soundtrack of the film.

ANOTHER SLOW NIGHT IN MODESTO

* *

Filming proceeded with virtually no input or interference from Universal. *American Graffiti* was a low-budget project, and studio executive Ned Tanen had only modest expectations of its commercial success. However, Universal did object to the film's title. The executives had long been baffled about what "American Graffiti" actually meant, and Lucas was dismayed when some people at the studio assumed he was making a film about feet. Universal therefore submitted a long list of alternative titles to the *Graffiti* production office. The studio's favorite was *Another Slow Night in Modesto*, and they pushed very hard to get Lucas to adopt the title. However, Lucas considered all of them to be dreadful and persuaded Tanen to delay the decision on the film's title until he had finished shooting.

The following are about half of Universal's preferred titles, as preserved in a memo from the period:

1962 Was Some Year
Ask Wolfman Jack
Birth of the Sixties
The Boys and Their Girls
Buddies No More
Burger City Blues
Color Them Wild
A Crowded Evening
The Drag Years
The Fast and the Deadly
The First Time Is the Worst Time
The Frantic Heart
Goodbye Burger City
High School's Over
It'll Never Be Like This Again
Last Night to Make Out
Love on Wheels
Looking for Trouble
Make Out at Burger City
No More Cotton Candy
Rock Generation
The Savage Heart
Something to Do
That Crazy Time
The Toy Dreams Gone
Those Sweet and Sour Sixties
To Learn about the World
The Violent Four
Wake Me Up, I'm Getting Older
Whatever Happened to My Childhood
Wine, Women, and Song
You Go Your Way . . .
The Young and Doomed
Young and Foolish
The Yesterday People

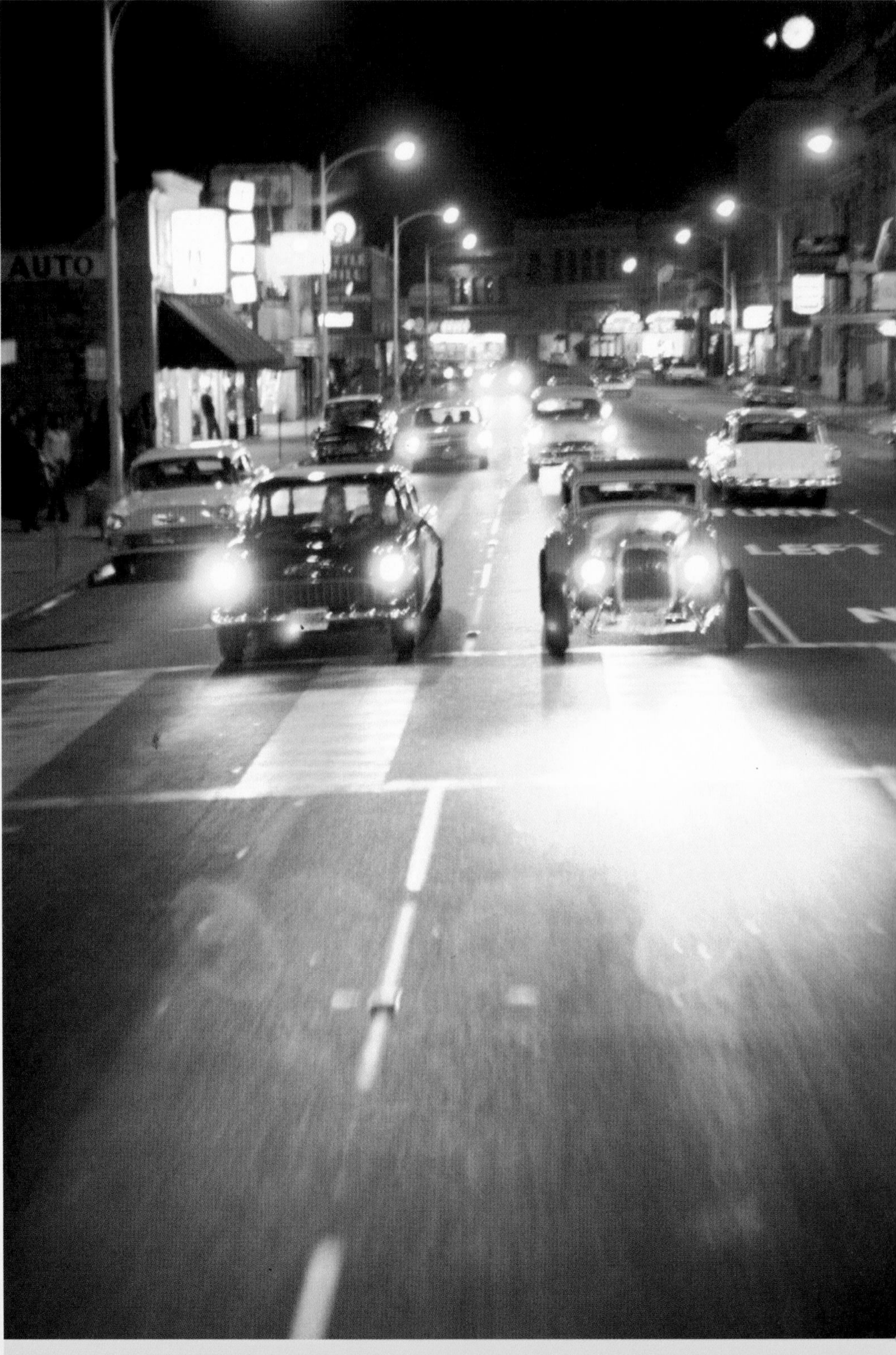

Ostensibly depicting his hometown of Modesto, Lucas shot *American Graffiti* primarily in Petaluma (Petaluma Boulevard is pictured above), with much of the cruising filmed during three nights on San Rafael's 4th Street. Both towns are located in northern California.

Lucas chose San Rafael, a relatively small town in Marin County, north of the Golden Gate Bridge, and ten minutes away from his home, to double for Modesto. Production got underway on Monday, June 26, with the filming of John and Carol's story on 4th Street. Lucas knew that every day of his limited schedule was precious, and he soon became frustrated at the amount of time it was taking to fix camera mounts to the cars. The crew started attaching the mounts at 4:00 P.M., but the daily production reports indicate that filming did not start until 11:40 P.M. Momentum then stalled as the crew broke for "lunch" between 1:00 and 2:00 A.M. By the time the company wrapped at 5:30 A.M., Lucas had achieved just ten setups—only half of what was on the shooting schedule.

Paul Le Mat and Mackenzie Phillips were called back to 4th Street at 8:00 P.M. the following day, but Lucas found his progress once more interrupted. He was unable to clear or control the regular street traffic as planned because of a City Council order to the San Rafael police department. The council was concerned about the disruption that filming caused the local businesses and had therefore withdrawn permission for Lucas to shoot beyond a second day. Location manager Nancy Giebink hastily opened negotiations with the city council of Petaluma, a similarly small town approximately twenty miles north of San Rafael, which was more cooperative. Lucas was able to relocate nearly all of the subsequent filming there, without the loss of a single day of shooting. Lucas did manage to persuade the San Rafael city council to allow two further nights of filming (on July 3 and 23) for general cruising shots, which he used to evoke as much of the intended location as possible in the finished film.

Shooting in Petaluma began on Wednesday, June 28, and proceeded at a much quicker pace. Before long, however, Lucas became aware of another problem. He had elected to shoot *Graffiti* using two camera operators (as he had done in *THX 1138*) and no formal director of photography. "I shot the film very much like a documentary," he says. "I would set the scene up, talk to the actors about what was going to happen, where they were going to go and what they were going to do, set the cameras up with long lenses,

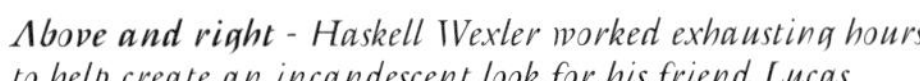

Above and right *- Haskell Wexler worked exhausting hours to help create an incandescent look for his friend Lucas.*

and let the actors run through the scenes with each other." The use of Techniscope, which preserved some of the grainy quality of 16mm in a widescreen frame, added to the documentary feel. Lucas had shot much of *THX 1138* using only available light but found it difficult to adopt the same approach on *Graffiti*. Most of the shops were closed by the time filming began, leaving only street lamps and car headlights to illuminate the actors. Cameramen Ron Eveslage and Jan D'Alquen were hard-pressed to hold a useful depth of field in the low light; an actor had to move only a few inches before he went out of focus.

Lucas decided to ask Haskell Wexler for help. Wexler was working in Los Angeles at the time: "I was scheduled to do a lot of commercials, so I flew up to San Francisco every evening and worked until daylight, then came back to Los Angeles and worked. It was incredible fun, but there was no money. I was so spaced out from not having any sleep that at one point I said to George, 'Point me in the right direction and I'll shoot!'"

Lucas told Wexler he wanted *American Graffiti* to "look like a jukebox," and Wexler did his best to oblige. He simulated street lighting by adding 1,000- or 2,000-watt lights to the existing lamps and asked shop owners to leave their lights on overnight as that would also help to illuminate the sidewalk scenes. Wexler placed twelve-volt lights inside the cars, powered directly from the batteries, to light the faces of the actors while they were cruising.

Wexler was not the only one who occasionally buckled under the strain of the schedule. Cindy Williams recalls that after one scene she shared with Howard, the two looked up to see that Lucas had fallen asleep during their performance. Lucas also succumbed to the flu. Lucas's disenchantment was clear when he told his friend John Milius, after one particularly rigorous night of filming, "I don't think I can last at this."

Ron Howard recalls that if Lucas was not behaving like a traditional director, it was perhaps because he felt that he had not started directing yet. "He said, 'I'm not really getting a chance to direct this film now—I don't have time. I'm really going to direct it in the editing room. That's where I'm going to make all my choices.'" Howard also remembers Lucas's unusual documentary-style

Right *-Jana Bellan (as carhop waitress Budda) and Lucas prepare to shoot take 3 of scene 4, in which Budda rejects an overly enthusiastic Toad. On shoot day 10, work began for most of the actors at 6:45 P.M. and continued until 4:50 A.M., with a break for "dinner" from 12:30 A.M. to 1:30 A.M.*

prod no:
7-10-72
TAKE 3
147
Camera-
G. Lucas

approach to the shoot: "Often we couldn't tell where the cameras were. You didn't know if it was a long lens getting you in close-up at any given moment. If you asked George, he wouldn't tell you, and would say just keep doing the scene. But I'd been trained to know all about the camera, to interact with the camera. So at first it was disorienting—but ultimately it was incredibly liberating. When I saw the performances, I realized that he'd achieved a complete honesty and naturalism that made all the characters so real. He'd taken the pressure off—there wasn't a moment for the big close-up—while also keeping you on your toes for every take."

"We took this movie really seriously," says Charles Martin Smith. "We would sleep until two in the afternoon, have something that resembled breakfast in the Holiday Inn, and then we would all get together, run the scenes, and rehearse and rehearse. . . . We worked hard. [The film is] a combination of that and mistakes, all of which George put in. Every time we screwed up, after all that hard work, he cut it in!"

The very first scene in the movie showed Terry arriving on his moped to meet Steve outside Mel's Drive-in. "I thought I would ride it in, bump up over a curb, put the thing into third, and let the clutch out so it would jerk," Smith recalls. "I thought that would be funny. . . . But instead it took off with me still hanging onto it. It banged into a trash can before it stalled and died." Smith didn't hear Lucas cry "cut" so he got off the stalled moped and carried on with the scene. Ron Howard similarly failed to hear any instructions, so he acted nonchalant throughout. To the actors' amusement, this was the take that Lucas used to open the movie. He knew that such minor mistakes, combined with the slightly grainy film stock and a cast of relative unknowns, would all contribute to the documentary feel he favored. "I'd let the action live unto itself, without playing to the camera," says Lucas.

On August 3, Lucas took his crew to Buchanann Field in Concord to film the final scene in the film: Curt boarding the DC-7 that would take him to a new life away from Modesto. Lucas found an authentic prop-driven plane still in service, and was perhaps satisfied that the name of the company that supplied it—Magic Carpet Travel Services—served his metaphorical purposes. With some careful repainting, the logo on the side of the aircraft was altered to read, "Magic Carpet Airlines." It was a fitting end to a grueling twenty-nine-day shoot.

Lucas knew from the outset that editing *American Graffiti*'s intertwining narratives into a coherent whole would represent a significant challenge. "There's no message or long speech," he said in 1973. "But you know that when the story ends, America underwent a drastic change. The early sixties were the end of an era. It hit us all very hard." He approached Verna Fields, who at the time was editing a film for director Peter Bogdanovich. Universal agreed with the choice, and Fields began work on the footage while Lucas was still shooting. Fields completed a rough cut of the movie before she returned to Rome to resume work on *What's Up, Doc?* (1972).

Above - *Debbie Dunham (Candy Clark), Terry "The Toad" Fields (Charlie Martin Smith), and Steve Bolander (Ron Howard) regroup after the "goat killer" scene, on the fourteenth shooting day.*

Left - *Lucas, Mackenzie Phillips, and Paul Le Mat.*

Opposite - *Lucas, in his USC varsity jacket, and crew prepare another setup.*

Following Fields's departure, Lucas struggled with the film's structure. He had written the script so that the four storylines were always presented in the same sequence. This ABCD, ABCD structure meant that a scene featuring John Milner would always be followed by a scene featuring Terry, which would always be followed by a scene featuring Steve, then Curt, and so on. Lucas persevered with his original vision until pragmatism dictated a compromise. The first cut of the movie was three-and-a-half hours long; and, in the process of removing an hour and a half, numerous scenes were cut and many others were shortened and combined. The film became increasingly loose, with the result that the presentation of scenes no longer resembled the ABCD sequence.

Wexler had achieved a warm and incandescent look for the film that complemented the nostalgic atmosphere—at times the cruising sequences in particular resemble a colorful, half-remembered dream. Lucas wanted to create the same ambience with the soundtrack, and consequently turned once again to sound designer Walter Murch. "In *American Graffiti*, the problem in search of a solution was George's initial irrevocable desire to have over forty songs in the film," he says. "The way the screenplay was written, every scene had the name of the song that was playing in the background next to it. It created a technical problem, which was that you would drive your audience mad if you did that. Two songs, four songs, that's fine, but forty-two songs back-to-back is too much, unless you do something with them. Nobody had ever done this before, so the problem had never been confronted."

Murch decided that the best way to keep the music Lucas wanted was to "worldize" its addition to the soundtrack, in much the same way he had treated the wedding scene in *The Godfather*. "George and I did some tests and found the most practical places to do the recordings. For special events such as the sock hop, we went to the basketball court at Tamalpais High School in Mill Valley and rerecorded the music in that environment and in a couple of other places that had special sounds."

The recording sessions would often begin in the backyard of Lucas's Mill Valley house, where *Graffiti* was edited. Lucas and Murch would stand about fifty feet apart from each other, with Lucas moving a speaker back and forth in a slow-moving arc while the music played. Murch would record the sound with a microphone. Sometimes they would face each other and other times they would stand at 180-degree angles. The result was two hours of tape featuring the entire Wolfman Jack show, including all the records he played, and all the commercials in between. "It turned out to be the audio equivalent of depth of field in photography," says Murch. "We had infinite flexibility."

The results of Murch's "worldizing" are remarkable. The sound of Herby and the Heartbeats (Flash Cadillac and the Continental Kids) singing "At the Hop" in the school gymnasium is as cavernous and indistinct as you'd expect from a primitive PA system in an unsuitable venue.

Clearing the music copyrights had cost approximately

Above - *At the sock hop, Herby and the Heartbeats perform what have become known as "golden oldies"—a tradition of nostalgia that* American Graffiti *began.*

Left - *With Kurtz (left) and Marcia Lucas (middle), Lucas prepares to film the sock hop on the twenty-sixth day of shooting, Tuesday, August 1.*

$80,000, and as a result there was no money left for a traditional score. "I used the absence of music, and sound effects, to create the drama," says Lucas, highlighting the scene where Terry fears he is being stalked by the infamous goat-killer. "Normally, you use the music to create the drama and the sound effects to create the realism. I used the music to create the realism and the sound effects to create the drama."

By December 1972, *American Graffiti* was complete. Lucas had risen to Coppola's challenge, creating a warm and poignant coming-of-age comedy-drama.

A radio tunes in to a rock-and-roll radio station as the sun sets over Mel's Drive-in. Terry "The Toad" Fields (Charlie Martin Smith), Steve Bolander (Ronny Howard), Curt Henderson (Richard Dreyfuss), and John Milner (Paul Le Mat) meet in the parking lot. Steve and Curt are preparing to leave town to attend college on the East Coast—this is the last night they will spend with their friends.

Steve and Curt are going to the freshman sock hop, but John goes off to cruise the streets. Terry drives away in Steve's Chevy. While cruising down 10th Street, Curt sees a beautiful blonde in a white Thunderbird. She mouths "I love you" before disappearing.

Above - *Laurie (Cindy Williams) tells Steve (Ron Howard) to "go to hell" while they dance to "Smoke Gets in Your Eyes."*

Right - *Curt Henderson (Richard Dreyfuss, center) nervously contemplates his standing with the Pharaohs: Joe Young (Bo Hopkins) and Carlo (Manuel Padillo Jr.), far left.*

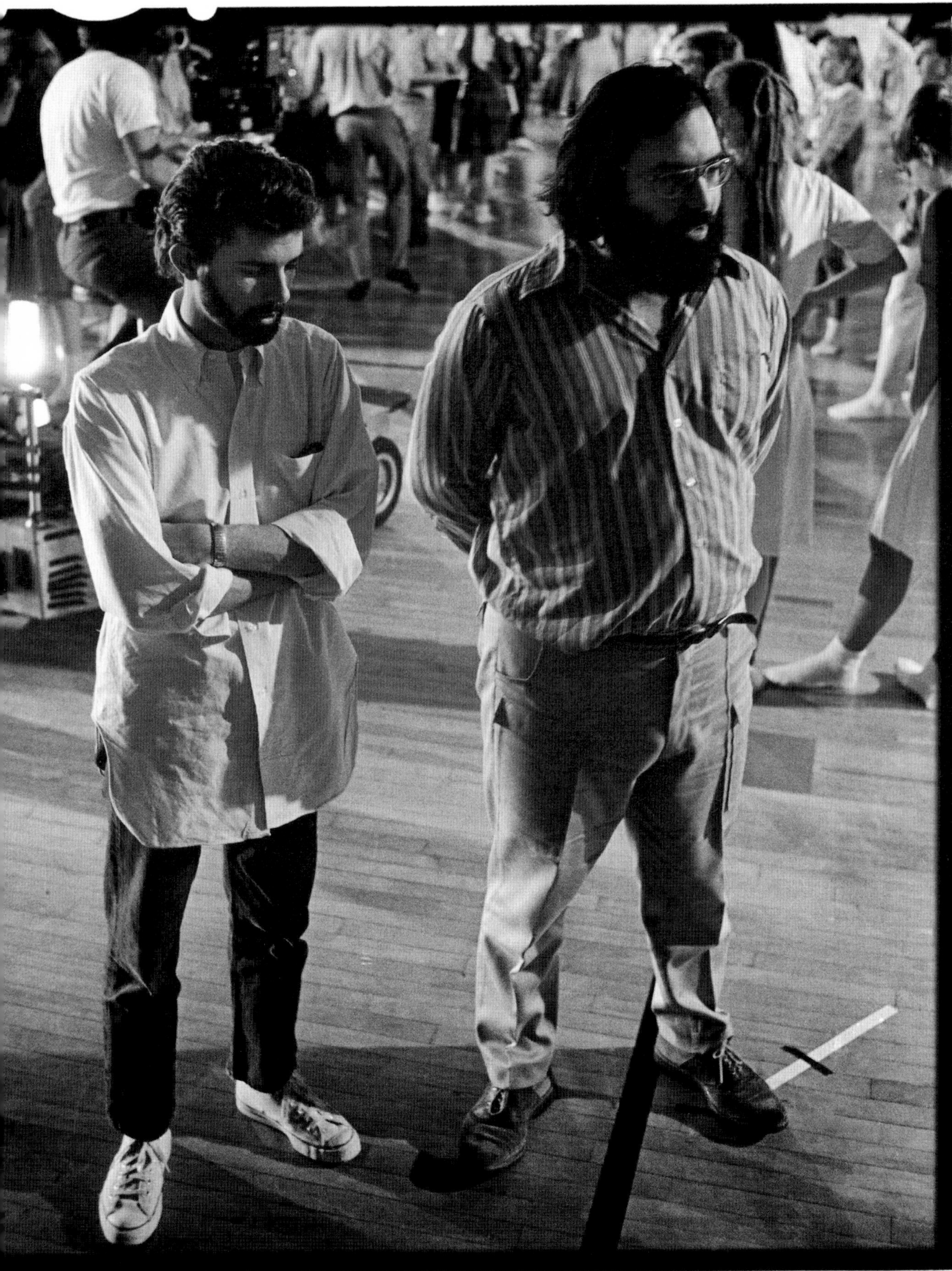

After leaving the hop, Curt is coerced into riding with a gang of would-be tough guys who call themselves The Pharaohs. He learns that Wolfman Jack broadcasts from just outside of town. Inside the dark, eerie radio station he encounters a bearded man he assumes to be the manager. Curt hands the manager a message to the blonde in the Thunderbird. As he walks away, Curt hears the voice of the Wolfman and looks behind him. The manager was Wolfman Jack all along.

The other three story lines involve breakups and reunions, and their stories intertwine until Toad and Steve end up on Paradise Road to watch John race against Bob Falfa (Harrison Ford)—with Laurie (Cindy Williams) as a passenger. The sound of "Green Onions" by Booker T and the MGs pumps out of the radio as the cars and spectators gather. Within seconds, it is all over—Falfa's car blows a tire and plunges into a ditch. Steve and John run over to the wreck, and a dazed Bob and Laurie stagger out before it explodes. Distraught, Laurie grips Steve tightly and begs him not to leave her.

The sound of a phone ringing in a booth wakes Curt from his sleep. He grabs the receiver and speaks excitedly to the mysterious blonde. She tells him she might see him cruising tonight. He says that's not possible. At the airfield Curt says goodbye to his parents, his sister, and his friends. The plane takes off and Curt gazes out of the window at the town and the life he is leaving behind. On the road beneath him, a white Thunderbird roars along.

Left - *Lucas and Coppola in the gym at Tamalpais High School in Mill Valley, California, during the filming of the sock hop. In a nod to Coppola, a briefly glimpsed marquee in* American Graffiti *bears the title of his debut film,* Dementia 13 *(1963).*

As if to underline the fact that *Graffiti* was no simpleminded cruise down memory lane, Lucas uses the final shot of the film for some thought-provoking mini-biographies. As Curt's plane disappears into the blue sky, each character's yearbook cameo appears alongside a brief account of their further exploits:

> *John Milner was killed by a drunk driver in December 1964.*
> *Terry Fields was reported missing in action near An Loc in December 1965.*
> *Steve Bolander is an insurance agent in Modesto, California.*
> *Curt Henderson is a writer living in Canada.*

Those who had failed to recognize the emotional story at the heart of *THX 1138* were probably surprised that the same writer/director had created *American Graffiti.* But Curt's departure from Modesto has the same metaphorical significance as the moment *THX* realizes he can simply walk out of prison. "There's a great big beautiful world out there," the Wolfman tells Curt.

The first public screening of *American Graffiti* took place on the morning of Sunday, January 28, 1973, at San Francisco's expansive Northpoint Theater. The event represented Lucas's first opportunity to experience the movie with a packed audience. It was also Universal executive Ned Tanen's first viewing of the film. "[The studio] hadn't seen dailies, they hadn't seen anything," says Lucas. "They'd forgotten about us."

Other attendees were Coppola and Lucas's old friends Matthew Robbins and Hal Barwood, who were writing Steven Spielberg's debut feature *The Sugarland Express* for Universal. Tanen was also in charge of *The Sugarland Express*, and Robbins recognized him as soon as he and Barwood boarded the plane in Los Angeles to travel north. "We greeted him and he greeted us, but I remember vividly how unfriendly he was," says Robbins. "He was unhappy. [Universal] had put most of their time and attention into another movie under his supervision, which was *Jesus Christ Superstar. American Graffiti* was an afterthought. In some circles at the studio it was, I think, considered a mistake."

DELETED SCENES

American Graffiti's preoccupation with radio and escape meant it shared much in common with Lucas's student film _The Emperor_ and his first feature, _THX 1138_. During its development, Lucas had to discard or alter a number of scenes that were integral to the expression of their shared thematic concerns of escape and the fantasy of radio.

A discussion between Steve and Curt, which reappeared in altered form in the shooting script as a debate between Steve and Laurie, offers another take on the theme of departure/escape. The exchange takes place as Steve and Curt push the latter's car, shortly before he visits the radio station.

STEVE

Why leave home to find a new home. Why leave friends you love to find . . .

CURT

All right already, I heard it. But, you can't back out now. There comes a time when you gotta leave the nest . . . Pull your head out of the sand, look around[:]the real world is waiting out there . . . somewhere.

STEVE

Who says this isn't the real world.

When Curt arrives at the radio station he finds the door locked, and his reaction highlights the listener/DJ dynamic. Concerned that he won't get the opportunity to meet Wolfman Jack, he complains to a character initially described as just a "voice":

CURT

Listen, I got a right to talk to him. I listened to him every night for as long—for 12 years almost. I know him and it's personal and it'll only take a minute and I bet Wolfman would be upset if he knew a friend couldn't get in touch with—

After Curt's plea, a buzzer sounds and he is admitted.

As the end credits rolled to the sound of the Beach Boys' "All Summer Long," the theater erupted. "It was one of those moments where the audience is so exhilarated that by the end of the film everyone is kind of high," says Robbins. "There was applause and there was cheering and chatter, a feeling of such generous goodwill and astonishment. It was a fabulous screening."

Lucas, Kurtz, and Coppola were delighted, and their enthusiasm was seemingly shared by everyone in the auditorium—everyone, that is, except one. Tanen was furious at what he'd seen, and said as much. He felt major revisions were required to bring the film up to the standard he expected. An appalled Lucas stood in the auditorium as people filed past, overwhelmed by the feeling that history was repeating itself. Lucas was at a loss for words, but Coppola was not. "We became aware of a lot of people standing at the back, and Francis histrionically tearing at his clothes," says Robbins. "It was a terrible scene."

Robbins and Barwood pushed forward to find out what was going on and heard Coppola ask, "Weren't you seated in this theater when the audience went absolutely crazy?" To which Tanen reportedly responded, "I'm not talking about that." At that point Coppola reached for a (probably metaphorical) checkbook and offered to buy the film from Universal then and there. Tanen refused to rise to Coppola's challenge, but Coppola insisted he was prepared to reimburse all of Universal's costs. "I had the money, yeah, and I

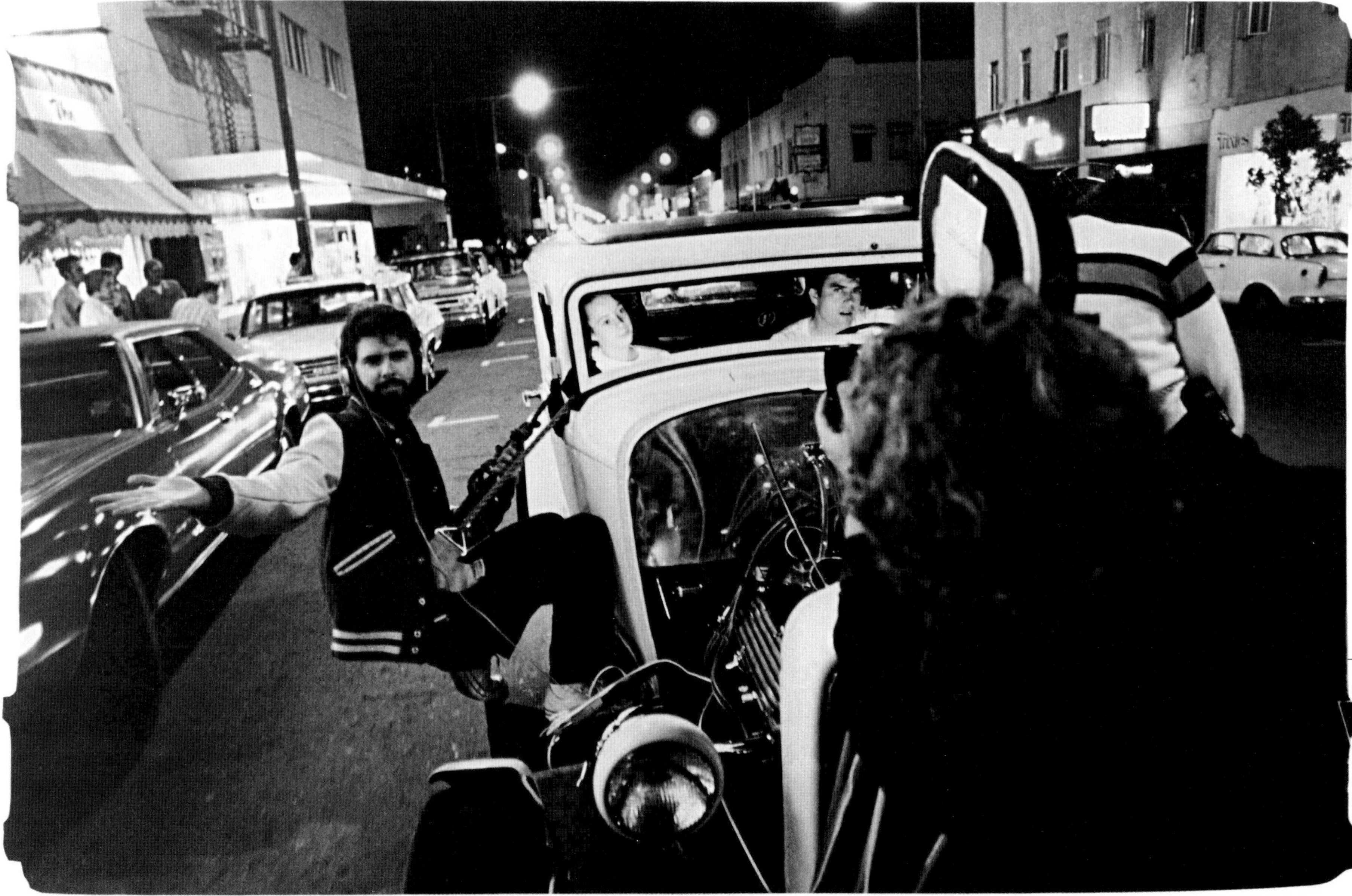

would've," Coppola would recall. "I told the executive, 'You should get on your knees and thank this kid for saving your career.'" Lucas left the theater in a daze.

"It was a very public incident," says Robbins, reflecting on an argument that is now infamous in Hollywood history. "That the studio, with a capital 'S,' could still represent itself in such a blind, insensitive, and obtuse way only reaffirmed so many of George's feelings about what Hollywood was made of."

For Lucas, there followed another dispiriting round of negotiations with studio executives. To his mind there could be no mutually acceptable compromise over any further editing of his film, but he knew it was beyond his power to refuse. Coppola brought his post-*Godfather* influence to bear and managed to reduce the studio's demands to about four-and-a-half minutes of edits. Three scenes were lost entirely: Terry's encounter with a fast-talking car salesman; an argument between Steve and his former teacher Mr. Kroot; and Bob Falfa's effort to break the ice with Laurie by serenading her with "Some Enchanted Evening."

Universal told Lucas that the film, in its edited form, was finally fit for release—as a TV movie. Lucas, however, was determined to show them they were mistaken. "We started to show it to people in Hollywood—secretaries, production assistants, basically anybody who would look at it," he recalled. "Word got out and eventually they changed their minds."

American Graffiti was released in the United States on August 1, 1973, and soon outperformed even Lucas's highest expectations. His critics at Universal were silenced when their $775,000 investment yielded a worldwide box-office gross that topped $118 million. Aside from returning one of the most phenomenal cost-to-profit ratios, *Graffiti* received a number of mixed reviews. The *San Francisco Chronicle* published a damning critique, but *Los Angeles Times* critic Charles Champlin appreciated that *Graffiti* was much more than a rose-tinted rock-and-roll movie. "That night is a comment, not a refuge," he wrote in the July 29 edition.

Opposite - *On a side mount, Lucas enjoys a moment of relaxation during the intense twenty-nine-day shoot.*

Above - *Lucas and Wexler.*

Right - *After a few botched attempts, Bob Falfa's car meets a spectacular demise during the film's climactic drag race, as the sun rises over Paradise Road.*

"The retrospective mirror in which Lucas and his friends studied themselves and their summer of '62 revealed that there had been plenty of bragging and hoping, and naiveté along with the savvy, but more loneliness and uncertainty than lust and/or wrath beneath the ducktails and the beehives.

"The great and satisfying significance of *American Graffiti* is that it marks one of the first attempts, and by a long shot the most impressive, by a new generation of filmmakers to look at their own experience. I am not much given to superlatives, but I think *American Graffiti* is one of the most important American films of the year, as well as the one most likely to move you to tears."

Lucas had been paid $65,000 for the two years' work, but his percentage of the film's net profits made him a millionaire. Perhaps recalling the offers he had received—and rejected—before making his film, he said in 1973, "*Graffiti* was successful because it came entirely from my head. It was my concept. And that's the only way I can work." He shared the spoils of the movie's success by giving lucrative percentage points of its profits to diverse participants, such as Haskell Wexler and Wolfman Jack. By the end of the year, Lucasfilm Ltd. was worth approximately $4 million and had begun to hire its first employees. Lucas set aside a working fund of $300,000 to help him develop his science-fantasy project independently. He had already given that project an evocative name: *The Star Wars.*

Right *- The Toad (Charlie Martin Smith) encounters a persistent car salesman (John Brent) in one of three scenes cut by Universal from* American Graffiti*'s original theatrical release.*

THIS
LAZY ME
USED CARS
ER BLVD. NO.
WHOLESALE
and

Shooting Schedule
American Graffiti
as shot

Information provided here is taken from the daily progress reports. Dialogue excerpts are from: "Rock Radio. . . is . . . AMERICAN GRAFFITI. . . saga of the low-riders, by George Lucas, Gloria Katz, Willard Huyck, May 10, 1972"

SHOOT DAY 1: Monday, June 26, 1972
Call: 7.00pm **Wrap:** 5.30am
Location: 4th Street (between C Street and Lincoln), San Rafael, California
Scenes: EXT. STREET & COUPE [John and Carol], Sc. 22 [John: "I don't like that surfing crap. Rock-n-roll's been going downhill ever since Buddy Holly died."]
Pages: 2-6/8
Setups: 10

SHOOT DAY 2: Tuesday, June 27
Call: 8.00pm **Wrap:** 6.40am
Location: 4th Street (between C Street and Lincoln), San Rafael
Scenes: EXT. STREET & COUPE [John and Carol], Sc. 13 [John: "How old are you?" Carol: "Old enough. How old are you?" "Too old for you."]
Pages: 4-7/8
Setups: 19
Notes: Unable to clear or control street as planned due to City Council Order to San Rafael Police Dept.

SHOOT DAY 3: Wednesday, June 28
Call: 7.30pm **Wrap:** 5.40am
Location: Oakhill Park and Petaluma Blvd., Petaluma, California
Scenes: EXT. STREET (Couple/Water Balloon/Park)
Pages: 3-2/8
Setups: 29
Cars: 32 Coupe, Studebaker, 24 Atmos. cars

SHOOT DAY 4: Thursday, June 29
Call: 7.30pm **Wrap:** 5.30am
Location: Petaluma Streets, Petaluma
Scenes: EXT. STREET (Coupe & Falfa), Sc. 54 [Carol: "He's fast." John: "But he's stupid."]
Pages: 2-7/8
Setups: 28

SHOOT DAY 5: Friday, June 30
Call: 6.30pm **Wrap:** 5.40am
Location: Rusty's Auto Wrecking 21481 8th St. East, Sonoma 563 2nd St. East, Sonoma
Scenes: EXT. AUTO WRECKING YARD, Sc. 30 [song indicated: "It's Just a Matter of Time"]
EXT. CAROL'S HOME
Pages: 3-7/8
Setups: 23
Livestock: 1 dog

SHOOT DAY 6: Monday, July 3
Call: 7.30pm **Wrap:** 5.40am
Location: 4th Street, San Rafael
Scenes: EXT. STREET (Coupe/B.A./Bozo etc.) Sc. 24 ["Travelling—Terry—Mercury"; song indicated: "Almost Grown"] Sc. 27 [Driver: "Toad—? Is that you in that beautiful car?" Terry nods casually. "Jeez, what a waste of machinery."]
Pages: 4
Setups: 16

HOLIDAY: July 4, 1972

SHOOT DAY 7: Wednesday, July 5
Call: 7:30pm **Wrap:** 5.30am
Location: Wilson's App. Store, 145 Kentucky Ave., Petaluma, Chamber of Commerce Parking Lot, Petaluma Blvd.
Scenes: EXT. TV APPLIANCE STORE, Sc. 36 [Curt is shanghaied by the "Pharoahs"]
EXT. PARKING LOT
EXT. STREET
Pages: 6
Setups: 13

SHOOT DAY 8: Thursday, July 6
Call: 7.30pm **Wrap:** 5.45am
Location: Richmond Streets, Richmond, California Miniature Golf Course/Office, Pinole
Scenes: EXT. STREET (Hoods/Curt/Merc)
EXT. MINIATURE GOLF COURSE
INT. HOLE-IN-ONE OFFICE: Sc. 48 [Joe: "We're outta gas." Curt: "They don't sell gas here." "We're outta money, too."]
Pages: 6-1/8
Setups: 16

SHOOT DAY 9: Friday, July 7
Call: 7.30pm **Wrap:** 5.15am
Location: Chamber of Commerce Lot, Petaluma Blvd. North, Petaluma, Petaluma Blvd.
Scenes: EXT. PARKING LOT, Sc. 62 [the patrol car loses its "trans-axle and two rear wheels"]
EXT. STREET/MERC.
Pages: 1-7/8
Setups: 26

SHOOT DAY 10: Monday, July 10
Call: 7.00pm **Wrap:** 6.00am
Location: Mel's Drive-In, Mission near Van Ness, San Francisco
Scenes: EXT. DRIVE-IN, Sc. 2 ["A large neon sign buzzes in the foreground, 'Burger City,' while in the background, 'Rock Around the Clock' blares from the radio of a beautiful decked and channeled, candy-apple red, tuck and rolled '53 Merc that glides into the Drive-In."]
Pages: 4
Setups: 15
Cars: Citroen
Sp. Equipment: (1) Jeep Crane #4

SHOOT DAY 11: Tuesday, July 11
Call: 7.00pm **Wrap:** 6.00am
Location: Mel's Drive-In, San Francisco
Scenes: EXT. DRIVE-IN, Sc. 42 [John orders Carol a Coke; song designated: "In the Still of the Night"]
Pages: 8
Setups: 23

SHOOT DAY 12: Wednesday, July 12
Call: 6.30pm **Wrap:** 5.30am
Location: Mel's Drive-In, San Francisco
Scenes: EXT. DRIVE-IN, Sc. 72
Pages: 5-2/8
Setups: 24

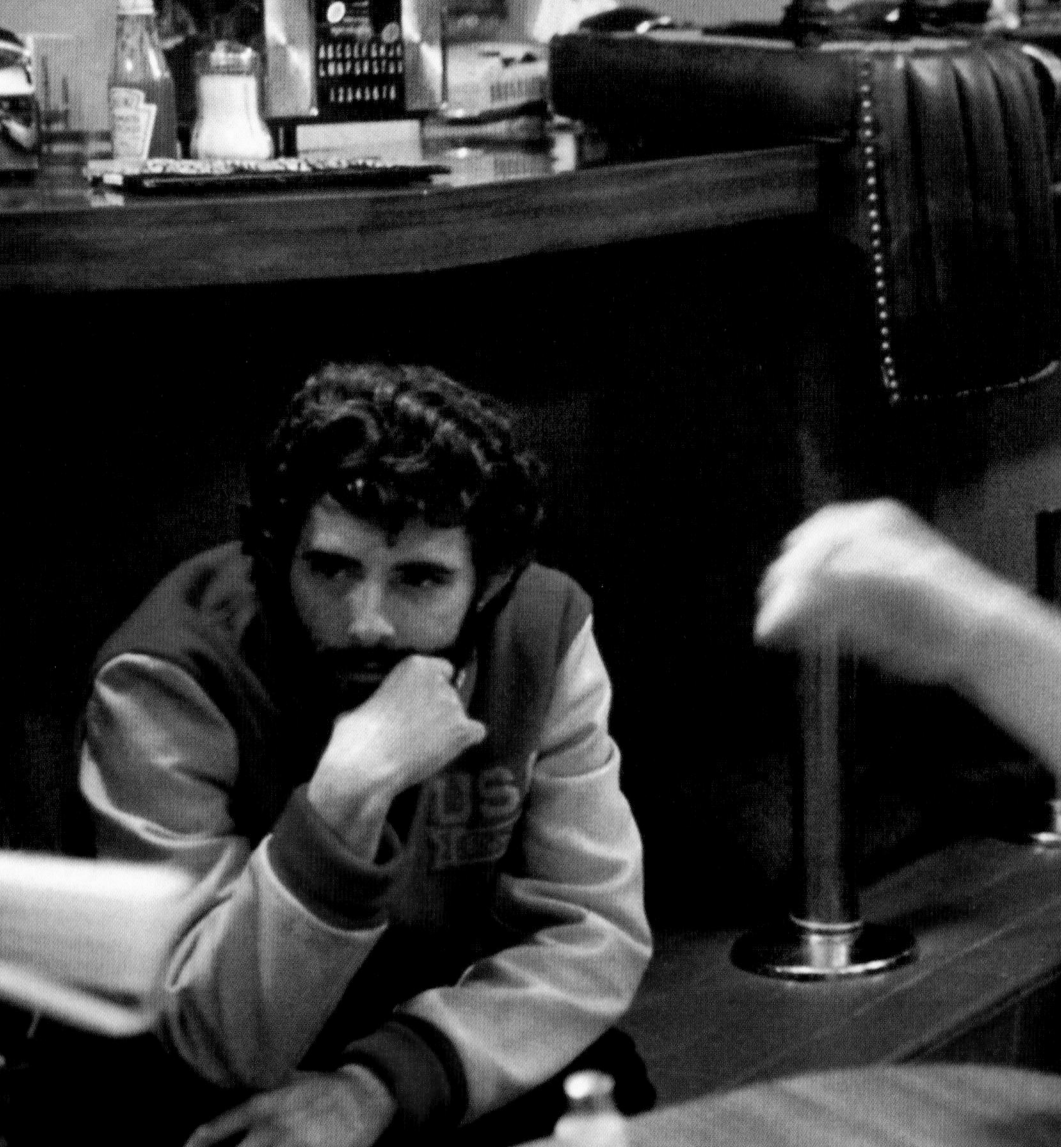

SHOOT DAY 13: Thursday, July 13
Call: 7.30pm **Wrap:** 5.30am
Location: C. OF C. Lot, Petaluma Petaluma Streets
Scenes: EXT. STREET
EXT. CAR LOT & STREET
EXT. CAR LOT/COPS (retake)
Pages: 1-2/8
Setups: 20

SHOOT DAY 14: Friday, July 14
Call: 6.30pm **Wrap:** 5.26am
Location: Marin Memorial Cemetery, Novato
Scenes: EXT. CANAL [Laurie gets angry with Steve; the Merc is stolen; talk of the "Goat Killer"]
Pages: 4-2/8
Setups: 8

SHOOT DAY 15: Monday, July 17
Call: 6.00pm **Wrap:** 7.49am
Location: Mel's Drive-In, San Francisco
Scenes: INT. DRIVE-IN
EXT. DRIVE-IN, Sc. 77 [Curt, speaking on the phone to the blonde in the white T-bird: "It's important to me. You're the most perfect beautiful creature I've ever seen and I don't know anything about you. Could we meet someplace?" Voice: "I cruise 3rd Street every night. Maybe I'll see you again tonight." "I don't think so. . . I'm leaving. . . in a couple of hours."
Pages: BAL. OF SEQ.
Setups: 30
Notes: (1) Éclair camera fell off tripod—badly damaged

SHOOT DAY 16: Tuesday, July 18
Call: 6.30pm **Wrap:** 5.26am
Location: Marin Memorial Cemetery, Novato Petaluma Streets, Petaluma
Scenes: EXT. CANAL
EXT. STREET (Terry/Falfa)
EXT. STREET (Laurie/Falfa)
Pages: 2-4/8
Setups: 12
Notes: Light rain from 1.30am to wrap prevented completion of scheduled scenes, streets too wet.

SHOOT DAY 17: Wednesday, July 19
Call: 7.30pm **Wrap:** 5.37am
Location: Petaluma streets (Petaluma Blvd., Kentucky, Washington, Western)
Scenes: EXT. STREETS (Curt/V.W./T-Bird/Kip) Sc. 29

[shouting from one car to another, Kip: "Henderson, long time no see. What'ya been doing?" Curt: "Not much, just wanted to let you know that Bobbie here is hopelessly in love with you and trembles at the sight of your rippling biceps . . ." Bobbie turns in the V.W. and "starts flailing at Curt with her purse"]
Pages: 1-2/8
Setups: 20

SHOOT DAY 18: Thursday, July 20
Call: 7.30pm **Wrap:** 5.45am
Location: Rowena Lane (KTOB transmitter), Petaluma
Lazy-Me Used Cars, 320 Petaluma Blvd. North
Petaluma streets
Scenes: EXT. RADIO STATION, Sc. 70 [Manager: "The Wolfman is everywhere. . . . Listen—no offense to your hometown here, but this place ain't exactly the hub of the universe. . . .Hell, here I sit while there's a whole big beautiful world out there."]
EXT. CAR LOT
EXT. STREETS
Pages: 2
Setups: 18
Friday, 7-21-72—COMPANY DID NOT WORK

SHOOT DAY 19: Saturday, July 22
Call: 12.00pm **Wrap:** 8.45pm
Location: Marin Memorial Cemetery, Novato
Scenes: EXT. CANAL & CANAL ROAD, FILTER DAY-FOR-NIGHT
Pages: 4-1/8
Setups: 11

SHOOT DAY 20: Sunday, July 23
Call: 7.30pm **Wrap:** 5.40am
Location: 4TH Street, San Rafael
SCENES: EXT. STREETS—MONTAGE SEQUENCES
Pages: 2
Setups: 27
Note: 4 cameras used . . . one Jeep crane

SHOOT DAY 21: Monday, July 24
Call: 8.30pm **Wrap:** 6.30am
Location: Sanderson's Used Cars (B St. and Petaluma Blvd. North) EZ Pickins Gas Station, U.S. 101 (south of Petaluma)
Frates Road, Sonoma County
Scenes: EXT. CAR LOT
EXT. STREETS
EXT. GAS STA., Sc. 66 [Attendant (to John): "Why do they even try. . . . Hell, you've been number one longer than I can remember . . ."]
EXT. PARADISE ROAD, Sc. 75 ["Both cars roar off the starting line, tires smoking and screaming."]
Pages: 2-4/8
Setups: 23

SHOOT DAY 22: Tuesday, July 25
Call: 8.30pm **Wrap:** 6.40am
Location: Petaluma High School
Pet. Streets
Frates Road
Scenes: EXT. GYM PARKING LOT, Sc. 21 [Wendy: "Same old Curt. All the time we went together you were never sure what you were doing."]
EXT. STREETS
EXT. PARADISE ROAD (cont'd)
Pages: 2-2/8
Setups: 22
Note: Blew reverse gear in 32 Coupe

SHOOT DAY 23: Wednesday, July 26
Call: 8.30pm **Wrap:** 6.30am
Location: Rear of Beasley's Rest. (Petaluma Blvd. N. & Washington)
Pet. Streets
Frates Road
Scenes: EXT. BAR PARKING LOT
EXT. STREETS (Curt/T-Bird)
EXT. PARADISE ROAD (cont'd)
Pages: 4
Setups: 26
Note: 1ST attempt to roll car failed . . . approx. 6.10am. Continued to shoot until wrap. Car unable to repeat run due to broken tie rod.

SHOOT DAY 24: Thursday, July 27
Call: 8.30pm **Wrap:** 6.40am
Location: EZ Pickins Gas Station, U.S. 101
Public Parking Lot, Petaluma Blvd.
Streets and sidewalk, Petaluma
Frates Rd.
Scenes: EXT. GAS STATION (pick-up c.u. "John")
EXT. ACME LOT
EXT. STREET AND SIDEWALK
EXT. PARADISE ROAD (cont'd)
Pages: 3-3/8
Setups: 25
Note: 2ND attempt at car stunt failed . . . bent right tie rod.

SHOOT DAY 25: Monday, July 31
Call: 8.00am **Wrap:** 8.00pm
Location: Petaluma High School
Marin Memorial Cem., Novato
Scenes: INT. HALL
INT. BOYS LAVATORY
INT. GIRLS LAVATORY
EXT. CANAL AND CANAL ROAD (retake)
Pages: 1-5/8
Setups: 13
Note: Retakes needed at Canal location due to under-exposed film.

SHOOT DAY 26: Tuesday, August 1
Call: 10.00am **Wrap:** 10.10pm
Location: Mt. Tamalpais High School—Boys Gym, M.V. [Mill Valley]
Scenes: INT. GYM (Sock hop), Sc. 14 [designated song: "At the Hop"]
Pages: 6-1/8
Setups: 38
Note: 4 cameras used

SHOOT DAY 27: Wednesday, August 2
Call: 8.30pm **Wrap:** 6.15am
Location: Petaluma High School
Pet. Streets
Scenes: EXT. GYM PARKING LOT
EXT. STREETS
EXT. DRIVE IN (retake)
Pages: 2-7/8
Setups: 18

SHOOT DAY 28: Thursday, August 3
Call: 8.30pm **Wrap:** 6.40am
Location: KRE Radio, Berkeley
Buchanan Field, Concord
Scenes: EXT./INT. RADIO STATION
EXT. AIRPORT
INT. AIRPLANE
Pages: 4-2/8
Setups: 16
Note: Airplane unable to taxi or take off due to flat left tires. Did not get shot of plane airborne.

SHOOT DAY 29: Friday, August 4
Call: 8.30pm **Wrap:** 9.30am
Location: 884 Bodega Ave., Petaluma
Frates Road
Buchanan Field (2ND unit)
Scenes: EXT./INT. LIQUOR STORE, Sc. 44 [Toad tries to buy the elusive bottle of "Old Harper"; designated song: "Teenager in Love"]
EXT. PARADISE ROAD (retake)
EXT. AIRPORT/AIRPLANE, Sc. 79: ["Curt listens to the radio as the plane takes off. As it climbs and banks out over the valley, the music fades and the station drifts between static and other stations and then it's gone. Curt turns off the radio and looks out the window. As the plane banks, the wing tips down and through the window Curt sees the yellow Thunderbird crossing beneath on the small grey ribbon of highway. Curt leans up, watching it—the plane shadow ripples over the car and then it's gone."]
Pages: 4-1/8
Setups: 26
Note: Low overcast prevented shooting at Frates Road location until 8.40am. Stunt again failed to work. "A" arm and tie rods bent. (1) cameraman & (1) asst. cameraman to airport to film plane take off after company wrap at Frates Road location. Wrap 1st unit shooting "*AMERICAN GRAFFITI*."

2nd UNIT SHOOTING: Monday 8/7/72
Call: 4.00am **Wrap:** 10.42am
Location: Frates Road
Scenes: EXT. PARADISE ROAD (retake stunt and explosion only)
EXT. ROAD/T-BIRD (aerial shot)
Note: Used Cessna as camera plane f/aerial shot. (4) cameras used on stunt.

Above - Lucas, Wexler (behind camera), and Ron Howard.

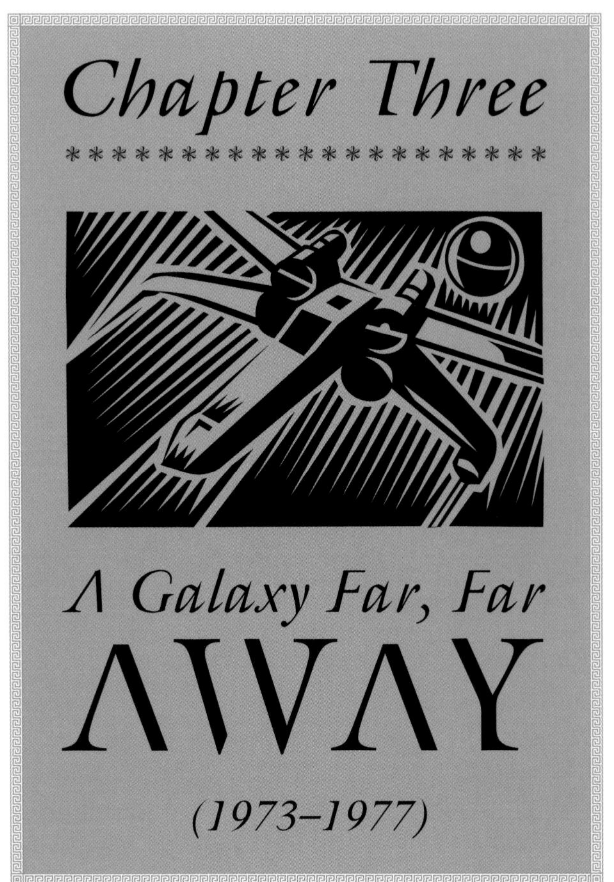
Chapter Three
A Galaxy Far, Far
AWAY
(1973–1977)

From 1973 onward Lucas dedicated himself to *The Star Wars*, but this new endeavor represented just one of the possibilities open to him in the wake of *American Graffiti*'s huge success.

During the filming of *Graffiti*, Lucas had approached Willard Huyck and Gloria Katz with an idea for a story called *Radioland Murders*, a screwball comedy thriller set in the 1930s. "We came up with this idea of doing *Ten Little Indians* in a radio station," says Lucas, who remembers that, at the time, the story was considered a thematic sequel to *Graffiti*. In 1974, Lucas began work on a treatment and held the first of many story discussions with Huyck and Katz.

Following the completion of *Graffiti*, Lucas also renewed his efforts to film *Apocalypse Now*. However, its disturbing exploration of America's occupation of Vietnam proved alarming to a Hollywood whose depiction of the conflict had yet to evolve beyond the gung-ho propaganda of *The Green Berets* (1968). "Nobody wanted to have anything to do with it," says Lucas. "We couldn't get any cooperation from any of the studios or the military, but once I had *American Graffiti* behind me I tried again and pretty much got a deal at Columbia. We scouted locations in the Philippines and we were ready to go." However, Columbia wanted all the rights American Zoetrope controlled, and Coppola refused to relinquish them. "The deal collapsed," remembers Lucas. "And when that deal collapsed, I started working on *Star Wars*."

Like *Graffiti* before it, the inspiration for *Star Wars* lay in Lucas's anthropology studies. While at college, he had read Joseph Campbell's 1949 book, *The Hero with a Thousand Faces*, an illuminating survey of religions and myths that identified and classified a number of threads common to them all.

"When I was ten years old, I asked my mother, 'If there is only one God, why are there so many religions?'" remembers Lucas. "I've been pondering that question ever since. The conclusion I've come to is that all the religions are true—they just see different parts of the elephant. Religion is basically a container for faith. Faith is the glue that holds us together as a society. Faith plays a very important part in allowing us to remain stable, remain balanced."

Campbell claimed: "The artist is the one who communicates myth for today," and Lucas was determined to rise to that challenge. His next immaculate reality would adopt the vernacular of Saturday matinee serials like *Flash Gordon* as the vehicle for a synthesis of reinvented mythological motifs. "The original inspiration for *Star Wars* was to try to create a modern myth," he says. "Westerns were the last mythological genre we had, but they had died out in the late 1950s/early 1960s and nothing had replaced them."

This undertaking would be the most exacting challenge yet for Lucas's talents. The backdrop for the story would have to be as compelling and

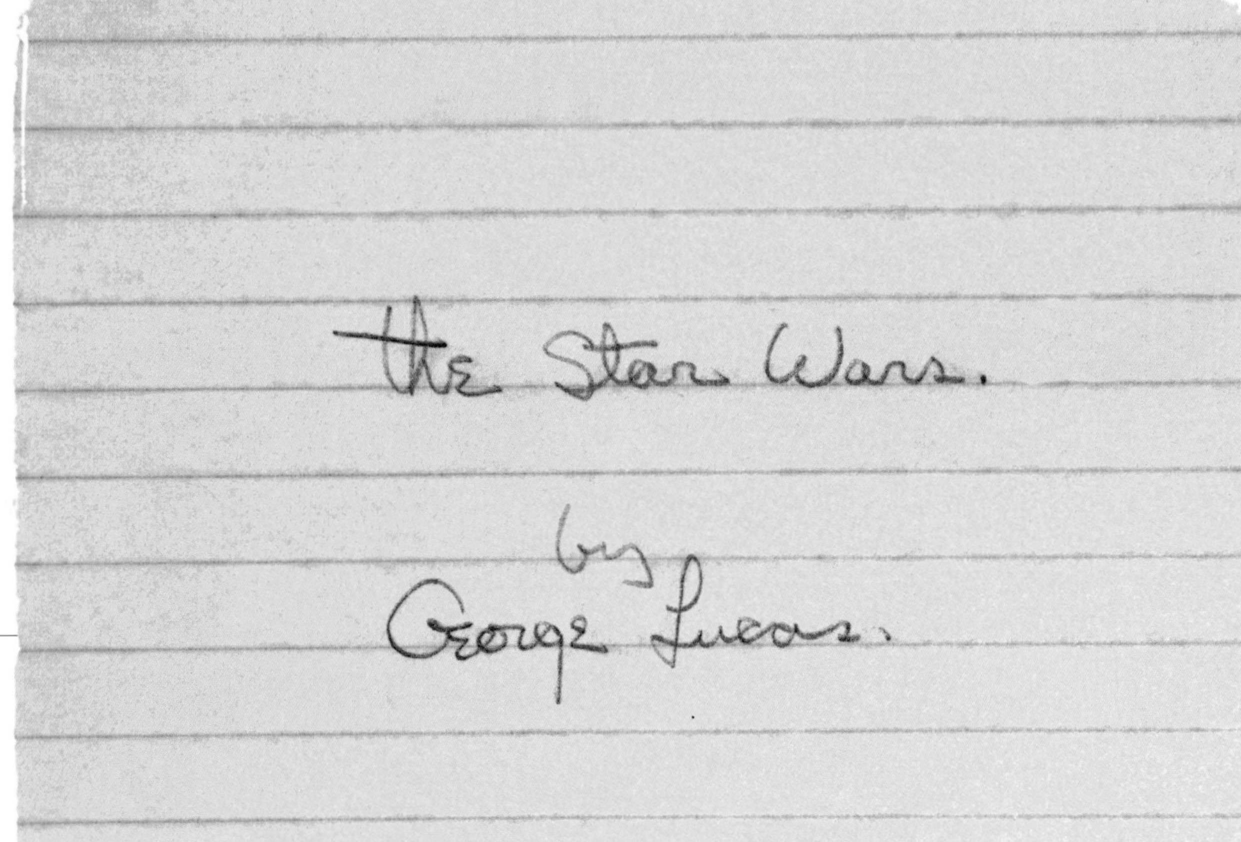
the Star Wars.

by

George Lucas.

Previous - *Lucas and Anthony Daniels (dressed as C-3PO) on what turned out to be a difficult location shoot in Tunisia for* Star Wars *in March 1976.*

Left - *The original handwritten first page of Lucas's May 1973 treatment of* The Star Wars.

RADIOLAND MURDERS FIRST DRAFT

* *

Lucas negotiated a deal to produce *Radioland Murders* for Universal shortly after the completion of *American Graffiti*. Willard Huyck and Gloria Katz prepared a rough draft based on Lucas's treatment in 1974, and Universal was confident enough to begin placing trade advertisements announcing preproduction soon after.

Huyck and Katz's first draft, dated July 1976, begins on the opening night of America's fourth radio network, WKGL. Studio assistant Penny Parker and her on-off boyfriend, writer Roger Henderson, work at a frantic pace to ensure the opening night's entertainment goes smoothly—but things get off to a bad start when trombonist Ruffles Reedy is poisoned. There are six more murders during the course of the evening, each one preceded by a warning from an eerie, disembodied voice. Each victim is killed in bizarre circumstances: one dies in an apparent accident with a revolving stage; one is electrocuted at his microphone stand; and one chokes on poisonous gas while watching a performance ("That . . . show . . . stinks!" he gasps, before collapsing).

In July 1978 Lucas revealed that *Radioland Murders* was still in development, and that Steve Martin had been approached to star as Roger Henderson. "He and Cindy [Williams] would be the ideal team," he said. "We have a script that is in the process of being shortened and we should start shooting early next year." It would be more than fifteen years, however, before production of *Radioland Murders* actually began.

In 1974, Lucas and Gloria Katz stand in front of the step-outline cards of the earliest version of the *Radioland Murders* script, at Willard Huyck and Katz's home office at Studio City.

APOCALYPSE NOW ALTERNATE ENDING

* *

The version of *Apocalypse Now* that Lucas was planning to make differed from the film ultimately shot by Francis Ford Coppola in a number of key respects. The screenplay's most radical difference occurs in the final act. "In the original script that John Milius did," Lucas recalls, "Willard reaches the end of his journey and the Viet Cong surround Colonel Kurtz's compound. But whenever helicopters are sent in to rescue these guys, Kurtz shoots them down. Kurtz tells Willard: 'My friends have died on this land. I have fought for this land. Our community has suffered to own this land, to be on this land, to have this be our land. We have an emotional investment in this. The Viet Cong don't. And the United States doesn't. But we do.' There are air strikes, and there is a huge battle with the Viet Cong. Kurtz gets killed, and only Willard and three or four other soldiers are left. The movie ends as headquarters sends a helicopter to get them out of there—and Willard shoots it down. He takes Kurtz's place and it continues, because he fought for the land."

"That wasn't a good ending," considers Milius, reflecting on what could have been. "I think my version's much too obvious. Some people liked it, but I prefer the ending that's there now."

convincing as anything Lucas had already realized on the screen. In 1972 he had begun work on a handwritten document he called the *Journal of the Whills*, devising a narrative vehicle with which to explore some thirty-five themes.

The *Journal of the Whills* was related by "C. P. Thorpe, Padawan learner of the famed Jedi," describing the exploits of "Mace Windy, a revered Jedi Bendu of Ophuchi." A separate list of planets included the desert world Aquilae, the jungle world Yavin, a "cloud planet" called Ophuchi, and a "city planet" called Alderaan. To embody his themes Lucas added a list of characters, which included General Luke Skywalker, General Vader, Han Solo, C-3PO, R2-D2, and Chewbacca. The latter was a giant apelike creature, or Wookiee, inspired by Lucas's Alaskan malamute Indiana, who would often sit in the passenger's seat of his car, looking very much the copilot.

After *Graffiti* was released, Lucas returned to these notes and, in between efforts to develop *Radioland Murders* and *Apocalypse Now*, developed a detailed synopsis for the saga of *The Star Wars* as well as the *Adventures of Indiana Smith* (see box on page 115).

Following its rejection by United Artists back in 1971, however, Lucas was obliged to offer his space fantasy to Universal, which, under the terms of the *American Graffiti* deal, had a number of options on his future work. *The Star Wars* was submitted to Universal in February 1973, immediately after the tumultuous Northpoint screening of *Graffiti*. Three weeks later Mel Sapper, Universal's head of business affairs, rejected it.

That summer, Lucas's agent, Jeff Berg, met with Alan Ladd Jr. at Twentieth Century-Fox and told him about *Graffiti*. Ladd was sufficiently intrigued to ask to see a print of *Graffiti* along with a treatment of Lucas's new idea. In May, Gary Kurtz smuggled a copy of the as-yet-unreleased *American Graffiti* to Ladd at Fox. At about the same time, Lucas completed a new treatment of *The Star Wars* for Ladd, narrowing the scope of the story to bring the projected budget under the $3 million mark that Ladd considered acceptable.

"The story was too big for one movie," says Lucas. "I had $3 million and I thought, 'No way—I have got to cut this down.' So I broke it down, making the first act as the first film and putting the second and third acts on the shelf to film later. It was the only way I could carry on with the script."

The treatment that Ladd read introduced sixteen-year-old Annikin Starkiller, his father, Kane, and his ten-year-old brother, Deak. Kane, one of the last of the Jedi, has gone into hiding with his children on the fourth moon of Utapau. A Sith warrior wearing black robes, his face obscured by a mask, murders Deak with a lasersword, and Kane uses his own lasersword to kill the warrior. Kane buries his son and takes Annikin to Aquilae, where he is reunited with his old

Above - *At Lucas's home: (from left) Hal Barwood, Lucas's dog Indiana (her name was the inspiration for one of Lucas's later, well-known characters), Lucas, a visitor, and Jane Bay, Lucas's executive assistant. Barwood is seated just outside Ben Burtt's office.*

Left - *Lucas with his father.*

Opposite - *At work in the office where much of* Star Wars *was written.*

friend General Skywalker. Kane is dying—electronic limbs and organs have replaced everything but his head and right arm—so he asks Skywalker to complete Annikin's training. A sinister creation known as the Death Star was moved up into this first act, though originally Lucas had placed it at the very end of the roughly two-hundred-page saga's third act.

Berg arranged a meeting between Lucas and Ladd, during which Lucas felt he had finally found a studio executive on his wavelength. "He understood what talent was, he respected talent, and he was able to say, 'I think this guy is talented, I think we're going to invest in him.' So Alan Ladd Jr. invested in me; he did not invest in the movie," Lucas recalls.

Lucas felt that his new relationship with Ladd would afford him the opportunity to realize his ambition to direct an old-fashioned Hollywood-style movie. "Mostly everything I'd done at that point was street films," he explains. "I wanted to make a movie on soundstages, with art directors and sets, before I went off to do my own stuff, my own stuff being abstract films. I figured that I'd barely managed to get another job after *THX*, and if *American Graffiti* went down the tubes—at this point they were just going to release it as a TV movie—this could be my last opportunity."

When it became clear that *American Graffiti* was in fact going to be huge hit, Fox moved quickly to close a deal to finance and distribute *The Star Wars.* Lucas had already agreed to Fox's offer of $150,000 to write and direct, plus a degree of profit participation. "We had a meeting to decide what to do," recalls Tom Pollock. "Jeff Berg told George, 'You're now a $500,000 director, if not more.' George said, 'I don't want to be a $500,000 director—I will write and direct the movie for the price I agreed to write and direct the movie.' He didn't change his points either, but there were a few things he did want—ownership

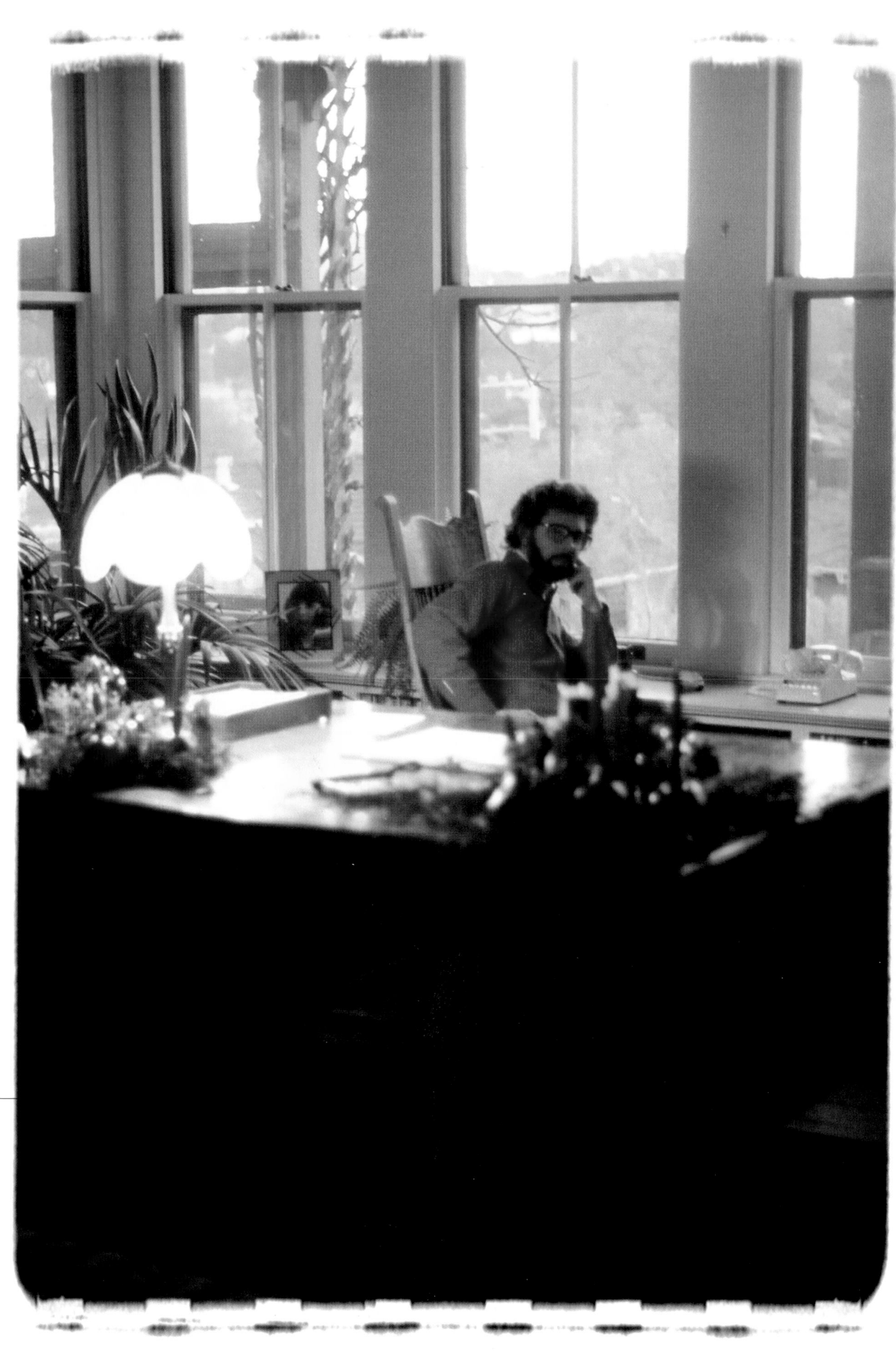

of the sequel rights, ownership of the television rights, and the eventual ownership of the merchandise rights, the music, and the soundtrack album. George made the decision that these things were more important to him than the money. He felt that not because he thought *Star Wars* was going to be a huge hit and was going to sell all the merchandise that it eventually sold—it was more about control. George had always imagined it as three movies, and he wanted to control his vision and his future."

Pollock recalls that Lucas's negotiating points surprised the studio. "I think Fox was relieved that all we were asking for were things nobody wanted. Who cared about sequel rights? They had first option on them anyway. Who cared about merchandising? In those days that meant posters and T-shirts." The deal was signed on August 20, 1973, just nineteen days after the release of *American Graffiti.*

In 1974, Lucas used some of his profits from *Graffiti* to buy a large Victorian house in San Anselmo, California. Christened "Parkway," the house was the first permanent headquarters for Lucasfilm. In an effort to re-create the atmosphere and ideals of USC and American Zoetrope, Lucas offered space within the house to other Bay Area filmmakers and old friends such as Carroll Ballard, Hal Barwood, Philip Kaufman, Michael Ritchie, Matthew Robbins, and, briefly, Walter Murch. "It was a little filmmaking complex," remembers Lucas fondly. "We had editing rooms, a sound department down in the basement, and a screening room that we built on the back."

Right - A very early poster concept by John Solie.

Barwood and Robbins helped Lucas renew his acquaintance with Steven Spielberg following their brief meeting in 1968. "George was the kind of maverick from northern California, and an independent filmmaker who was always extremely proud that he had very few attachments to Hollywood," says Spielberg. "And I was essentially a test-tube baby, incubated at the lot at Universal Studios and raised inside the establishment. I was very proud of that. I was given my start inside the industry, and George was very proud that he was given his start outside. I think that difference attracted us to each other."

While Spielberg developed his next movie, an adaptation of the Peter Benchley novel *Jaws*, Lucas continued working on *The Star Wars*. By July 1974, he had progressed his rough draft into a first-draft screenplay, preserving familiar core themes such as man's relationship with machines, the importance of friendship and social obligations, and, crucially, the importance of choosing the correct path. These were all familiar meditations from Lucas's student work as well as his first two feature films, but never had they been articulated against such a carefully constructed and ambitious milieu. "It started off in horrible shape," says Barwood. "It was hard to discern there was a movie there. It was both kind of futuristic and funny and endearing and exciting all at once, but that combination of possibilities just didn't dawn on us reading these words on the page. But George never gave up and he worked and worked and worked."

In 1977, Lucas revealed something of this tortuous writing process to French journalist Claire Clouzot: "*THX 1138* was a nonnarrative film, without a framework," he said. "*American Graffiti* was similar; it was a juxtaposition of various sequences rather than one coherent story. On the other hand, *Star Wars* is a classic story, an old-style narrative, even blatantly old-fashioned. I wanted to know if I could do it. I wanted to explore this creative field that I had consciously avoided. . . . It's really what I wanted to do: be the sole architect of a traditional story where everything was linked by cause and effect."

Lucas was aware that some of the concepts and characters he was devising were so bizarre that it was very difficult for anyone else to visualize them. The treatment he had shown Ladd in May 1973 was illustrated with the occasional picture cut from a magazine, but he now wanted to present illustrations showing actual scenes from the first draft. To this end, Lucas hired freelance artist Ralph McQuarrie to paint what would be referred to as concept artwork based on four key scenes. "He wanted the pictures to be idealist," said McQuarrie in 1977. "In other words, don't worry about how

Above *- In 1974 at Universal Studios, on the set of Steven Spielberg's* Jaws *(1975): Gloria Katz (to Lucas's right), Lucas, Gary Kurtz, Willard Huyck. (on far right).*

Far left *- At famed illustrator Frank Frazetta's house in Pennsylvania: (from left) Edward Summer, Frazetta, and Lucas. According to Summer, Lucas was interested in having Frazetta do the cover of the* Art of Star Wars *book he envisioned. (from the Edward Summer collection)*

Left *- At Lucas's home, accountant Lucy Wilson (at the typewriter), and assistant film editor Todd Boekelheide (at table).*

things are going to get done or how difficult it might be to produce them—just do them how you'd like them to be."

Though the story evolved and changed with every draft, McQuarrie's pictures played a crucial part in convincing Fox executives to keep their faith in the project as its scope—and projected budget—assumed new proportions. It was not until Lucas's second-draft script (dated January 28, 1975) that the story began to closely resemble the final film. This script was entitled *Adventures of the Starkiller. Episode I: The Star Wars*, and opened with the quote:

> *". . . And in the time of greatest despair there shall come a savior, and he shall be known as: THE SON OF THE SUNS."*
> –Journal of the Whills, 3:127

Lucas's intention to borrow from the style of Saturday matinee serials, with their episodic structure and recaps at the beginning of each installment, fitted perfectly with his plan to divide *The Adventures of the Starkiller* into a series of films. Although the titles of *The Star Wars* indicated that it was "episode one" in this saga, the second-draft script began with a story recap in the form of a "roll-up" seen against a backdrop of stars:

> *The Republic Galactica is dead. Ruthless trader barons, driven by greed and the lust for power, have replaced enlightenment with oppression, and "rule by the people" with the First Galactic Empire.*
>
> *Until the tragic Holy rebellion of "06," the respected Jedi Bendu of Ashla were the most powerful warriors in the Universe. For a hundred thousand years, generations of Jedi Bendu knights learned the ways of the mysterious Force of Others, and acted as the guardians of peace and justice in the Republic. Now these legendary warriors are all but extinct. One by one they have been hunted down and destroyed by a ferocious rival sect of mercenary warriors: The Black Knights of the Sith.*
>
> *It is a period of civil wars. The Empire is crumbling into lawless barbarism throughout the million worlds of the galaxy. From the celestial equator to the farthest reaches of the Great Rift, seventy small solar systems have united in a common war against the tyranny of the Empire. Under the command of a mighty Jedi warrior known as the Starkiller, the Rebel Alliance has won a crushing victory over the deadly Imperial Star Fleet. The Empire knows that one more such defeat will bring a thousand more solar systems into the rebellion, and Imperial control of the Outlands could be lost forever. . .*

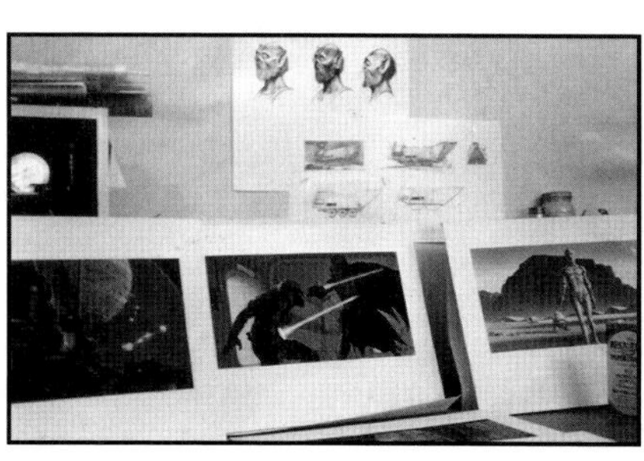

Above - Key production illustrator Ralph McQuarrie at work on the concept paintings that would prove so influential in the making of Star Wars. *McQuarrie began his career in advertising design, although subsequent work included illustrations for film posters and* CBS News' *coverage of* NASA's Apollo *flights. He was introduced to Lucas by their mutual friends Hal Barwood and Matthew Robbins.*

Far left *- The cover of the January 28, 1975 draft of* Star Wars, *entitled* Adventures of the Starkiller.

Left *- McQuarrie's studio, showing some of his early concept paintings (with sketches above). (from the Edward Summer collection)*

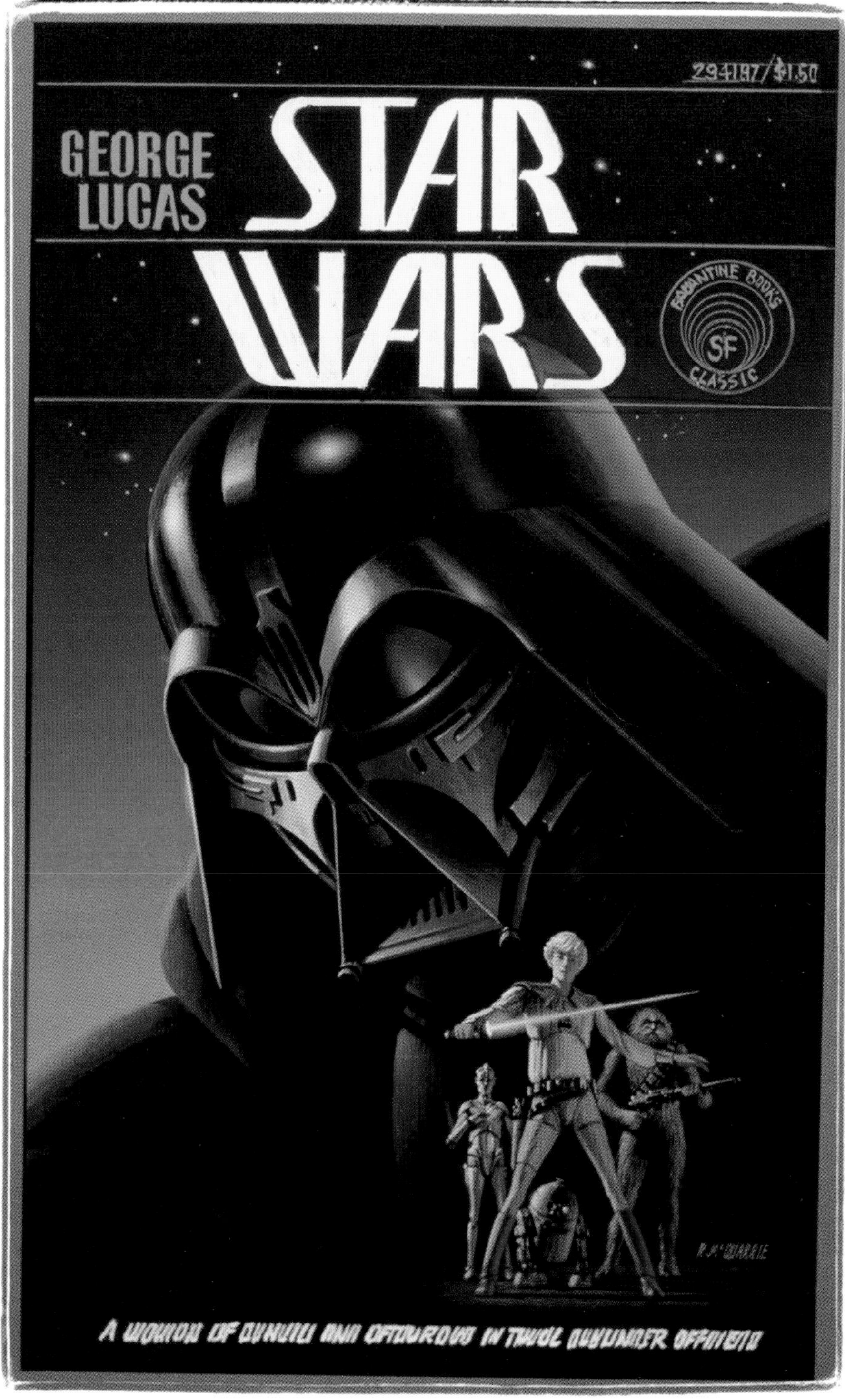

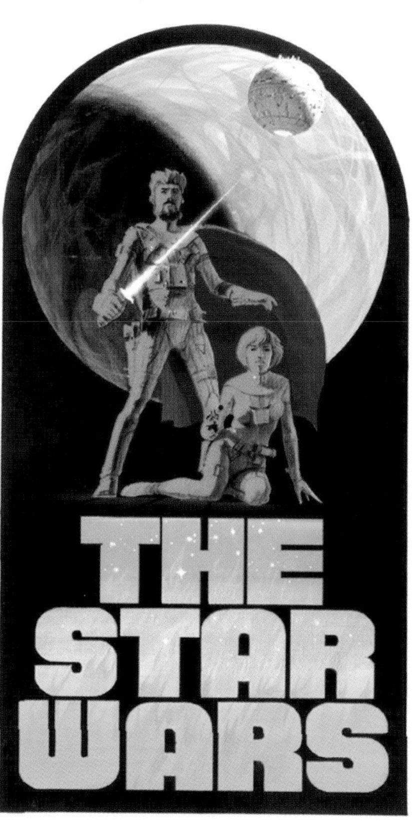

Above - Early Star Wars *logos and poster concepts by McQuarrie.*

Right *- The droids, which were named in an early draft A-2 (R2-D2) and C-3 (C-3PO), explore the surface of the mysterious desert planet Utapau in the first* Star Wars *production painting completed by Ralph McQuarrie in 1974.*

Far right *- From Akira Kurosawa's* The Hidden Fortress *(1958), the two peasants (Minoru Chiaki and Kamatari Fujiwara), who served as Lucas's inspiration for R2-D2 and C-3PO.*

This draft introduces the reader to a bewildering array of characters and technology, described in a disarmingly matter-of-fact style. Characters communicate with each other over long distances via devices called "com-links" and batons that hang from the belts of Imperial soldiers can be "ignited" into long, glowing "laserswords" that spark into life "with a sharp hum."

Much of the story is seen through the electronic eyes of two lowly characters—a short, claw-armed triped robot called R2-D2 and his bronze-colored robotic companion C-3PO. (R2-D2 was named after an abbreviation for "Reel 2, Dialogue 2" that had intrigued Lucas during the sound mix for *Graffiti*.) In the second draft's first act, a farm boy called Luke Starkiller explains an important part of the back story during a conversation with two of his brothers: many years before, a holy man called the Skywalker became aware of the Force of Others, a powerful energy field that he believed influenced the destiny of all living creatures.

Lucas had first introduced the idea of a spiritual energy, or "Force," in an early draft of *THX 1138*. That idea would gain more significance and a focal point in the form of a powerful crystal. Lucas recalls that he introduced the Force to *The Star Wars* in an effort to awaken the spirituality of the film's young audience. "I don't see *Star Wars* as profoundly religious," he nevertheless says. "*Star Wars* takes all the issues that religion represents and tries to distill them into a more modern, more easily accessible construct so that people can accept the fact that there is a greater mystery out there."

> *Adventures of the Starkiller. Episode I:* The Star Wars *begins as a small Rebel space fighter is overwhelmed by a giant Imperial Star Destroyer . . .*
>
> *Aware that his capture is inevitable, Deak Starkiller, the captain of the Rebel ship, sends a number of R2 droids from his starship to the surface of the nearby desert planet Utapau to search for his brother Luke. R2-D2 embarks on the mission, closely followed by the whining C-3PO.*
>
> *Deak is taken prisoner by the seven-foot Lord Darth Vader, a Black Knight of the Sith. On Utapau, the two droids are captured by the dwarflike Jawas. The droids eventually find their way to a moisture ranch owned by Luke's uncle and aunt, Owen and Beru Lars. The droids meet Luke's young brothers, Biggs and Windy, and his sixteen-year-old sister, Leia. When the droids meet Luke Starkiller, he interrupts his lasersword training to introduce himself as "the Skywalker." R2-D2 projects a holographic message from Deak—he is lost, and their father desperately needs Luke's help. Luke's father is waiting for his son to bring the restorative Kiber Crystal to the planet Ogana Major, which is under siege by the Imperial Legions of Alderaan.*
>
> *Luke would partly rather stay and complete his archaeology studies, but he decides to accept the challenge. He visits his mother's grave and takes the unique, diamondlike Kiber Crystal from his uncle. The crystal will amplify the power of the Ashla force a hundredfold, but could also intensify the power of the dark Bogan. It must not fall into Sith hands.*
>
> *At the Mos Eisley spaceport, Luke meets Corellian pilot Han Solo and his two-hundred-year-old Wookiee first mate, Chewbacca. Solo agrees to take Luke and the two droids to Ogana Major with the understanding that Luke's father will pay the balance of the million [credit] fee on arrival. Han does*

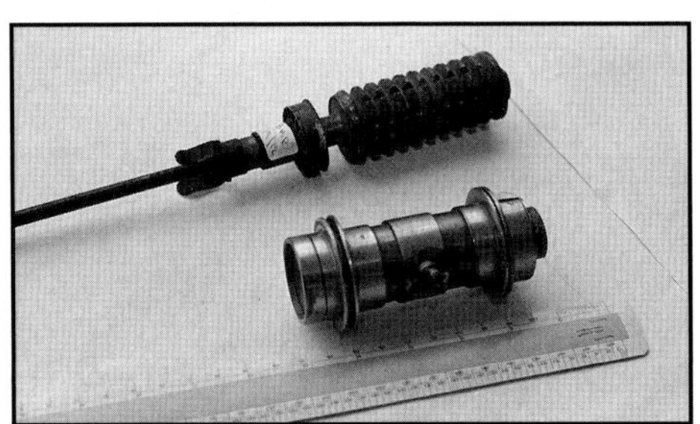

Above *- In a McQuarrie production painting, Darth Vader and an assailant duel with lightsabers—one of* Star Wars' *unique weapons and one that posed unique production problems. "I soon had my camera assistants fighting with triangular strips of wood covered with 3M material," remembers DP Gil Taylor. "A small motor was incorporated in the lightsaber handles so that the blade would spin, giving it a fluorescent effect when the light was projected onto its surface. This was done by placing a 50-percent mercury-surfaced mirror in front of the camera lens at a 90-degree angle. Using a small projector we passed a beam through the axis of the lens onto the 3M material."*

Far left *- Prototype lightsaber props, created at Elstree Studios.*

not, however, have a ship of his own. He fakes a reactor overload on a pirate ship he serves on, causing the captain and other crew members—including one Jabba the Hutt—to flee in terror. Han then steals the ship, maintaining Chewbacca and science officer Montross Holdaack as his only crew mates. Holdaack is almost entirely robotic—only his head and right arm remain. Luke and the two droids get aboard, and the starship heads for Ogana Major.

But Ogana Major has mysteriously vanished—destroyed in an enormous attack—so Luke asks Han to instead make for Alderaan, the dwelling place of the Bogan Master, Prince Valorum. Luke suspects that Deak is being held on Alderaan, in a city suspended in a sea of cirrus methane. On Alderaan, Luke and Han steal the white uniforms of Imperial stormtroopers and rescue the dying Deak. They have a close encounter with vicious

Above - Early concept drawings for Princess Leia and Annikin Skywalker (McQuarrie). The latter bears a resemblance to George Lucas.

Right - Lucas explains his ideas to McQuarrie. (From the Edward Summer collection)

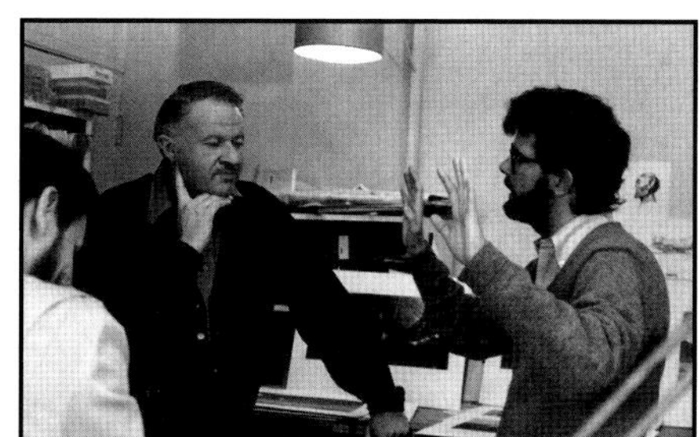

JOSEPH CAMPBELL

* *

In the 1949 book *The Hero with a Thousand Faces*, author Joseph Campbell noted: "The hero must separate from the ordinary world of his or her life up to the point at which the story begins; then, in the new world through which the journey takes place, the hero must undergo a series of trials and must overcome many obstacles in order to achieve an initiation into ways of being hitherto unknown; finally, the hero returns to share what he or she has learned with others."

If this sounds like a description of Luke Skywalker's path from farm boy to hero of the Rebel Alliance, it is no coincidence. Campbell's research into mythology and comparative religion had been a major influence on Lucas since his college days. Referring to Campbell's books, among many other sources, Lucas carefully constructed his screenplay for *Star Wars* as a cinematic expression of mythological archetypes that could be traced back thousands of years.

Lucas was intrigued to see that *Time* magazine interviewed Campbell following the release of *Star Wars*, but he did not get to meet the author until 1984, when he attended one of his lectures in San Francisco. Campbell was unfamiliar with *Star Wars*, but the two soon became friends. Campbell recalled being "thrilled" to see the film for the first time: "Here the man understands the metaphor," he said, in the posthumously published *The Hero's Journey* (1990). "What I saw was things that had been in my books but rendered in terms of the modern problem, which is man and machine. . . . That young man opened a vista and knew how to follow it and it was totally fresh."

Lucas believed that Campbell's lectures were even more compelling than his books. Over the summers of 1985 and 1986, he filmed a number of discussions between Campbell and journalist Bill Moyers, with the primary aim of preserving a private visual record of Campbell's work. Following Campbell's death in 1987, edited highlights of those discussions were used as the basis of the acclaimed PBS television series *The Power of Myth* (1988).

Dai Noga creatures in the bowels of the city and almost get squashed in a huge trash compactor before escaping Alderaan and heading back into space. The heroes are pursued by four fin-winged Imperial TIE fighters, but Han and Chewbacca manage to evade them, as well as what seems to be a giant space station. The Kiber Crystal revitalizes Deak on the journey to their next destination—the Rebel stronghold on the fourth moon of Yavin.

On the fourth moon's Masassi Outpost Luke and his friends meet such Rebels as Bail Antilles, General Dodana, and the Grande Mouff Tarkin. The Kiber Crystal revitalizes Luke's father, the impossibly aged Starkiller, who tells his son that he intends to train him as a Jedi. Luke joins a mission to strike at an exhaust port on the surface of the Death Star—the immense Imperial space station that destroyed Ogana Major. Han receives eight million in payment for his services, but refuses to join the Rebels.

Luke heads for the Death Star, with C-3PO, R2-D2, and Antilles aboard his ship. He keeps the Kiber Crystal in his pocket. Darth Vader, leading the defense of the Death Star, soon senses the presence of the Kiber Crystal. He is about to close in on Luke when Han, Chewbacca, and Montross come to the rescue. As Luke pilots his ship with expert precision, Antilles and C-3PO fire the shots that enter the exhaust port and destroy the Death Star.

Back on the fourth moon of Yavin, the Starkiller tells his son: "Your achievement will be sung through the ages. The Kiber Crystal has stopped the onslaught of the Bogan forces so that brave warriors can once again show their merit. . . . The revolution has begun."

Lucas indicated that the roll-up at the end of the movie would lead into episode two of the saga:

. . . And a thousand star systems joined the rebellion, causing a significant crack in the great wall of the powerful Galactic Empire. The Starkiller would once again spark fear in the hearts

of the Sith knights, but not before his sons were put to many tests . . . the most daring of which was the kidnapping of the Lars family, and the perilous search for "The Princess of Ondos."

Lucas continued recruiting the preproduction team for *The Star Wars*. As Walter Murch was unavailable, Lucas asked Kurtz to visit USC and evaluate the emerging talent. "They said, 'We're looking for another Walter Murch,'" says Ben Burtt, the student they eventually chose. "I met Gary Kurtz first for an interview. He basically said that they were doing a science-fiction movie. . . . This was prior to shooting the movie, and they really wanted to develop a sound for Chewbacca so they would know on the set how to make the actor behave."

Burtt graduated from USC in June, but before reporting for duty at Lucasfilm in July he taped the first of many sounds for the new film: the motor on a projector in the department of cinema became the basis of the "sharp hum" of the laserswords. "In my initial conversations with George, he made it very clear that he didn't want to just draw upon stock sounds or previously thought-out science-fiction sounds they'd done for other movies," says Burtt.

Having established his one-man sound department, Lucas turned his attention to the film's visual effects. He knew that some sequences in *The Star Wars*—notably the attack on the Death Star in the final act—were so unlike anything that had been seen before that he would have to develop groundbreaking techniques. "I had some images in mind," he recalls. "I'd never seen a space battle. I'd seen flying around in serials like *Flash Gordon*, but they were really dopey. And in *2001*, it was slow. Very, very brilliant, but not what I was interested in. I wanted to see this incredible aerial ballet in outer space."

In June, Lucas asked John Dykstra—who had collaborated with *2001* pioneer Douglas Trumbull on the impressive effects for *The Andromeda Strain* (1971) and *Silent Running*–to supervise the special photographic effects for *The Star Wars*. Lucas established his own special-effects house in a thirty-thousand-square-foot warehouse in Van Nuys, sixteen miles northwest of Los Angeles, and put Dykstra in charge of what he named Industrial Light & Magic.

To give Dykstra an idea of the dynamic qualities he wanted to attain for the space combat, Lucas gave him a 16mm copy of a sequence of dogfights he had cut together from World War II documentary films. Dykstra assembled a team of young experts to help him, and one of the company's first employees was designer and storyboard illustrator Joe Johnston. The motion-control system developed for *The Star Wars* was designed by July, and named the "Dykstraflex." The freedom the system offered to repeat precise camera/model

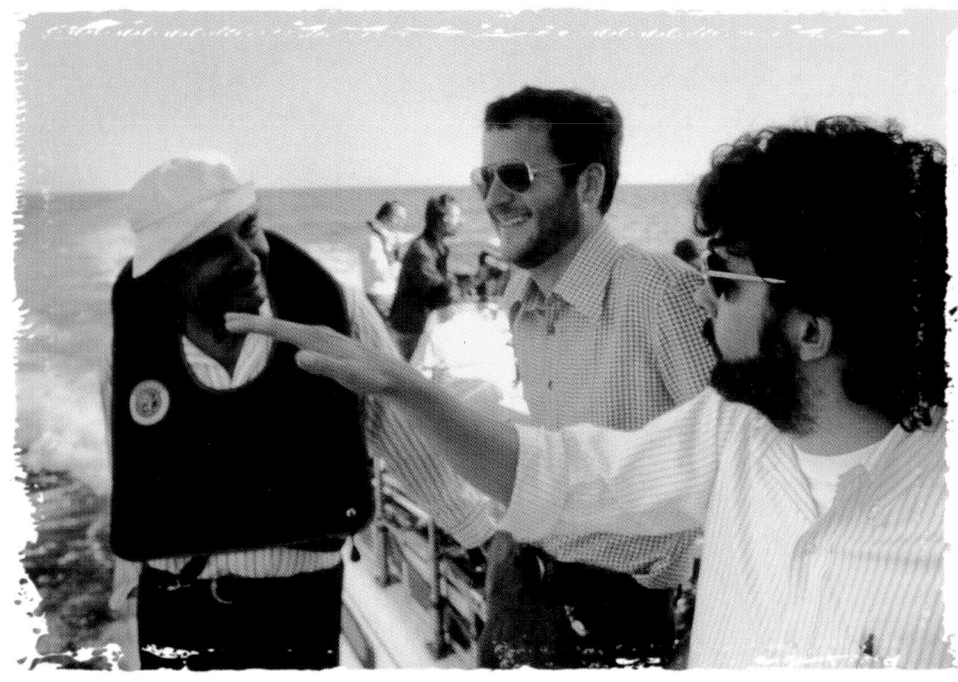

Opposite *- One of the first four McQuarrie concept paintings features the twin suns of the planet that would eventually be called Tatooine.*

Above *- Also one of the first four, this painting shows an Imperial pilot in his fighter tracking the* Millennium Falcon *as it approaches the Death Star.*

Above right *- In 1974, Lucas and Willard Huyck traveled to the set of* Lucky Lady *(1975) in Mexico to talk with cinematographer Geoffrey Unsworth (in hat) about filming* Star Wars.

Right *- Another one of the four initial McQuarrie paintings reveals the Jawa sand crawler.*

Above *- At Lucas's home, playing bocce ball on the occasion of a baby shower for Ben Burtt's first daughter, Alice: (from left) Walter Murch, Hal Barwood, Lucas, Joe Johnston, and Bill Bryant (a friend of Burtt's).*

Left *- On the steps of Lucas's Medway house (from left to right, sitting): Lucy and Sam Wilson, Marcia Lucas, Sophie Robbins (young girl), Maggie and Beatrice Murch, Janet Robbins, Jane Bay, and Chantal; (standing) Kathy Bryant and Barbara Barwood.*

Opposite above *- Concept art of the Death Star trench run.*

Opposite right *- A concept illustration of an X-wing starfighter by designer and storyboard artist Joe Johnston.*

movements allowed for fast-moving foreground action to be played out against perfectly synchronized backgrounds. "This allows complex, matched-move, multielement matte shots by shooting the foreground against [a] blue screen and then taking that program of motions to a twin camera system. A separate background element can then be photographed with matching motions," explained Dykstra in 1977. "When the two elements are combined, the appearance is that of real-time photography—allowing pans, tilts, rolls, and accelerations on shots having a multitude of elements that were shot at different times, on separate cameras."

One of the other founding members of ILM was Dennis Muren, who was recruited as a cameraman and was one of the first to come to grips with motion control. "Here was a place where they were spending money to build a camera, which was unheard of," recalls Muren.

The design of the Dykstraflex was merely the beginning of almost eight months of development work that was undertaken while Lucas continued writing *The Star Wars.* His third-draft screenplay was dated August 1, and while it retained the same essential structure as the previous version, it shuffled the characters around.

In the third draft, sixteen-year-old Rebel Princess Leia Organa is captured by Darth Vader, a Dark Lord of the Sith, while C-3PO and R2-D2 escape to the desert planet Utapau. The droids encounter sixteen-year-old Luke Starkiller in much the same way, and Luke is intrigued to discover that they have been involved in the "Clone Wars" against the Empire. . .

R2 projects a message from Princess Leia, saying that she is to be taken to Ogana Major. After deliberating over the risks, Luke leaves a "video-slate" message that says "Aunt Beru, Uncle Owen, I don't mean to hurt you and I know you've been good to me, but I'm leaving. There are important things I must do. . . . I've also taken my father's lightsaber. . ." Owen, dismayed that Luke has left, tells Beru: "That boy is going to get himself killed. . . . He's just like his father."

Following a skirmish with aggressive creatures called Tusken Raiders, Luke and the two droids encounter an elderly character called Obi-Wan (Ben) Kenobi. "You're General Kenobi?!? The Jedi Knight! The commander of the White Legions?" asks a disbelieving Luke. Luke introduces himself as the son of Annikin Starkiller and says he knows Ben's Diary of the Clone Wars *by heart. But Ben is old and, as he illustrates following an accident with his arm, now partly mechanical. Ben fixes his arm but admits he has little of the Force left in him: "Let's just say the Force is something a Jedi Warrior deals with," he explains. "It is an energy field in oneself, a power that controls one's acts, yet obeys one's commands. It is nothing, yet it makes marvels appear before your very eyes. All living things*

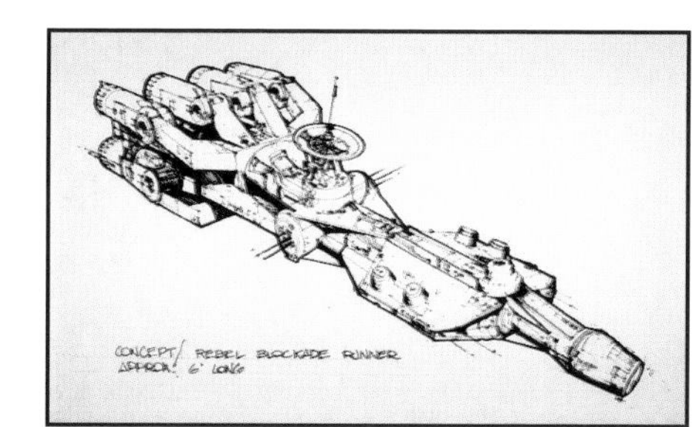

Middle *- Johnston acting out the X-wing/TIE fighter dogfight. "George didn't hire film-industry veterans," says Johnston. "Most of the people working at ILM came from disciplines—there were artists, machinists, and so on. They didn't know what they were doing. I don't think that I knew what I was doing half the time."*

Far right *- A concept illustration of the Blockade Runner* Tantive IV *by designer Colin Cantwell.*

generate this Force field, even you. . . . When a creature dies, the Force it generated remains. The Force is all around us. It can be collected and transmitted through the use of a Kiber Crystal. It's the only way to amplify the power of the Force within you."

Ben explains that his Kiber Crystal was taken at the Battle of Condawn—which was where Luke's father was killed. One of his disciples, Darth Vader, took the crystal and became a Sith Lord.

The few crystals that remain are in the possession of the Sith Lords on Alderaan. "The negative side of the Force is called the Bogan," continues Ben, "and it is the part that is used by the Dark Lords to destroy their opponents. Both halves are always present. The Force is on your right, the Bogan is on your left."

Ben, Luke, and the droids commission Han Solo and Chewbacca in much the same way, and use Han's pirated ship to travel to Ogana Major. The planet has, however, already been obliterated by the Death Star. Ben tells Han to go instead to Alderaan so they can rescue the Princess. Ben is confident that Leia will not submit to mind control on account of the fact that she is "a swan sensana." On the journey, Ben begins Luke's Jedi training using a lightsaber and a remote droid.

TIE fighters follow Han's ship to the Imperial city of Alderaan. When the ship touches down, Ben leaves to find the Kiber Crystal, telling Luke: "May the Force be with you," before he leaves. Han and Luke disguise themselves as stormtroopers and eventually find the Princess: "Suspended inside the cell by invisible rays, a bloody and mutilated Leia Organa hangs upside down. A strange yellow glow radiates from her eyes."

Ben finds the pedestal on which the Kiber Crystal rests and gains renewed strength from its presence. Luke, Han, and Chewie encounter a vicious Dia Nogu creature before the resourceful Leia regains consciousness and takes charge. They slide down a garbage chute, and Han declares: "I've got a very bad feeling about all this."

Ben is intercepted by Darth Vader, who tells the old man, "I've been waiting . . . At last we meet again . . . It could only have been you . . ." Ben replies: "The Force of the Bogan has grown strong with you. I expected your master . . ." Vader responds: "You were once my master, but I am the master now . . . the crystal will be of little use to you . . . " Their lightsabers clash, and Ben is badly injured by stormtroopers before his friends can get him back aboard the pirate starship. The ship takes off and the crew defend themselves from marauding TIE fighters. Leia then reveals that R2-D2 is carrying the plans for a giant battle station—the Death Star.

They head for the fourth moon of Yavin, where they are met in the Masassi Outpost's war room by General Aay Zavos and Grande Mouff Tarkin. Han is paid off and leaves with Chewbacca. Ben gives Luke the glowing Kiber Crystal. Tarkin briefs the rebel pilots, and the attack on the Death Star commences. During the raid, Luke grasps the Kiber Crystal and Han

Above - Sand People hunt their quarry in this illustration by McQuarrie.

Left - A McQuarrie illustration of Darth Vader and an early production painting of a stormtrooper holding a lightsaber.

to crush the rebellion once and for all the empire has sent its most sinister ~~messenger~~ knight of ~~doom the Dark lord~~, Darth Vader, to ~~discover~~ find and destroy the rebels ~~the location of the rebels~~ hidden base, ~~and destroy it~~ with ~~its~~ the Empire ultimate weapon, ~~the death Star.~~ an armored space station powerful enough to destroy an entire planet.

Powerful enough to destroy an entire planet, its completion spells certain doom for ~~the~~ champions of freedom.

makes a surprise return to save Luke from the pursuing Darth Vader. Luke fires the shots that destroy the Death Star, and Vader's ship spins off into space.

Back on Yavin 4, Princess Leia hands out medals to the new heroes of the Rebellion.

The script was becoming more ambitious with each draft, and Lucas had already asked Kurtz to give some consideration to where the film would be shot. "In Hollywood, the stages were so full of television shows and disaster epics we couldn't get near them," Kurtz recalled in 1976. "It was unbelievable to me that [in the U.K.] there was so much space, so much talent, and so much opportunity going

Above - A page from one of Lucas's early Star Wars *drafts shows his editing of the now well-known opening crawl.*

Right - In a McQuarrie production painting, rodent Jabba draws a gun on Luke Starkiller. A-2 and C-3 are to the left. These characters would change and take on different shapes and names.

Hollywood celebrities Eddie Fisher and Debbie Reynolds, for the role of Princess Leia. Earlier that year, *Variety* had praised Fisher's brief but memorable performance in Hal Ashby's *Shampoo*, and Roos felt she could provide the balance of feminine and feisty for which Lucas was looking. In a previously unpublished interview recorded in January 1977, Fisher recalled that she was asked to learn dialogue for two scenes. "I was caught by my mother and some of my family rehearsing it in my underwear. I would come out of the bathroom and say things like 'General Kenobi . . .' and 'A battle station with enough firepower to destroy an entire system.' They thought I was crazy."

Fisher was sent the third-draft script and asked to report to the Goldwyn Studios. Three weeks later, Fisher was told she had the part and found herself particularly looking forward to filming the scene showing her rescue from the prison cell on Alderaan. "I wanted to have a still of me hung upside down with yellow eyes and bleeding. I couldn't figure out how the hell they were going to do all that. I wanted to be involved in that. And I wanted to have lunch with monsters."

Since appearing in *Graffiti*, Harrison Ford had made a small appearance in Coppola's *The Conversation* and had secured some television roles, but by late 1975 he was once more working as a carpenter. Roos hired him to do some work at the Goldwyn Studios in order to bring him to Lucas's attention for the role of Han Solo. "We wanted a fancy door with a section of glass and the Zoetrope logo," says Roos. "We got Harrison to put it in. George came over one day when Harrison was doing this. I think George got a different view of him that day, even though he had been in *Graffiti*. I guess he saw Harrison in a different light. It just clicked for him."

"Finally, they made me an offer," Ford would recall. "This was promoted as a low-budget movie. It certainly was for the actors; I can attest to that."

Toward the end of the casting process the role of Luke was awarded to twenty-four-year-old Mark Hamill, who had appeared in more than fifty episodes of ABC's long-running soap opera *General Hospital* and alongside Lisa Eilbacher in the TV comedy series *The Texas Wheelers*. "I was just lucky," said Hamill in an interview conducted in September 1976. "I tested, and for some reason [Lucas] liked me."

to waste." Lucas was most impressed by Elstree Studios, a deserted nine-stage facility in Borehamwood, northwest of London. All nine stages were reserved for a planned shooting date of spring 1976, while additional space was booked at Shepperton. By fall 1975, the studio and the locations had been chosen and an art department was established at Elstree.

In November 1975, amid simultaneous development work at ILM and Elstree, Lucas began three months of casting in Los Angeles. Neither Lucas nor Ladd envisioned the film as a star picture, so Lucas embarked on a search for talented unknowns to play the film's young leads, consulting Fred Roos and casting director Diana Crittenden. The casting sessions were held at the Zoetrope offices at the Goldwyn Studios in Los Angeles. The most promising contenders for Princess Leia, Han Solo, and Luke Starkiller were invited back for screen tests recorded on black-and-white videotape.

Roos suggested Carrie Fisher, the nineteen-year-old daughter of

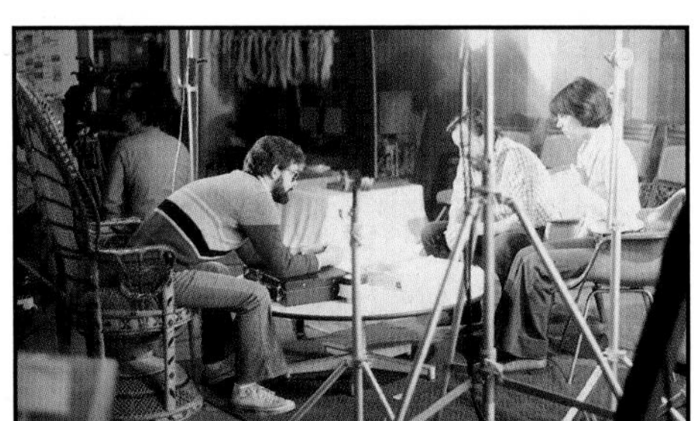

Above - An aerial shot of Elstree Studios (EMI Studios) in Borehamwood, England.

Left - In October–November 1975, auditions were held for Star Wars *at Dove Films, a small off-Hollywood studio usually used for shooting commercials. Here, Lucas conducts the auditions of Freddie Forrester and Cindy Williams (who played Laurie in* American Graffiti*).*

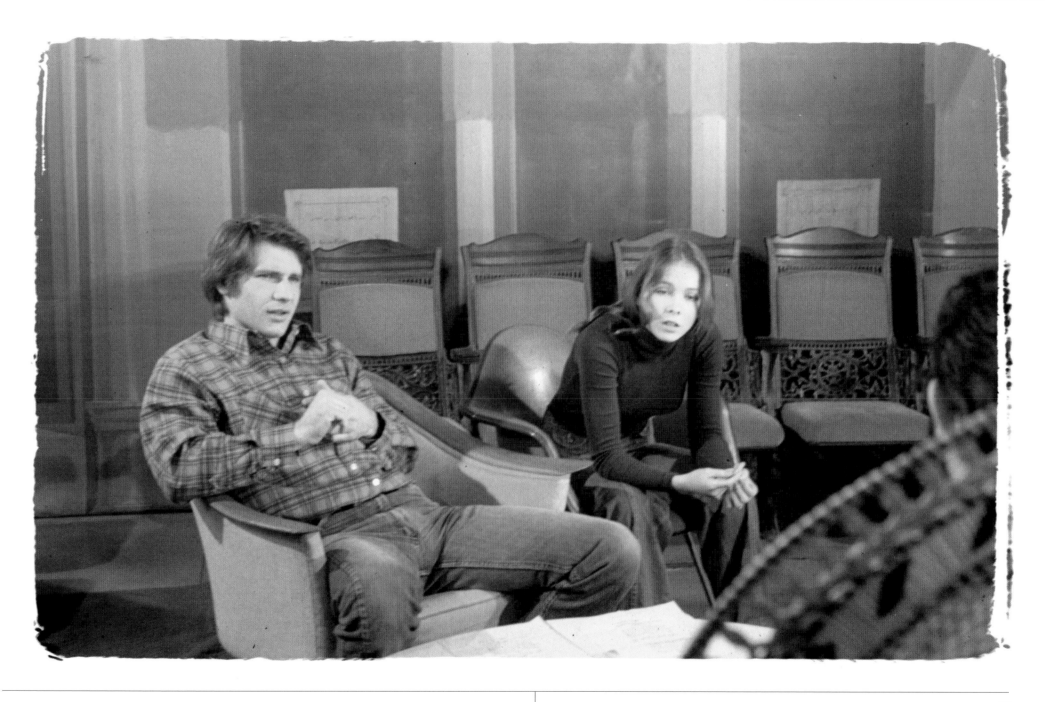

Above *- Harrison Ford and Terry Nunn during casting auditions.*

Right *- Lucas with Mark Hamill (and Harrison Ford, sitting) at the latter's first casting audition. Just before Hamill's audition, while Lucas was having lunch, sound designer Ben Burtt had auditioned clandestinely for the role of Luke Skywalker. "I was young, and I was videotaping all these auditions, and I thought, 'Hey, I could do that!'" However, after viewing the results, Burtt thought better of a career change.*

Far right *- Mark Hamill and Carrie Fisher in a relaxed publicity shot.*

The casting for the film's ageing Jedi Knight, Ben Kenobi, was rather more straightforward. Lucas had originally suggested to Ladd that Toshiro Mifune, the Kurosawa mainstay who had played the General in *The Hidden Fortress*, would be right for Kenobi. By late 1975, however, Lucas had decided on Sir Alec Guinness for the role. One of Britain's most respected theatrical knights, Guinness had forged a distinguished career in the cinema. He had won his first Academy Award for his portrayal of Colonel Nicholson in David Lean's *The Bridge on the River Kwai* (1957), but his film appearances had become infrequent by the early 1970s.

The casting of Guinness was the first thing about *The Star Wars* to interest the press. Guinness told the *Sunday Times* in May 1976 that he was impressed by the quality of Lucas's screenplay. "The characters aren't cardboard. There's more to them than that. The story is gripping. There's a quest, encounters with other forms of life. There's more than a touch of Tolkien about it. But what I'm supposed to be doing I can't really say. I simply trust the director." One thing Guinness did not reveal was that he had been further enticed to join the production by the offer of profit participation. In 1975, however, there was little to suggest that accepting such an offer represented anything other than a calculated risk.

Before Lucas could relocate to Elstree on a more permanent basis, there was still another battle to be fought in Los Angeles. "About the time we finished the preproduction, we did a budget on it," recalled Lucas in 1977. "The first budget actually came out at $16 million, so I threw out a lot of designing new equipment and said, okay, we'll cut corners and do a lot of fast filmmaking, which is really where I come from. . . . We got it down to $13 million, which was really about as cheap as that script could possibly be made by any human being." However, the studio insisted that the budget be under $10 million. "When we finally got the budget down to $9,999,999, we knew it couldn't be done. I was practically working for free and my only hope was that if the film paid off, my net points might be worth something."

Lucas had unveiled the fourth draft of his screenplay on January 1, 1976, and Fox had given its go-ahead to commence principal photography soon after. There were changes apparent on the very first page. The full name of the film was now *The Adventures of Luke Starkiller*, as taken from the *Journal of the Whills*. This installment of the adventure was called *Saga I: Star Wars*. The "Son of the Suns" quote that had opened previous drafts was replaced with:

> *A long, long time ago in a galaxy far, far away an incredible adventure took place. . . .*

In the third draft, Montross was no longer a friend of Han Solo's, but rather one of the pirates that Han duped into leaving his ship before he blasted off from Mos Eisley. In the fourth draft, Montross became an Imperial bureaucrat whom Han had to get rid of in a similar way. Han's ship, while still unnamed, now possessed incredible speed thanks to its ability to jump to "hyperspace."

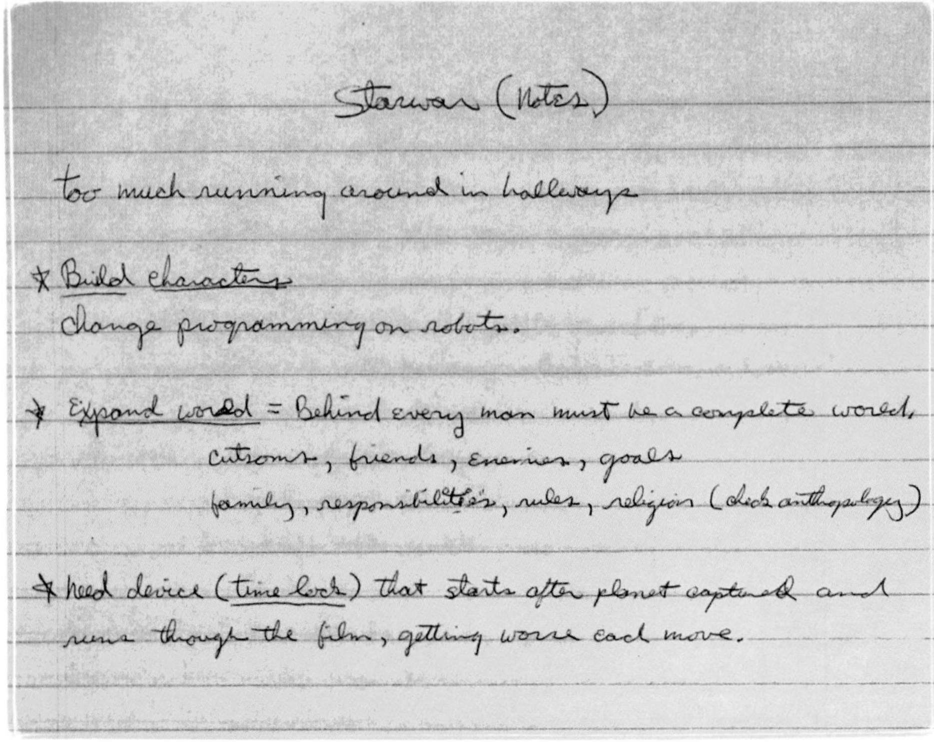

Starwar (Notes)

too much running around in hallways

* Build characters
change programming on robots.

* Expand world = Behind every man must be a complete world,
customs, friends, enemies, goals
family, responsibilities, rules, religion (check anthropology)

* need device (time lock) that starts after planet captured and
runs though the film, getting worse each move.

Above - Undated script notes written by Lucas to aid in his writing of subsequent drafts of Star Wars.

Left - Sir Alec Guinness was cast as Obi-Wan Kenobi.

Opposite - Lucas and director of photography Gil Taylor, who came on board when Geoffrey Unsworth proved unavailable.

Presumably much to Carrie Fisher's dismay, Princess Leia's interrogation scene had fallen victim to Lucas's cost-cutting, and she was now menaced by a floating "black torture droid." Another change partly motivated by budgetary restrictions was the complete removal of the Alderaan location and the shifting of those scenes to the Death Star. The fourth draft also saw Lucas discard the mysterious Kiber Crystal coveted by Jedi and Sith alike. "I felt the Kiber Crystal was a way of articulating what was going on," says Lucas, "but I decided that I didn't need it. It was better to make the Force more ethereal than to have it solidified in a thing like the crystal."

In England, casting for the film continued. Peter Cushing was selected by Lucas to play Governor Tarkin, now the commander of the Death Star. Bodybuilder David Prowse was offered the role of either Darth Vader or Chewbacca. Balking at the idea of wearing a furry body suit, Prowse opted for the former (whom Lucas had by now decided should be the film's half-mechanical man). While his tree-trunk physique was impressive, his thick West Country brogue meant that his voice was rarely heard in films. *The Star Wars* would be no exception.

The role of Chewbacca therefore went to towering hospital porter Peter Mayhew. Although Mayhew had recently completed filming an appearance in *Sinbad and the Eye of the Tiger*, he had no particular aspirations to become an actor. He decided to visit Lucas at Elstree to discover more about the role. "George came into the office, and at that time I'd been sitting down on a chair, so I stood up and his eyes almost popped out of his head," recalls Mayhew. "Within twenty minutes, we were on our way down to one of the costumers to get the costume fitted. It was as simple as that."

Like Darth Vader and Chewbacca, the golden droid C-3PO was another character that required an all-encompassing costume. Lucas cast Anthony Daniels, at that time appearing in a Young Vic production of *Rosencrantz and Guildenstern Are Dead*, on the strength of his experience in mime.

"I felt that the physical embodiment of the character was only half the performance," says Daniels. "George and I discussed the voice on and off during the making of the costume. I took my lead from George's script. The dialogue suggested that this was a highly strung, rather neurotic character, so I decided to speak in a higher register, at the top of the lungs."

C-3PO's counterpart R2-D2 was to be largely realized using a mechanical prop developed by John Stears. Close-ups of the droid betraying excitement or agitation did, however, require some human input. Lucas hired Kenny Baker, a cabaret artist and occasional actor, to inhabit the droid. Not wishing to split up Baker's musical double act, he cast his similarly diminutive friend Jack Purvis as Chief Jawa.

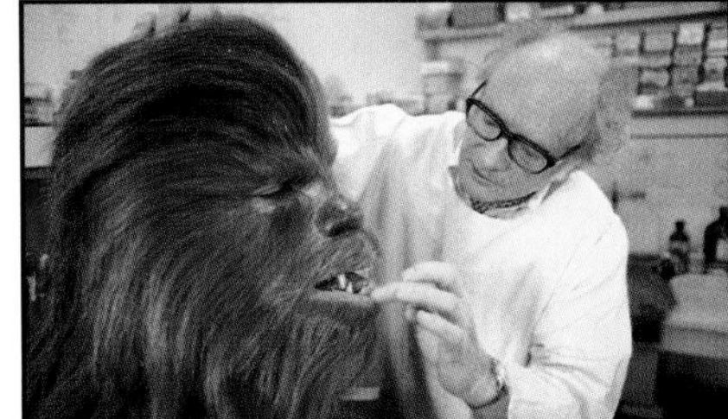

Above - Mark Hamill and Peter Cushing between takes at Elstree Studios.

Far left *- Veteran makeup supervisor Stuart Freeborn prepares the elaborate Chewbacca mask. Freeborn had, earlier in his career, helped transform Alec Guinness into Fagin for* Oliver Twist *(1948) and created the disguises that aided Peter Sellers in playing three roles in* Dr. Strangelove *(1964).*

Middle left *- Peter Mayhew, wearing the Chewbacca costume Freeborn created.*

Left *- Anthony Daniels, wearing parts of a prototype C-3PO costume at Elstree.*

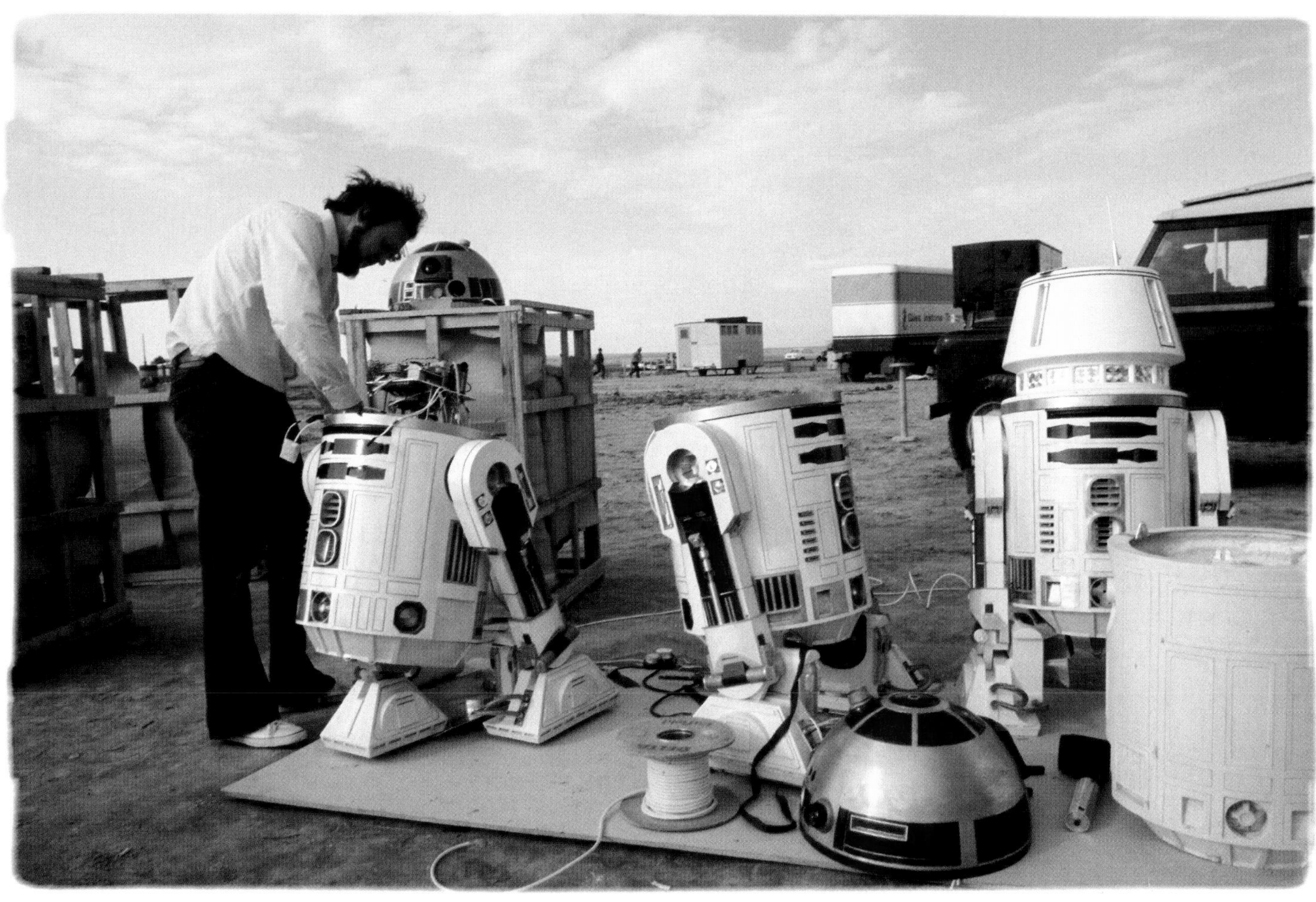

hile the sets were completed, Lucas put the finishing touches to a revised fourth draft of his screenplay, which bears the date March 15, 1976. The script opened with the shortened legend:

A long time ago in a galaxy far, far away........

The story contained a number of interesting additions (Han Solo's ship had a name—the *Millennium Falcon*) and some minor changes. At the last minute, Lucas had asked Huyck and Katz to polish the script, and they rewrote less than a quarter of the dialogue. Their touch is most apparent in the wisecracking exchanges between Han Solo and the newly liberated Princess Leia:

Leia
Listen. I don't know who you are,
or where you came from,
but from now on, you do
as I tell you. Okay?

Han
Look, your holiness, let's get
something straight! I take orders
from one person . . . me.

Leia
It's a wonder you're still alive.

The biggest change, however, introduced in the revised fourth draft was the result of a decision that would dramatically alter the climax of the film's second act. Lucas had long been concerned that, following the heroes' escape from Alderaan/The Death Star, Ben Kenobi's story was essentially over. Following their arrival on the Rebel base on the Yavin moon, Ben had little more to do than hand Luke the Kiber Crystal. Once that had been removed in the fourth draft, all Ben could offer his protégé was advice as the attack on the Death Star commenced without him. With mere weeks to go before filming was to begin, Lucas decided that Kenobi would allow himself to be killed by Darth Vader; he would thereafter become one with the Force and offer Luke advice from the spirit world.

Above *- R2-D2 and various droids being prepared for shooting by effects supervisor John Stears.*

Right *- The hovering effect of Luke's landspeeder was one of the more difficult effects to achieve. Although work began during preproduction in London, success would have to wait until postproduction in California.*

Far right *- Hamill, Guinness, producer Gary Kurtz, and Lucas on location in Tunisia.*

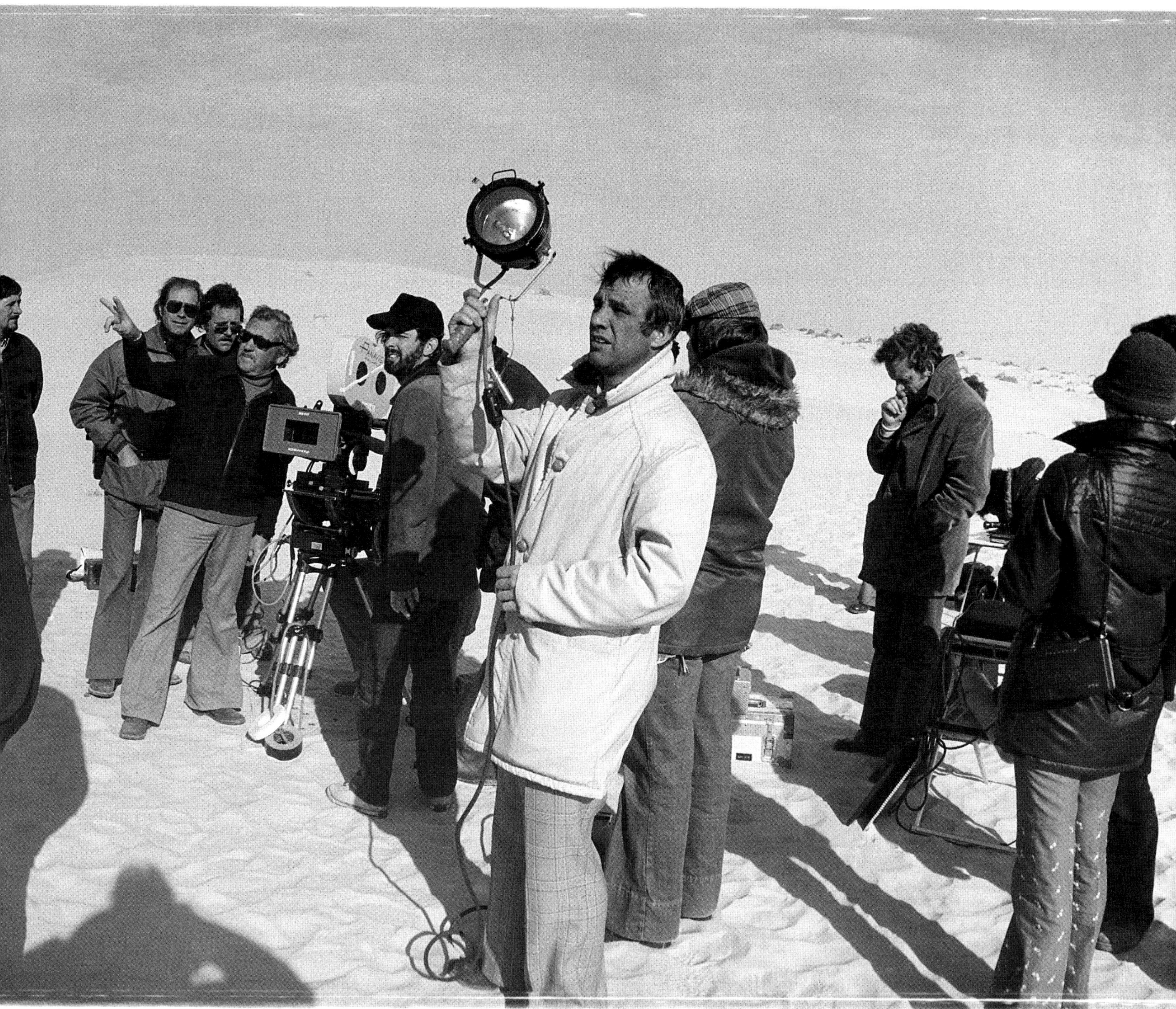

Lucas broke the news to Guinness before the revised fourth draft was circulated. "He could have walked away," says Lucas, "but we had lunch and I told him, 'We're doing this for an important reason.' We looked through the script together and I pointed out that he didn't have anything to do for the last third. I felt it would be much more powerful to have him become a spirit. He didn't like it and he was unsure, but he accepted that I had to make the film work. He agreed with me in the end. He was very talented and intelligent, and I was glad I was able to explain my decision to him."

Less than a week later, on March 22, 1976, Lucas called "Action" in Tozeur, Tunisia. "We went at the wrong time," says director of photography Gil Taylor. "Instead of getting hard sun, we got terrible weather. Tunisia hadn't had rain for seven years, and we had rain for four days." These were hardly the conditions Lucas had expected for his arid desert planet. It would prove a challenging two weeks for other reasons: Mark Hamill had injured his left arm before filming began, a damaged Panaflex lens would cast doubt over the quality of some of the shots, and one of the unit's Land Rovers would be seized by a local court following a dispute over a canceled hotel reservation.

The first scene filmed was the sale of the droids R2-D2 and C-3PO to Luke and his Uncle Owen (Phil Brown). The mechanisms powering R2-D2 proved temperamental on the uneven desert surface, and Anthony Daniels experienced significant discomfort inside the fiberglass and aluminium C-3PO costume. "We'd been up since just after midnight trying to finish it," says Daniels, recalling the first day of filming. "We started putting it on at 6:30 in the morning, and it took about two

OBI-WAN KENOBI DELETED SCENES

In Lucas's fourth draft, dated January 1, 1976, Ben Kenobi does not die when he confronts Darth Vader aboard the Death Star. Instead, the two are separated when a "heavy blast door slams down between them." Luke then helps the "old man" to the pirate ship, Princess Leia blasts the safety lock, and they all escape to Yavin 4. Upon their arrival at the Rebel base, Ben is greeted by Commander Dodonna.

Ben Kenobi (Alec Guinness).

DODONNA

General Kenobi! This is a great honor. I thought you were . . .

BEN

There were many who thought I was dead . . . perhaps I was.

It is Ben who then explains the weakness of the Death Star to the assembled starpilots. After the attack commences, he stays in the war room, giving tactical instructions to various pilots—and instructing Luke to "trust your feelings on this run. Use the Force." In this draft, Luke makes two attack runs on the exhaust port. The first time, he does not use the Force and fails. The second time, Ben again tells Luke to "trust the Force." After hesitating, Luke finally decides not to use his targeting computer—and succeeds in blowing up the Death Star. Upon his return, "the crowd thins, revealing Ben. Luke goes to him and bows from the waist."

BEN

You have stepped into your father's shoes. You will become a powerful Jedi.

At the subsequent awards ceremony, "Ben is sitting to the right of the Princess."

hours. . . . I had a respectful attitude to the costume because I knew what had gone into its creation, but I also hated it. I felt like I was being stabbed with a pair of scissors every time I made a gesture."

Kurtz's assistant Bunny Alsup remembers that Alec Guinness felt that the "used universe" look Lucas was striving for should extend to Obi-Wan Kenobi. "Sir Alec arrived in a brand new, clean costume," she remembers. "He laid down in the sand and dirtified himself before his first scene. I thought that was unique and wonderful."

Ultimately, the Tunisian location shoot proved more difficult than anyone had expected–at one point a storm destroyed the standing sets and jeopardized the entire shoot–but Lucas finally wrapped on Sunday, April 4. "I though the film was in trouble," Lucas would say when recalling that he'd filmed only about half of what he had wanted. "I wasn't over schedule, but I didn't have the movie." The footage was handed over to the film's British editor John Jympson, who was charged with creating a rough assembly as soon as possible.

Previous *- Lucas directs stormtroopers in the Tunisian desert. Tunisia had been chosen after Persia, Libya, and Nigeria had been ruled out. Nearly all the scenes shot there were within thirty minutes of the centrally located Tozeur, on the edge of the Sahara desert.*

Far left *- Lucas, Daniels, and Guinness discuss the scene in which Obi-Wan Kenobi explains the Force to Luke Skywalker.*

Above *- Toward the end of the location shoot in April 1976, despite the scorching heat of Djerba, Tunisia, Lucas shoots the scene in which Luke (Mark Hamill), C-3PO (Anthony Daniels), and R2-D2 arrive in Mos Eisley.*

Right *- Lucas directs stormtroopers in the Tunisian desert.*

Lucas began shooting interiors on Stage 7 at Elstree Studios on Wednesday, April 7, picking up exactly where he had left off in Tunisia. With the arrival of Harrison Ford and, a few days later, Carrie Fisher, for the first time the entire *Star Wars* cast was together. "That was almost like a whole separate movie," Mark Hamill would say. "It was like getting a fresh start."

By the time filming began at Elstree, Fox executives had seen dailies of the footage Lucas had shot in Tunisia and had expressed dissatisfaction with the soft focus adopted by Gil Taylor at Lucas's request. That problem was rectified by giving greater clarity to the studio-bound lighting setups—however, the atmosphere on set became increasingly fraught. In the face of numerous technical and labor-relations problems, the average amount of screen time Lucas was able to film slipped from almost two minutes per day in early April to one minute forty-five seconds in early May, and just over one minute thirty seconds by June. By July, it was even less. "Every day it was like trying to push a ball up a hill," says Lucas, who still has vivid memories of the painful summer of 1976. "The crew saw it as a dopey film made by this American kid. Nobody went any distance to try and help. It was a tough schedule and they didn't really sympathize with my situation."

When Huyck and Katz decided to visit Lucas at Elstree Studios, they were made to feel unwelcome. "We were met by one of the assistant directors," says Huyck. "He asked us who we were, and I said we were two of George's friends. He said, 'That's all we need, George's friends.' When we got inside, I remember Gil Taylor was lighting a scene with Chewbacca. I heard him say, 'Put some more light on the dog, whatever it's called.'"

In the evenings, a dejected and homesick Lucas would wander around the deserted sets and gather his thoughts. His vision was being compromised by an inadequate budget and a rebellious crew. He also had anxious Fox executives breathing down his neck. By the third week of June, the director had lost his voice and was struggling to make his directions heard in a virtual whisper. Stuart Freeborn also fell ill and was unable to complete work on the cantina alien costumes. Hamill's arm improved, but he then suffered from swollen lymph glands and an infection of his right foot that made it difficult for him to walk. Toward the end of the shoot, he suffered a burst blood vessel that made the white of one his eyes so red that filming of certain close-ups had to be postponed.

By July, with the studio in a panic and threatening to shut the film down, desperate measures were being taken to claw back some of the lost time—three units filmed simultaneously on different stages at Elstree, while the interiors of the Rebel base on Yavin 4 were filmed at Shepperton Studios. Certain exteriors of the base, to be used in matte paintings, were also filmed outside an aircraft hangar at the Royal Air Force base at Cardington in Bedfordshire.

Above - *At Elstree Studios, Lucas and continuity supervisor Ann Skinner (holding script) run through the ultimately abandoned encounter between Jabba the Hutt (Declan Mulholland) and Han Solo (Harrison Ford). Peter Mayhew can be seen, minus his Chewbacca mask, at the right. Gil Taylor, in a pale-colored cap, is at the back.*

Far left - *Lucas on a crane in Shepperton Studios, films Luke emerging from his X-wing after destroying the Death Star.*

Middle left - *Guinness and David Prowse rehearse the final encounter between Obi-Wan Kenobi and Darth Vader under the supervision of stunt coordinator Peter Diamond (far left).*

Left - *Obi-Wan Kenobi (Alec Guinness) and Han Solo (Harrison Ford)—Luke and Chewbacca are barely visible—in the cockpit set of the* Millennium Falcon *as they become entrapped by the Death Star's tractor beam.*

Lucas flew back to the United States on Saturday, July 17. Seeking a sympathetic friend, Lucas paid a visit to Spielberg, who was on location in Alabama. "I'd just finished shooting the movie and I was exhausted," Lucas would recall, "but I had to go right from the shooting into the finishing without a break."

There was little to reassure Lucas back in southern California. Industrial Light & Magic (ILM) had more than 360 effects shots to prepare for *Star Wars*, and he was relying on Dykstra and his seventy-five-strong team to have made significant progress by the time the British shoot had wrapped. Unfortunately, Lucas discovered that research and development had swallowed up most of the company's time and money. When he visited Van Nuys in summer 1976, he found that ILM had already spent half its budget but had just one acceptable shot in the can. Lucas was appalled. Back in the Bay Area that night, he suffered such crippling chest pains that he was rushed to Marin General Hospital. During an overnight stay, it was established that he had not suffered a heart attack, but that extreme stress and a punishing schedule were placing his health at risk. Lucas left the hospital the following morning.

Unwilling to accept that the effects shots could not be produced on time, Lucas appointed production supervisor George Mather to institute a strict new regime at ILM. The technicians were divided into two teams—one working a day shift and the other working at night—and Lucas personally supervised the work on Mondays and Tuesdays.

Lucas was not feeling quite as conciliatory toward editor Jympson, whom he fired at the end of the British shoot. "I'd started to see things cut together, and I wasn't happy with it," Lucas remembers. "I tried to get the editor to cut it my way and he didn't really want to, and so I had to let the editor go. I had no editor, I was behind schedule, and I had to race to finish the movie."

Editing of the film resumed at Parkway in August, with the attack on the Death Star the priority, in an effort to provide ILM a work print featuring the studio-based footage. This was the first time Lucas had seen many of the scenes from this section of the film, as the lab at Elstree had not been able to prepare 35mm reductions of VistaVision footage. He spent days sifting through many thousands of feet of film, attempting to match the VistaVision scenes shot against a blue background to the 35mm

Above right - *Exterior shots of the surface of the Death Star during the final attack were filmed in the parking lot outside Industrial Light & Magic in Van Nuys, California. Optical effects cameraman Richard Edlund, with assistant cameraman Douglas Smith standing in foreground, records an explosion.*

Above left - *Lucas prepares to shoot Darth Vader's dramatic boarding of the* Tantive IV *at Elstree during the eighty-second day of shooting on Wednesday, July 14.*

Right - *Carrie Fisher and Mark Hamill talk things over with Lucas at Elstree, shortly before swinging over the chasm during their characters' escape from the Death Star.*

Far right - *Special photographic effects supervisor John Dykstra examines miniature X-wing and Y-wings on a table at ILM's model shop. Some of these models were specially designed to be blown up, while others were designated "cherry" or "hero" models for close-ups.*

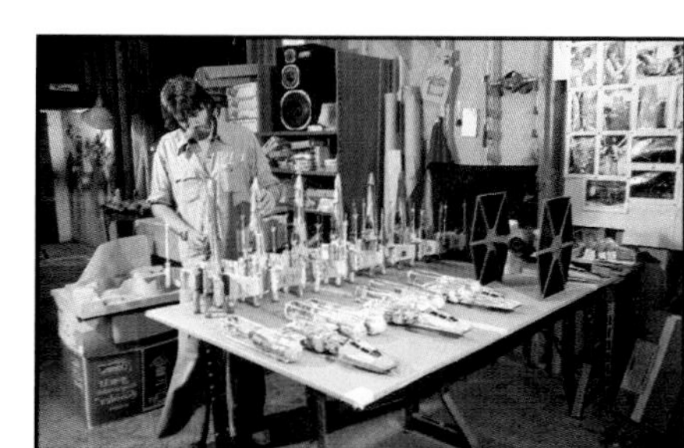

footage. Richard Chew was hired to recut Jympson's footage from earlier in the film, while Lucas, with his editor and wife, Marcia, pieced together the attack on the Death Star.

The cutting of this climactic attack took between three and four months. At one point, Fox argued that the attack on the Death Star should be removed from the film altogether, but Lucas persevered. The first cut of the space battle lasted thirty-five minutes but had to be abridged in order to reduce ILM's optical costs. In this first version, Luke made two runs through the Death Star trench. As editing continued, a number of the peripheral characters involved in the raid were cut and Luke's two attacks were combined into one.

"One of the biggest contributions I made to the film was a suggestion to George to intercut Princess Leia and the Rebels in their station with Luke making the run to destroy the Death Star," remembers Richard Chew. "I had the idea that if we could put Princess Leia in jeopardy and then simultaneously have Luke try to destroy the Death Star in order to save her and the Rebels, it would just provide much more tension to the ending. Originally, these were not simultaneous events; they were separate." Luke's Death Star attack was also intercut with footage of a seemingly anxious Governor Tarkin, although the absence of dialogue specific to the attack in these scenes betrays the editors' sleight of hand. Like the Leia footage, much of this Tarkin material was culled from scenes that were originally supposed to occur elsewhere in the film. The sequence was ultimately made to work by intercutting new second-unit footage of Death Star personnel preparing to fire the battle station's giant laser.

Above - In this deleted scene, Lucas experiments with differentiating scales—an interest that runs throughout his work.

Left - An anxious Princess Leia (Carrie Fisher) in the war room at the Rebel base on Yavin 4. Extra non-utilized footage such as this was cut together late in postproduction to create new scenes in which Princess Leia and the Rebel base are seen to be in danger of being obliterated by the Death Star.

DELETED SCENES

The earliest surviving cut of *Star Wars* is the assembly compiled by British editor John Jympson in summer 1976. This relatively crude work-in-progress, preserved in Lucasfilm's archive on black-and-white 35mm film, contains numerous deleted and alternate scenes. Its principal points of interest are three consecutive scenes that Lucas had deleted by early 1977.

The first of these scenes introduces the audience to Luke Skywalker as he carries out maintenance work on one of his uncle's moisture vaporators. Luke is distracted by a space battle he glimpses in the sky (the skirmish between the Imperial Star Destroyer and Princess Leia's Blockade Runner) and takes a closer look with a high-powered surveillance device.

The second deleted scene has Luke hurrying to a power station at Anchorhead to tell his young friends about the battle he has just seen. Camie (Koo Stark), Biggs (Garrick Hagon), and Fixer (Anthony Forrest) join Luke on the roof of the building to see for themselves, but the battle is now over.

In the third deleted scene, Biggs takes Luke into his confidence, telling him that he intends to join the Rebel Alliance before he is drafted into the service of the Empire. The two part company, with Luke telling Biggs: "I'll be at the Academy next season . . . after that who knows. I won't be drafted into the Imperial Starfleet, that's for sure. . . . Take care of yourself; you'll always be the best friend I've got."

"The first cut of the film had the intercuts of Luke on the planet with what was going on in space," Lucas would recall. "But it just wasn't the movie I wanted to make. At the time, to have the first half-hour of the film be mainly about robots was a bold idea."

In one of *Star Wars*' deleted scenes, Luke (Mark Hamill), Camie (Koo Stark), Fixer (Anthony Forrest), and Biggs (Garrick Hagon) climb onto the roof of the power station at Anchorhead in an effort to catch a glimpse of the space battle.

With the possibility that Fox would pull the plug on the final battle sequence, Lucas insisted that the first rough cut of *Star Wars* be ready by October 1976. "During postproduction, *Star Wars* gained a rather ominous reputation within the studio because the costs were exceeding what had originally been estimated," recalls Fox vice president of creative affairs Gareth Wigan. "A lot of the studio administration became increasingly nervous about it. Nobody in the studio knew how to do the groundbreaking special effects George was doing, or indeed knew what he was doing."

At ILM, visual-effects techniques were progressing faster than anyone at Fox could have imagined. Model maker and matte painter Paul Huston recalls one particularly momentous meeting with Lucas: "They had taken plans we had made and used a Cray Super Computer to make an 8x10 still image of a virtual X-wing. It looked great. Of course, as model makers, we looked at that and said, 'Oh my God, are you gonna give me my pink slip today or tomorrow?' At that time it was too expensive to incorporate computer images into the film, but Lucas told Huston, 'This is the way of the future. Some day we'll be able to fly through matte paintings.'"

For honest feedback on the first rough cut, the director gathered an audience that included Hal Barwood, Jay Cocks (film critic for *Time* magazine), Brian De Palma, Willard Huyck, Gloria Katz, John Milius, Matthew Robbins, and Steven Spielberg. As the lights were raised in the Parkway screening room, only Cocks and Spielberg spoke up to claim the film would be a success. "I don't know why George chose to show it in that shape," remembers Spielberg. "The reaction was not a good one, but I loved the movie, and I told George how much I loved it." After the screening a nervous Ladd called Spielberg and asked him for a private opinion. Spielberg told him: "I think this film is going to make a fortune."

Another editor, Paul Hirsch, had joined the team in September. A rough cut of the attack on the Death Star was delivered to ILM in November 1976, and Marcia Lucas moved on to edit Martin Scorsese's *New York, New York.* Chew stepped down in the third week of December and Hirsch carried on alone, cutting in the optical-effects scenes from ILM and working toward the creation of a final cut.

Star Wars' temporary music track included music from composers such as Gustav Holst, Antonin Dvorák, and William Walton. Kubrick's *2001* had already presented a powerful combination of classical music and futuristic imagery, and Lucas seemed keen to pursue the same idea in *Star Wars.* Spielberg had suggested early on that he approach John Williams, who had composed the music for *The Sugarland Express* and had won an Academy Award for *Jaws.* Lucas explained to Williams that he wanted an old-fashioned, romantic-sounding score befitting the 1930s serial atmosphere that had inspired the mood of the film. To prepare, the composer read the script and visited the set. "It's very challenging," Williams recalls, "when someone says to a composer, 'do a score like Wagner.'"

Above *- In this deleted scene, Grand Moff Tarkin (Peter Cushing), General Motti (Richard LeParmentier), Darth Vader (David Prowse), and General Taggi (Don Henderson) discuss the possible threat posed by the Rebels. The schematic behind the actors was one of a handful of computer-generated images used in the film.*

Right *- Ben Burtt, above in the box, with optical unit second cameraman Dennis Muren below. Burtt and Muren acted almost as a "third unit," according to Burtt, while Lucas was out of the country during principal photography. Burtt is using a 4x5 camera to photograph the model of the Death Star. These photographs were then duplicated about 100 times, put together optically, and applied to a curved Plexiglas surface that became the Death Star exteriors seen in the film.*

In January 1977, Lucas hosted a screening of the latest cut of *Star Wars* at Parkway, largely for Williams's benefit. Gareth Wigan took the opportunity to view the film for the first time. "It was in a pretty rough state," he says. "I remember the final attack on the Death Star didn't exist. He had cut in footage of dogfights from World War II movies and occasional storyboard drawings. Even in that primitive state the effect of the film was astonishing. I flew back to L.A. that night. I went home and I sat my wife and two children down around a table and said, 'I want you to remember this day. This has been an extraordinary day that I will always remember.' I knew that something astounding was happening."

As Williams worked on his score, Lucas tidied up the other aspects of the film's soundtrack. Acclaimed actor James Earl Jones agreed to voice Darth Vader. Jones's chilling baritone invested Vader's huge presence with a suitably sinister resonance.

Ben Burtt offered Lucas a number of different options for the sound of R2-D2. "The breakthrough came when we were working on the sound of another droid," remembers Burtt. "I was trying to make the sound of this binocular robot, and in discussing it with George we started making little vocal sounds between each other to get a feeling for it. And it dawned on us that the sounds we were making were actually not so bad. Out of that discussion came the idea that the sounds a baby makes as it learns to talk would be a direction to go; a baby doesn't form any words, but it can communicate with sounds."

Lucas found it much more difficult to find a voice for C-3PO. Burtt felt that Anthony Daniels's own voice would work perfectly for C-3PO, but Lucas was dubious. It was only after he had auditioned about thirty other actors, including Richard Dreyfuss, that Lucas invited Daniels to add his own voice to the soundtrack.

While overseeing the editing and supervising the work at ILM, Lucas patched in extra scenes to the film. *Star Wars* was already $2 million over budget, so Ladd was unwilling to finance the shooting of these second-unit additions. He eventually released only an extra $20,000. Lucas had no choice but to accept yet another compromise.

Above *- Lucas joins composer John Williams for a scoring session in London. Lucas produced the soundtrack recordings himself.*

Far left *- Sound effects designer Burtt in his ground-floor office at Parkway house. Among the equipment on the table, which would be deemed primitive by today's standards, are a four-track tape recorder, a two-track tape recorder, amplifiers, a patch bay, and processing machines. To Burtt's right is the sound-effects library (the black ones are for* Star Wars*) and on the walls are the storyboards for the film's opening shots.*

Left *- C-3PO (Anthony Daniels) and R2-D2 (Kenny Baker) in Luke's room. Originally, the protocol droid was going to have a more American-style used-car-salesman voice, until trial and error convinced Lucas that Daniels's voice and performance would work the best.*

windshield of his BMW. He had undergone plastic surgery to reconstruct his face—specifically his badly damaged nose—and would be unavailable for the filming. Lucas went ahead, using a double and filming the landspeeder in long shots. He used a mirror to disguise the vehicle's wheels: "The reflection of the ground in the mirror made it look as if the car was floating," Dalva recalls. "I asked them to build a mirror longer than the car, so the edge of the mirror wouldn't be at the same edge as the landspeeder. If the two lines were offset, your eye wouldn't connect them."

Starting on Saturday March 5, 1977, John Williams conducted the London Symphony Orchestra over eight days of recording sessions at the Anvil Studios. The result was a soundtrack that ran to approximately eighty-eight minutes of *Star Wars*' 121-minute running time. In the final edit of *Star Wars*, it became clear that Lucas had created a film that betrayed few of the compromises made to bring it to life. He had fashioned a fantasy so purely cinematic that its epic story barely needed dialogue to unfold. Williams acknowledged this by creating a score that conveyed the story of the film independently of pictures. His sweeping theme heralded an eclectic array of character signatures and evocative cues that celebrated the Wagnerian leitmotif technique beloved of such composers as Franz Waxman and Bernard Herrmann.

Delighted with Williams's music, Lucas returned to England to produce the recordings himself. Between sessions he called Spielberg in Los Angeles and proudly played him half an hour of music over the phone. "To hear Johnny play the music for the first time was a thrill beyond anything I can describe," Lucas recalls.

The most notable of these extra shots were those Lucas added to the cantina sequence, which he felt had never been fully realized following Stuart Freeborn's illness. Additional second-unit filming was also shot by Carroll Ballard in California's Death Valley (doubling for Tunisia), where most of the material for the R2-D2-in-canyon and Sand People scenes was captured. "I shot out in the desert for about two weeks," Ballard recalls. "And then we went back to a little, tiny stage right across from Kodak in Hollywood where we shot the bar scene and added the new creatures."

Lucas had planned to replace Declan Mulholland's Jabba the Hutt with a matted-in stop-motion character, but by now it was clear that he would not have the time or money to make that happen. He reluctantly decided to cut the Jabba scene from the film. Meanwhile, ILM's Richard Edlund took a small crew to the Tikal National Park in Guatemala to film the exteriors for the jungle planet Yavin 4.

In mid-January 1977 a second unit–photographed by another of Lucas's old friends, Robert Dalva—was due to shoot additional scenes of the landspeeder at China Lake Acres, north of Los Angeles. In the morning of filming, news arrived that Mark Hamill had been involved in an accident, and had been hurled through the

Above left - *Lucas directs Han's cinematic point-of-view of the bounty hunter Greedo during additional shooting for the cantina sequence in Hollywood, California. Carroll Ballard is the camera operator, while production assistant Miki Herman (right) checks the script.*

Above right - *The score for* Star Wars *was recorded at the Anvil Studios in Denham, England, in March 1977.*

Right - *Scenes featuring Luke's landspeeder were filmed at the Tunisian salt flats in March 1976 and then again, as shown here, in mid-January 1977 at China Lake Acres, where the hovering problem was finally resolved.*

Far right - *With remnants of fast food in the foreground, Lucas prepares to shoot a bantha—i.e., "Marjorie the Elephant" in disguise—during additional shooting in California's Death Valley.*

In April, the score was mixed and added to *Star Wars'* Dolby Stereo soundtrack and the first prints were struck. Lucas could see only compromises, claiming that, "*Star Wars* is about 25 percent of what I wanted it to be."

The first public screening of *Star Wars* took place in San Francisco's Northpoint Theater on Sunday, May 1, 1977. The audience at the test screening did not seem to mind that the sound in the last three reels had still not been mixed properly, and applauded enthusiastically.

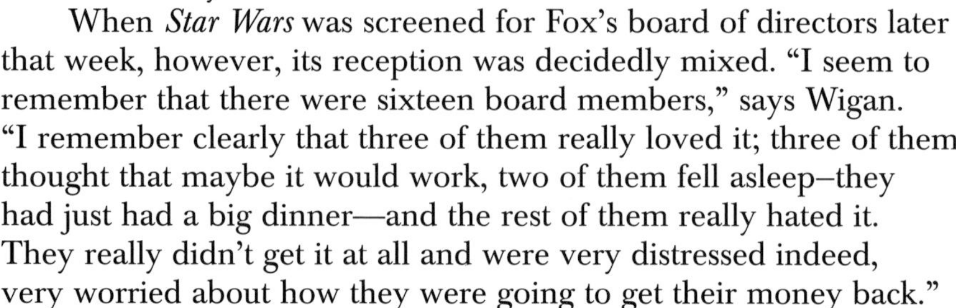

When *Star Wars* was screened for Fox's board of directors later that week, however, its reception was decidedly mixed. "I seem to remember that there were sixteen board members," says Wigan. "I remember clearly that three of them really loved it; three of them thought that maybe it would work, two of them fell asleep–they had just had a big dinner—and the rest of them really hated it. They really didn't get it at all and were very distressed indeed, very worried about how they were going to get their money back."

In the summer of 1977, the smart money was on *Sorcerer*, William Friedkin's remake of *The Wages of Fear* (1953), and *The Other Side of Midnight*, a melodrama based on a Sidney Sheldon novel. Exhibitors were dubious about *Star Wars.* In the late 1970s, it was usual for a major studio release to open on six hundred to eight hundred screens across the United States. *Star Wars* would open on just thirty-two.

"People have funny visions about *Star Wars* and what happened," Lucas would recall. "They always say that it changed the movie business. *Star Wars* didn't change the movie business. The big weekend to release movies was Christmas, which people have forgotten; it's always been Christmas ever since movies began. The second time to release your movies is the fourth of July weekend. But I said I want my film to be released in May for Memorial Day weekend. And the studio said, 'But the kids aren't out of school'—and I said, 'Well I don't want the kids out of school; I want the kids to be able to see the movie and then talk about it, so we can build word of mouth.' And they thought I was out of my mind. So the film was released in thirty-two theaters. Nobody thought of it as a hit movie; everybody thought of it as a kind of crazy, modest science-fiction film."

Star Wars began its discreet general release on the morning of Wednesday, May 25, 1977. Venues such as the Astor Plaza in New York City and the Coronet in San Francisco were besieged. For a whole generation of filmgoers, *Star Wars* would be a dazzling, majestic miracle, quite unlike anything they had ever seen before.

One of the people most surprised at the film's impact was Lucas, who at the time was engrossed in preparing the foreign-language versions in Los Angeles. He was in a hamburger restaurant on Hollywood Boulevard when he gazed out of the window at the crowd forming outside Grauman's Chinese Theater. "It was like a mob scene," says Lucas. "One lane of traffic was blocked off. There were police there. There were limousines in front of the theater. There were lines, eight or nine people wide, going both ways around the block. I said, 'My God, what's going on here? It must be a premiere or something.' I looked at the marquee, and it was *Star Wars.*"

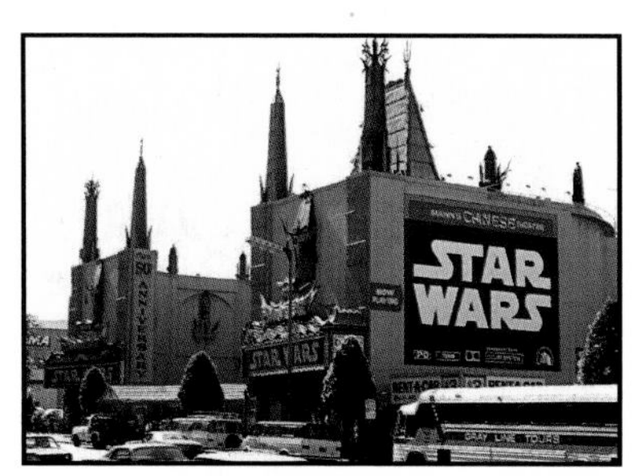

Above *- Darth Vader (David Prowse) casually surveys the Rebel casualties aboard the* Tantive IV *as he stalks his real prey: the princess and the stolen plans to the Death Star.*

Far left *- At Parkway house, a group has gathered in the afternoon to evaluate the* Star Wars *test screening at the Northpoint Theater of that morning: (from left) Marcia Lucas, woman in bandanna, assistant film editor Colin Kitchens, film librarian Pamela Malouf, Ben Burtt, publicist Charles Lippincott, (leaning back) assistant to the producer Bunny Alsup.*

Left *- Grauman's Chinese Theater in Los Angeles during the unexpected euphoria that greeted* Star Wars*' release on May 25, 1977.*

Opposite, left *- This American one-sheet, featuring artwork by Drew Struzan and Charles White III, paid homage to the matinee serials that had partly inspired* Star Wars.

Opposite, right *- This Japanese poster was based on the artwork for the British posters. Artist Tom Chantrell had enjoyed a long association with Hammer Film Productions, and his was the only poster design to incorporate former Hammer star Peter Cushing.*

STAR WARS

A LONG TIME AGO IN A GALAXY FAR, FAR AWAY. . .

Starring MARK HAMILL HARRISON FORD CARRIE FISHER
PETER CUSHING
and ALEC GUINNESS

Written and Directed by GEORGE LUCAS Produced by GARY KURTZ
Music by JOHN WILLIAMS

PG PARENTAL GUIDANCE SUGGESTED

PANAVISION® PRINTS BY DE LUXE® TECHNICOLOR®
Original Motion Picture Soundtrack on 20th Century-Fox Records and Tapes

DOLBY STEREO

STAR WARS

海運・百樂・京都・麗聲

盛大獻映

老少咸宜

雄奇偉大・不可思議
千變萬化・耳目一新

影壇奇才 佐治洛卡斯 震世之作

麥咸美
嘉麗菲莎
夏里遜福 領銜主演
亞歷堅尼斯
彼得古城 客串主演

特藝七彩
超藝透視體

星球大戰

20th Century Fox

電影有史以來最賣座影片！美加收入超過二億三千萬美元，壓倒任何影片

霍士公司
震驚全球
包羅萬有
驚險奇趣
娛樂片王

DOLBY STEREO

* *

Prior to the release of *Star Wars*, only twenty films had used the Dolby noise-filtration system to enhance their soundtracks. Lucas approached the British sound specialist Dolby Laboratories in 1975 to discuss its potential involvement in the soundtrack for *Star Wars*. Engineers from Dolby consulted the film's sound mixers at Elstree Studios before filming began, and the process was completed during the final mixing sessions at the Goldwyn Studios in April 1977. Dolby-encoded stereo was applied to the film's 35mm prints, while a new stereo surround system with extended bass response was applied to the 70mm prints.

In July 1977, *American Cinematographer* magazine noted that more than half of the first-wave release theaters playing *Star Wars* were equipped with compatible Dolby playback equipment, including noise-reduction decoders and equalizers that could make precise adjustments to each venue's loudspeaker system. "In this way," noted the magazine, "for the first time ever, the sound heard in the theater should to all intents be identical to that heard by the director during the mix."

The commercial success of *Star Wars* prompted unprecedented demand for Dolby equipment from movie theaters across America, as audiences gained a new appreciation for the way sound effects and music could enhance a movie. "George knew how to use Dolby," said Alan Ladd Jr. in 1977. "Other people were just using a process."

The band at the Mos Eisley cantina performed two specially composed jazz-style numbers in John Williams's *Star Wars* score.

Those thirty-two screens generated a record-breaking $254,809 in opening-day revenue. Exhibitors soon realized they had underestimated demand, and Fox immediately provided prints for another ten screens. The film spread like wildfire across the United States, and the most perceptive critics were quick to analyze its appeal. In the *New York Times*, Vincent Canby overestimated the size of Lucas's budget when he described *Star Wars* as "the most elaborate, most expensive, most beautiful movie serial ever made."

For the keen-eyed, *Star Wars* contains elements of the director's previous work–Luke, like Curt and THX 1138 before him, goes on a journey of self-discovery, mustering the courage to leave his home. (And Luke was clearly the character with whom Lucas most closely identified; during filming in Tunisia, Hamill even introduced some of Lucas's mannerisms and vocal inflections into his performance.) However, Luke's journey differs in an important way from those of the other two characters. By ending at the beginning of the journey, the previous films were, in a sense, meditations on the decision to leave. *THX 1138*, for example, ends with THX gazing into the sun; Luke, however, gazes into twin suns at the beginning of *Star Wars* and then continues his adventure, revealing his journey and the ongoing decisions that must be made while out in the world.

The film also demonstrates Lucas's penchant for cultural disorientation, traceable from his early experiences watching Kurosawa films through *THX 1138*, which throws the spectator into worlds and situations without a lot of explanation. "When it was first released, people felt *Star Wars* moved very, very fast," Lucas says. "Part of that is you're introduced to a world you've never seen before. One of the premises is that I would assume this was a natural world for everybody, so I wouldn't dwell on setting this up, trying to explain what a droid is and so on."

The exhausted figure in the eye of the storm allowed himself only cautious optimism. In late May, Lucas began a vacation in Maui, where he was accompanied by Huyck and Katz, and later by Spielberg and his girlfriend Amy Irving. Lucas took the opportunity to escape from *Star Wars*, and Spielberg was seeking refuge from his postproduction woes on *Close Encounters of*

Above - *Luke (Mark Hamill, far left) watches as Princess Leia (Carrie Fisher) awards Han Solo (Harrison Ford) a special medal for his bravery. Rebel strategist General Dodonna (Alex McCrindle) stands to the right. Still photographer John Jay is behind Fisher. Continuity supervisor Ann Skinner, taking notes, is on far right.*

Right - *Luke (Mark Hamill) contemplates his future outside the Lars homestead on Tatooine.*

Far right - *The heroes of the Rebel Alliance turn to face the applause in the final shot of* Star Wars.

the Third Kind. The two were sitting on a beach, building a sand castle, when Lucas was asked to return to his hotel nearby and take a phone call from Los Angeles. He returned with the good news that *Star Wars* had done incredible business during its first seven days. Lucas's relief was palpable. He allowed himself only a few moments, however, before asking Spielberg what he wanted to do when *Close Encounters* was finished. Spielberg replied that he wanted to direct a James Bond film. Lucas told him he had something better. He then recounted the story he had devised for *Raiders of the Lost Ark* some two years before. Lucas felt that globetrotting adventurer Indiana Smith was more than a match for Bond. Spielberg agreed, though the archaeologist's surname was eventually changed to "Jones."

Star Wars grossed $2.89 million in its first seven days, and, by mid-June, was playing in 350 theaters. The value of shares in Twentieth Century-Fox hit their highest level since 1970. By August, *Star Wars*' domestic box office hit $78 million. In November, its domestic gross surpassed that of *Jaws.* It was official—*Star Wars* was the fastest-selling, highest-grossing ticket in Hollywood history. And the film had yet to open in most major foreign territories. Eventually, Lucas would give percentages of the film's profits to his principal actors. "We ended up earning what we were worth," Ford recalls. He also gave most of his crew huge bonuses.

In December of 1977, Lucas was invited to give a lecture at USC, where division cochairman Mort Zarcoff introduced him as "the first cinema student ever to direct the most profitable movie in film history." Lucas screened excerpts from his films and fielded questions from an audience of more than 350 students—who were eager to discover what Lucas planned to do next.

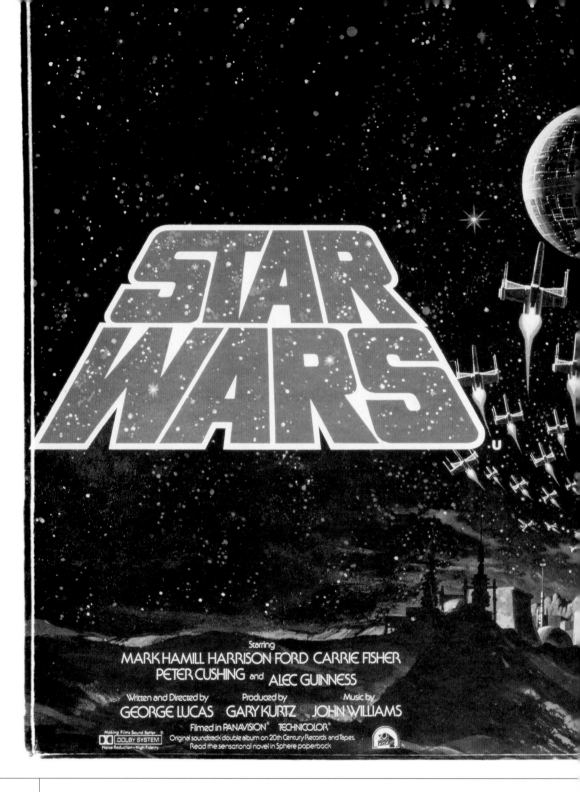

Above - A British quad poster featuring an iconic illustration by American artists Greg and Tim Hildebrandt.

Far left - The Howard Anderson Optical Printer. Commissioned at ILM in 1975; decommissioned at ILM in 1993. Although this printer had been used for films such as Cecil B. DeMille's The Ten Commandments *(1956) and Alfred Hitchcock's* North by Northwest *(1959), as the VistaVision format waned, it had fallen into disuse by the time work began on* Star Wars. *In 1975, however, Lucas purchased it from Paramount because he needed an optical printer that would be able to duplicate images many times without loss of quality. It was set up at the Van Nuys ILM facility and was eventually used for ILM's visual-effects works on films such as* Raiders of the Lost Ark *(1981) and* Who Framed Roger Rabbit? *(1988).*

The VistaVision widescreen process offered a negative area 2.66 times greater than that of standard 35mm film with an aspect ratio of 1.66:1, which made it ideal for Star Wars' *complex visual-effects shots.*

Left - A specialized camera and mount films the opening crawl.

May the force be with you
HILDEBRANDT
©1977 Twentieth Century-Fox

INDIANA SMITH

Such was Lucas's enthusiasm for the Saturday matinee serials that had inspired *Star Wars*, he felt there were other ways to reintroduce their action-adventure ethos to a medium that had all but forgotten such simple pleasures. Luke was an aspiring archaeologist in the second draft of *The Star Wars*, but years before Lucas had created a full-fledged archaeologist—an intrepid relic hunter called Indiana Smith. (The character's first name was a reference to Lucas's dog, Indiana.)

Lucas discussed his story idea with Philip Kaufman, hoping he would direct it. Kaufman spent several weeks working with Lucas on ideas for a script. Kaufman's major contribution to Indiana's first adventure was suggesting that the object with supernatural powers in Lucas's treatment, which Smith and his prewar Nazis enemies were fighting for, should be the Hebrews' Lost Ark of the Covenant—the chest containing the fragments of the Ten Commandments.

Progress stalled, however, when Kaufman was contacted by Clint Eastwood, who invited him to write his new Western *The Outlaw Josey Wales* (1976). Kaufman's collaboration with Eastwood prompted Lucas to shelve *Raiders*—but it would ultimately find another director.

Lucas and *Indiana Jones* director Steven Spielberg.

Shooting Schedule

Star Wars: Episode IV A New Hope

* * * * * * * * * * * * * * * * * *as shot* * * * * * * * * * * * * * * * * *

Scenes in boldface were cut from the final version. Not all scenes filmed are listed for each day. All spellings are verbatim from the daily progress reports and dialogue is taken from the revised fourth draft, dated March 15, 1976. This schedule does not include pick-ups filmed in the United States.

REPORT NO. 1 SFX: January 14, 1976
Where Working: EMI Studios, Borehamwood
Today's shooting comprised special effects tests on: laser swords, R2-D2, model and illuminated control boards

REPORT NO. 2 SFX: January 23
Where Working: EMI Studios
Today's shooting comprised special effects tests on: laser swords, Jawa "eyes"

REPORT NO. 1: Monday, March 22
Call: 06.30 **Unit Dismissed:** 19.20
Where Working: Tunisian Location: Salt Flats at Nefta, NR. Tozeur
Sets: EXT. Lars' Homestead
Scene Numbers: 26 PART [purchase of C-3PO and R2-D2]; 29 PART [Luke and giant twin suns]; B29 [Luke and C-3PO rush out of the homestead to look for R2-D2]
Scs. Completed Today: 1
Screen Time Taken To-day: 2m. 43s.
Daily Status: _ day over
Remarks: Commencement of principal photography today. The UK unit travelled from London to Djerba on Saturday March 20 and after staying overnight in Djerba travelled to the Tozeur location on Sunday March 21, with the exception of Sir Alec Guinness.

REPORT NO. 2: Tuesday, March 23
Call: 06.30 **Unit Dismissed:** 18.16
Where Working: **Salt Flats at Nefta, Sand Dunes, Nefta**
Sets: EXT. Lars' Homestead
Scene Numbers: 26 PART [purchase of C-3PO and R2-D2]
Scs. Completed Today: Nil
Screen Time Taken To-day: 1m. 00s.
Daily Status: 1 day over

REPORT NO. 3: Wednesday, March 24
Call: 06.30 **Unit Dismissed:** 17.57
Where Working: Sand Dunes, Nefta
Sets: EXT. Edge of Dune Sea
Scene Numbers: 15 [C-3PO and bleached bones of beast]; 14 PART [C-3PO and R2-D2 argue about which way to go]
Scs. Completed Today: 1
Screen Time Taken To-day: 12m. 31s.
Remarks: Sir Alec and Lady Guinness arrived in Tozeur this afternoon.

REPORT NO. 4: Thursday, March 25
Call: 06.30 **Unit Dismissed:** 18.40
Where Working: Tozeur
Sets: EXT. Dune Sea, EXT. Lars' Homestead, EXT. Desert Wasteland, EXT. Sandcrawler
Scene Numbers: B32 [stormtroopers find evidence of droids]; C42 [Luke discovers his aunt and uncle have been killed]; **3 PART [Luke in wasteland with droid that malfunctions]**
Scs. Completed Today: 3
Screen Time Taken To-day: 1m. 32s.
Remarks: Two units working separately this morning with 2nd unit covering Jawa activity shots with robots in front of Sandcrawler.

REPORT NO. 5: Friday, March 26
Call: 07.00 **Unit Dismissed:** 18.15
Where Working: Canyon in Tozeur
Sets: EXT. Rock Canyon Set
Scene Numbers: 37 [Luke and C-3PO find R2-D2]; 38 PART (some of this to be shot in USA) [Luke attacked by Tusken Raiders]
Scs. Completed Today: 1
Screen Time Taken To-day: 1m. 20s.

REPORT NO. 6&7: Saturday & Sunday, March 27/28
Call: 08.00 **Unit Dismissed:** 18.12
Where Working: Canyon in Tozeur
Sets: EXT. Rock Canyon Set
Scene Numbers: 39 PART [arrival of Ben Kenobi in canyon]; 40 [Luke finds injured C-3PO]
Scs. Completed Today: 1
Screen Time Taken To-day: 2m. 54s.
Remarks: Although Call Sheet No. 6 was issued for 3/27, weather conditions made it impossible to shoot; therefore call was cancelled and Sunday working was decided upon instead.

REPORT NO. 8: Monday, March 29
Call: 06.30 **Unit Dismissed:** 19.12
Where Working: Canyon, Tozeur; Salt Flats, Nefta
Scene Numbers: 47 [they view Mos Eisley, a "wretched hive of scum and villainy"]; 35 [Tusken Raiders spot Luke in landspeeder]
Scs. Completed Today: 5
Screen Time Taken To-day: 52s.

REPORT NO. 9: Tuesday, March 30,
Call: 07.00 **Unit Dismissed:** 20.45
Where Working: Canyon in Tozeur
Sets: EXT. Rock Canyon Set
Scene Numbers: 17 PART [Jawas neutralize R2-D2]; 18 [Jawas carry R2-D2 to Sandcrawler]
Scs. Completed Today: 1
Screen Time Taken To-day: 1m. 20s.

REPORT NO. 10: Wednesday, March 31,
Call: 08.00 **Unit Dismissed:** 17.35
Where Working: Canyon in Tozeur
Sets: EXT. Rock Canyon Set
Scene Numbers: B42 [Luke and Ben discover killed Jawas]; E42 [Jawa bonfire]
Scs. Completed Today: 2
Screen Time Taken To-day: 1m. 45s.
Remarks: Today was the last shot of shooting on the Tozeur locations. Unit moves to Gabes tomorrow.

REPORT NO. 11: Thursday, April 1
Call: 05.00 **Unit Dismissed:** 18.36
Where Working: Hotel Sidi Driss, Matmata (Gabes Loc.)
Scene Numbers: 26 COMPLETED [purchase of droids]; A28 [Lars' homestead—kitchen]
Scs. Completed Today: 4
Screen Time Taken To-day: 2m. 29s.

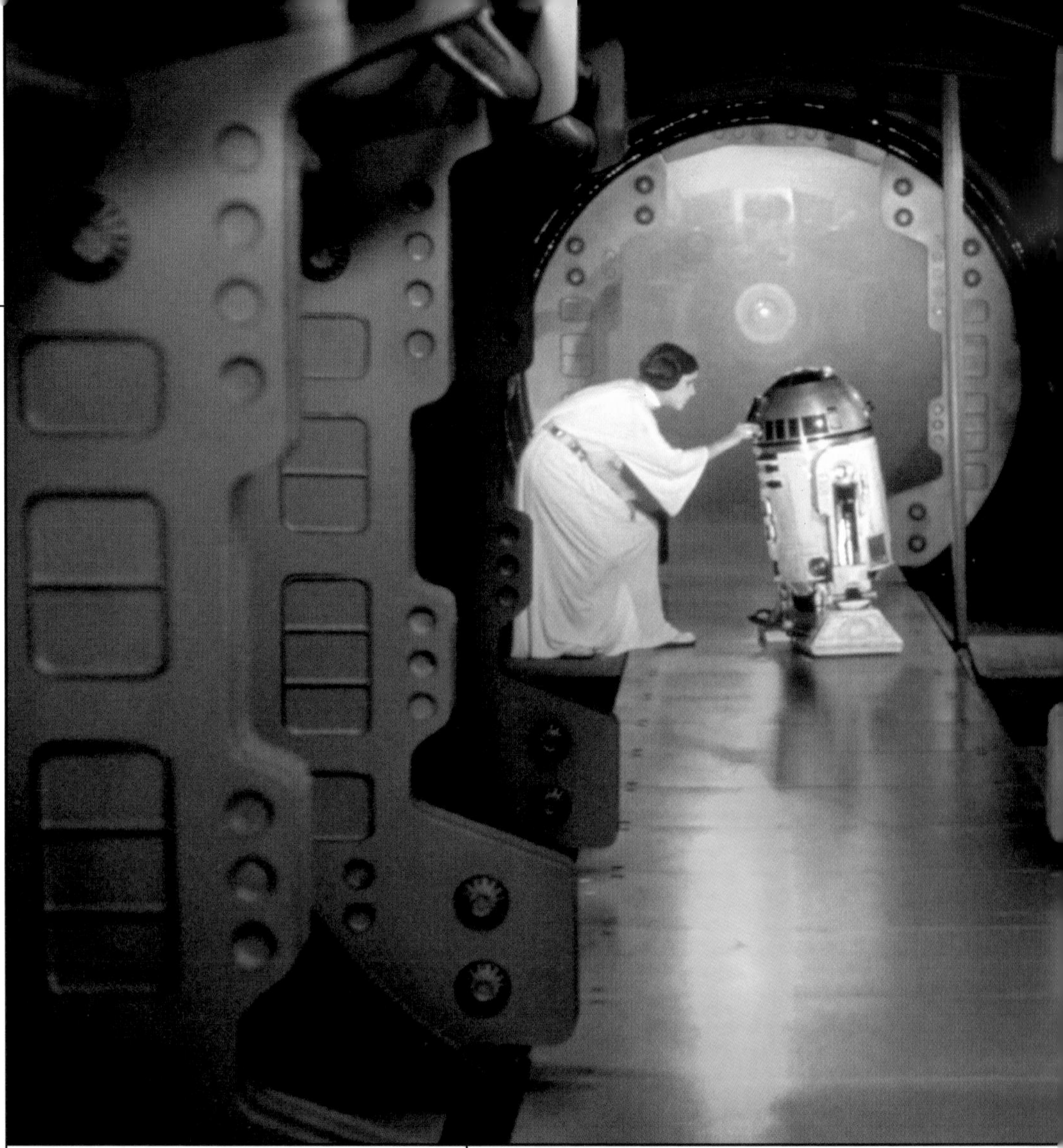

REPORT NO. 12: Friday, April 2
Call: 07:30 **Unit Dismissed:** 17.46
Where Working: Ajim, Djerba
Scene Numbers: 48 [Ben: "These are not the droids you're looking for"]; 59 [Mos Eisley: stormtroopers watch Millennium Falcon blast off]
Scs. Completed Today: 2
Screen Time Taken To-day: 52s.

REPORT NO. 13: SATURDAY, April 3
Call: 06:30 **Unit Dismissed:** 17.45
Where Working: Ajim, Djerba
Scene Numbers: ZA50 (EXTRA)[droids in front of the Cantina]; A50 [Ben tells Luke he'll have to sell his landspeeder]
Scs. Completed Today: 3
Screen Time Taken To-day: 1m 19s.
Remarks: Unit completed shooting on Ajim location today, and will move to mosque location tomorrow A.M.

REPORT NO. 14: SUNDAY, April 4
Call: 07:30 **Unit Dismissed:** 17.46
Unit Dismissed: Mosque, Djerba
Scene Numbers: **8 [Luke in landspeeder almost runs down a woman]; 10 [Biggs and Luke look up into the sky]; 16 [Biggs reveals that he's going to join the Rebellion]**
Scs. Completed Today: 4
Screen Time Taken To-day: 4m 11s.
Remarks: Unit completed shooting on Tunisian locations today.

REPORT NO. 15: Wednesday, April 7
Call: 08:30 **Unit Dismissed:** 17.25
Where Working: EMI Studios; Borehamwood, Stage 7
Sets: INT. Lars' Kitchen; INT. Anchorhead Power Station
Scene Numbers: 28 [Beru fills pitcher with blue milk]; **9 [Biggs/Luke reunion]**
Scs. Completed Today: 3
Screen Time Taken To-day: 1m 21s.
Remarks: Today is the first day of studio shooting in U.K.
Retrospective Nite: Harrison Ford ("Han Solo") arrived in the U.K. from U.S.A. on Thursday April 1, 1976.

REPORT NO. 16: Thursday, April 8
Call: 08.30 **Unit Dismissed:** 18.05
Where Working: Stage 1
Sets: INT. Lars' Homestead (garage)
Scene Numbers: 27 PART [Luke discovers R2-D2'S message]

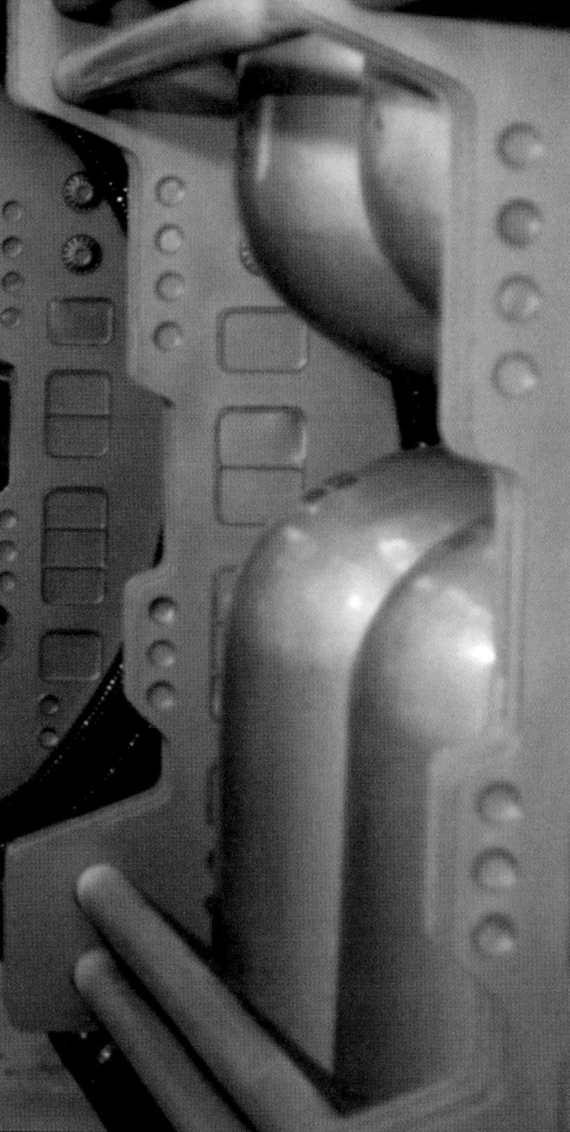

Scs. Completed Today: –
Screen Time Taken To-day: 3m 46s.

REPORT NO. 17: Friday, April 9
Call: 08.30 **Unit Dismissed:** 17.30
Sets: Stage 1–INT. Lars' Homestead Garage
Scene Numbers: A29 [Luke finds C-3PO hiding]
Scs. Completed Today: 2
Screen Time Taken To-day: 27s.

REPORT NO. 18: Monday, April 12
Call: 08.30 **Unit Dismissed:** 17.45
Sets: Stage 3–INT. Docking Bay 94
Scene Numbers: EXTRA SC. AA53 [Jabba and Han Solo in Docking Bay]
Scs. Completed Today: 1
Screen Time Taken To-day: 2m 28s.
Nite: SCS. deleted from draft dated 1/1/76: A53, 54, 55, 57 [these scenes featured Han's outsmarting of Imperial bureaucrat MONTROSS, who tries vainly to enforce an edict that would prevent the Falcon from flying out of Mos Eisley]

REPORT NO. 19: Tuesday, April 13
Call: 08.30 **Unit Dismissed:** 17.45
Sets: Stage 3–INT. Docking Bay 94; Stage 6–INT. Cantina
Scene Numbers: 50 PART [Obi-Wan uses lightsaber in the Cantina]
Scs. Completed Today: 1
Screen Time Taken To-day: 48s.

REPORT NO. 20: Wednesday, April 14
Call: 08.30 **Unit Dismissed:** 17.35
Sets: Stage 3–INT. Docking Bay 94; Stage 6–INT. Cantina
Scene Numbers: AA53 RETAKE; 50 PART
Scs. Completed Today: –
Screen Time Taken To-day: 10s.

REPORT NO. 21: Thursday, April 15
Call: 11.00 **Unit Dismissed:** 18.12
Sets: Stage 6–INT. Cantina
Scene Numbers: 50 PART
Scs. Completed Today: –
Screen Time Taken To-day: 30s.
Daily Status: 1 day behind

REPORT NO. 22: Tuesday, April 20
Call: 11.00 **Unit Dismissed:** 18.06
Sets: Stage 6–INT. Cantina
Scene Numbers: ZB50 (EXTRA SCENE) [Luke and Obi-Wan meet Han Solo]; 50 PART (EXTRA SCENE) [Han and Greedo]
Scs. Completed Today: 1
Screen Time Taken To-day: 2m 00s.
Remarks: Carrie Fisher (Princess Leia) arrived from U.S.A. on Monday, April 19TH.

REPORT NO. 23: Wednesday, April 21
Call: 08.30 **Unit Dismissed:** 18.12
Sets: Stage 3–INT. Docking Bay 94 (retake); Stage 6–INT. Cantina
Scene Numbers: AA53, etc.
Scs. Completed Today: 1
Screen Time Taken To-day: 1m 22s.

REPORT NO. 24: Thursday, April 22
Call: 08.30 **Unit Dismissed:** 18.05
SETS: Stage 8–EXT. Mos Eisley Spaceport, Alleyways
Scene Numbers: 53 [Luke has sold his landspeeder]; 56 [spy transmits info]
Scs. Completed Today: 4
Screen Time Taken To-day: 2m 01s.

REPORT NO. 25: Friday, April 23
Call: 08.30 **Unit Dismissed:** 18.20
Sets: Stage 7–INT. Ben Kenobi's Cave
Scene Numbers: 42 PART [Obi-Wan views Leia's message]
Scs. Completed Today: –
Screen Time Taken To-day: 4m 00s.

REPORT NO. 26: Monday, April 26
Call: 08.30 **Unit Dismissed:** 17.30
Sets: Stage 7–INT. Ben Kenobi's Cave; Stage 2–INT. Death Star
Scene Numbers: 42 COMP.; 111 [Vader espies Kenobi]
Scs. Completed Today: 3
Screen Time Taken To-day: 57s.

REPORT NO. 27: Tuesday, April 27
Call: 08.30 **Unit Dismissed:** 17.30
Sets: Stage 2–INT. Death Star
Scene Numbers: BA53 (REPLACES BA50 DELETED) [Vader okays more stormtroopers to search for droids on Mos Eisley; he hopes that if they're found, it will break Princess Leia's spirit]
Scs. Completed Today: 1
Screen Time Taken To-day: 1m 17s.

REPORT NO. 28: Wednesday, April 28
Call: 08.30 **Unit Dismissed:** 17.30
SETS: Stage 2–INT. Death Star
Scene Numbers: B110 PART [Luke and Leia arrive at precipice]
Scs. Completed Today: 1
Screen Time Taken To-day: 1m 01s.

REPORT NO. 29: Thursday, April 29
Call: 08.30 **Unit Dismissed:** 19.40
Sets: Stage 4–INT. Death Star Control Room
Scene Numbers: A124 PART [Vader: "This will be a day long remembered . . ."]; D42 PART [Vader and Tarkin discuss Leia's resistance to the mind probe]; SS225 PART [Tarkin: "Evacuate! In our moment of triumph?"]; 66 PART [Leia: "The more you tighten your grip . . ."]
Scs. Completed Today: --
Screen Time Taken To-day: 3m 07s.

REPORT NO. 30: Friday, April 30
Call: 08.30 **Unit Dismissed:** 17.30
Sets: Stage 2—INT. Death Star
Scene Numbers: B110 PART [Luke and Leia swing across the precipice]
Scs. Completed Today: --
Screen Time Taken To-day: 14s.

REPORT NO. 31: Monday, May 3
Call: 08.30 **Unit Dismissed:** 17.30
Sets: Stage 1 & 4–Death Star Interiors
Scene Numbers: 22 [Vader: "I find your lack of faith disturbing"]; 89A [Vader reports Obi-Wan's presence to Tarkin]; 66 PART [Tarkin to Leia: "Charming to the last . . ."]
Scs. Completed Today: 3
Screen Time Taken To-day: 3m 52s.

REPORT NO. 32: Tuesday, May 4
Call: 08.30 **Unit Dismissed:** 17.30
Sets: Stage 4 & 2–INT. Death Star
Scene Numbers: A124 COMP.
Scs. Completed Today: 3
Screen Time Taken To-day: 17s.
[Peter Cushing's last day]

REPORT NO. 33: Wednesday, May 5
Call: 08.30 **Unit Dismissed:** 17.30
Sets: Stage 2–INT. Death Star, Stage 1–INT. Conference Room
Scene Numbers: 84, 109 [action scenes in Death Star]
Scs. Completed Today: 4
Screen Time Taken To-day: 1m 10s.
Daily Status: 4 days over

REPORT NO. 34: Thursday, May 6
Call: 08.30 **Unit Dismissed:** 17.25
Sets: Stage 2–INT. Death Star, Stage 7–INT. Ben Kenobi's Cave, Stage 9–INT. Pirate Starship Hallway
Scene Numbers: 80 [emerging from smuggling compartments in *Falcon*]
Scs. Completed Today:: 4
Screen Time Taken To-day: 1m 14s.

REPORT NO. 35: Friday, May 7
Call: 08.30 **Unit Dismissed:** 17.30
Sets: Stage 9–INT. Pirate Starship Hallway
Scene Numbers: 67 PART [Luke training with seeker; hologram board game]
Scs. Completed Today: –
Screen Time Taken To-day: 2m 50s.

REPORT NO. 36: Monday, May 10
Call: 08.30 **Unit Dismissed:** 17.30
Sets: Stage 9–INT. Pirate Starship
Scene Numbers: 63 [C-3PO: "I forgot how much I hate space travel"]
Scs. Completed Today: 4
Screen Time Taken To-day: 33s.

REPORT NO. 37: Tuesday, May 11
Call: 08.30 **Unit Dismissed:** 17.30
Sets: Stage 2–INT. Death Star, Stage 9–INT. Pirate Starship Hallway (2ND UNIT)
Scene Numbers: A42 PART [Leia and torture robot], 89 PART [Leia to Luke: "Aren't you a little short for a stormtrooper?"]
Scs. Completed Today: 2
Screen Time Taken To-day: 1m 12s.

REPORT NO. 38: Wednesday, May 12
Call: 08.30 **Unit Dismissed:**17.35
Sets: Stage 4–INT. Death Star
Scene Numbers: 88 PART [detention level fight]
Scs. Completed Today: 2
Screen Time Taken To-day: 1m 30s.

REPORT NO. 39: Thursday, May 13
Call: 08.30 **Unit Dismissed:** 17.30
Where Working: Shepperton Studios
Sets: H Stage–INT. Masassi Outpost, Throne Room
Scene Numbers: 252 PART [celebration–last scene of film]
Scs. Completed Today: –
Screen Time Taken To-day: 1m 18s.
Remarks: Today is the first day of shooting on "H" Stage at Shepperton Studios.

REPORT NO. 40: Friday, May 14
Call: 08.30 **Unit Dismissed:** 17.40
Sets: H Stage–INT. Masassi Outpost, Throne Room
Scene Numbers: 252 COMPLETED
Scs. Completed Today: 1
Screen Time Taken To-day: 15s.
Remarks: Anthony Daniels this morning complained of a sore right hand, caused by his costume chafing.

REPORT NO. 41: Monday, May 17
Call: 08.30 **Unit Dismissed:** 17.30
Sets: H Stage–INT. Masassi War Room
Scene Numbers: 135 PART [Death Star attack briefing]
Scs. Completed Today: –
Screen Time Taken To-day: 1m 52s.
Daily Status: 6 days over

Above - Princess Leia (Carrie Fisher) inserts the Death Star plans—and an important mission—into the saga's unsung hero, R2-D2.

REPORT NO. 42: Tuesday, May 18
CALL: 08.30 **UNIT DISMISSED:** 19.35
SETS: H Stage–INT. Masassi War Room
SCENE NUMBERS: 137 PART, etc.
SCS. COMPLETED TODAY: 8
SCREEN TIME TAKEN TO-DAY: 3m 33s.

REPORT NO. 43: Wednesday, May 19
CALL: 08.30 **UNIT DISMISSED:** 17.25
WHERE WORKING: EMI Studios, Borehamwood
Stage 4–INT. Death Star
SCENE NUMBERS: 91 PART [Han to Leia: "Maybe you'd prefer it back in your cell?"]
SCS. COMPLETED TODAY: –
SCREEN TIME TAKEN TO-DAY: 27s.

REPORT NO. 44: Thursday, May 20
CALL: 08.30 **UNIT DISMISSED:** 17.37
WHERE WORKING: EMI Studios & Shepperton Studios (2ND UNIT)
SETS: INT. Death Star & 2ND Unit doing pick-up shots on INT. Masassi War Room
SCENE NUMBERS: 91 PT.; 2ND Unit: 137 COMPLETED, 190 & 135 COMP.
SCS. COMPLETED TODAY: 4
SCREEN TIME TAKEN TO-DAY: 1m 24s.

REPORT NO. 45: Friday, May 21
CALL: 08.30 **UNIT DISMISSED:** 17.35
WHERE WORKING: EMI Studios
SETS: Stage 4–INT. Death Star Prison Corridor, Stage 8–INT. Pirate Starship Cockpit
SCENE NUMBERS: 91 COMP. [Han to Luke: "Watch your mouth, kid, or you'll find yourself floating back home"]
SCS. COMPLETED TODAY: 5
SCREEN TIME TAKEN TO-DAY: 54s.
DAILY STATUS: 7 days over

REPORT NO. 46: Monday, May 24
CALL: 08.30 **UNIT DISMISSED:** 17.30
SETS: Stage 8–INT. Pirate Starship Cockpit
SCENE NUMBERS: A74 PT. [Luke: "He's heading for that small moon"]
SCS. COMPLETED TODAY: 2
SCREEN TIME TAKEN TO-DAY: 2m 15s.

REPORT NO. 47: Tuesday, May 25
CALL: 08.30 **UNIT DISMISSED:** 18.45
SETS: Stage 8–INT. Pirate Starship Cockpit
SCENE NUMBERS: 62 COMP.
SCS. COMPLETED TODAY: 6
SCREEN TIME TAKEN TO-DAY: Nil [SIC]

REPORT NO. 48: Wednesday, May 26
CALL: 08.30 **UNIT DISMISSED:** 17.40
SETS: Stage 3–INT. Death Star–Main Forward Bay
SCENE NUMBERS: A101 [R2-D2 tries to shut down garbage masher]
SCS. COMPLETED TODAY: 3
SCREEN TIME TAKEN TO-DAY: 2m 13s

REPORT NO. 49: Thursday, May 27
CALL: 08.30 **UNIT DISMISSED:** 17.40
SETS: Stage 3–INT. Death Star–Main Forward Bay
SCENE NUMBERS: 117 PART [Obi-Wan is cut down]
SCS. COMPLETED TODAY: –
SCREEN TIME TAKEN TO-DAY: 29s

REPORT NO. 50: Friday, May 28
CALL: 08.30 **UNIT DISMISSED:** 17.20
SETS: Stage 3–INT. Death Star–Main Forward Bay
SCENE NUMBERS: 117 PART
SCS. COMPLETED TODAY: –
SCREEN TIME TAKEN TO-DAY: 16s

REPORT NO. 51: Tuesday, June 1
CALL: 08.30 **UNIT DISMISSED:** 20.45
SETS: Stage 3–INT. Death Star–Main Docking Bay
SCENE NUMBERS: 116 PART [Vader to Obi-Wan: "We meet again at last"]
SCS. COMPLETED TODAY: –
SCREEN TIME TAKEN TO-DAY: 1m 39s
DAILY STATUS: 9 days over

REPORT NO. 52: Wednesday, June 2
CALL: 08.30 **UNIT DISMISSED:** 17.21
SETS: Stage 2–Death Star Command Office
SCENE NUMBERS: 82PT. [Luke convinces Han to help rescue Leia]
SCS. COMPLETED TODAY: 2
SCREEN TIME TAKEN TO-DAY: 37s

REPORT NO. 53: Thursday, June 3
CALL: 08.30 **UNIT DISMISSED:** 17.30
SETS: 1ST Unit: Stage 2–INT. Command Office 2ND UNIT: Stage 3–INT. MAIN FORWARD BAY
SCENE NUMBERS: 117 PART, etc.
SCS. COMPLETED TODAY: 2
SCREEN TIME TAKEN TO-DAY: 1m 34s

REPORT NO. 54: Friday, June 4
CALL: 08.30 **UNIT DISMISSED:** 20.45
SETS: Stage 2–INT. Power Trench, Stage 3–INT. Main Forward Bay (2ND Unit)
SCENE NUMBERS: A105 PART [Obi-Wan shuts down the tractor beam]
SCS. COMPLETED TODAY: 1
SCREEN TIME TAKEN TO-DAY: 1m 36s

REPORT NO. 55: Monday, June 7
CALL: 08.30 **UNIT DISMISSED:** 17.35
SETS: Stage 8–INT. Pirate Starship Cockpit, INT. Command Office on Stage 2
SCENE NUMBERS: A105 PART, etc.
SCS. COMPLETED TODAY: –
SCREEN TIME TAKEN TO-DAY: 2m 09s
DAILY STATUS: 10 days over

REPORT NO. 56: Tuesday, June 8
CALL: 08.30 **UNIT DISMISSED:** 18.10
SETS: Stage 2–INT. Command Office, Stage 8–INT. Sandcrawler, 2ND Unit Shooting INT. Power Trench
SCENE NUMBERS: 82 PART, etc.
SCS. COMPLETED TODAY: 3
SCREEN TIME TAKEN TO-DAY: 1m 40s

REPORT NO. 57: Wednesday, June 9
CALL: 08.30 **UNIT DISMISSED:** 19.30
WHERE WORKING: Shepperton Studios
SETS: "H" Stage–INT. Masassi Main Hangar Deck
SCENE NUMBERS: 136 PART [Luke reproaches Han]
SCS. COMPLETED TODAY: –
SCREEN TIME TAKEN TO-DAY: 1m 05s

REPORT NO. 58: Thursday, June 10,
CALL: 08.30 **UNIT DISMISSED:** 19.28
SETS: "H" Stage–INT. Masassi Main Hangar Deck
SCENE NUMBERS: 136 PART
SCS. COMPLETED TODAY: –
SCREEN TIME TAKEN TO-DAY: 1m 47s

REPORT NO. 59: Friday, June 11
CALL: 08.30 **UNIT DISMISSED:** 17.30
SETS: "H" Stage–INT. Masassi Main Hangar Deck
SCENE NUMBERS: A132 [arrival on Yavin 4]
SCS. COMPLETED TODAY: 1
SCREEN TIME TAKEN TO-DAY: 49s

REPORT NO. 60: Monday, June 14
CALL: 08.30 **UNIT DISMISSED:** 21.05
SETS: "H" Stage–INT. Masassi Main Hangar Deck
SCS. COMPLETED TODAY: 2
SCREEN TIME TAKEN TO-DAY: 1m 14s
DAILY STATUS: 13 days over

REPORT NO. 61: Tuesday, June 15
CALL: 08.30 **UNIT DISMISSED:** 19.30
WHERE WORKING: 1ST Unit–EMI Studios; 2ND Unit–Shepperton Studios
SCS. COMPLETED TODAY: 1
SCREEN TIME TAKEN TO-DAY: 36s

REPORT NO. 62: Wednesday, June 16
CALL: 08.30 **UNIT DISMISSED:** 19.10
WHERE WORKING: EMI Studios
SETS: Stage 8–INT. Pirate Starship (2ND Unit working on Stages 3 & 4)
SCS. COMPLETED TODAY: –
SCREEN TIME TAKEN TO-DAY: 5s
REMARKS: Sir Alec Guinness (Ben Kenobi) completed his role.

REPORT NO. 63: Thursday, June 17
CALL: 08.30 **UNIT DISMISSED:** 17.30
SETS: 1ST Unit–Stage 8, 2ND Unit–Stage 2
SCENE NUMBERS: 1ST Unit: A125PT. [Han: "Not a bad bit of rescuing"]
239PT. [Han: "You're all clear, kid. Now blow this thing so we can go home."]; 245PT. ["Good shot, kid. That was one in a million."]
SCS. COMPLETED TODAY: –
SCREEN TIME TAKEN TO-DAY: 2m 44s

REPORT NO. 64: Friday, June 18
CALL: 08.30 **UNIT DISMISSED:** 17.30
SETS: 1ST Unit: Stage 8; 2ND Unit: Stage 2 & 8
SCENE NUMBERS: 1ST Unit: A122 [Leia and Chewbacca hug after Falcon/TIE fight]
SCS. COMPLETED TODAY: 11
SCREEN TIME TAKEN TO-DAY: 57s

REPORT NO. 65: Monday, June 21
CALL: 08.30 **UNIT DISMISSED:** 17.45
SETS: Stage 4–INT. Garbage Room
SCENE NUMBERS: A97 PART [Han: "What an incredible smell you've discovered."]
SCS. COMPLETED TODAY: –
SCREEN TIME TAKEN TO-DAY: 2m 05s

REPORT NO. 66: Tuesday, June 22
CALL: 08.30 **UNIT DISMISSED:** 21.42
SETS: Stage 4–INT. Garbage Room
Stage 2–INT. Disused Hallway & INT. Command Office (2ND Unit)
SCENE NUMBERS: A100 [walls close in]
SCS. COMPLETED TODAY: 6
SCREEN TIME TAKEN TO-DAY: 1m 22s

REPORT NO. 67: Wednesday, June 23
CALL: 08.30 **UNIT DISMISSED:** 17.30
SETS: Stage 8–INT. Gun Port; 2ND Unit: Stage 2–Unused Hallway, Stage 4–Garbage Room
SCENE NUMBERS: B120 [Falcon/TIE fight]
SCS. COMPLETED TODAY: 10
SCREEN TIME TAKEN TO-DAY: 1m 05s
REMARKS: ILM personnel (J. Dykstra, R. Edlund, R. Blalack) arrived today from Los Angeles.

REPORT NO. 68: Thursday, June 24
CALL: 08.30 **UNIT DISMISSED:** 17.30
SETS: Stage 8–INT. Gunport Pirate Starship, Stage 2–INT. Death Star (both units)
SCENE NUMBERS: G163 [Vader: "We'll have to destroy them ship to ship"]
SCS. COMPLETED TODAY: 16
SCREEN TIME TAKEN TO-DAY: 49s
REMARKS: Harrison Ford ("Han Solo") today completed his role. Mark Hamill's eye still shows no improvement [this injury occurred during his scene in the trash compactor].

REPORT NO. 69: Friday, June 25
CALL: 08.30 **UNIT DISMISSED:** 17.25
SETS: Stage 2–INT. Death Star Corridor (both units)
SCENE NUMBERS: F163, etc.
SCS. COMPLETED TODAY: 3
SCREEN TIME TAKEN TO-DAY: 1m 04s

REPORT NO. 70: Monday, June 28
CALL: 08.30 **UNIT DISMISSED:** 17.45
SETS: Stage 8–INT. Cockpit (with blue backing); 2ND Unit on Stages 2 & 4
SCENE NUMBERS: 140, 143, 152, etc.
SCS. COMPLETED TODAY: 15
SCREEN TIME TAKEN TO-DAY: 1m 02s
REMARKS: Please note that Harrison Ford returned to Los Angeles on Sunday, June 27th on flight BA 599. Also on same flight was Carrie Fisher, who will return next week for further filming. Peter Mayhew ("Chewbacca") completed his role today.

REPORT NO. 71: Friday, June 29
CALL: 08.30 **UNIT DISMISSED:** 17.45
SETS: 1ST UNIT: Stage 8–INT. Cockpit; 2ND Unit: Stages 4 & 2 (Garbage Room & INT. Corridor)
SCENE NUMBERS: 148 [Wedge: "Look at the size of that thing"]
SCS. COMPLETED TODAY: 24
SCREEN TIME TAKEN TO-DAY: 1m 03s

REPORT NO. 72: Wednesday, June 30
CALL: 08.30 **UNIT DISMISSED:** 17.25
SETS: Stage 8–INT. Cockpit
SCENE NUMBERS: N220, etc. [attack on Death Star]
SCS. COMPLETED TODAY: 8
SCREEN TIME TAKEN TO-DAY: 1m 12s

REPORT NO. 73: Thursday, July 1
CALL: 08.30 **UNIT DISMISSED:** 17.25
SETS: Stage 8–INT. Cockpit
SCENE NUMBERS: 240 [Luke switches off his targeting computer]
SCS. COMPLETED TODAY: 21
SCREEN TIME TAKEN TO-DAY: 2m 31s

Remarks: Mark Hamill's eye still red & it is therefore not possible to shoot close-ups on him.

REPORT NO. 74: Friday, July 2
Call: 08.30 **Unit Dismissed:** 17.25
Sets: Stage 8–INT. Cockpit & Luke'S Speeder on EXT. Desert Wasteland (FP)
Scene Numbers: 34 [Luke spots fugitive R2-D2]
Scs. Completed Today: 3
Screen Time Taken To-day: 1m 37s
Remarks: Carrie Fisher arrived back in the U.K. on Sunday July 4TH, 1976.

REPORT NO. 75: Monday, July 5
Call: 08.30 **Unit Dismissed:** 17.45
Sets: Stage 8–INT. Cockpit
Scene Numbers: B219, etc. [attack on Death Star]
Scs. Completed Today: 10
Screen Time Taken To-day: 56s

REPORT NO. 76: Tuesday, July 6
Call: 08.30 **Unit Dismissed:** 17.46
Sets: Stage 8–INT. Y-Wing Fighter, Stage 4–INT. Sandcrawler & INT. Hologram
Scene Numbers: COMPLETED: 215, etc.
Scs. Completed Today: 3
Screen Time Taken To-day: 1m 26s

REPORT NO. 77: Wednesday, July 7
Call: 08.30 **Unit Dismissed:** 17.30
Sets: 1ST Unit: Stage 2–Gun Emplacements, Stage 8–INT. Cockpit; 2ND Unit: Stage 4 & Stage 2
Scene Numbers: COMPLETED: 158, etc.
Scs. Completed Today:6
Screen Time Taken To-day: 43s

REPORT NO. 78: Thursday, July 8
Call: 08.30 **Unit Dismissed:** 17.30
Sets: 1ST Unit: Stage 8–INT. Cockpit, Stage 4–INT.
Gunport 2nd Unit: Stage 2–INT. Death Star
Scene Numbers: Sequence A120-A123 (close-ups of Mark Hamill)
Scs. Completed Today: 22
Screen Time Taken To-day: 1m 16s

REPORT NO. 79: Friday, July 9
Call: 08.30 **Unit Dismissed:** 17.30
Sets: 1ST Unit: Stage 9–INT. Rebel Starfighter; 2ND Unit: Stage 8–Luke'S X-Wing
Scene Numbers: 11 [Leia: "Lord Vader . . . only you could be so bold."]
Scs. Completed Today: 4
Screen Time Taken To-day: 2m 37s
DAILY STATUS: 18 days over

REPORT NO. 80: Monday, July 12
Call: 08.30 **Unit Dismissed:** 17.37
Sets: Stage 9–INT. Rebel Starfighter, Stage 8–Various Fighter Shots
Scene Numbers: 6 ["The Dark Lord begins to squeeze the officer's neck"]; A6 PT. [C-3PO: "Don't call me a mindless philosopher"]; 4 PT. ["We'll be sent to the spice mines of Kessel . . ."]
Scs. Completed Today: 6
Screen Time Taken To-day: 1m 53s

REPORT NO. 81: Tuesday, July 13
Call: 08.30 **Unit Dismissed:** 17.30
Sets: Stage 9–INT. Rebel Spacefighter, Stage 8–Traveling Matte (2ND UNIT)
Scene Numbers: C6 [stormtroopers stun Leia]; 2 PT. [C-3PO: "Did you hear that? They've shut down the main reactor."]
Scs. Completed Today: 23
Screen Time Taken To-day: 1m 34s

REPORT NO. 82: Wednesday, July 14
Call: 08.30 **Unit Dismissed:** 17.37
Where Working: 1ST Unit: EMI Studios; 2ND Unit: Cardington Air Establishment in Bedfordshire (Location Masassi Hangar)
Scene Numbers: A3 ["The awesome, seven-foot tall Dark Lord of the Sith makes his way into the blinding light of the main passageway. This is Darth Vader, right hand of the Emperor. His face is obscured by his flowing black robes and grotesque breath mask which stands out next to the fascist white armored suits of the Imperial stormtroopers. Everyone instinctively backs away from the imposing warrior and a deathly quiet sweeps through the rebel troops. Several of the rebel troops break and run in a frenzied panic."]
Scs. Completed Today: 2
Screen Time Taken To-day: 1m 55s

REPORT NO. 83: Thursday, July 15
Call: 08.30 **Unit Dismissed:** 18.52
Sets: Stages 8 & 9–3 Units working INT. Rebel Starfighter & Traveling Matte (on Stage 8)
Scene Numbers: 2 PART, A6 PT, 4 PT., etc.
Scs. Completed Today: 31
Screen Time Taken To-day: 2m 51s
Daily Status: 20 days over

REPORT NO. 84: Friday, July 16
Call: 08.30 **Unit Dismissed:** 17.30
Sets: 3 Units working on various Stages
Scene Numbers: 4 PT. [Leia and R2-D2]
Scs. Completed Today: 3
Screen Time Taken To-day: 20s
Scenes Completed To Date: 344
Daily Average Screen Time: 1m30s
Taken To Date 124m02s
Total Exposed Film Footage: 322,704
Total Sound Magnetic Footage: 219 ROLLS
Remarks: Completion of principal photography in U.K. today. Mark Hamill [Luke Skywalker] and Carrie Fisher [Princess Leia] completed their roles today and will travel to Los Angeles tomorrow, Saturday, July 17, 1976. George Lucas will travel to USA on July 17. Anthony Daniels [C-3PO] and Kenny Baker [R2-D2] also completed their roles today.

REPORT NO. 1 POST PRODUCTION: Friday, July 23
Call: 08.30 **Unit Dismissed:** 17.36
Where Working: EMI Studios, Borehamwood
Sets: Stage 9–INT. Corridor, Rebel Spacefighter, Stage 3–INT. TIE Fighter
Scene Numbers: 8 & 2 (extra shots)
Remarks: Today's shooting completes quote of scs. for UK/Tunisian location shooting. Remainder of scs. to be shot in USA per last progress report.

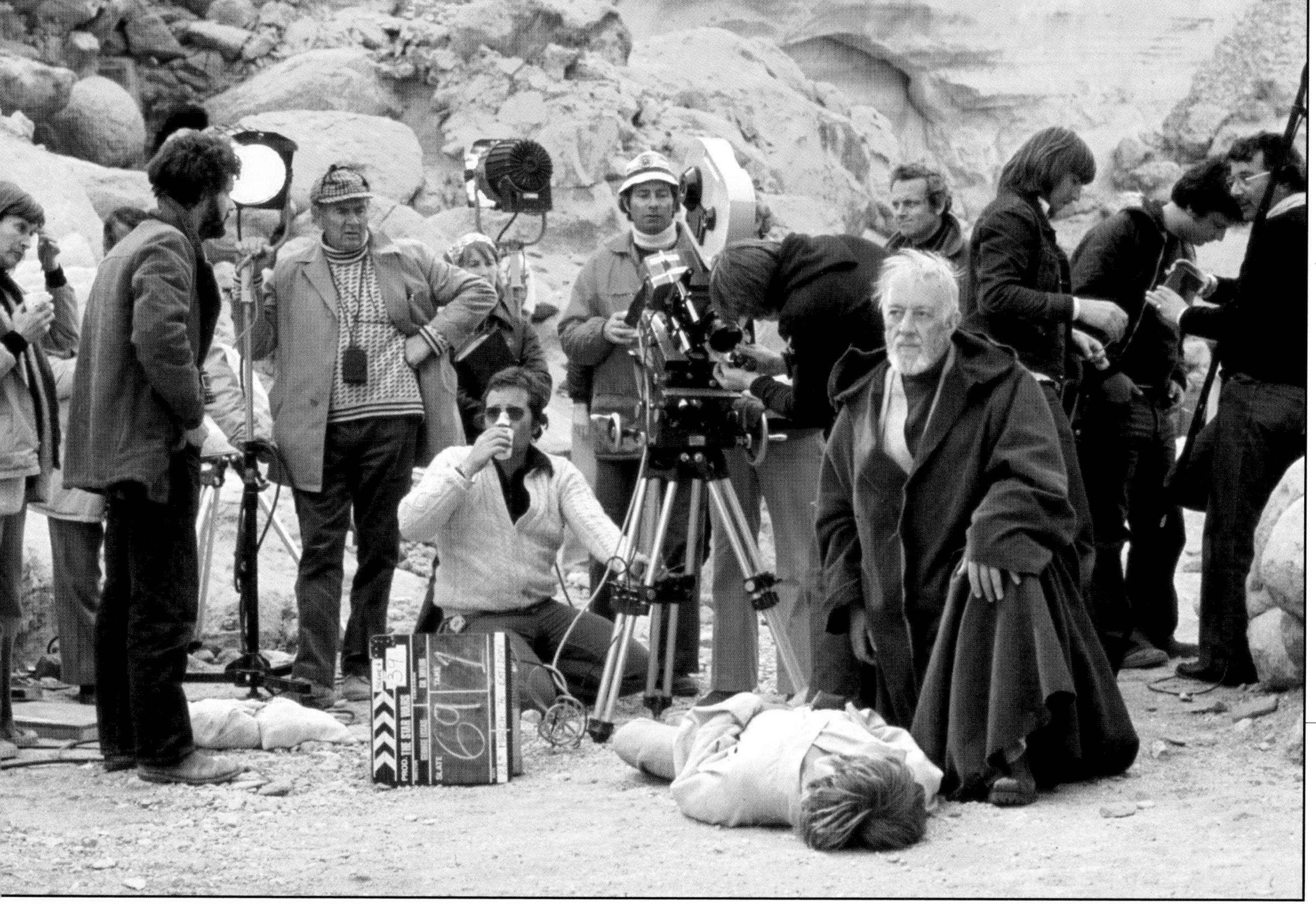

Left - On Sunday March 28, 1976, on shoot day 7, Lucas films scene number 39, in which Obi-Wan Kenobi (Alec Guinness, kneeling) finds an injured Luke Skywalker (Mark Hamill, on ground). Slate #69 indicates that it is Take 1 in Tozeur, Tunisia.

Chapter Four

Cliffhanging

(1977–1989)

Few of Lucas's friends and colleagues believed he could stay "retired" for long. Indeed, in March 1978, Lucas told *Time* magazine that he might one day direct another *Star Wars* movie: "I've always thought that sooner or later . . . I will go back and [direct] another one. But it will be toward the end of the cycle of films, about twenty years from now." Aside from his share of the box-office grosses from his last two films, Lucas was enjoying other, equally unforeseen, benefits. In September 1977, Warner Bros. reissued his first film, the new posters exploiting the director's recent success: "Before George Lucas explored the outer regions of space in *Star Wars*, he explored the inner regions of society in *THX 1138*." And in May 1978, Universal rereleased *American Graffiti*, enabling Lucas to reinstate the three cut sequences and remix the soundtrack in stereo.

In 1978, the future of Lucasfilm seemed clear: the company would nurture and support the work of talented filmmakers, whose efforts would be coordinated from a dedicated headquarters. In addition, three movies vied for Lucas's attention: the sequels to *American Graffiti* and *Star Wars*, and *Raiders of the Lost Ark*.

Lucas devoted much of 1978 to developing *Raiders* and the sequel to *Star Wars*. He needed a producer to oversee development of *Raiders* while he waited for its director, Steven Spielberg, to finish work on his World War II comedy *1941*.

In early 1978 Frank Marshall, at that time best known for being Peter Bogdanovich's associate producer, received a call asking him to meet Lucas at the office Steven Spielberg still occupied on the Universal lot. "I went to this little office and we started talking about the movies I'd made with Peter," says Marshall. "George told me that his vision for Lucasfilm included having three movies in production at all times. *More American Graffiti* and *The Empire Strikes Back* were underway, and he was looking for a third person to produce the next film. He told me a little about the film, and I said I'd love to be considered. I was about to leave and he said, 'You know, why don't you wait a minute? Steven's coming back in a few minutes and you can say hi.'"

Spielberg was accompanied by Lawrence Kasdan, a young screenwriter who had come to his attention in 1977 with a script for a comedy called *Continental Divide* (1981). Marshall was pleased to see Spielberg again—the two had last met five years before. "Then another production person came in," remembers Marshall, "and George started introducing everybody. George said, 'This is Steven, and this is Larry Kasdan, he's the writer of *Raiders of the Lost Ark*.' And then he said, 'This is Frank Marshall, he's the producer of *Raiders of the Lost Ark*,' and we all shook hands. I was stunned. About six months later I was having lunch with Larry Kasdan and he said, 'Remember that first day we met?' I said, 'Yeah.' He said, 'Did you know that you had the job of producer?' I said, 'No.' He said, 'Well neither did I! I didn't know I was the writer.' I think this shows how George goes with his instincts. He's always been great like that."

Following the initial meeting, Lucas chaired three days of intensive story discussions between himself, Spielberg, and Kasdan. The

Previous - *During the shoot of* Indiana Jones and the Last Crusade, *Lucas (in ILM T-shirt) and Spielberg (in "Stunts Indy III" baseball cap).*

Above - *Storyboard drawings for the* Star Wars *sequel* The Empire Strikes Back, *prepared by Ralph McQuarrie.*

Far left - *Concept illustration by McQuarrie.*

Left - *On the ice cave set, screenwriter Lawrence Kasdan, Lucas, and Mark Hamill.*

the Empire Strikes back.
story treatment by George Lucas.
11/28/77

Open on the bleak white planet of Hoth. Luke is riding across the windswept ice slopes on a large snow lizard (taun taun) He reins up on the shaggy two-legged creature when he spots something on the horizon; a strange ice formation, or meteorite hit. Luke talks into his walkie-talkie which is on his helmet. He lifts his snow goggles as he says: "Han, ol buddy everything's OK here, but I saw a glint on the next ridge, and I want to check it out." Over the com link we hear Han say "OK but don't take too long kid, there's a storm coming up." Luke says a few kind words to his lizard, sinks his spurs in, and the beast leaps forward. He rides over the ridge when suddenly, out of nowhere, a giant snow creature jumps up in front of him, causing the lizard to rear back and throw Luke to the icy ground. The monster grabs the taun taun by its neck, killing the poor snow lizard, then bashes Luke in the face. Unconscious, covered with blood, the young warrior from Tatooine is dragged across the snow by the horrible snow monster.

conversations were recorded, and Kasdan used the resulting 100-page transcript as the basis for his first draft of *Raiders.*

Lucas had already hired a writer for *The Empire Strikes Back.* In the fall of 1977, he had approached sixty-one-year-old Leigh Brackett, cowriter of the Howard Hawks classics *The Big Sleep* (1946) and *Rio Bravo* (1959). Given Lucas's penchant for 1940s-style dialogue in the *Star Wars* films, Brackett was a fine choice.

Brackett began work on the screenplay, based on a transcript of her story conferences with Lucas and his treatment, with the knowledge that she was suffering from cancer. She nevertheless completed her first draft in late February 1978. The script was titled "Star Wars Sequel, from The Adventures of Luke Skywalker." Lucas had no opportunity to discuss the draft with the ailing writer, who died a few weeks later. Saddened and left with no choice except to continue himself, Lucas wrote the second draft.

Lucas had prepared handwritten notes on a proposed third draft by the time Kasdan finished work on the first draft of *Raiders,* which he hand-delivered to Lucas at Parkway. Later that day, Lucas took Kasdan out for lunch and asked him to take *Empire* to a third draft. Kasdan was astonished that Lucas should make such an offer without even having read the *Raiders* script. Lucas told him he would read the *Raiders* script that night and withdraw the offer if he did not like it. The following day Kasdan received a call—and was formally hired.

Darth Vader ruthlessly pursues the Rebels to their outpost on Hoth. Rebel troops are no match for Imperial machinery, and they are forced to evacuate. The spirit of Ben Kenobi tells the injured Luke Skywalker to go to the Dagobah System, while Han, Leia, Chewbacca, and C-3PO head for the sanctuary of Cloud City on Bespin.

On Dagobah, Luke and R2-D2 encounter an eccentric hermit called Yoda, who begins to train Luke as a Jedi Knight. On Cloud City, Han is betrayed by his former friend Lando Calrissian. Han and his friends are captured by Darth Vader, who uses them as bait to trap Luke.

Sensing that something is wrong, Luke interrupts his training to go to Cloud City. Vader freezes Han in carbonite and hands the trophy to bounty hunter Boba Fett, who is working for Jabba the Hutt. When Luke arrives, he duels with the waiting Vader, who attempts to lure him to the dark side of the Force. When these attempts fail, Vader reveals the awful truth that he is Luke's father . . .

With Kasdan writing *Empire,* Lucas now had more time to concentrate on the financial aspect of his growing business—that is, Lucas intended to self-finance *Empire.* By the

Above - The first page of Lucas's handwritten story treatment for The Empire Strikes Back, *dated November 28, 1977.*

Right *- An unused environment concept by McQuarrie, in which Han Solo is held captive while Lando Calrissian (in white cape), Boba Fett (in poncho), and Darth Vader discuss his fate.*

Far right *- A flying creature concept that did not make it into* Empire, *but which would be revamped for a subsequent* Star Wars *film.*

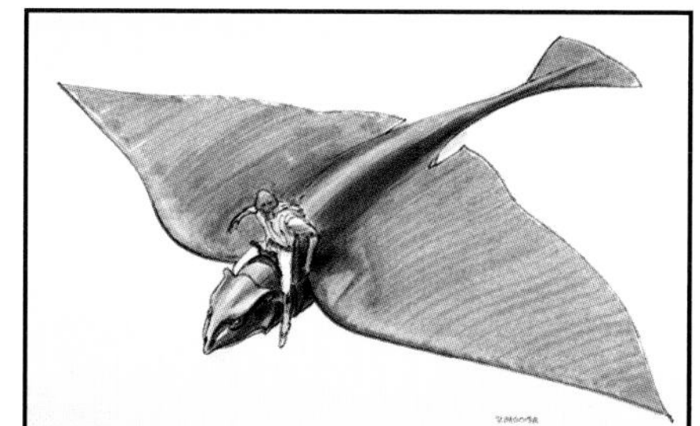

Choosing the right director was clearly crucial. Lucas's search came to an end with fifty-six-year-old Irvin Kershner, who had studied anthropology and history at USC—and who had also studied under Slavko Vorkapich, the montagist whose work Lucas admired. Kershner came to prominence as a documentary filmmaker, writing, directing, and shooting the pioneering television documentary series *Confidential File.* His career was subsequently distinguished by highly regarded, if infrequent, films, which included *The Luck of Ginger Coffey* (1964), *The Flim-Flam Man* (1967), and *The Return of a Man Called Horse* (1976). Kershner first connected with Lucas in the 1960s when, as a visiting lecturer to USC, he had been greatly impressed by *6.18.67* and *THX 1138 4EB.* He was one of the first to recognize Lucas's emerging talent, later discovering that they shared an admiration for the films of Kurosawa.

end of 1978, *Star Wars* had earned approximately $400 million worldwide, but Lucas's share was a relatively small fraction of that overall amount. After setting aside a sum as a deposit on land he wished to purchase for the Lucasfilm headquarters, he used what remained as collateral against which to borrow the budget for *Empire*, which was initially estimated at $15 million. By the end of the year, it stood at a more realistic $18.5 million.

The loan represented the greatest risk of Lucas's career. "I'm faced with a situation where everything I own, everything I ever earned, is wrapped up in this picture," he revealed in 1979. "If it isn't a success, not only could I lose everything but I could also end up being millions of dollars in debt, which would be very difficult to get out from under. It would probably take me the rest of my life just to get back even again. That worries me. Everybody says, 'Oh, don't worry, the film will be a huge success,' and I'm sure it will be. But if it is just one of those mildly successful film sequels, I'd lose everything. It has to be the biggest grossing sequel of all time for me to break even."

Fox re-released *Star Wars* in July 1978, this time with the subtitle Episode IV: *A New Hope* atop the opening crawl. While the preparations for Episode V continued, Lucas searched for a suitable piece of land on which to build his new headquarters. "I'm trying to develop a place that is designed to stimulate activity, especially among writers," he told *Time* magazine. Kershner had seen the designs for the new facility pinned to the wall when Lucas interviewed him. Lucas explained that not only was there a huge amount of money at stake, but the future of the dream envisioned in those sketches was also dependent on *Empire's* success.

In summer 1978, Lucas viewed a piece of land in Nicasio's Lucas Valley, between Petaluma to the north and San Rafael to the south. (The valley and adjoining road were named for John Lucas,

Above *- Luke crash-lands on the surface of Hoth, pursued by an Imperial AT-AT vehicle in this McQuarrie gouache painting.*

Far left *- A patch for* Empire.

Left *-* Empire *director Irvin Kershner talks with Harrison Ford, who reprised his role as Han Solo.*

who, in the 1880s, inherited much of the surrounding valley from his uncle, an early settler of Marin County.) "I walked into the valley and I just said, 'Okay, this is it. I'm buying it,'" remembers Lucas. Lucas bought Bulltail Ranch in September 1978, although he would have to wait until early 1980 before the County Planning Commission would approve the plans and construction work could begin. It would take much more time to transform the ultimately 2,500-acre creative retreat into what he would name Skywalker Ranch.

Kershner relocated to London in the same month and began casting actors to play the new characters in *Empire.* Notable among these were Billy Dee Williams, as Han Solo's untrustworthy friend, Lando Calrissian. Another new character was Yoda, the diminutive Jedi Master. Although there would be attempts to perform some of Yoda's scenes using a short actor wearing a mask designed by Stuart Freeborn, he was ultimately realized by a combination of complex puppetry, "animatronic" engineering, and the vocal skills of Frank Oz, best known at that time for the numerous voices he contributed to Jim Henson's television programs *Sesame Street* and *The Muppet Show.* "That was a real leap, because if that puppet had not worked, the whole film would have been down the tubes," Lucas would recall.

Mark Hamill, Carrie Fisher, and Harrison Ford reprised their roles, as did Anthony Daniels and Kenny Baker as the droids, Peter Mayhew as Chewbacca, and David Prowse as the physical embodiment of Darth Vader.

Principal photography on *Empire* got underway with location shooting for the exteriors of Hoth in Finse, Norway, on March 5, 1979. Inhospitable weather conditions initially made filming almost impossible—the temperature was twenty-six degrees below zero and blizzards made access to and from the two base camps treacherous. Lucas was at Elstree for

Above - *Puppeteer Frank Oz (who can be seen in the mirror) demonstrates his portrayal of Jedi Master Yoda for Lucas and Kershner at Elstree Studios.*

Right - *A concept illustration of Yoda by visual effects art director Joe Johnston.*

Far right - *In March 1979, location filming in Norway was hampered by extreme cold and blizzards.*

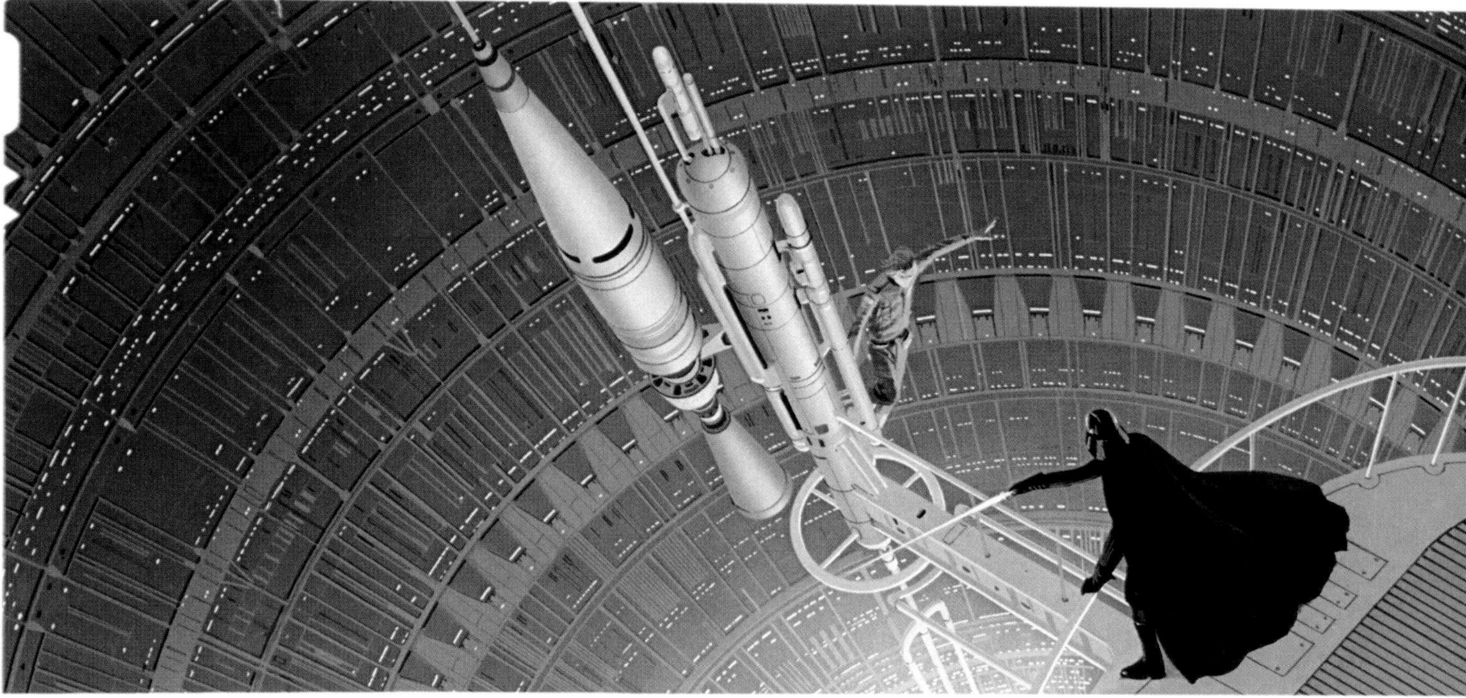

the beginning of studio shooting on March 13, and his concerns were already mounting over the budget and the schedule. The weather conditions at Finse and a recent fire on Elstree's Stage 3 had already caused delays, which increased the budget from $18.5 million to $22 million.

By July, the budget stood at $25 million, and Lucas calculated that he would need another $3 million to complete the picture. "I was just hoping the bank would allow me to finish without going back to Twentieth Century Fox and giving away all my rights, because that's ultimately what my choice was: to simply let them own it and lose my independence. But I wanted my independence so badly, we managed to switch banks and get a new loan. If I had to pay Fox a few extra points in order to get them to guarantee a loan with the bank, I could do that. And I think Fox was just as concerned as we were that the movie get finished."

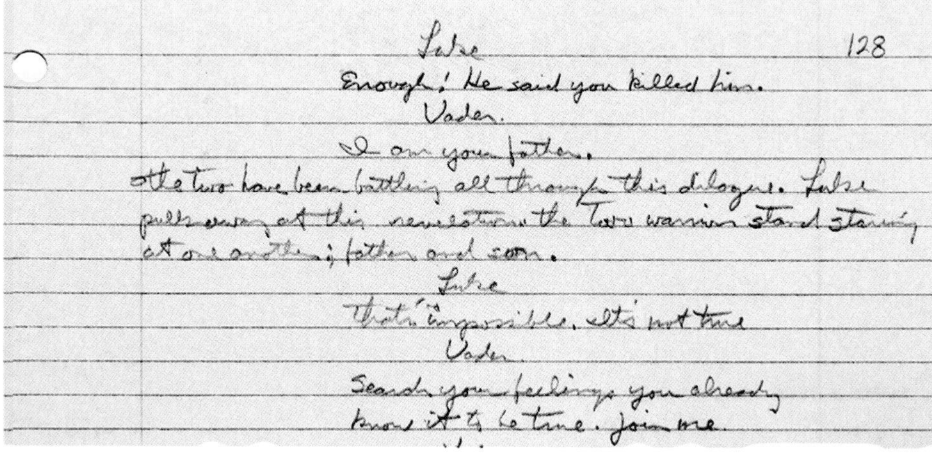

Luke 128
Enough! He said you killed him.
Vader.
I am your father.
The two have been battling all through this dialogue. Luke pulls away at this revelation. The two warriors stand staring at one another; father and son.
Luke
That's impossible. It's not true
Vader
Search your feelings. you already know it to be true. join me.

For the scene in which Vader reveals his paternity to Luke, secrecy was still paramount. "At the time, I knew that Mark [Hamill] had a father and it was Darth Vader, but this was not in the script," Kershner would recall. "There was a false page inserted. . . . It was a total secret." In order to get the reactions he needed on set, Kershner did tell the truth to Hamill the day of the scene. But, according to Hamill, what he was hearing from Vader that day were the words, "You don't know the truth: Obi-Wan killed your father." Vader's real dialogue would be recorded in postproduction under conditions easier to control.

Toward the end of August, as filming at Elstree neared completion, Sir Alec Guinness filmed his scenes against a velvet backing in just one day, on September 5. Principal photography finally wrapped a week later.

As editing and postproduction of *Empire* commenced, Lucas sought a distribution deal for a proposed trilogy of adventures starring whip-cracking archaeologist Indiana Jones.

Opposite - *Kershner braves the elements in Finse, Norway.*

Above left - *Lucas's handwritten page 128 contains Darth Vader's words to Luke: "I am your father."*

Above right - *Page 128's conceptual visualization by Ralph McQuarrie.*

Right - *Father and son.*

Far right - *A logo treatment.*

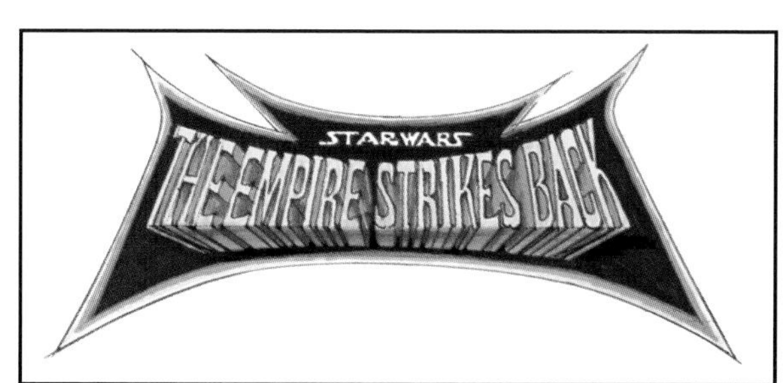

The prospect of a collaboration between the directors of *Jaws* and *Star Wars* would normally have proved irresistible to any enterprising production executive, but almost every studio balked at Lucas's terms, which, in 1978, were perceived as radical: he proposed a partnership whereby the studio would simply distribute the finished product and the filmmakers would enjoy a more equitable share of the box-office receipts. The only studio that stepped up to the plate was Paramount, which at that time was under the chairmanship of Michael Eisner. A budget of $20 million was agreed upon and a production office was established at Elstree Studios. Associate producer Robert Watts and production designer Norman Reynolds resumed their familiar responsibilities from *The Empire Strikes Back*, while Lucas balanced the budget with his coproducers Frank Marshall and Howard Kazanjian. The U.S. production office for *Raiders* was established in a building generally referred to as the Egg Company, a former egg warehouse on Lankershim Boulevard, across the street from Universal Studios.

Above *- Concept art from* Raiders of the Lost Ark *by artist Jim Steranko.*

Far left *- An early logo concept.*

Left *- A Steranko production painting depicting the truck chase.*

MORE AMERICAN GRAFFITI

* *

Lucas asked Howard Kazanjian, his old friend from USC, to produce the sequel to *American Graffiti.* He turned to Bill L. Norton, best known for his acclaimed drama *Cisco Pike* (1972), to write the screenplay and eventually direct the film.

More American Graffiti tells four stories, each set on New Year's Eve of a different year. New Year's Eve 1964 follows John Milner's efforts to become a professional drag racer; New Year's Eve 1965 depicts Terry "The Toad" Fields's experiences as a soldier in Vietnam; New Year's Eve 1966 sees Debbie Dunham hit the road with rock group Electric Haze; and on New Year's Eve 1967 Steve and Laurie deal with marriage difficulties and student protests.

Curt's place in the 1967 sequences is taken by Andy, his brother, played by Will Seltzer. Harrison Ford makes a brief uncredited appearance as Bob Falfa (who has become a traffic cop), and all the other principal cast members from the first film reprised their roles.

Each story strand in *More American Graffiti* was filmed using a different film format. The 1964 sequences were shot in a 2.35:1 aspect ratio to reproduce the CinemaScope feel. Lucas suggested shooting the Vietnam sequences on 16mm film, and personally photographed a lot of the action on location near Stockton, California. (In the Vietnam sequences, we see glimpses of what the Lucas/Milius *Apocalypse Now* might have looked like.) He also suggested shooting the 1966 story in a scope aspect ratio with numerous split-screen sequences. The 1967 segment was shot in 1:85 widescreen. "It was a crazy idea," says director of photography Caleb Deschanel, "but we had a great deal of fun. It was really a continuation of the atmosphere at USC, where there had been a lot of experimentation."

The editing of *More American Graffiti* followed the strict ABCD pattern that Lucas had originally tried on the first film. A 1964 sequence is always followed by an installment of the 1965 story, then a sequence of the 1966 story, and finally a piece of the 1967 story, before the cycle begins again. What unites the characters is their disillusionment. Terry is disillusioned with his role in Vietnam, Debbie with the free-love scene, and Laurie with her marriage. In a brief but poignant scene, John Milner finds his advances toward a beautiful European girl rejected. She storms out of his trailer, leaving him alone to contemplate his behavior. He casts a baleful eye at the radio and switches it off—even the Wolfman is not immune to the cold realities of 1964.

Top right - In *More American Graffiti*, Steve Bolander (Ron Howard) and Laurie Bolander (Cindy Williams) witness the subjugation of an anti-war protest on New Year's Eve, 1967; **Bottom left** - Lucas films hand-held aerial shots over forests near Stockton, California, for the Vietnam sequences; **Bottom right** - The film's logo treatment recalls certain posters for rock concerts of the 1960s.

Following five revisions, Kasdan's shooting script was ready by April. "The script was a real page-turner," says Marshall. "It was fantastic—all the things Steven and George had talked about."

The year is 1936, and the power of Adolf Hitler's Third Reich is growing. The U.S. government learns that Hitler has embarked on a quest for the fabled Ark of the Covenant, believing that possession of the holy relic will afford him invincibility. Dr. Indiana Jones, a professor of archaeology with an adventurous streak, is dispatched to find the Ark before the Germans do.

In Nepal, Indy is reunited with ex-girlfriend Marion Ravenwood. Marion's late father had knowledge crucial to Indy's quest, so she reluctantly accompanies him on his quest. Marion is abducted in Cairo, where Jones discovers that rival French archaeologist Belloq is helping the Nazis locate the Ark. Indy rescues Marion from the lecherous clutches of Belloq, but the Nazis escape with the Ark. Indy and Marion begin a desperate attempt to retrieve the relic, but just when it seems they have failed, it transpires that the Ark has the power to discriminate between those who seek to harness its power . . .

Raiders had relatively few special-effects demands in comparison to the *Star Wars* films, but one sequence of storyboards illustrated a fight beneath an experimental Luftwaffe "flying wing" aircraft. "George flew down from San Francisco one day to see how everything was going," Kazanjian remembers. "I told him, 'There's one thing I haven't been able to figure out, and that's the flying wing. It's going to cost a million dollars and we have $750,000 to spend on it.' George didn't say another word, but walked with me to the conference room where Steven was waiting. In the conference room there were a bunch of models, including a model of the flying wing, which had two engines on each side. George picked it up and then broke the end off each wing, leaving one engine on each side. He said, 'Looks good this way. How much can we save if we do this?' and I said, 'Probably a quarter of a million dollars.' And he said, 'I like this. Do it this way.' Everybody was shocked, but that was George's way of coming up with an answer."

T*he Empire Strikes Back* opened on May 21, 1980, and any fears that Lucas may have had about recouping his unexpectedly large budget soon evaporated as the public, and critics, responded with enthusiasm to the sequel.

Audiences immediately identified a brooding, introspective feel to the adventure, enhanced by the subtle and often subdued lighting

Above - Scenes from Indiana "Smith"'s first adventure depicted in concept illustrations by Jim Steranko. On the "flying-wing" plane in the background, there are more engines than on the one ultimately built for the film (four as opposed to two); budget considerations reduced their number.

Far left *- A storyboard panel showing Indy at the moment the ark is excavated. The text underneath reads, "Cut to extreme up angle of Indy with fierce storm clouds gathering behind him . . . Indy tells workers to 'Open it!!'"*

Left *- A Steranko production painting of Indy among the snakes.*

Opposite *- The Rebels crumble under the firepower of an Imperial onslaught in* The Empire Strikes Back.

of cinematographer Peter Suschitzky. Kershner had also been mindful not to stray too far from the kinetic pace Lucas had established on *Star Wars.* "I was trying to keep the convention that George Lucas set up where you stay with no scene very long, where you have a constant shifting of scenes, and where the editorial rhythm is in a way more important than the camera moves or the actors saying their lines. I tried to push everything to where it was almost too fast—and then back it off."

Empire would present no challenge to *Star Wars'* box-office supremacy but would briefly reign as the most commercially successful sequel ever made. Lucas plowed much of the money into the construction of Skywalker Ranch. He also shared profits with every one of his employees, handing out more than $5 million in bonuses. The profits from *Empire* would ultimately secure Lucas's independence from Hollywood—but, unexpectedly, the filmmaker found himself temporarily mired in Hollywood politics. To preserve the dramatic opening sequences of his films, Lucas wanted the screen credits to come at the end of the movies. And for the first *Star Wars,* the Writers Guild and Directors Guild had allowed it. But when Lucas did the same for the sequel, they fined him more than $250,000 and even attempted to pull *Empire* from theaters. The DGA also went after Kershner. To protect his director, Lucas paid all of Kershner's fines to the guild, but the situation left him feeling frustrated and persecuted. "Lucas was so upset that he dropped out of the Directors Guild, the Writers Guild, and the Motion Picture Association," remembers Kazanjian.

As the start of principal photography on *Raiders* loomed, Lucas and Spielberg had yet to find anyone to play Indiana Jones. Some of the screen tests were recorded in the courtyard of the Egg Company, the most successful of which was that of Tom Selleck. Lucas and Spielberg offered Selleck the role, but his participation was blocked by CBS. The network, encouraged by what it saw as Selleck's imminent promotion to A-list status, invoked a clause in Selleck's contract that committed him to the television series *Magnum P.I.*

"*The Empire Strikes Back* was opening and Steven, Frank, George, and I all went together," says Kathleen Kennedy, who was Spielberg's executive assistant on *Raiders.* "We came out of the movie, looked at each other, and said, 'Harrison *is* Indiana Jones.' It was an epiphany. We moved very quickly and the rest is history." Ford signed a contract for three *Indiana Jones* films and negotiated terms for his appearance in the forthcoming *Revenge of the Jedi* at the same time (he had originally been contracted for only the first two *Star Wars* films).

The role of Marion went to Karen Allen. A strong supporting cast of British character actors included Paul Freeman as Belloq; Ronald Lacey as Toht, the sadistic Nazi; John Rhys-Davies as Sallah, Indy's Egyptian friend; Denholm Elliott as Dr. Marcus Brody, Indy's cautious colleague; and Alfred Molina as Satipo, his rather less trustworthy accomplice.

Filming began on June 23, 1980, at a former German submarine pen at La Rochelle in France. Anxious not to repeat the experience of *Empire,* Lucas told Spielberg that *Raiders* should be shot in the "quick and dirty" style of the Saturday matinee serials, and the two agreed on an extremely tight schedule. Spielberg, who was still smarting from the critical and commercial failure of *1941,* had his own demons to exorcise. While extremely successful, both *Jaws* and *Close Encounters* had gone over schedule and over budget. "*Raiders* was a film to clean out

Above - Romance grows between Princess Leia (Carrie Fisher) and Han Solo (Harrison Ford) in a city above the clouds.

Far left - Indiana Jones (Harrison Ford) takes on a bad guy while rescuing Marion Ravenwood (Karen Allen).

Left - Director Steven Spielberg consoles Karen Allen during the particularly arduous scenes that called for hundreds of snakes in Raiders of the Lost Ark.

Opposite - Indiana Jones (Harrison Ford) practices his reckless approach to archaeology. The object about to be seized is actually a fertility statue of a woman kneeling while giving birth.

my system, blow the saliva out of my mouthpiece," he later said.

The main unit went from France to Elstree to conduct the studio filming, before heading to some familiar locations in Tunisia, which Norman Reynolds had ingeniously suggested could double for Cairo. Tunisia thus became the location for the Tanis archaeological digs, an incredible fight-on-a-speeding-truck sequence, and the flying-wing punch-up. "Steven really wanted to do this fast," says Marshall. "On the day of the flying-wing sequence I think we did forty-seven setups in 130-degree heat. Day after day we were pushing, but it was fun. Steven did a lot of storyboards and it was all very well planned, but it was on the edge—and I think that shows."

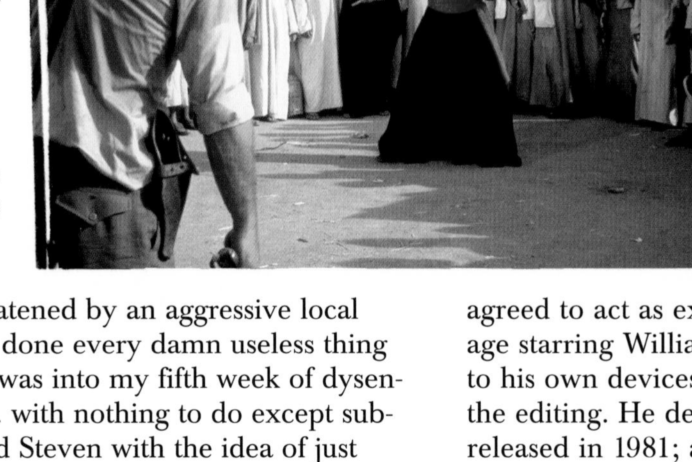

Many of the cast and crew succumbed to stomach upsets in Tunisia, although Spielberg, who subsisted exclusively on a diet of tinned food he had brought from England, remained immune. Illness and the stifling heat caused tempers to fray, and Ford was out of patience the day he was supposed to shoot a scene in which he is threatened by an aggressive local brandishing a scimitar. "I'd already done every damn useless thing in the world," said Ford in 1981. "I was into my fifth week of dysentery and I was riding in at 5:30 A.M. with nothing to do except submit to wild imaginings. So I stormed Steven with the idea of just dismissing this maniac. I'd never unholstered my gun in the whole movie, so I said, 'Let's just shoot [him].' And we did. That's getting character in action."

For the final part of the filming, the main unit went to Kauai, Hawaii, to shoot the exteriors for the film's opening sequence. By the time principal photography wrapped in September, Spielberg had shaved off twelve days from the schedule and had still managed to film more scenes than had been included in the script. "We were averaging, outside, forty setups a day and inside, under difficult lighting conditions, fifteen shots a day," said Spielberg after filming was complete. "That's the fastest I've ever shot, next to my experience in television. I never shot a picture this quickly without having to compromise quality." Some of those shots were the work of Lucas, who helped his friend by filming certain second-unit scenes. "I think he was doing it just to be nice to me," he jokes.

Following postproduction work at ILM, *Raiders of the Lost Ark* opened on June 12, 1981, and became the highest-grossing film of the year, ultimately earning more than $242 million from its American box office alone.

In 1980, Kasdan had sold a script called *Body Heat* to Alan Ladd Jr., who by this time was running his own company, producing films for Warner Bros. Ladd agreed to back Kasdan's directorial debut on the condition that he find a more established director to oversee him. Lucas agreed to act as executive producer on *Body Heat*, a film noir homage starring William Hurt and Kathleen Turner. Lucas left Kasdan to his own devices on the film, although he offered advice during the editing. He declined to take a credit when *Body Heat* was released in 1981; although he had helped bring the film to the screen, he had no wish to inadvertently detract from what was primarily Kasdan's achievement.

The next outside project Lucas became involved with was *Twice Upon a Time*, an animated feature produced and directed by John Korty and Charles Swenson. In 1981, Korty showed Lucas a ten-minute showreel for a project featuring animated cut-outs lit from beneath to lend them a glowing quality. Korty called the process "Lumage" animation (an abbreviation for "Luminous

Above *- Indiana Jones's (Harrison Ford) encounter with an Arab swordsman (Terry Richards) was abridged with amusing effect.*

Far left *- The scheming Matty Walker (Kathleen Turner) in Lawrence Kasdan's steamy thriller* Body Heat *(1981), for which Lucas was the (uncredited) executive producer.*

Middle and left *- Images from John Korty's pioneering "Lumage" feature* Twice Upon a Time *(1983), for which Lucas was also executive producer.*

image"), and Lucas was sufficiently intrigued to act as executive producer, brokering a finance and distribution deal with the Ladd Company. After three years of painstaking production, *Twice Upon a Time* received only a limited release. "Our mistake, I suppose, was to try to make a film that would appeal to everybody, all ages," says Korty. "There was a lot of slapstick in it, but it was much too sophisticated for the four- and five-year-olds. . . . George gave us a lot of great feedback, mainly in the postproduction stages, but nobody knew quite how to sell it."

For Lucas, 1981 was also distinguished by an important personal milestone. He adopted a baby girl whom he named Amanda. His daughter's arrival would soon lead Lucas to reassess his priorities.

Above - *Lucas, Spielberg, and assorted extras on location in Kauai for* Raiders of the Lost Ark.

Right - *The climactic scene in which the Ark of the Covenant is opened, with visual effects realized by ILM.*

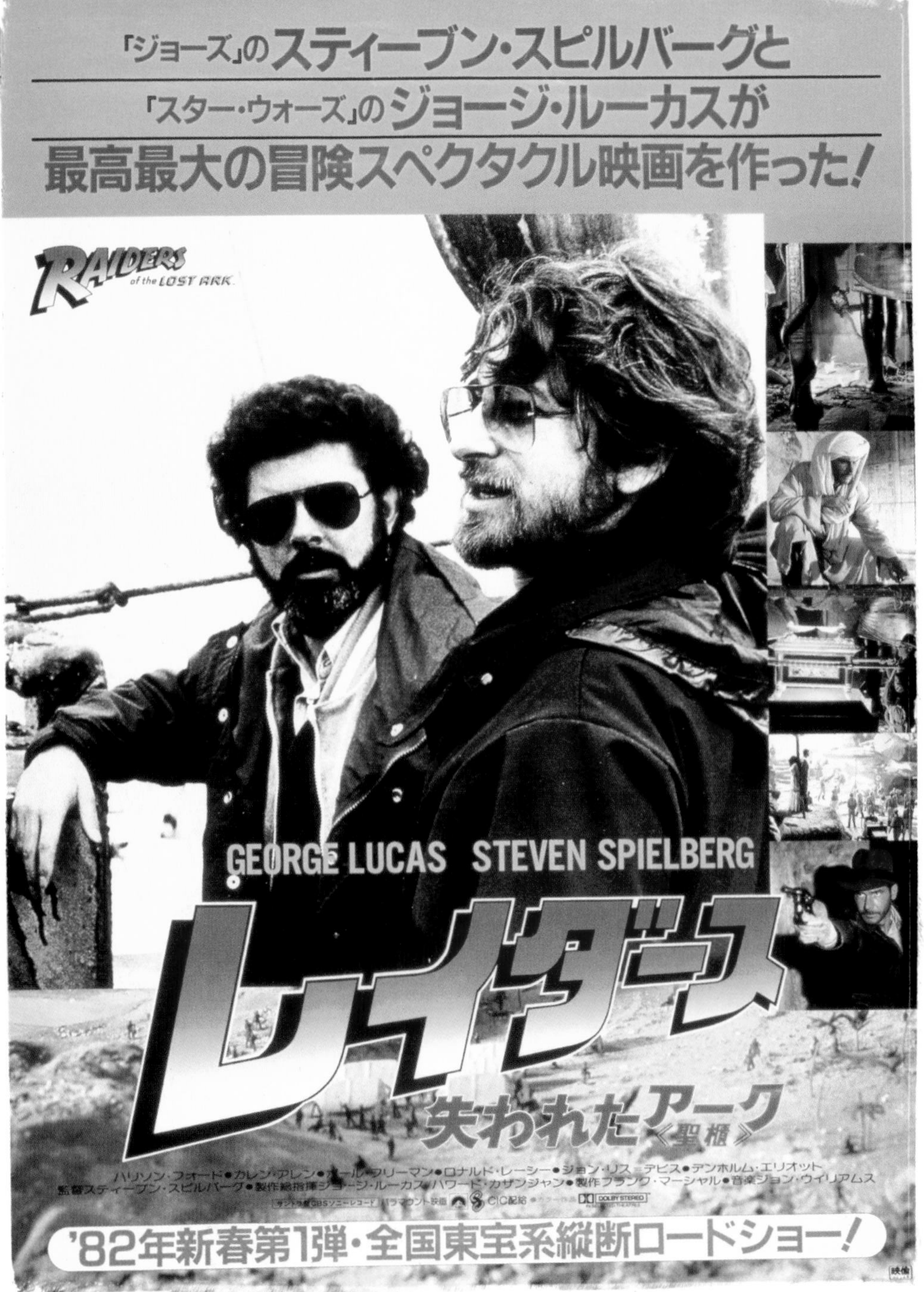

Four posters for the Indiana Jones *films:* ***Above, from left*** *- An Asian* Raiders of the Lost Ark *poster that features its famous collaborators as its main selling-point, and an American poster that hypes their films without mentioning them by name. Drew Struzan's striking artwork for* Temple of Doom *was used extensively throughout many international campaigns, but this imagery would see only limited use in the U.S., appearing on an exclusive one-sheet available to Star Wars Fan Club members in 1984. Since then, it has been widely used in many of the video release campaigns. On the far right is a* Temple of Doom *enticement.*

Below right - A Raiders poster for Poland, with artwork by Jakob Erol (who previously illustrated the Polish posters for Star Wars and The Empire Strikes Back), and a Temple of Doom poster for Yugoslavia, both featuring skulls.

KAGEMUSHA

* *

During the 1980s, Lucas would continue to use his status and influence to help his friends, old and new. "I met Coppola and Lucas in America," said Akira Kurosawa in 1980. "They approached me, and said that they'd learned a lot from my films. Lucas, in particular, said that he would like to assist me in any way that he could." Lucas used his influence to help secure international distribution for Kurosawa's 1980 film, *Kagemusha*, or *The Shadow Warrior*. Lucas shared the executive producer credit on the international version of the film with Francis Ford Coppola.

Kagemusha **was Kurosawa's first Japanese production in ten years and represented something of a comeback in a country whose critics resented what they perceived to be his Western influences. The film won the Palme d'Or at the Cannes film festival, which enabled Kurosawa to find a French producer for his next film, *Ran* (1985). When Lucas introduced Spielberg to the Japanese director, Kurosawa found in Spielberg another benefactor, who helped him make the elegiac *Yume* (*Akira Kurosawa's Dreams*, 1990), whose visual effects were created at ILM.**

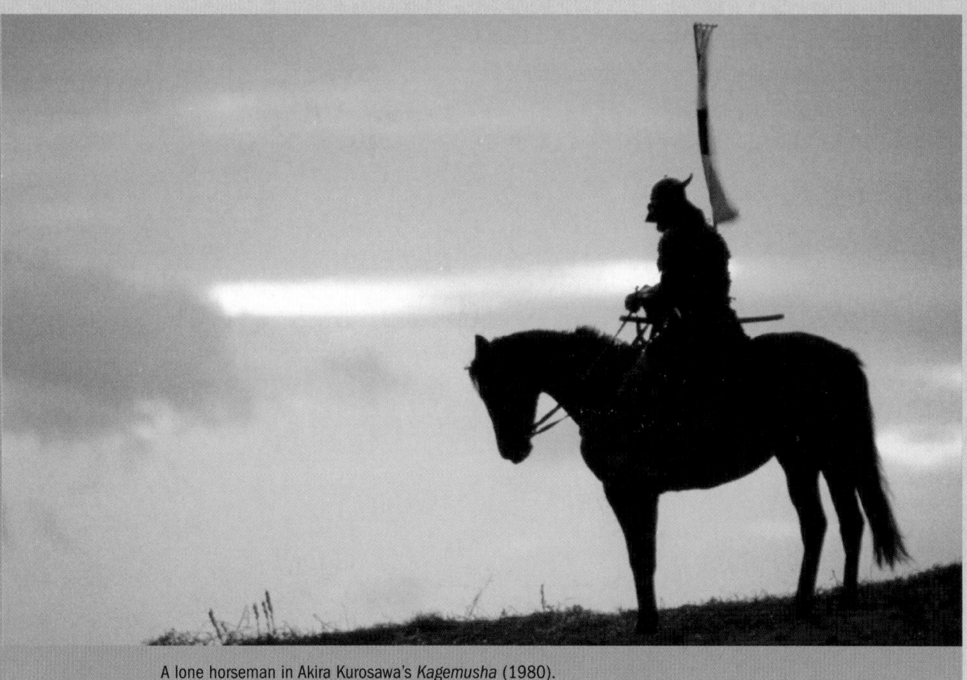

A lone horseman in Akira Kurosawa's *Kagemusha* (1980).

In the meantime, a conclusion was needed for the *Star Wars* trilogy. Work on Episode VI began as soon as filming on *Raiders* was complete. Welsh-born Richard Marquand first discovered that he was a contender for the director's job in October. The forty-two-year-old Marquand may have seemed an unlikely choice—he had directed the BBC documentary *The Search for the Nile* and the little-seen horror film *The Legacy* (1978). But his TV movie *Birth of the Beatles* (1979) had brought him wider acclaim, and he was currently working on the World War II espionage thriller *Eye of the Needle* (1981). Lucas asked to see the rough cut and was sufficiently impressed to request a meeting with Marquand at England's Twickenham Studios in early 1981. Lucas hired Marquand, who brought along two key members of his usual British crew: cinematographer Alan Hume and editor Sean Barton.

The obvious choice to write the final draft of *Revenge of the Jedi* was Kasdan, who joined Lucas, Kazanjian, and Marquand for a five-day story conference in July. Kazanjian remembers what followed: "Larry Kasdan went back to Hollywood and wrote his draft of the screenplay based on a first-draft screenplay George had written. Months later, we met again and discussed the screenplay."

Above - The three Star Wars *directors united on the set of* Return of the Jedi *at Elstree Studios: Irvin Kershner, Lucas, and Richard Marquand.*

Left - Early promotional art featuring the title Revenge of the Jedi.

Han Solo's body encased in carbonite has been delivered to the palace of crime lord Jabba the Hutt on Tatooine. C-3PO and R2-D2, and then Leia and Chewbacca, are all taken prisoner by Jabba, and it falls to Luke to rescue them. His Jedi training is almost complete; Luke is a more sober figure and a formidable warrior.

Following the demise of Jabba and Boba Fett on Tatooine, Luke and R2-D2 return to Dagobah, where Yoda is dying. Before joining the Force, he hints that Luke may not be the last hope for the Jedi. Luke intuits that the other Skywalker Yoda referred to is his sister . . . Leia.

Luke catches up with his friends, and the other Rebels, as they attempt to destroy a shield generator protecting a new, partially built Death Star. The shield generator is located on the Forest Moon orbiting the planet Endor. The Rebels' efforts against Imperial stormtroopers are eventually aided by the moon's indigenous life form: small furry creatures called Ewoks.

To save his friends, Luke surrenders to the Imperial forces. Luke's father, Darth Vader, escorts him to the Death Star to confront his master, the Emperor. Luke refuses to kill his father, foiling the Emperor's plan. Vader then refuses to turn on his son, instead killing the Emperor. Luke's father dies, not as Darth Vader but as the redeemed Anakin Skywalker.

Aboard the Millennium Falcon, *Lando Calrissian destroys the Death Star. On the Forest Moon there is a party to celebrate the demise of the Empire. Amid the celebrations, the spirits of Obi-Wan Kenobi, Yoda, and Anakin Skywalker appear before Luke.*

The principal cast members of *The Empire Strikes Back* all reprised their roles. "We had the same crew for all three films, for the most part, so it was a family," Carrie Fisher recalls. The most notable newcomer in the cast was thirty-four-year-old Ian McDiarmid, who would endure many hours of makeup to become the wizened Emperor. Meanwhile, Harrison Ford was lobbying Lucas to kill off Han Solo in the heroic attack on the new Death Star. "He would have best served the situation by giving it the weight of sacrifice, but that was the one thing I was unable to

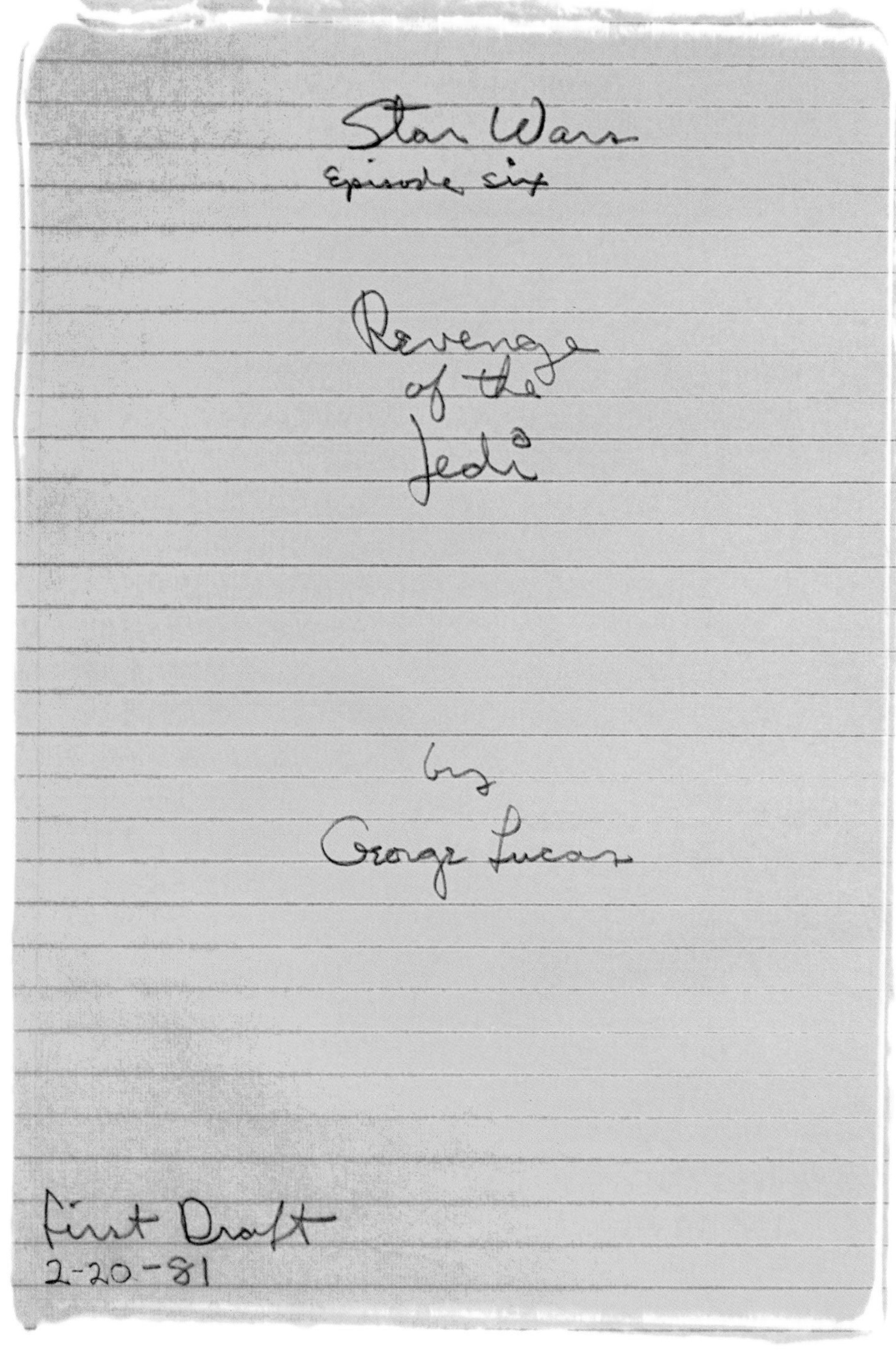

Star Wars
Episode six

Revenge
of the
Jedi

by
George Lucas

First Draft
2-20-81

Above - The first page of Lucas's handwritten first draft, dated February 20, 1981.

Right - Lucas with Coppola and Kurosawa, whose films so inspired Lucas when he was a student at USC—and long afterward.

Far right - Concept illustration by Ralph McQuarrie showing a scene from Return of the Jedi*'s speeder bike chase on the Forest Moon of Endor.*

convince George of," said Ford prior to the film's release.

Norman Reynolds's sets occupied all nine stages at Elstree Studios when shooting began on January 11, 1982. The first scene to be shot at Elstree—a sandstorm that engulfs the heroes before they depart Tatooine—was ironically the only major scene to be dropped during editing. Marquand encountered none of the serious scheduling problems that had dogged *Empire*, and Lucas maintained a more conspicuous presence at the studio. "It is rather like trying to direct *King Lear*—with Shakespeare in the next room!" joked Marquand.

A veil of secrecy shrouded the entire shoot, with certain actors given intentionally misleading dialogue. Even the title of the film—*Revenge of the Jedi*—was replaced with *Blue Harvest*. The title switch had an added benefit, as coproducer Jim Bloom explains: "Any time you would go in and try and negotiate for production facilities [for a *Star Wars* film], people would say, 'Oh, well, that will cost $2,' when it might normally cost a dollar. So I suggested that we change the name of the picture to *Blue Harvest*, with the subtitle '*Horror Beyond Imagination*.'"

The greatest secrecy surrounded the filming of the scene in which Luke removes Darth Vader's helmet to reveal the dying Anakin Skywalker (Sebastian Shaw). Only a handful of people knew about the scene, which Lucas supervised as cameraman and director once all other work on the Death Star set was completed.

In April 1982, cast and crew went to Buttercup Valley in the Yuma Desert, Arizona, to film the Tatooine exteriors. Yuma offered spectacular sand dunes as a backdrop to Jabba the Hutt's demise. Following the experiences of *Raiders of the Lost Ark*, nobody was in a hurry to return to Tunisia. The scenes set on the Forest Moon of Endor were filmed in the giant redwood forest near Crescent City, California, from late April onward. Principal photography came to an end in May—on schedule and on budget at $32.5 million.

Lucas would later admit, however, that he had found the filming of *Jedi* almost as grueling as the shoot for *Star Wars*. "I hadn't realized that ultimately it's probably easier for me to do these things than to farm them out," he would say. "Because it was even more complex than the last one, I really did end up being there every day on the set and working very closely with Richard, and shooting second unit. It was really more work than I thought it was going to be."

Following a year of postproduction work at ILM, *Return of the*

Above - Chewbacca, C-3PO, and the others escape Tatooine amidst a sandstorm in this deleted scene from Return of the Jedi.

Left - The Blue Harvest *logo was designed for call sheets, caps, and T-shirts used during the secretive filming of* Jedi.

Opposite, left - Two ILMers examine a matte painting by Chris Evans of the landing pad on Endor, which now hangs in the reception area of ILM in San Rafael.

Jedi was released on May 25, 1983—the day had been deliberately chosen to coincide with the sixth anniversary of the debut of *Star Wars.* "Three is not enough," decided Gene Siskel, writing in the *Chicago Tribune.* "For the professional moviegoers, it is particularly enjoyable to watch every facet of filmmaking at its best. For example, I can't think of another recent picture whose sound I enjoyed so much. . . . It's almost flawless."

The public was similarly enthusiastic about a *Star Wars* sequel that offered a more optimistic take on the galaxy far, far away than did Episode V. *Jedi's* domestic box office would top $309 million, displacing *Empire* as the most lucrative sequel in cinema history.

Although *Return of the Jedi* brought the original trilogy to an end, few people expected that it would be the last *Star Wars* film. "I'd like to do one of the early ones," said Marquand in 1983, anticipating the production of the prequel trilogy. "I'm already fascinated with them, the way the society works in these early ones is something that appeals to me very much. It sounds like a very intriguing world." Sadly, Marquand would not live long enough to see the prequels—he died of a heart attack in 1987, at the age of forty-nine. For cast and crew, there was a sentiment of finality mixed with possibilities, as Mark Hamill recalls: "As we were finishing the third one, we really had the sense of, it was the end. . . . Part of me was saying, 'Oh, I'm so glad to put this behind me,' and the other aspect was, 'Well, what about all the adventures that Luke could have?'"

SPROCKET SYSTEMS

While Industrial Light & Magic was established to create the visual effects for *Star Wars*, Lucas founded another company, Sprocket Systems, to edit and mix the sound for the film. Sprocket spawned a number of spin-off companies, each with a fine reputation in its specialist area of postproduction.

Lucas had paid close attention to sound design since his earliest student films, and his belief that "sound is 50 percent of the motion-picture experience" led to research into ways that the public presentation of films could be improved. Sound engineer Tom Holman worked alongside Sprocket Systems staff to develop a unique configuration of loudspeakers integrated with the specific room acoustics of the Sprocket Systems dubbing stage. The THX Sound System was launched in June 1982 and subsequently tailored to the design and construction of individual theaters. THX became world renowned as a benchmark for quality soundtrack reproduction in theaters and home-cinema systems.

Sprocket lives on as Skywalker Sound, which oversees numerous Lucasfilm and outside projects. By 2002, Skywalker Sound had received seventeen Academy Awards for Best Sound and Best Sound Effects Editing.

On the recording stage of Skywalker Sound.

As had become customary during the week of a *Star Wars* release, Lucas took a vacation in Hawaii. Upon his return, Lucas began work on the follow-up to *Raiders of the Lost Ark*. Fortunately, Spielberg was keen to direct the sequel, but there was still a script to write. The foundation for the movie would be two elaborate stunt sequences that had been dropped from the incident-packed script for *Raiders*: a treacherous whitewater raft journey and an epic mine-cart chase. Around these two set pieces, Lucas wove a fairly dark story.

"My job and my challenge were to balance the dark side of this *Indiana Jones* saga with as much comedy as I could afford," said Spielberg in 1984. "In many ways, the visual style of the film was conceived when George told me the whole story, which was a very rough sketch of the movie he wanted us to help him construct. I heard a couple of things. I heard Kali Cult and Thuggees. I heard temple of doom, black magic, voodoo, and human sacrifice."

The scriptwriting job went to Willard Huyck and Gloria Katz, whom Lucas remembered had a special interest in India and its culture. Their screenplay was a prequel to *Raiders*, and began with a spectacular musical number in Shanghai's Club Obi Wan . . .

The year is 1935. Indiana Jones narrowly escapes the clutches of ruthless Oriental gangsters and escapes to the nearby Nang Tao airport with nightclub singer Willie Scott and his twelve-year-old sidekick, Short Round.

En route to India, their sabotaged plane crashes in the mountains, but Indy, Willie, and Short Round survive. They come across a village whose beleaguered inhabitants are the victims of a mysterious cult. The Thuggee have stolen the village's sacred stone and abducted their children. Unable to resist the lure of "fortune and glory," Jones leads his companions on a journey to the home of the cult, the young Maharajah's palace at Pankot. He finds a sinister underground temple and learns that the abducted children have become part of a scheme to recover other sacred stones that will bring the cult enormous power. Indy engineers a revolt, but safety from the furious cultists lies beyond the waterlogged mines and across a dangerous rope bridge . . .

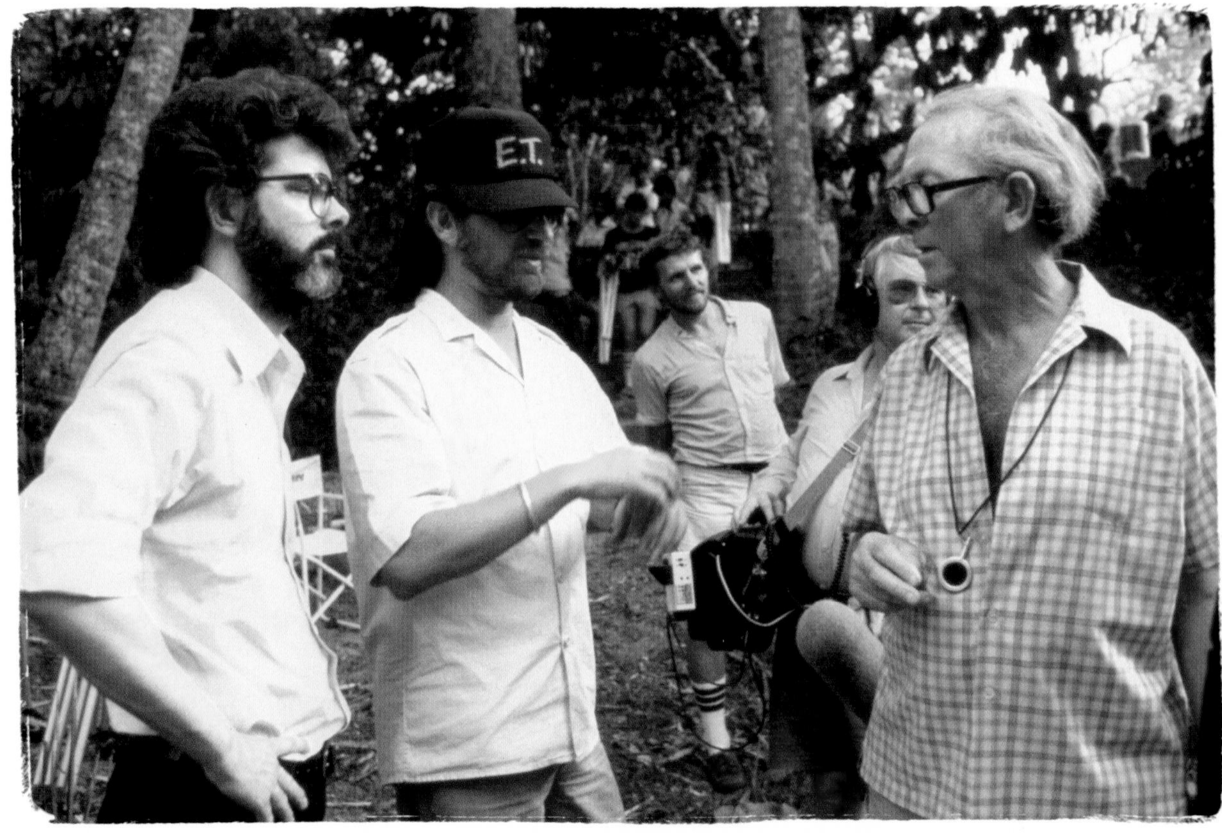

Harrison Ford reprised his role as Indiana. Willie Scott was played by Kate Capshaw. (The actress made quite an impression on Spielberg; Capshaw became his second wife a few years later.) Orphaned street urchin Short Round was played by newcomer Ke Huy Quan. The character names were an in-joke, following the tradition started by Lucas when he named Indiana after his dog—Willie was the name of Spielberg's dog, and Short Round was the name of the dog owned by the Huycks.

Previous - Luke accompanies his father, Darth Vader, to a meeting with the Emperor aboard the new Death Star in this concept painting by Ralph McQuarrie.

Above - Lucas, Spielberg, and director of photography Douglas Slocombe on location in Sri Lanka for Temple of Doom.

Far left - Jones (Harrison Ford) battles more bad guys.

Left - Ke Huy Quan (Short Round), executive producer Frank Marshall, director Spielberg, and executive producer Lucas.

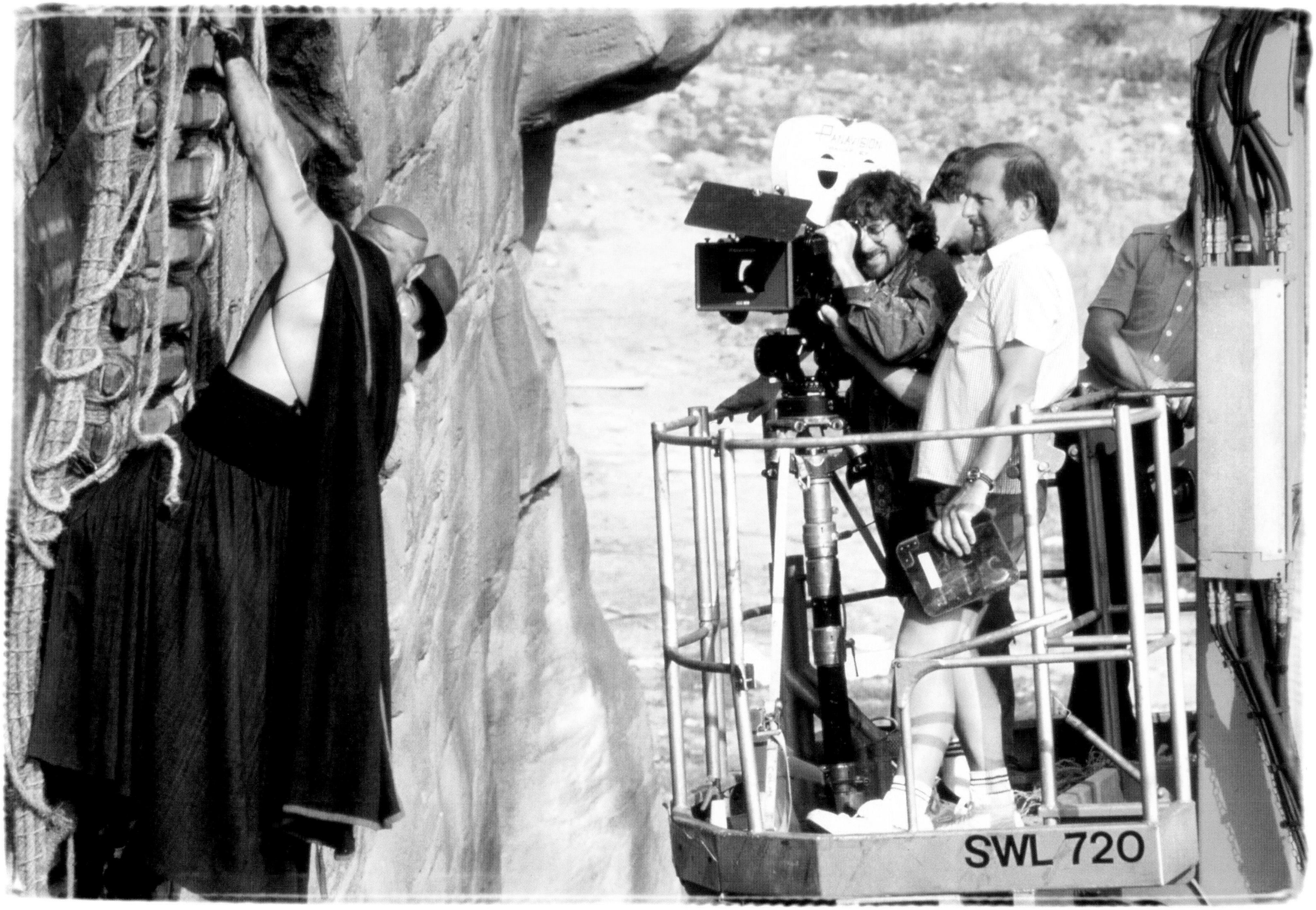

Above - *Spielberg films Amrish Puri (Mola Ram) as he clings to the collapsed rope bridge at Elstree Studios.*

Right - *Spielberg and Lucas brave the rope bridge in Sri Lanka.*

Far right - *Logo design for* Temple of Doom.

The film's production designer Elliot Scott created elaborate and expansive sets that occupied eight of Elstree's nine stages (the crew used the other stage as a workshop). Set construction continued as location shooting began in and around the Sri Lankan village of Kandy in April 1983. Sri Lanka provided many of the script's required locations, including the village and the gorge connected by the rope bridge, but a second unit would also spend six days in Macau filming the Shanghai streets, which served as a backdrop to the escape from Club Obi Wan. Other locations were found in California, such as the Mammoth Mountain and the American and Tuolumne rivers, where the scenes of whitewater rafting were shot. The rope bridge sequence required a multipronged approach: long

and medium shots of the bridge were filmed in Sri Lanka, shots of the alligator-infested river below were filmed in Arizona, and close-ups following the bridge's collapse were shot at Elstree. Douglas Slocombe's skillful lighting helped disguise the fact that about 80 percent of *Indiana Jones and the Temple of Doom* was studio-bound.

During the filming at Elstree, Harrison Ford suffered a herniated back during a particularly rigorous fight scene. He soldiered on in considerable pain, resting on a bed between shots, but was eventually flown back to Los Angeles for surgery. Despite the difficulties, Spielberg finished five days short of the eighty-five-day schedule and within the $28 million budget.

The rough cut prepared by editor Michael Kahn came in at two hours and ten minutes. The first cut Spielberg showed Lucas was fifteen minutes shorter, but both men were still able to identify an obvious problem. "We looked at each other, and the first thing out of our mouths was 'too fast,'" said Spielberg in 1984. "We needed to decelerate the action. I actually did a few matte shots to slow it down. We reestablished the palace outside in a night shot before going back inside again, for example. We made it a little bit slower . . . by putting breathing room back in so there'd be a two-hour oxygen supply for the audience."

The finished film was still a little too breathless for some reviewers—and a little too disturbing for others. The Motion Picture Association of America was concerned enough to initiate discussions that would lead to the creation of a new rating that sat between PG (Parental Guidance) and R (Restricted). *Indiana Jones and the Temple of Doom* was released on May 23, 1984, with a PG rating, but future borderline cases would be issued with the new PG-13.

The public seemed unconcerned. *Raiders* had played in some theaters for over a year, and audiences lapped up the sequel. *Temple of Doom* grossed a record-breaking $45.7 million in its first week of release in North American theaters and went on to earn almost $180 million in domestic takings.

A third *Indiana Jones* adventure was inevitable—but it would have to wait. Lucas closed down the British production office run by Robert Watts after work was completed on *Temple of Doom.* He had closed his American production office at the end of *Jedi.* "Lucasfilm is not a production company," Lucas said in 1983. "We don't have a studio, we don't have production heads. We have a producer who produces a movie. . . . The rest of Lucasfilm is really a series of companies. Each one somehow grew out of the films or what we were doing. And now they're service organizations for other people who make movies."

Much later, Lucas would look back upon this period of intense activity and recall, "The challenge is always trying to do something that's all consuming while having a private life. I had made the decision, after *Star Wars*, that I had certain goals in my private life: one was to be independent of Hollywood, the other was to have a

Opposite *- Kate Capshaw (Wilhelmina "Willie" Scott), Spielberg, Lucas, and Ford take a break in the shade during location filming.*

Above *- Behind the scenes during shooting of* Temple's *climactic battle in the mines.*

Right *- Lucas and Ford in Sri Lanka.*

Far right *- Surrounded by children, Indiana Jones (Harrison Ford) and Willie Scott (Kate Capshaw) embrace.*

family. I finished *Return of the Jedi* and I figured that was the end of it for me. And it was overwhelming and difficult, but fate has a way of stepping in. I ended up getting divorced right as *Jedi* was finished, and I was left to raise my daughter."

The remainder of the decade would see a disparate variety of productions released under the Lucasfilm banner. The plucky Ewoks that helped the Rebels in *Return of the Jedi* had been a big hit with younger audience members. In 1984, Lucas wrote a story that became the basis of *The Ewok Adventure: Caravan of Courage*, a live-action TV movie set on the Forest Moon of Endor. Directed by John Korty from a screenplay by Bob Carrau, the production was transmitted as an "ABC Sunday Night Movie" on November 25 and received the network's second-highest ratings for a movie that year. The film was released theatrically outside the U.S. under the shortened title *Caravan of Courage.*

In November 1985, ABC transmitted a follow-up film, *Ewoks: The Battle for Endor*, written and directed by Jim and Ken Wheat from a story by Lucas. The production designer on both movies was Joe Johnston, who worked on *Caravan of Courage* in between semesters at USC. "I told George I had been working for him for almost ten years, and that I'd like to take some time off to travel," he remembers. "George suggested I use the time to go to film school, and said that if I went to USC he would keep me on at half salary and pay my tuition fees. That way, I could go to the front of the line and pick any classes I wanted. It was a very generous offer."

Johnston was keen to preserve a visual link between *Caravan of Courage* and the *Star Wars* films, but was obliged to work within a relatively limited budget of $3 million. "The effects we did were pretty primitive," he recalls. "We did forced perspectives and glass paintings, back-to-basics things that had been around since the 1920s. George just told us to go out there and have some fun."

The two Ewok movies were successful enough for ABC to commission two animated television series based on *Star Wars* characters. Thirty-five episodes of *Ewoks* were transmitted between 1985 and 1986. (One of the first-season episodes was entitled *Blue Harvest.*) Another animated series, *Droids*, depicted the adventures

Above - At the table, Cindel Towani (Eric Walker) and Mace Towani (Aubree Miller) make friends with Ewoks in The Ewok Adventure: Caravan of Courage.

Far left - Director Wheat.

Left - Cindel (Aubree Miller) and Wicket (Warwick Davis).

of C-3PO and R2-D2, and featured the voice of Anthony Daniels. Thirteen episodes of *Droids* were aired in 1985, one of which was cowritten by Joe Johnston and another of which was storylined by Ben Burtt. The following year ABC broadcast *The Great Heep*, an hour-long spin-off from *Droids* based on a screenplay by Burtt and featuring production design by Johnston. "That was my favorite episode," says Daniels. "Ben has a particular affection for me as C-3PO and has a natural empathy toward R2-D2."

While Lucas had been working on his *Star Wars* sequels, his old friend and colleague Walter Murch was working on a sequel of his own. Walt Disney Pictures had asked if he would be interested in directing a film for them, and he used the opportunity to make a sequel to *The Wizard of Oz*. Murch based *Return to Oz* on *The Land of Oz* (1904) and *Ozma of Oz* (1907), L. Frank Baum's first two sequels to his original book. Shooting began at Elstree in spring 1984, with Norman Reynolds as production designer and Gary Kurtz as executive producer. When Murch encountered budgetary and production difficulties, however, he asked Lucas for help. Lucas and Robert Watts consequently acted as consultants on the production, joining Murch on the set.

As filming continued, Lucas took the opportunity to see what else was being shot at Elstree. One of the neighboring soundstages was hosting Gavin Millar's film *Dreamchild*, an unorthodox biopic about Lewis Carroll written by controversial British playwright Dennis Potter. Lucas struck up a conversation with the film's producer Rick McCallum. "I only met George briefly," says McCallum, "but I could tell he was very interested that we had about eighteen people making our film, where he had about 250 working on his. I could see there was a yearning; he really wanted to be on our set more than he wanted to be on his set."

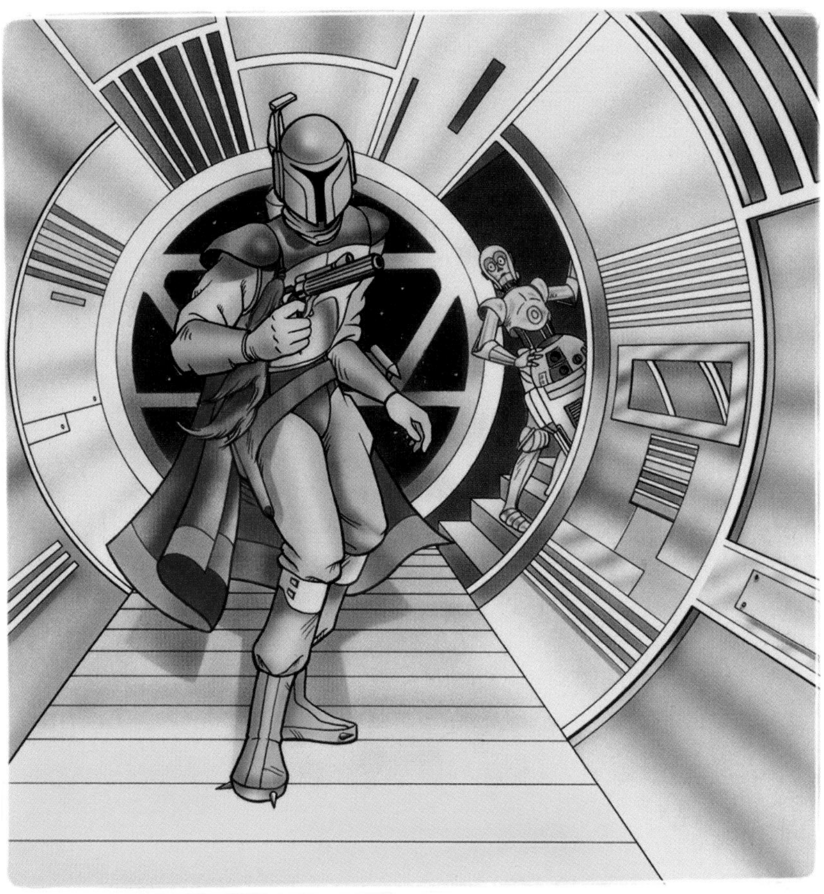

Another project that Lucas helped shepherd to the screen in 1984 was *Mishima: A Life in Four Chapters*, an exquisite study of the life, work, and suicide of Japanese writer Yukio Mishima. The film was directed and cowritten by Paul Schrader, who had originally sought help getting it made from Francis Ford Coppola under the Zoetrope banner. Lucas was enthused about the project and joined Coppola as coexecutive producer, helping Schrader raise half of the film's financing from Warner Bros.

Above left *- Robot Tik-Tok (played by Timothy M. Rose and Michael Sundin) from Walter Murch's* Return to Oz. *The robot first appeared in L. Frank Baum's third book in the series,* Ozma of Oz.

Above right *- Bounty hunter Boba Fett, C-3PO, and R2-D2 from the animated series* Droids.

Right *- A frame from the* Ewoks *cartoon.*

Middle *- A frame from* Droids.

Far right *- Blues icon Long John Baldry did the voice for* The Great Heep, *seen here alongside the droids and their master, Mungo Baobab (on the rock hopper creature).*

Since working on *American Graffiti*, Haskell Wexler had kept in touch with Lucas. Despite his success as a cinematographer, Wexler had been frustrated in his attempts to direct another picture since the groundbreaking *Medium Cool* (1969). He was just as politically aware as he had been in the 1960s, and had thus become outraged by America's involvement in Nicaragua. Wexler devised a story about a Hispanic Green Beret who finds his loyalty divided when he falls in love with a Nicaraguan girl whose father is an insurgent. Wexler called his film *Latino*, and became so determined to bring it to the screen that he financed the production with his own money. "George knew the facts about this politically sensitive situation," says Wexler, "[but] I think he mostly went along with this out of friendship to me."

Lucas offered Wexler the use of his postproduction facilities and arranged specialist distribution under the Lucasfilm banner. "The film won an award at the Cannes Film Festival," recalls Wexler, "but it didn't make any money because there wasn't any money to publicize it, and the media—which was still covering for Reagan's Contra activities—said it wasn't true."

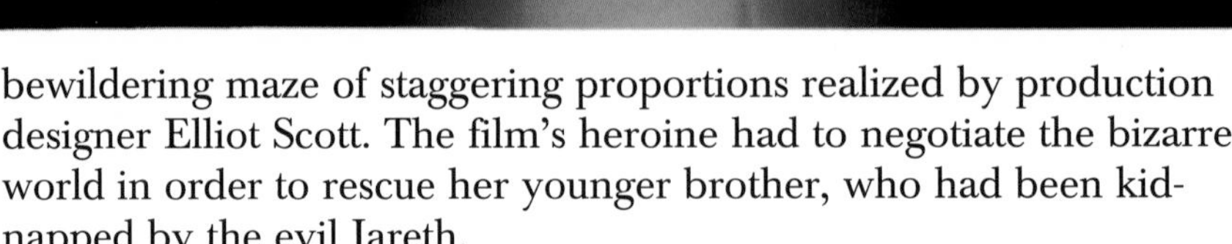

Latino was released in February 1986, a year that saw the release of three other productions bearing the Lucasfilm name. Lucas had great respect for Jim Henson, the creator of *The Muppet Show*, and had consulted with him on the techniques that had helped bring Yoda to life in *The Empire Strikes Back* and *Return of the Jedi*. When Henson asked Lucas if he'd like to work with him on an elaborate fantasy film that would develop those techniques further, Lucas agreed to get involved. *Labyrinth*, based on a script by Monty Python's Terry Jones and starring David Bowie as Jareth the Goblin King and Jennifer Connelly as Sarah, began shooting at Elstree Studios in 1985. The labyrinth of the film's title was a bewildering maze of staggering proportions realized by production designer Elliot Scott. The film's heroine had to negotiate the bizarre world in order to rescue her younger brother, who had been kidnapped by the evil Jareth.

Henson directed the film himself, and Lucas flew over to England to watch him work. Lucas recognized Henson as a kindred spirit who created his own immaculate realities through a combination of artistry and engineering ingenuity. "Jim and I both wanted to work with each other, and that was a movie that nobody really wanted," says Lucas. "We had to do a real song-and-dance to get people behind it."

While *Labyrinth* was being filmed in England, ILM was having problems trying to create a Muppet-style character of its own: the comic-book character *Howard the Duck*. Lucas was one of the character's earliest fans and had showed Willard Huyck an issue of *Howard the Duck*. Over the next few years Huyck and Katz wrote numerous drafts of a live-action comedy based on the duck's exploits. Such was their faith

Top - *A moment from Paul Schrader's* Mishima.

Above - *Jim Henson (second from left) and friends, both human and Muppet.*

Far left - *A surreal shot from* Mishima.

Middle - *Director Haskell Wexler during the making of* Latino. *Wexler and his crew took significant personal risks to shoot* Latino *on location in Nicaragua.*

Left - *A scene from* Latino.

in the idea that Huyck nominated himself as director, and Katz wanted to produce. The project did the rounds of the major studios, but by the time it arrived at Universal the character's popularity had waned (the comic was canceled in 1981). Universal nevertheless promised to back the picture—on the condition Lucas allowed his name to be attached as executive producer.

An extremely tight schedule began in late 1985, with studio and location filming kept within close proximity to ILM and its technicians. Huyck and Katz felt that their original intentions for the film were waylaid by Universal; while they struggled in vain with the studio, the film ended up 20 percent over budget. *Howard the Duck* opened in August 1986 to merciless reviews. "If I hadn't been identified with the project, the reviews might have been a little gentler, at least," Lucas says.

The final Lucasfilm release of 1986 was also the most successful, even though it never played in conventional theaters. *Captain EO* was a seventeen-minute, 70mm 3-D production designed for screening at Disney's Anaheim and Orlando theme parks. The project had an unusual history. In 1984, the ailing Disney corporation had been rescued from corporate predators when members of the Texan Bass family became major shareholders. Lucas had been asked to run the revitalized company but had declined the offer. "It wasn't what he wanted to do with his life," says Howard Roffman, who was acting as Lucasfilm's chief operating officer during the Disney shake-up. "Disney had never let outside properties in [to their theme parks] but when the Bass brothers came in, they thought it was the best idea they'd ever heard. They wanted to do a deal really quickly, so we locked ourselves in a room and came up with something they put to their shareholders."

The Disney Board, consulting with Sid Bass, offered the job of Disney chief executive to Michael Eisner (who, while at Paramount, had green-lit *Raiders of the Lost Ark*), and he began discussions with Lucas over a new exclusive production for screening at Disneyland and Disney's Epcot. Lucas became executive producer of *Captain EO*, an ambitious fantasy marrying Disney animation and ILM visual

Above *- One of strange creatures that populate* Captain Eo.

Right *- Lucas, David Bowie (who played the King of the Goblins), and Muppets creator Jim Henson collaborated on the epic* Labyrinth *in 1985.*

Far right *- Critics were unkind to* Howard the Duck, *and the film failed to make an impact with the public. This scene was shot on Nicasio Valley Road, not far from Skywalker Ranch in Marin County.*

effects, as a vehicle for Michael Jackson, the decade's most successful pop star. Lucas asked Coppola to direct the film, which began production in July 1985. The experiment used a new type of 70mm stock from Eastman and a 3-D process developed by Disney, and the result was a spectacular, enveloping experience. *Captain EO* opened in September 1986 and continued at Disneyland until 1997.

Toward the end of the 1980s, Lucas focused his creative energies on initiating new projects. *Powaqqatsi* was the second in a trilogy of remarkable experimental films by avant-garde director Godfrey Reggio. The first film in the trilogy, *Koyaanisqatsi* (1983), comprised an engrossing collage of blended and interwoven images against a hypnotic score by Philip Glass to evoke "life out of balance" (a translation of the film's Hopi-language title).

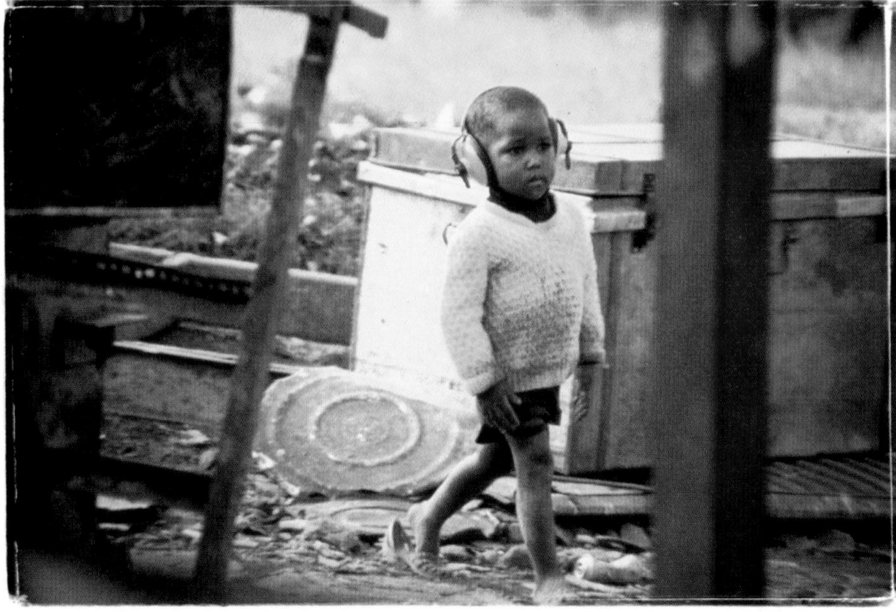

Koyaanisqatsi had been preceded by the caption "Francis Ford Coppola presents," but Coppola found that his name, on its own, was not enough to help Reggio secure distribution for *Powaqqatsi* (which used the same technique to depict "life in transformation").

Above and left - "Life in transformation" from Godfrey Reggio's Powaqqatsi.

STAR TOURS

In 1984, Lucasfilm and Disney began negotiations to create a theme-park ride. In 1986, thirty years after Lucas first visited Disneyland, it was announced that Tomorrowland would play host to a space simulator based on the characters and events from the *Star Wars* trilogy.

Star Tours took the form of a tour through the galaxy in the period following the Rebels' triumph in *Return of the Jedi*. Passengers strapped themselves into the hydraulically mounted StarSpeeder shuttle before C-3PO and R2-D2 assumed the roles of intergalactic tourist guides. The images seen through the vessel's windows were projected from 70mm film and boasted effects that were specially created by ILM. The journey's unpredictable course was partly the fault of the inexperienced pilot, a hapless droid called Rex. Lucas's original notes for the pilot described him as a reckless Clone Wars veteran called "Crazy Harry."

Lucas and Disney chief executive Michael Eisner formally opened the ride on January 9, 1987. Prior to the opening ceremony, Lucas said, "I've been approached to do many amusement parks—develop them from scratch or be a part of them—and I've always felt that there's only one first-class amusement park operation and this is it. When I did something, I've always wanted to make sure it was done right and it was maintained right, operated correctly . . . and this is the only place in the world like that."

At Disneyland, people line up for Star Tours while C-3PO debriefs them on their ride to come.

Lucas was happy to add his name to Coppola's, using his influence to secure a distribution agreement from Cannon's Menahem Golan and Yoram Globus. *Powaqqatsi* was released in April 1988 and found a small but appreciative audience.

Later in 1988, Lucas joined Steven Spielberg as coexecutive producer of an animated feature by Don Bluth, who had broken away from what he considered to be the stifling atmosphere at Disney to create his own animation work. Spielberg had provided the inspiration for Bluth's project about baby dinosaurs struggling to reach their promised land as climate changes and larger dinosaurs threaten them. *The Land Before Time* was released in November 1988 and would combine appealing Disney-style creatures with uncompromising imagery of a prehistoric Earth in turmoil. The film was a big commercial success, and has to date spawned no fewer than nine straight-to-video sequels.

Aside from the gestating *Star Wars* prequels, Lucas also harbored ambitions to produce an epic sword-and-sorcery fantasy that had been in the back of his mind since the mid-1970s. Lucas first called his idea *Munchkins*, but it would become better known by its ultimate title: *Willow*.

At the heart of *Willow* was Lucas's desire to once again reinvent a number of well-known mythological situations for a young audience. The medieval-style world of *Willow* would also be predominantly populated with little people. During the production of *Return of the Jedi*, Lucas had approached Warwick Davis, one of the actors sweltering inside the Ewok costumes, about playing the eponymous lead in *Willow*. Five years passed, during which time Davis played the Ewok named Wicket in *Caravan of Courage* and *Battle for Endor*, before he was finally cast in the film. "I thought it would be great to use a little person in a lead role," said Lucas in 1989. "A lot of my movies are about a little guy against the system, and this was just a more literal interpretation of that idea."

Lucas had similarly firm ideas about who should direct the movie. Shortly after appearing in *American Graffiti*, Ron Howard had attended film school at USC and, in 1977, made his directorial debut with *Grand Theft Auto* for producer Roger Corman. Howard then gave Michael Keaton his first starring role in *Night Shift* (1982) and scored major commercial successes with *Splash* (1984) and

Above - Willow Ufgood (Warwick Davis) determines to save his newfound baby from the clutches of evil Queen Bavmorda in Ron Howard's Willow.

Right - Climatic upheaval threatens the dinosaurs in Don Bluth's animated adventure The Land Before Time, *for which Lucas acted as coexecutive producer.*

Cocoon (1985), the latter of which featured visual effects by ILM. It was while Howard was supervising postproduction at ILM that Lucas first brought up the idea of Howard directing *Willow*. Lucas felt that he and his former star shared a simpatico relationship similar to the one he enjoyed with Spielberg.

"One of the reasons I got involved in this project was because of George," recalled Howard in 1988. "He knew I was looking for something to do in this genre. He came to me with this idea about two-and-a-half years ago and said, 'Let's just both commit to this.' There was no development deal, it was just a case of, 'Let's just start making this movie.' I immediately felt a loyalty to George and the project. We weren't flirting with this movie to see if we could fall in love while we developed it; we were going to get down to the brass tacks and solve it."

Howard nominated Canadian writer Bob Dolman to write the script. The two had worked together on an unsold television pilot called *Little Shots*, and both Howard and Lucas admired Dolman's work on the TV sitcom *W.K.R.P. in Cincinnati*. Dolman joined Howard and Lucas at Skywalker Ranch for a series of lengthy story conferences and wrote seven drafts of his script between spring and fall 1986. The final draft of the screenplay was clearly infused with the spirit of *Star Wars* and read like a blueprint for a new series of adventures in the same vein:

> *Bad-tempered sorceress Queen Bavmorda is warned that a newborn girl bearing a special mark will grow up to depose her. When just such a child is born, she is smuggled away from Bavmorda's kingdom and ends up in a community of little people called Nelwyns.*

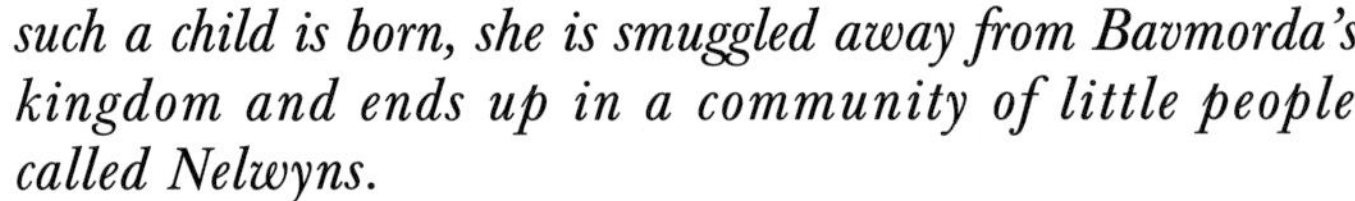

> *Nelwyn farmer and would-be necromancer Willow Ufgood determines to return the child to her own kingdom so her destiny can be fulfilled. He conquers his fears and embarks on the long journey, recruiting a roguish swordsman called Madmartigan and a pair of tiny bickering Brownies. Things get complicated when Madmartigan falls in love with Bavmorda's daughter Sorsha, but Willow and his friends are helped in their struggle by Fin Raziel, a good sorceress trapped in the body of a muskrat (and later a goat).*
>
> *The baby falls into the hands of Bavmorda, but Sorsha decides to desert her evil mother. The scene is set for a climactic confrontation when Bavmorda transforms Willow's army of warriors into pigs. As the child's life hangs in the balance, Willow restores Fin Raziel to human form so she can face her archenemy Bavmorda for the last time . . .*

Preproduction began at the end of 1986, as producer Nigel Wooll worked alongside Robert Watts to assemble a team that included cinematographer Adrien Biddle. The cast included Val Kilmer as Madmartigan and the British actress Joanne Whalley as the tempestuous Sorsha. Queen Bavmorda was played with obvious relish by Jean Marsh.

Lucas once again found an ally in Alan Ladd Jr., the newly appointed chief executive officer of M-G-M. The cash-strapped studio had long since gained a reputation as Hollywood's most

Above - Director Ron Howard reviews visuals from Willow *with executive producer Lucas, director of matte photography Craig Barron, and matte painter supervisor Chris Evans.*

Far left - Queen Bavmorda (Jean Marsh).

Left - Howard and Lucas on location for Willow.

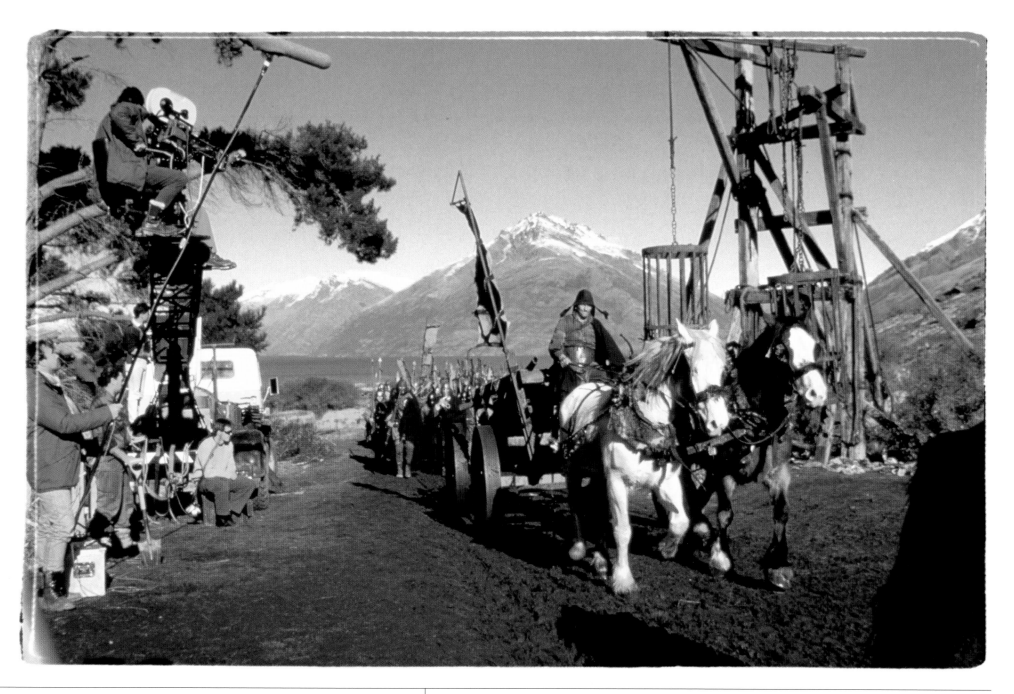

Above *- A behind-the-scenes shot of* Willow *on location in New Zealand.*

Right *- Lucas, Howard, and visual effects technicians Phil Tippett and Dennis Muren examine a brazier that is to be stop-motion animated for* Willow.

Far right *- Another ILM visual effect results in* Willow*'s forest fairy visitation.*

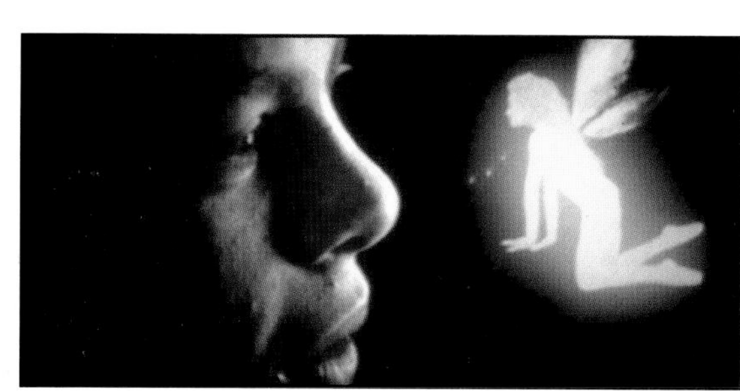

SKYWALKER RANCH

* *

The purchase of the 1,700-acre Bulltail Ranch was only the beginning of Lucas's ambitious plans to create a headquarters for Lucasfilm and a creative retreat for his employees, colleagues, and friends. The subsequent addition of adjoining land was the next step toward creating the impressive 6,500-acre complex that exists today.

Skywalker Ranch is dominated by the impressive Main House. Designed in a Victorian style, the Main House is generally the first port of call for visitors. In an effort to help the architects reconcile the Mission, Arts and Crafts, Art Nouveau, and Art Deco influences he wanted to incorporate, Lucas devised a fictional history for the Main House, dating various sections of it to different periods between 1869 and 1934. Construction of the building took place between 1982 and 1984, using redwood milled from old bridge timbers. The Main House was subsequently joined by a number of ancillary buildings such as the Brook, Gate, and Carriage Houses, and a Storage Barn. The Technical Building was designed in the style of an old brick winery. A vineyard was planted on the grounds of the building in 1987; its first Merlot and Chardonnay wines were bottled for private consumption in 1992.

Highlights of Skywalker Ranch: (clockwise from top) the Main House, the Solarium, the Lucasfilm research library, and the Tech Building (where Skywalker Sound is located).

troubled major and its investment in a fantasy film was perceived as a risk. Ladd advanced half the $36 million budget in return for theatrical and television rights, leaving Lucasfilm with home-video and pay-TV rights to offer in exchange for the other half.

Principal photography began in spring 1987. While Elstree hosted the interiors, Howard filmed the expansive location scenes in Wales and New Zealand. Despite it being Howard's first production on such a large scale, he was unperturbed by the scope of the film's battle scenes. "There really isn't much difference between shooting a fight scene between four hundred people and between four people," he said in 1988. "I really viewed it as an epic on a secondary level. First and foremost, it is a character story about some very unlikely heroes being emotionally involved in an issue, to the point where they're willing to risk their lives."

While Howard continued shooting, Lucas assumed responsibility for the film's postproduction. In summer 1987, Dennis Muren found time to introduce a major innovation. Dolman's script called for *Willow* to restore Fin Raziel (Patricia Hayes) from a goat to her original human form. Willow recites what he thinks is the appropriate spell, but turns the goat into an ostrich, and then a tortoise, and finally a tiger, before returning Raziel to her human body. "This was our first chance to try something we called morphing," says Muren, who proposed filming each animal, and the actress doubling for Patricia Hayes, and then feeding the images into a computer program developed by Doug Smythe. The program would then create a smooth transition from one stage to another before outputting the result back onto film. The traditional way to execute such a shot would have been through the use of an optical dissolve with cutaways at various stages, but Muren thought that by digitally morphing the transformation, the effects of the spell could appear almost seamless. Smythe began development of the necessary software in September 1987; by March 1988, the impressive result Muren and his fellow designer David Allen achieved would represent a breakthrough for digital effects.

Willow was released on May 20, 1988. Certain critics recognized the film's obvious virtues: "The story is pleasing and the climax terrifically intense," wrote Mike Clark in *U.S.A. Today*. "The rainstorm wrap-up, in which Good edges Evil 12-11 in extra innings, is like Led Zeppelin Meets the Wild Bunch. . . . *Willow* is probably too much for young children and possibly too much of the same for cynics. But any 6- to 13-year-old who sees this may be bitten by the 'movie bug'—and for life."

Willow was filmed concurrently with another project that was close to Lucas's heart. His emotional attachment to *Tucker: The Man and His Dream*, however, was derived not only

Above - Lucas on a snow-laden location in New Zealand.

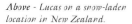

Right *- Thanks to ILM, the backing of Lucas, and the pioneering work of programmer Doug Smythe, the revolutionary process of morphing first saw the light of day in this sequence from* Willow, *in which a woman changes into various creatures before regaining her human form.*

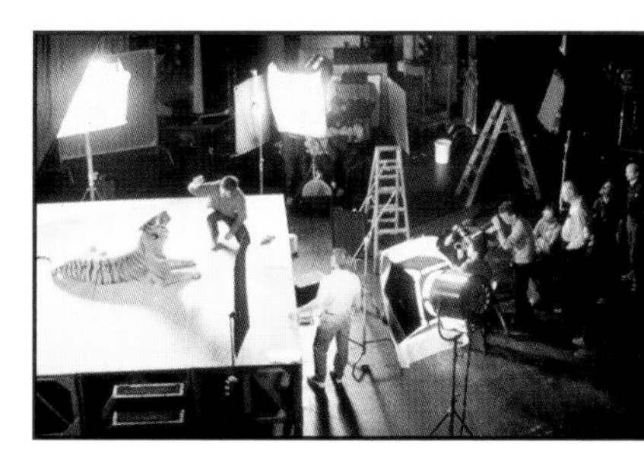

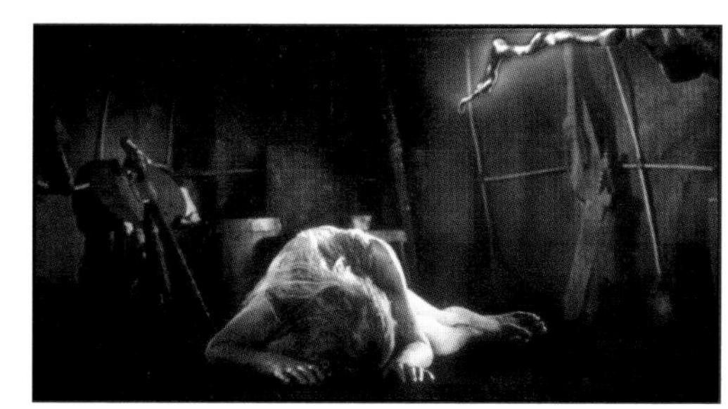

from the story, but also from his longstanding friendship with the film's director. Coppola had first seen a Tucker Torpedo on display in 1948. His father, Carmine, was so impressed that he ordered a car and invested $5,000 in the Tucker Corporation. The company collapsed and the car never arrived, but Francis never forgot about the futuristic vehicle he had glimpsed as a small boy. He later acquired one of his own.

Lucas was well aware of Coppola's fascination with Tucker's rise and fall. During the production of *Captain EO*, Coppola had reminded Lucas about his ambition to film Tucker's life story. "George's fortunes were rising just as mine were falling," says Coppola, "so it created a dramatic situation in that the person that had always been the sponsor of things was no longer able to do that. We always saw each other socially, and one time my kids had the Tucker out and George said to me, 'I always liked that idea you had of making *Tucker*. Why don't you do it?' And I said, 'Well, I'm not quite sure. . . . Who'd want to do it or who'd finance it?' He said, 'I'll help you,' and he did."

Lucas agreed to act as executive producer and resolved to come up with the film's $24 million budget himself. In a 1988 interview, Lucas downplayed his contribution. "I started out as his creative assistant and I guess that's still what I am, when it really comes down to it. It's just that now I'm helping to fund him, and then he was helping to fund me."

Coppola asked Arnold Schulman (who had recently completed work on *A Chorus Line*) to write the final-draft screenplay, but Schulman initially refused, protesting that he hated cars. Schulman recalls that Lucas persuaded him by explaining, "This film is not about cars. It's about Francis." *Tucker* was produced by Fred Roos and Fred Fuchs, and starred Jeff Bridges as the charismatic Preston Tucker. Jeff's father, Lloyd, played the scheming Senator Ferguson, and Martin Landau would be nominated for an Oscar for his portrayal of Tucker's business partner, Abe Karatz. More than twenty original cars were borrowed from the forty-six surviving models owned by members of the Tucker Automobile Club of America.

Filming began on April 13, 1987 and, three weeks later, Lucas finally persuaded Paramount to distribute the film. Coppola recalls that Lucas had to "twist a few arms" to get a commitment from the studio, but he was helped by the fact that Paramount was courting Coppola to direct a third installment of *The Godfather*.

"It's about the life of an entrepreneur and the fate of creativity in a modern, financially oriented America," said Lucas in 1987; when the film was released on August 12, 1988, however, few critics drew the obvious parallel between Coppola's and Lucas's struggle for independence from the major studios and Tucker's battle with Detroit's "big three" car manufacturers.

The final Lucasfilm production in a turbulent decade represented the end of an era for several reasons. The third *Indiana Jones* movie would bring the original trilogy of films to a close, and would be the final film that Lucas mounted at Elstree—the studio he had come to regard as his "lucky charm."

The approved script included no elements of Lucas's original idea of a film set in a haunted house. Instead, Lucas decided to return to an old idea: "the search for the Holy Grail." Spielberg suggested that Indiana Jones should be reunited with his estranged father: "I did not want Indy on a headlong pursuit without a subplot that was almost stronger than the actual quest itself," said Spielberg in 1989. "So I came up with the father/son story, because the Grail

Opposite - Preston Tucker (Jeff Bridges) unveils the "The Car of Tomorrow—Today" in Tucker: The Man and His Dream, *directed by Coppola and executive produced by Lucas.*

Above left - Lucas on location for Tucker *with cinematographer Vittorio Storaro.*

Above right - Behind the scenes of Tucker.

Right - Storaro, Coppola, Lucas, and producer Fred Roos during the filming of Tucker *in 1987.*

Far right - A still from Tucker.

HI-WIRE ACTS and ACROBATS
DUNN & DUFFY COMBINED CIRC
RAGING!

SIDE SHOWS
of STRANGE PEOPLE

is symbolic of finding the truth in one's life—the truth we are always looking for, consciously or unconsciously."

Spielberg's suggestion resonated with Lucas, who had of course used a father/son relationship as a major theme in the *Star Wars* trilogy, and who had been raising his daughter Amanda. Both Spielberg and Harrison Ford had also recently become fathers, and, in 1988, Lucas would adopt a second daughter, Katie.

The role of Indy's father, Henry, was offered to Sean Connery, who was eager to join the cast of the new *Indiana Jones* film despite the fact there was a mere twelve-year age gap between him and his screen son. As Lucas was keen to begin the new film with a flashback showing the exploits of Indiana Jones as an idealistic boy scout, Harrison Ford suggested eighteen-year-old River Phoenix, who had recently played Ford's screen son in *The Mosquito Coast* (1986). The role of icy blonde Dr. Elsa Schneider went to Irish actress Alison Doody. British character actor Julian Glover, who had a cameo in *The Empire Strikes Back*, adopted an American accent to play devious industrialist Walter Donovan. Indy would call on old allies Marcus Brody and Sallah; Denholm Elliott and John Rhys-Davies, respectively, reprised their familiar roles.

Dutch-born writer Menno Mejes (who had worked on *The Color Purple* and *Empire of the Sun*) shared the film's story credit with Lucas, and the final-draft screenplay was prepared by Jeffrey Boam, who had cowritten the Spielberg-produced *Innerspace* (1987). Boam's script for this most character-driven of the Indy films would mark a return to the style of *Raiders of the Lost Ark* . . .

1912: Young Indiana Jones fails to wrest the Cross of Coronado away from an unscrupulous archaeologist, who intends to sell the artifact to a sinister businessman rather than donate it to a museum.

1938: During a fight aboard a freighter, Indy recovers the cross; the businessman dies when the boat explodes. Indy's teaching career is interrupted when Walter Donovan asks him to find the Holy Grail. Donovan's previous team leader was Indy's irascible father, Henry, who was close to discovering the location of the Grail when he went missing.

In Venice, Indy, Marcus Brody, and Henry's glamorous assistant, Dr. Elsa Schneider, discover the location of the temple where the Grail is hidden. Marcus heads to Iskendurun to find the temple, while Indy and Elsa go to a mysterious castle on the German-Austrian border to rescue Henry from his Nazi captors.

It transpires that Walter and Elsa are Nazi sympathizers. Indy and Henry escape—first by motorbike and sidecar and later by zeppelin, plane, automobile, and foot. Indy and Henry must reconcile their differences as they join Marcus and Indy's friend Sallah in the race to find the Grail. With the prize finally within Indy's grasp, he is forced to decide between possession of the cup and something even more important . . .

Lucas, Spielberg, and Paramount agreed on a budget of $36 million, and on May 16, 1988, filming began in the desert near Almería, Spain. Other locations included Venice, Jordan, Austria, Germany, Colorado, New Mexico, Utah, and Texas—all of which amounted to the greatest challenge yet for producer Robert Watts.

Previous - *Young Indy (River Phoenix) is pursued on a circus train.*

Above - *Sean Connery (Henry Jones) confers with Spielberg on the castle set at Elstree Studios during the shooting of* Last Crusade.

Far left - *Lucas and Spielberg on location in Venice, Italy.*

Middle - *"Junior" (River Phoenix).*

Left - *Professor Henry Jones (Sean Connery) and his son Indiana (Harrison Ford) are captured by Nazis on the German-Austrian border.*

Above - *Behind the scenes during the motorboat fight.*

Right - *Adolf Hitler (Michael Sheard) signs an autograph for a disguised Indiana Jones (Harrison Ford) at a book-burning rally in Berlin.*

Far right - *Dr. Elsa Schneider (Alison Doody) and Walter Donovan (Julian Glover) try to find the Hidden Valley of the Crescent Moon.*

Filming was conducted at the now-customary brisk pace. "I would guess that the average film is told in something like three hundred to five hundred setups," said cinematographer Douglas Slocombe in 1989. "But all three of the *Indiana Jones* films have to run to at least fifteen hundred setups, probably close to two thousand. . . . I can't remember the number of times when I was saying a few words to an electrician about where I wanted a lamp [when] I would hear Steven shout, 'Turn over!' So at that point I would know my time was up."

Highlights of *Last Crusade* include a sequence set in secret catacombs beneath Venice, where Indy and Elsa are besieged by a plague of rats. Months before filming began, more than seven thousand of the creatures were specially bred. For the most dangerous scenes, mechanical substitutes doubled for the rats that perish in a canal of flaming gasoline.

Following a three-week hiatus, principal photography came to an end with the prologue showing young Indy's struggle with greedy archaeologist Fedora (Richard Young). Although he was not required for filming, Ford joined Spielberg on location in order to coach Phoenix on his delivery of the lines and his body movements. "All of us would come back together on each of these movies," recalls Kathleen Kennedy. "All of us had such a good time making the movies. What I found to be so interesting and kind of extraordinary is that none of that got in the way of the work. Often those kinds of dynamics can be the very thing that rip things apart, but in this case, I think those dynamics brought everybody even closer and closer together."

The final scenes for *Last Crusade* were actually shot some time after principal photography had wrapped. When Spielberg viewed the rough cut compiled by Michael Kahn, he decided that there was not enough action, so he filmed a motorcycle-and-sidecar chase in Lucas Valley near Skywalker Ranch.

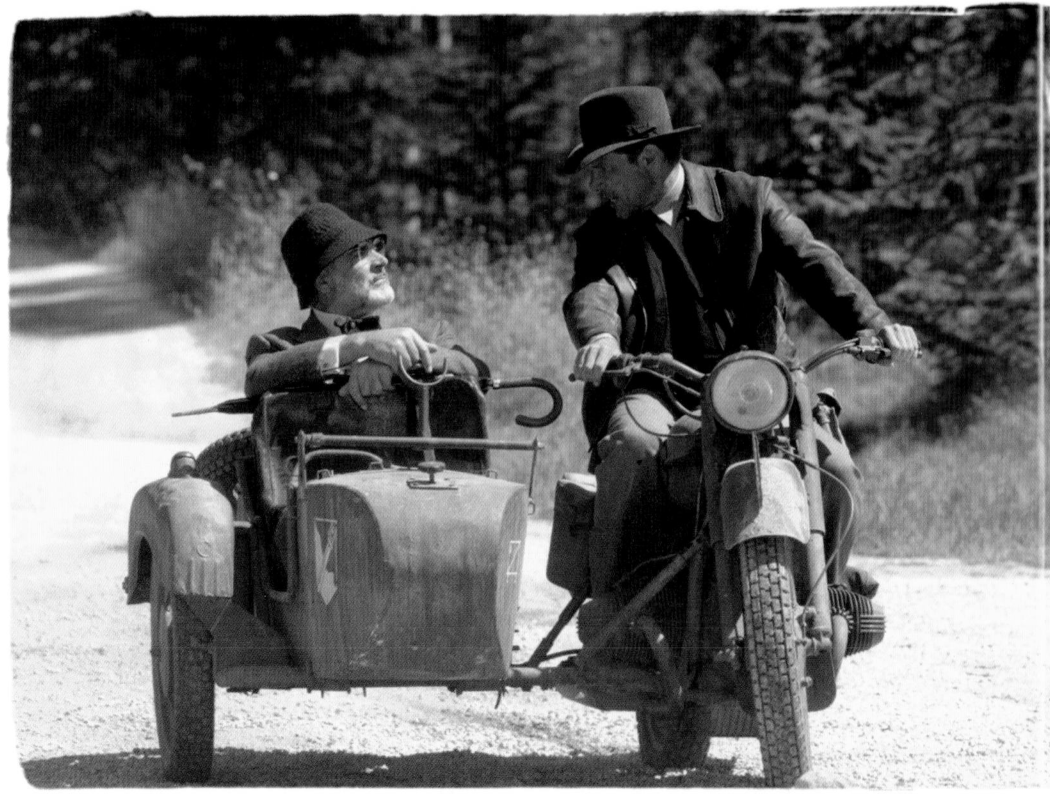

Above left *- Ford, visual effects supervisor Mike McCallister, and Lucas examine the German fighter planes to be used in another Indiana Jones cliffhanger.*

Above right *- Some late shots of the motorcycle sequence were filmed near Skywalker Ranch.*

Far left *- The Luftwaffe is in hot pursuit of Indiana Jones (Harrison Ford) and his father, Henry (Sean Connery), in this chase scene, filmed in Almeria, Spain.*

Left *- The traitorous Walter Donovan (Julian Glover) threatens Marcus Brody (Denholm Elliott), Sallah (John Rhys-Davies), Indiana Jones (Harrison Ford), and Henry Jones (Sean Connery) as the race to find the Holy Grail is seemingly lost.*

Opposite, left *- Drew Struzan's portrait of "the man with the hat" for the* Last Crusade *American advance poster. Like previous submissions to the trilogy, this poster saw more use in the post-theatrical home-video market than in general release.*

Opposite, right *- The American one-sheet for* Indiana Jones and the Last Crusade *also featured artwork by Struzan.*

Indiana Jones and the Last Crusade was released on May 24, 1989, and brought the original trilogy to a magnificent conclusion. Elliott Scott's production design, Douglas Slocombe's photography, the engaging performances, and the energy produced by the third Lucas/Spielberg collaboration conspire to make this the trilogy's most satisfying evocation of the era. *Last Crusade* may not offer action sequences to rival those of the previous two films, but the breathing space allows Ford and Connery to bicker their way across the world, resulting in something even more memorable.

The film grossed $197.2 million in North American theaters, placing it some way ahead of *Temple of Doom.* Paramount and the public were left clamoring for more, but Lucas maintained that the trilogy of films he first outlined to Spielberg in 1977 was now complete. An optimistic Lucas began planning a new project partially inspired by the flashback to Indy's youth in *Last Crusade.* In providing his most popular character with a history, Lucas was creating the foundations of a pioneering future.

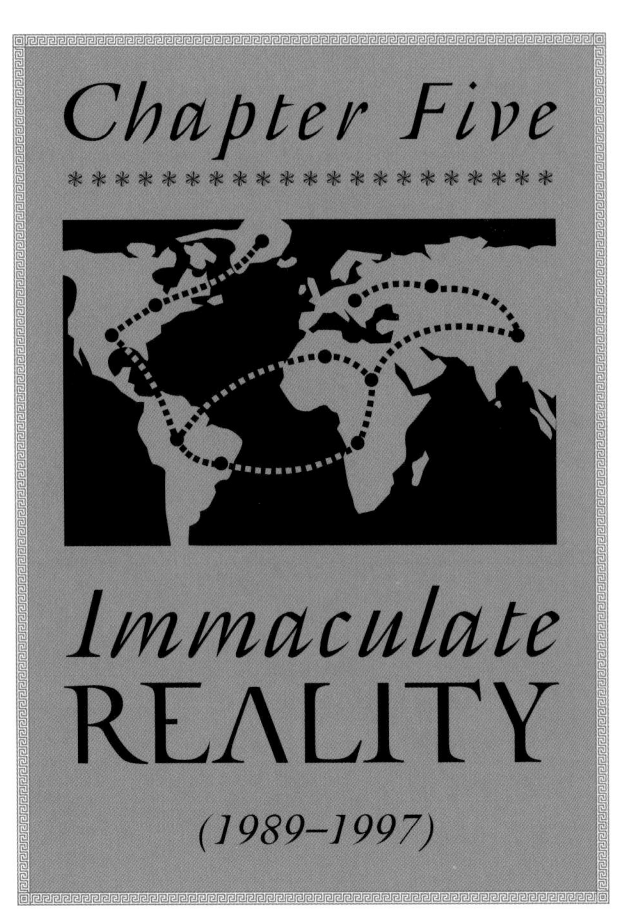
Chapter Five
Immaculate
REALITY
(1989–1997)

Lucasfilm's hard-won stability placed Lucas in an enviable position as he faced the new decade with an impressive production infrastructure in place. "I will get back to directing," he claimed in 1991. "Being an executive is fun in its own way, but it's like the difference between coaching and playing. Lately, I've been getting the itch to play."

Wary of jumping prematurely back into the fray, Lucas was methodically and tenaciously preparing a more satisfying life for himself as director. Since the early 1980s, he had been making predictions that movies would one day no longer be shot on film but recorded digitally. One of the first significant moves away from film came in 1984 when Lucasfilm unveiled the EditDroid, the first disc-based nonlinear editing system—i.e., a computerized system that enabled editors to cut and rearrange sequences working from a videodisc copy of celluloid footage. "I really wanted to build a system that allowed me to get around all the vulgarities of editing," he says. "The mindless, stupid things that slow you down, distract you, and aggravate you: things like tearing sprocket holes, breaking splices, and losing three frames at the bottom of the film bin or down in the depths somewhere. I knew that with a digital system, I would be able to feed 847,000 feet into it and then press a button to find the scene I wanted."

The EditDroid largely removed the actual handling of film from the postproduction equation, empowering editors to create more complex scenes and sequences in less time and, crucially, to view the results of their work almost instantaneously. The EditDroid was developed in Lucasfilm's Computer Division, which had been founded by Lucas back in 1979 and overseen by Ed Catmull. The EditDroid team was led by Ralph Guggenheim, while Andy Moorer was responsible for the development of the SoundDroid. This latter innovation enabled technicians to edit and manipulate soundtracks in computers before outputting them back onto film. The EditDroid revolutionized the process of film editing forever (it was later sold to Avid Tech).

Lucas had first used computerized visual effects as early as 1977, with a relatively primitive sequence illustrating the proposed attack run on the Death Star. By the early 1990s he had hopes of more fully implementing digital effects, which could improve upon traditional visual-effect techniques that had been in use since the days of silent filmmaking. An early problem had been one of resolution: the capacity of computers available in the 1970s limited the presentation of graphics to a television-size screen. By the 1980s, however, the morphing sequence ILM had created for *Willow* gave some indication of how far digital effects had progressed—but for Lucas, it was still not far enough. The settings he envisioned for Episodes I to III of the *Star Wars* saga would be far too expensive

***Previous** - Young Indy (Sean Patrick Flanery) carries Lily (Jayne Ashbourne) to safety in* Chapter 18: Treasure of the Peacock's Eye *from the third season of Lucas's TV series* The Young Indiana Jones Chronicles.

***Left** - Lucas visiting a* Young Indy *set in 1992.*

***Above** - In the early 1990s, Skywalker Ranch became what it had been designed for: a think-tank for writers and filmmakers plotting out fantastic stories (painting by Erik Tiemens).*

***Right** - Lucas's years of work created a suitable atmosphere for the seven writers of* Young Indy *to weave together romantic historical tales.*

Bicycles are omnipresent at the Ranch, as employees use them to pedal from one building to another.

PIXAR

* *

Lucasfilm's Computer Division was reorganized into three independent companies in the mid-1980s: Droid Works incorporated the technology and staff associated with the film and sound-editing technology; the Games Group remained part of Lucasfilm, ultimately becoming the acclaimed software house LucasArts; and the Graphics Group was renamed Pixar, after its Pixar Image Computer. The Pixar computer made its debut in 1985 and proved powerful and versatile enough to lend itself to numerous nonfilmmaking applications, such as medical imaging.

A frame from *The Adventures of André and Wally B.*

Lucas hired computer expert Ed Catmull in 1979. "Our charter at the time was to bring high technology into three areas—video editing, digital audio, and computer graphics," says Catmull, who alongside colleagues such as Andy Moorer, Alvy Ray Smith, and Ralph Guggenheim, made significant advancements in the technology Lucas knew his future film projects would require.

Around the same time the computer-graphics group was renamed Pixar, Catmull found a kindred spirit in former Disney animator John Lasseter, who was hired in 1984, four years after Smith was hired to head the graphics project. It was the latter's two-minute film *The Adventures of André and Wally B* (1984) that achieved a major breakthrough with the application of motion blur in 3-D computer animation.

"Once we had all the technology that we thought we needed from Pixar, I decided I didn't want to stay in the business of just manufacturing hardware and software, which is what they were doing," says Lucas, reflecting on his decision to sell the company. "I knew that John's ambitions and Ed's ambitions were not to be in that business either. They wanted to make animated movies."

In February 1986, Lucas sold Pixar to Steve Jobs, the cofounder of the Apple computer company. Already renowned for its award-winning commercials and short films, Pixar completed work on *Toy Story*, the first fully computer-animated feature film, in 1995. *Toy Story* was distributed by Disney, which also worked with Pixar on the similarly successful *A Bug's Life* (1998), *Toy Story 2* (1999), *Monsters, Inc.* (2001), *Finding Nemo* (2003), and *The Incredibles* (2004).

to realize by building sets and creating effects of the kind he had used in the original trilogy. When asked in 1989 if he had plans to commence production on a prequel trilogy soon, Lucas highlighted cost as a major obstacle: "It will be unbelievably expensive. And that's one of the things holding it up. If there was a way of doing them less expensively, it could make it easier to go ahead and do more."

In 1990, Lucas decided to put Skywalker Ranch at the center of a new project that would combine his love of history with a pioneering effort to educate children by entertaining them with fact-based adventures. Putting aside his previous aim of producing a number of feature films each year, he diverted his resources into a large-scale, long-term project that marked his first venture into live-action episodic television. The series that became known as *The Young Indiana Jones Chronicles* would expand on the 1912 prologue from *Indiana Jones and the Last Crusade* by depicting the youthful Indy's adventures and encounters with historical figures between 1908 and 1920. Lucas was determined that the various locations in Indy's globetrotting adventures should appear as authentic as possible, and asked ILM to accelerate its research by using the series to experiment with low-resolution digital effects. Lucas hoped that the result would be a show with a low budget but exemplary production values, the foundation for a multimedia educational package for schools and colleges, and a showcase for cutting-edge visual effects that he could then use for other projects.

The Young Indiana Jones Chronicles became a coproduction between Lucasfilm and the Network Television Division of Paramount Pictures. Lucas persuaded ABC to buy a first season of fifteen fifty-minute episodes sight unseen, based on his name and the *Indiana Jones* franchise. The next step was to find a producer who could coordinate the schedule and budget for what promised to be a lengthy international shoot. "I've always had the same relationship with my producers," says Lucas. "As executive producer, I hire the writers, the actors, the key people, and I hire the producer to pretty much hire everyone else and to keep the crew going from day to day and week to week."

Lucas consulted Robert Watts before traveling to London to interview the candidates. "I sat in a hotel for a week, interviewing around ten guys every day until I found who I needed," he says. The person who impressed Lucas the most had come highly recommended by Watts, and was someone whom he had encountered before. Rick McCallum reminded Lucas that the two had briefly met in 1984 on the set of *Dreamchild*, and Lucas recalled that he had been impressed by McCallum's low-budget filmmaking expertise.

During the 1980s, McCallum had produced films and television series for distinguished British writers and directors such as David Hare, Nicolas Roeg, and Dennis Potter (most notably the BBC production of Potter's *The Singing Detective*), but he was starting to tire of the constraints of the British film industry. "In England, it felt as though failure was a way of life," he says. "It was much easier to make movies at a very small cost, but ultimately nobody would see them."

Lucas spent about an hour explaining his plans for *Young Indy* and left the meeting with the impression that McCallum had an instinctual understanding of his aims. A month later, he called

Above *- Indy's mother, Anna Jones (Ruth de Sosa), and father, Professor Henry Jones Sr. (Lloyd Owen), with director Billie August, producer Rick McCallum, and child Indy (Corey Carrier) during the making of* Chapter 3: The Perils of Cupid *in 1992.*

Right *- Lucas nurses a broken arm on location for* Young Indy. *Producer Rick McCallum is by his side. Clapper loader Keegan O'Neill stands between them.*

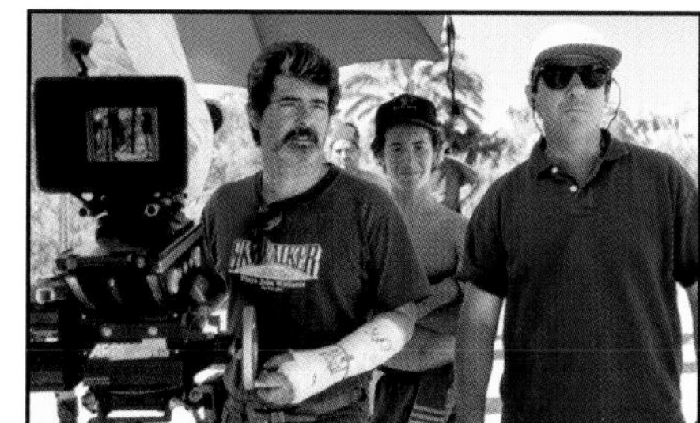

A WALK THROUGH HISTORY:
GEORGE LUCAS EDUCATIONAL FOUNDATION

* *

"The way we are educated is based on nineteenth-century ideas and methods," said Lucas in 1993. "Here we are, entering the twenty-first century, but you look at our schools today and say, 'Why are we doing things this way?' Our system of education is locked in a time capsule, and you want to say to the people in charge, 'Hey, you're not using today's tools. Wake up!'"

In 1991, Lucas's frustrations with the teaching methods that had failed to engage him as a youngster, coupled with the desire to explore how technology could improve classroom learning, led him to establish the non-profit George Lucas Educational Foundation (GLEF). Inspired by the educational potential in some of the interactive software being produced by the Computer Division, GLEF began exploring ways of enriching public education in the digital age. The philosophy of "Edutopia" (an environment where students and teachers can easily access information from beyond their school building) is promoted through TV programs, videos, CD-ROMs, and, more recently, the website www.glef.org.

Lucas: "All of us who make motion pictures are teachers."

One of Lucas's earliest aims was to use technology such as videodiscs (which were at the heart of the EditDroid system) to present multimedia lessons, accessed via computers in classrooms. The original videodisc project was given the title *A Walk through Early Twentieth Century History with Indiana Jones*, but Lucas soon saw the potential to develop the core of the idea as the television series *The Young Indiana Jones Chronicles*.

"We now realize that the best use of [GLEF's] time is as a clearing house," said Lucas in 2003, "taking the best examples of how technology is used in the educational system and disseminating that information to all the schools that want it. It's been very successful, because it's a need that hadn't been met by anybody else."

McCallum and asked him to produce the series. The working methods Lucas proposed were highly unorthodox: "What he wanted to do was to break the boundary between physical production and post-production," recalls McCallum. "He wanted to be able to have the opportunity, as a writer and creator, to send us out to do the most painful part—which for him is the shooting—then edit the film and rewrite it. To do that, we had to change the paradigm of how we make films. Normally, you get an idea, you raise the money, you shoot it, you go to postproduction, and you release it. He wanted to get rid of those divisions, add new scenes, write new dialogue, and reshoot sequences if possible. We set deals with our talent and crew that allowed us to shoot an episode, give George the time to edit it—and then add extra scenes that made the episodes better. Sometimes we would go back and shoot new scenes for an episode two or three times, which would allow him the chance to continue to write in the postproduction process. That was very exciting—and very dangerous—to do that at that particular time."

Lucas devised many of the basic stories for the series, then selected eight writers to expand those stories into teleplays. The group included Carrie Fisher, whose debut novel *Postcards from the Edge* (1987) had won widespread acclaim; veteran British film and TV writers Jonathan Hales and Rosemary Anne Sisson; and relative newcomer Frank Darabont. The writers were accommodated at Skywalker Ranch's guest quarters and given research "homework" to complete before each day's meetings.

"George had a very diverse group of writers," says Jane Bay. "They would come to the office every day and George would tell them these stories. They were based on historical information, most of which he knew but some of which came from research provided by the library. It was the first time he had collaborated with a group of people in this way, and I have never seen him happier in a creative environment."

"We all had enormous fun doing *The Young Indiana Jones Chronicles* and I think that reenergized George to a degree," says Jonathan Hales. "That and working with Rick McCallum, who was there at our first story conference before he started filming around the world. I remember Rick saying excitedly, 'We could go anywhere with this, do anything!' and that enthusiasm was certainly infectious. It was a unique working situation, and the Ranch was a fascinating working environment. I spent many years working on that series and it was a great experience. It was the best job I've ever had."

Some of Lucas's stories were quite detailed when he presented them, while others were more basic, such as, "Indy, aged nine, meets Tolstoy." As the story conferences continued, Lucas would flesh out one story per day on his favorite lined paper. "At the beginning, George had the outlines of most of the stories in mind," says Hales. "Later, he was much more open and the storylines emerged from the group working together."

"George had in mind an educational show that didn't play like an educational show but played as entertainment," Frank Darabont

Above - Three faces of the hero of The Young Indiana Jones Chronicles: *(left to right) child Indy, Corey Carrier (in* Chapter 2: Passion For Life*); Young Indy, Sean Patrick Flanery (in* Chapter 22: Hollywood Follies*); and elder Indy, George Hall (with Lucas).*

Far left *- Corey Carrier (front row) and crew on the Great Wall of China, during the location shoot of* Chapter 5: Journey of Radiance *in 1991. DP Giles Nuttgens is kneeling on far right.*

Left *- McCallum with director Robert Young during the making of* Chapter 14: Espionage Escapades *in 1991.*

says. "He wanted to let people know who Albert Schweitzer was, or who Pancho Villa was—things that we tend to ignore in this MTV-driven insane society we have, where attention spans are very short."

With Skywalker Ranch working as the creative hothouse Lucas had always hoped it would become, McCallum recruited directors and other crew members. "If you look at a normal American television show, you'll see between nine and thirteen producers," he says. "We weren't going to have that. We weren't going to have ten different companies and units; we were going to do them all as one film."

An ambitious shooting schedule was therefore devised for the first-season episodes, taking in London, Barcelona, Almeria, Kenya's Tana River, Nairobi, Prague, and various locations in India between May 1991 and January 1992. The original intention to find just two directors to handle all the filming was soon forgotten. "I couldn't find a single director who would do it for six months," says McCallum. "Then we got lucky with Carl Shultz—that was our

Above - *Young Indy (Sean Flanery) and his friend Remy (Ronny Coutteure) during the location shoot in Kenya for* Chapter 10: The Phantom Train of Doom *in 1992.*

Right - *Young Indy (left, Sean Flanery) with Colonel Paul Von Lettow-Vorbeck (Tom Bell) on location in Kenya for the* Phantom Train *episode.*

Far right - *At the post–World War I peace talks in Versailles, France: T. E. Lawrence (aka "Lawrence of Arabia," played by Douglas Henshall) and King Feisal (Anthony Zaki) in* Chapter 19: The Winds of Change.

breakthrough. He was Hungarian but had immigrated to Australia where he did a beautiful film called *Careful, He Might Hear You* (1983). We hired him to do five episodes for that first year. From that moment on, it clicked. I got all my friends: Nic Roeg, Gavin Millar, and David Hare."

Other directors would include stunt coordinator Vic Armstrong and Monty Python's Terry Jones. Mainstays of the series were British cinematographer David Tattersall and production designer Gavin Bocquet, both of whom had worked on the Yorkshire Television series *Yellowthread Street* (1990). Tattersall was at a very early stage in his career—McCallum had seen his work on a low-budget feature titled *The Bridge* (1992)—but Bocquet had been an art-department draftsman on *The Elephant Man* (1980) and *Return of the Jedi* before gaining more senior credits on *Empire of the Sun* (1987), *Dangerous Liaisons* (1988), and *Kafka* (1991). "I'd heard rumors about it before *Kafka*," says Bocquet. "So I found out who was producing it, which was Rick, and that he lived fifty yards from me in Fulham. So I went and put an envelope through his door on Christmas Eve. He'd gone on holiday to the Bahamas, so I didn't hear back for three weeks. Then he just rang out of the blue and said he was coming around; he dropped in on a Wednesday evening and looked at my portfolio—and I think he sold me to George. I think the understanding was that from *Young Indy*, George and Rick were trying to find a crew that could eventually move on to *Star Wars*. This would be a younger crew with a slightly different way of looking at it."

Lengthy auditions were held to find a Young Indy, and Lucas chose twenty-year-old newcomer Sean Patrick Flanery to play the teenage Indy. Flanery would endure an exhausting schedule as the

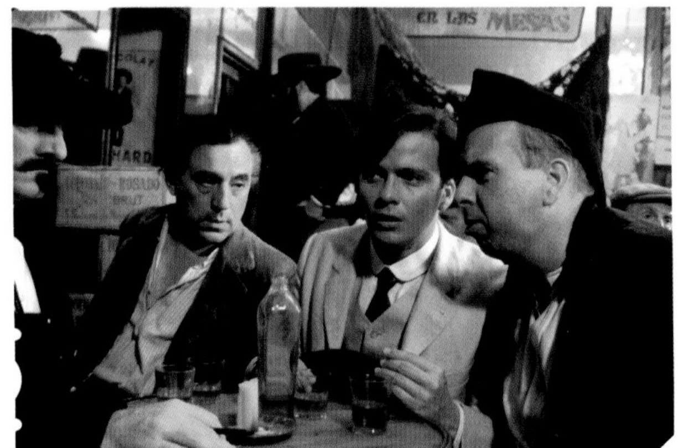

Above - Marcello (Terry Jones, who also directed) and Young Indy (Sean Flanery) flanked by other spies in Chapter 14: Espionage Escapades.

ILM AND THE DIGITAL REVOLUTION

* *

"*Jurassic Park* changed everything," says Lucas, recalling the profound impact made by the film's pioneering visual effects. Industrial Light & Magic had created a water creature for *The Abyss* (1989) and a robot that appeared to be made of liquid chrome for *Terminator 2: Judgment Day* (1991), but Steven Spielberg's dinosaur epic threw down a new gauntlet. The challenge this time was to use digital technology to create creatures that appeared to live, breathe, and move in believable ways.

Spielberg began production of *Jurassic Park* in fall 1992 with the intention of realizing the dinosaurs using a combination of puppets, animatronics, and stop-motion, with relatively little digital augmentation from ILM. He needed convincing before he would accept that technology had reached a stage where photorealistic dinosaurs were possible.

"We did a test for Steven," recalled Lucas in 1994, "and when we put [the dinosaurs] on the screen everyone had tears in their eyes. It was like one of those moments in history, like the invention of the lightbulb or the first telephone call. A major gap had been crossed, and things were never going to be the same. You just cannot see them as anything but real. It's just impossible. Maybe twenty years from now, fifty years from now, they will look clumsy. But I'm not sure even that will happen. I think we may have reached a level here where we have actually artificially created reality, which of course is what the movies have been trying to do all along." For Lucas, the success of *Jurassic Park* proved that the scenarios and creatures he envisioned for the *Star Wars* prequel trilogy were finally feasible.

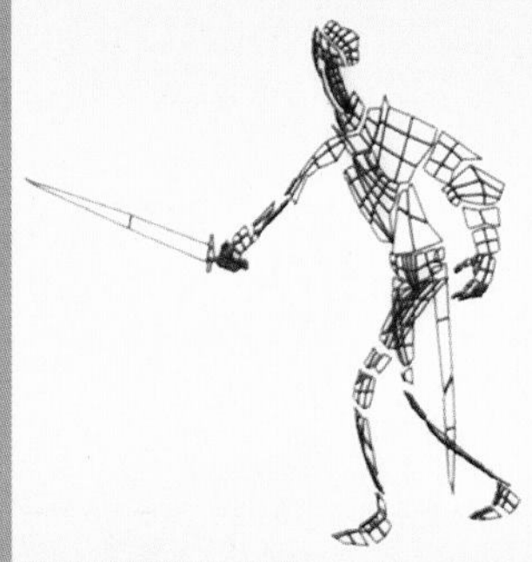

Above and right - Dennis Muren (left) works with Jeff Mann on ILM's groundbreaking "stained-glass man" from *Young Sherlock Holmes* (1985).

star of the series, while only a handful of episodes would feature ten-year-old Corey Carrier as junior Indy; flashback "bookend" scenes would show George Hall as the ninety-three-year-old Indy reminiscing.

From the outset, Lucas made it clear to his production partners that *Young Indy* would be more cerebral than the swashbuckling Spielberg/Ford trilogy. "There was a little bit of nail-biting when they actually read the scripts," he admitted in 1992, "but ABC and Paramount have been very supportive in allowing me to do what I want. This allowed me a lot of creative freedom, which I think is unique in this medium."

Lucas's plan for nonlinear filming and editing worked well from the start. Tattersall and his camera operators used 16mm film (in another effort by Lucas and McCallum to keep the budget low), and their footage was regularly dispatched to Skywalker Ranch, where it was scrutinized by Lucas and his editors. EditDroid allowed the swift and efficient preparation of rough cuts, which then evolved with the addition of extra material filmed by the roving crew.

"We shot six days a week," says McCallum. "Often from the time you left to the time you got back was fifteen, sixteen hours, day after day after day. We had to adapt to every culture. And you don't want to force them to adapt to yourself. We needed to achieve thirty or forty shots a day. That was the level—and nobody had ever worked liked that. We'd blow all our money in Italy, England, Spain, and all these expensive countries—and then we'd go back to Prague with whatever money we had left. We'd do Paris, Moscow, Vienna—every major European city there."

Young Indy also worked well in that it gave Lucas the hoped-for opportunity to experiment with low-resolution, inconspicuous digital effects. "It took a long time to transform ILM into a digital company," says McCallum, recalling some initial resistance to adapting to new methods and working in the unfamiliar medium of television. "It was a hard transformation for them, but they kept up and it happened." ILM worked alongside San Francisco–based computer-graphics company Western Images, which seamlessly extended or created buildings or added multiple horses, soldiers, and crowds.

Above left - Behind the scenes in Prague, Czechoslovakia (masquerading as Paris, France) in Chapter 19: The Winds of Change. *The train (which belonged to Archduke Franz Ferdinand, whose assassination catapulted much of the world into war in 1914) was a borrowed museum piece. Trevor Coop operates the camera being pulled by grip Pete Myslowski. Douglas Henshall plays T.E. Lawrence.*

Above right - Maya (Catherine Zeta-Jones) in Chapter 15: Daredevils of the Desert.

Right - Erich von Stroheim (Dana Gladstone) in Hollywood Follies.

Far right - Young Indy (Sean Flanery) and Albert Schweitzer (Friedrich Von Thun) in Chapter 11: Oganga, The Giver and Taker of Life.

It was decided that the show would debut with a movie-of-the-week comprising two adventures, one set in 1908 and one in 1916. Told in flashback by the ninety-three-year-old Indy, *Young Indiana Jones and the Curse of the Jackal* begins with the junior Indy accompanying his father (Lloyd Owen) on his lecture tour to Egypt, where T. E. Lawrence (Dougie Henshall) introduces him to the excitement of archaeology. The episode continues when the teenage Indy joins Mexican revolutionary Pancho Villa (Mike Moroff) and crosses paths with Lieutenant George Patton (Stuart Milligan). The two stories are linked by a precious artifact, which is stolen in one and recovered in the other.

The terms of Lucasfilm's deal with ABC gave the former no control over which day or time slot would be chosen for the new series. "ABC wanted to promote it as action-adventure," says Lucasfilm director of communications Lynne Hale, "but George kept saying, 'This is not an action-adventure show—this is a show about the intellectual growth of a boy.'"

The study guides and carefully targeted publicity campaign that Lucasfilm prepared to accompany each installment did help to build a substantial following for the show, but ABC was nervous enough about the viewing figures to take it off the air temporarily after just six episodes—though transmission of new episodes resumed in September with *Austria, March 1917*.

Filming of the second season had begun at the Carolco Studios in Wilmington, North Carolina, in May 1992. Following the initial shooting of bookend material, the first episode to go into production was *Princeton, February 1916*, in which Indy and his girlfriend Nancy Stratemeyer (Robyn Lively) investigate a theft from Thomas Edison's workshop. The episode was directed by Joe Johnston who, since being encouraged to attend USC by Lucas, had directed the feature films *Honey, I Shrunk the Kids* (1989) and *The Rocketeer* (1991). "We had a lot of fun," says Johnston. "We used historical characters, but I wouldn't say we were absolutely historically accurate, as I don't know if those two people ever met. But I think it was a valid thing to do, because we hopefully enlightened people, especially kids, about those characters."

Filming of subsequent episodes continued in diverse locations such as Ireland, England, Italy, Czechoslovakia, and Kenya; then, in December 1992, Lucas took a small crew to Wyoming to shoot bookends, featuring Harrison Ford as the fifty-year-old Indy, for the movie-length episode *Young Indiana Jones and the Mystery of the Blues.*

Above - *In 1993, Flanery and McCallum during the location shoot in Istanbul for* Chapter 17: Masks of Evil.

Above right - *Harrison Ford (Indiana Jones, age fifty) and Lucas during the former's appearance in* Chapter 20: Mystery of the Blues, *filmed on December 19–20, 1992, in Jackson Hole, Wyoming.*

Far left - *Christopher Lee as Count Ottakar, Graf Czernin, in* Chapter 13: Adventures in the Secret Service.

Left - *Camera operator Trevor Coop, first assistant director Nick Laws, and director Dick Maas on location in Istanbul, inspecting the impaled victims of Vlad IV the Impaler (aka Dracula), for* Chapter 17: Masks of Evil.

THE IRVING G. THALBERG AWARD

* *

Although Lucas is not a member of the Academy of Motion Picture Arts and Sciences, a very public recognition took place when he became the thirty-second recipient of the prestigious Irving G. Thalberg Award.

The Academy's Board of Governors offers the award in recognition of a "creative producer whose body of work reflects a consistently high quality of motion-picture production," and it does not necessarily select a recipient every year. Previous Thalberg winners include Walt Disney, Cecil B. De Mille, and Alfred Hitchcock.

Lucas received the award from Steven Spielberg—himself a winner in 1986—at the Academy Awards ceremony on March 30, 1992. A message of congratulations was later broadcast to Earth by the crew of the orbiting space shuttle *Atlantis*.

In his acceptance speech, Lucas thanked his teachers and made special reference to Francis Ford Coppola:

> ***I'd like to thank the Academy Members and the Board of Governors for this tremendous honor. Not only for myself, but for the thousands of talented men and women, robots and aliens, and others with whom I've been lucky enough to share the creative experience in the last few years.***
>
> ***Movies are not made in isolation, it's a group activity. And it's only because of the work, the very hard work, of many actors, writers, directors, producers, and creative technicians, thousands of assistants of all kinds, and projectionists, that I'm able to stand here and accept this award. I'm very, very grateful to them all.***
>
> ***I'd especially like to thank a group of devoted individuals who, apart from my parents, have done the most to shape my life—my teachers. From kindergarten through college, their struggle—and it was a struggle—to help me learn to grow and learn was not in vain. And it is greatly appreciated.***
>
> ***I've always tried to be aware of what I say in my films because all of us who make motion pictures are teachers. Teachers with very loud voices. But we will never match the power of the teacher who is able to whisper in a student's ear.***
>
> ***Thank you, Francis, for being my mentor.***
>
> ***And finally, thanks to my current and most important teachers, my two daughters. They have taught me more and enriched my life beyond anything imaginable.***
>
> ***After twenty years, this award comes at what I hope is the halfway point of my career. I assure you that I will strive to be worthy of all it signifies.***
>
> ***Thank you very, very much.***

Lucas receives the coveted Irving G. Thalberg Award from his friend Steven Spielberg at the 64th Annual Academy Awards in 1992.

FORD

ABC scheduled the 1992–93 second season of *Young Indy* after *Monday Night Football*, but the network brought its screenings of the series to a premature end with four episodes yet to air. ABC then sold its option on the series to the Family Channel, which requested four movie-length installments of the show. A third and final season was thus filmed especially for the cable channel between January and August 1994 in Thailand, Czechoslovakia, Greece, Austria, and Russia; studio work was conducted at Pinewood, England, and in the familiar Carolco Studios.

Scottish costume designer Trisha Biggar joined the team, and sound designer Ben Burtt diversified by directing and cowriting *Young Indiana Jones and the Attack of the Hawkmen*, in which Indy joins the Lafayette Escadrille flying squadron in the skies above France in 1917. "I asked George if I could do the editing on some of the episodes," says Burtt. "He knew I was interested in that, and that I had an aptitude for it. And then they gave me a chance to do some second-unit directing, which I did for several years. The directorial part of it gathered momentum and I was given whole segments of the shows with principal actors, as well as the second unit, and eventually I did one 'Movie of the Week.' I was one of the writers, I was the editor, and I was the director—so I got the chance to finally do my big student production!"

By the time principal photography on the third season came to an end, the forty-plus episodes of *The Young Indiana Jones Chronicles* had entailed over 150 weeks of shooting in more than twenty-five countries. The longest location shoot in history had generated enough 16mm film to stretch from New York to Phoenix. "The first year alone was fifty weeks of shooting," says McCallum. "There is no way to describe the relentlessness of it. There were marriages, divorces . . . unbelievable things went on."

Frank Darabont is similarly proud of his work on the show. "Like any television series, some of them were good, some of them were bad, some of them were in the middle. . . . The series was overlooked, really." Nevertheless, the series was awarded some of the television industry's highest accolades: it won ten Emmy awards and was nominated for thirteen others between 1992 and 1994, and in 1994 was nominated for a Golden Globe as Best Television Drama Series.

While the impact *Young Indy* will make on educational home entertainment remains to be seen, its impact on Lucasfilm was clear. Lucas's attempts to digitally augment and enhance live-action images were a resounding success. "There was really no such thing as digital-effects technology when we started to prep *Young Indy* in 1990, but by the first year we were achieving about a hundred digital effects shots in each episode," says McCallum. "That was an incredibly difficult period of time, because we lived in an analog world in terms of filmmaking. We did a lot of 2-D digital matte paintings. The effects were liberating—they helped us get away with things we never would have achieved with traditional filmmaking."

Left - *One of Lucas's goals for* Young Indy *was to inspire kids to learn more about historical figures. This selection features just some of the personalities sprinkled throughout the shows: (clockwise from top left) John Ford (Stephen Caffrey,* Hollywood Follies*), Al Capone (Nicholas Turturro Jr.,* Mystery of the Blues*), Prince Vlad IV the Impaler (aka Dracula, played by Bob Peck in* Masks of Evil*), Anthony Fokker (Craig Kelly,* Attack of the Hawkmen*), Lieutenant George Patton (Stuart Milligan,* Spring Break Adventure*), Halide Edib (Zuhal Olcay,* Masks of Evil*), Sidney Bechet (Jeffrey Wright,* Mystery of the Blues*), Ernest Hemingway (Jay Underwood,* Tales of Innocence*), Manfred Von Richthofen (aka The Red Baron, played by Marc Warren in* Attack of the Hawkmen*), Pancho Villa (Mike Moroff,* Spring Break Adventure*), Kemal Atatürk (Ahmet Levendoglu,* Masks of Evil*).*

Above - *Despite a limited budget,* Young Indy *managed to stage sequences such as this World War I battle from Chapter 8:* Trenches of Hell *with heightened production values.*

Right - *Young Indy (Sean Flanery) makes use of an early roadster in* Chapter 6: Spring Break Adventure.

Far right - *McCallum and Lucas behind the scenes.*

Lucas was ready to take the next step and apply what he and his collaborators had learned to a feature film. The ideal subject on which to experiment had been lying in wait for nearly twenty years—and so, in 1994, Lucas finally took *Radioland Murders* off the shelf. "Bill and Gloria started writing the scripts for it, and as time went on, we just couldn't crack it," says Lucas, who in the intervening years had commissioned Theodore Flicker to prepare a new draft. "It was a very tough film because it was a very fast-paced comedy, a throwback to a different kind of period. And it was a noncommercial idea in that it was about old-time radio and the advent of television, and these are just not hot topics. But it was a project I'd always cared about."

No longer stalled by the structural complications, montage-oriented style, and sheer scale that had made the story so daunting in 1974, Lucas confidently told Universal that ILM's newfound expertise could help bring the film in for a relatively low budget of about $10 million. Universal agreed and, on Ron Howard's recommendation, Lucas passed the project to Jeff Reno and Ron Osborn (writers and producers of the television series *Moonlighting*) for another rewrite. The final draft was prepared by Lucas, who combined his favorite elements of the Reno/Osborn draft with the original Huyck/Katz draft from 1976. The result was a riotous homage to 1930s screwball comedies:

> *Chicago, 1939: WBN is about to go national as America's fourth radio network. Chaos reigns behind the scenes as the station takes to the air, and resourceful secretary Penny Henderson struggles to hold things together. Sound engineer Max Applewhite runs the control booth with calm efficiency, and sound maestro Zoltan provides bizarre effects, but everyone else seems to let Penny down. The evening's live broadcast is hampered by ill-prepared stage performers and overworked writers (including Penny's estranged husband, Roger), but the audience is most confused by an ominous voice that interrupts the broadcast with mysterious warnings. Each message precedes a ghastly murder. As the bodies pile up, the police begin to suspect the hapless Roger. Station sponsor Bernie King is not amused.*

> *Can Roger convince Penny that he did not have an affair with the "va va va voom girl" Claudette Katsenback? Will General Walt Whalen live long enough to see his network win the war against its rivals? And will a dose of nitrous oxide give Bernie King the last laugh?*

Radioland Murders was directed by Mel Smith, a comedian well known in his native England as part of the team behind the popular sketch show *Not the Nine O'Clock News* (1979–82) and its spin-off, *Alas Smith and Jones* (1984–88). Smith then embarked on a career as a film director, beginning with *The Tall Guy* (1989). *Radioland Murders* required an emphasis on outrageous sight gags, and Lucas was convinced that Smith could handle the film's "rather extreme style."

Smith recommended Brian Benben for the role of Roger. Penny was played by Mary Stuart Masterson. The supporting cast included Ned Beatty as WBN owner General Walt Whalen; Christopher Lloyd, whose energetic performance as the seemingly

Above - *Lucas confers with director Mel Smith during a visit to the set of* Radioland Murders *in 1994.*

Far left - *Lucas with* Radioland Murders *newcomer Scott Michael Campbell (Billy).*

Left - *A zany radio play is performed with costumes, for the sake of the studio audience.*

Above - *(from left) From* Radioland Murders: *Anita Morris (Claudette Katsenback), Robert Klein (Father Writer), Brian Benben (Roger Henderson, seated), Bob Goldthwait (Wild Writer), Peter MacNicol (Son Writer), and Brion James (Bernie King).*

Right - *Christopher Lloyd as the frenetic sound effects man Zoltan.*

Far right - *Aided by two policemen, Lieutenant Cross (Michael Lerner) in a madcap search for the killer.*

possessed Zoltan was filmed in one day; and Broadway star Anita Morris as sultry chanteuse Claudette Katsenback.

Coproducer McCallum oversaw a tight schedule as *Radioland Murders* was filmed at the Carolco Studios in just seven weeks. Production designer Gavin Bocquet inventively disguised the film's limited budget by creating more than twenty architecturally interrelated rooms in a beehivelike structure. Larger areas, notably the exterior of the building and the transmission tower on the roof, were created or augmented with digital mattes added by visual-effects supervisor Scott Squires at ILM. "Fortunately, Mel had enormous faith in what we were doing," says McCallum. "Before we started shooting any scene, he would turn to us and say, 'Now tell me what I'm seeing.'"

Composer Joel McNeely started work on *Radioland Murders* unusually early, as he was required to compose and arrange some of the music performed during the inaugural broadcast. Like Lalo Schifrin many years before on *THX 1138*, McNeely demonstrated a keen attention to detail, even composing the advertising jingles that interspersed the acts, whose lyrics were provided by Jonathan Hales.

Following a break, in which Lucas, Smith, and editor Paul Trejo reviewed the footage using the new Avid digital editing system (the successor to EditDroid), the cast and crew were reassembled for a further two weeks of filming. Lucas worked alongside Smith and Trejo to prepare the final cut, and *Radioland Murders* was released on October 21, 1994.

There is a lot to admire in what must rank as one of Lucasfilm's most unusual productions. Aside from the technical innovations and glossy production values, Mary Stuart Masterson and Brian Benben are highly engaging leads, and there are numerous celebrity cameo appearances: ninety-eight-year-old George Burns makes his screen swansong as ancient stand-up comic Milt Lackey ("Retire? Who'd support my mother and father?"); Rosemary Clooney takes the stage to sing "That Old Feeling"; *Willow*'s Billy Barty is unmistakable; and *American Graffiti* stars Bo Hopkins and Candy Clark make a number of brief appearances as the proud parents of page boy Billy (Scott Michael Campbell).

"I loved the film but it went absolutely nowhere," says Lucas. "I like my movies, and I'm always surprised if they do very well or do terribly. But *Radioland Murders* was inexpensive and we learned quite a bit."

Ten days after the release of *Radioland Murders*, Lucas retreated to his office to pore over a bundle of carefully stored notes he had made more than twenty years before. With the *Journal of the Whills* by his side, Lucas started work on his next handwritten screenplay. The first page carried the title *Star Wars: Episode I.* "By this time, I was pretty much tuned in about what I was going to do and how I was going to do it," he says. "I didn't take seriously the idea of doing prequels to *Star Wars* until I had the digital technology with which to do it. I wasn't interested in doing another frustrating, imagination-inhibiting experience like *Star Wars*, where I was working around the technology and cutting back on the story. I wanted to walk around in a world I'd created, and mine its full potential. I was always interested in the backstory of where Darth Vader came from, although I never planned it to be the same kind of story as *Star Wars. Star Wars* is a plot-oriented film based on mythical motifs that had a beginning and a middle and an end. The back story is more of a résumé, it's more of a character piece about how people come to be what they are."

Lucas began to focus on the task ahead, but the writing of Episode I served as a constant reminder of the original trilogy's

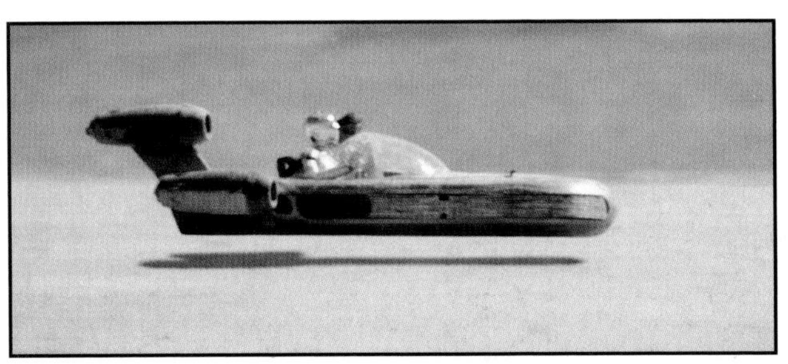

Above *- Han's encounter with a digitally composited Jabba the Hutt resolved a longstanding dissatisfaction with the original version of* Star Wars. *Boba Fett (far right) was also added to the mix.*

Left *- Lucas found a solution to another twenty-year-old problem when Luke's landspeeder was finally made to hover convincingly in the* Star Wars Special Edition.

technical shortcomings—especially *Star Wars.* The temptation to go back and fix the compromises and mistakes that pained Lucas each time he viewed the film became too strong to resist. Lucas decided to create a "Special Edition" of *Star Wars*, restored and enhanced by improved visual effects, to be rereleased on the film's twentieth anniversary in 1997. *Star Wars Special Edition* would be the most ambitious test yet of ILM's digital capabilities before Episode I entered production. "We called it an experiment in learning new technology," says Lucas, "and hoped that that the theatrical release would pay for the work we had done. It was basically a way to take this thorn out of my side and have the thing finished the way I originally wanted it to be finished."

In April 1995, Lucasfilm and Twentieth Century Fox agreed to collaborate on a new VHS video release of the *Star Wars* trilogy, with each film boasting digitally remastered picture quality and THX sound. Fox also agreed to the theatrical distribution of the *Star Wars Special Edition*, later committing to a deal that included the rerelease of *The Empire Strikes Back* and *Return of the Jedi* in "Special Edition" formats as well.

The *Star Wars Trilogy Special Edition* features a number of significant enhancements. For the entrance into Mos Eisley, Lucas was finally able to fix the "force field" area below Luke's floating landspeeder, replacing the blurry efforts to disguise the vehicle's wheels with digitally enhanced thin air. The landspeeder's approach to Mos

Above - Rebel X-wings swoop on the Death Star in another sequence that benefited from the addition of computer-generated imagery, in this case created by visual effects supervisor John Knoll (who had gained experience creating cheaper, quicker effects in ILM's work on Star Trek: Generations*, 1994).*

Right *- A computer-generated X-wing departs Yavin 4 in another augmented scene.*

Eisley received a radical overhaul, as the spaceport was transformed into a much larger area, teeming with cosmopolitan visitors, exotic droids, and lumbering beasts of burden.

Although achieved with the very latest digital technology, Lucas's efforts to draw the eye to activity at the edge of the frame and in the background dated back to *THX 1138*. Many of the other enhancements, such as those made to the Rebel attack on the Death Star, were simply efforts to create a more immaculate reality without matte lines.

The most surprising addition was the reinstatement of Han Solo's encounter with Jabba the Hutt. Lucas had reluctantly dropped the scene from Episode IV. Jabba's later realization as an obese sluglike creature in *Return of the Jedi* had given the public a distinctive image of the character, which Lucas determined to replicate in computer-generated form for the *Special Edition*. Aside from adding a satisfying symmetry to Han's storyline, the new Jabba would represent a landmark in cinema history as an entirely computer-generated character in the midst of a live-action film. The year ILM invested in the Jabba sequence would pay dividends in the making of Episode I.

The restoration of *The Empire Strikes Back* was largely restricted to upgrading the visual effects, in particular the occasional white matte lines that appear against the white snowscapes of Hoth. The Wampa ice creature is briefly glimpsed in the original film, but in the *Special Edition* a new costume with cable-controlled mechanisms was employed for additional close-ups. The *Millennium Falcon*'s approach to Cloud City was expanded with a new aerial panorama showing the bustling skylanes, in much the same way that Lucas had reconfigured Mos Eisley as a believable environment rather than simply a backdrop. The scenes set inside Cloud City were also augmented, with previously featureless corridors gaining large windows showing views of Bespin outside.

For the *Return of the Jedi Special Edition*, the Sarlacc, a subterranean creature whose gaping maw threatened Luke and his friends on Tatooine, was given extra writhing tentacles and a snapping beak. Lucas also asked John Williams to compose a new musical number—for a CG-enhanced scene that replaced the original revelries in Jabba's palace—and to write another new song to replace the one performed at the closing celebrations on the Forest Moon. Intriguingly, these celebrations now included a shot of the public rejoicing on the planet Coruscant, the seat of Imperial rule.

Above - A wide shot aboard Darth Vader's starship from The Empire Strikes Back Special Edition.

Left - The planets Bespin and Hoth receive digital makeovers in The Empire Strikes Back Special Edition, *as overseen by Lucas and visual effects supervisor Dave Carson. The trench is filled with extras shot at ILM.*

The *Star Wars Special Edition* was released on January 31, 1997. For a new generation of children and fans the event was seized as a rare opportunity to see the film on the big screen. The resulting box-office takings outstripped Lucas's wildest expectations, setting a new record for a January and February opening and taking *Star Wars*' cumulative gross to more than $400 million. The *Special Edition* soon earned the distinction of being the most successful rerelease in history. *The Empire Strikes Back Special Edition* followed it into cinemas on February 21, immediately beating its predecessor's record for a February opening, and the *Return of the Jedi Special Edition* premiered on March 14. The three films surpassed all expectations, collectively going on to become the fifth most successful domestic release of the year. It was an unprecedented feat that suggested an even more positive response awaited the release of Episode I in 1999.

The innovations in digital technology that Lucas had nurtured through *The Young Indiana Jones Chronicles*, *Radioland Murders*, and *The Star Wars Trilogy Special Edition* had helped revitalize his passion for filmmaking. "There was a cinematic innovation in the first *Star Wars* film that made people say, 'Gee, I've never seen that before,'" he said in 1997. "I have the opportunity to do that again with the prequels."

Above - The Return of the Jedi Special Edition *offers the first glimpse of the planet Coruscant, as the citizens celebrate the collapse of the Empire. Matte painter Brian Flora provided the sky and buildings.*

Right - *A computer-generated singer entertains the denizens of Jabba's palace.*

Far right - *The Emperor torments Luke aboard the Death Star with improved blue lightning.*

Shooting Schedule
The Young Indiana Jones Chronicles
* * * * * * * * * * * * * * * * *Around the World in 40+ Episodes* * * * * * * * * * * * * * * * *

Dates below are based on advanced shooting schedules and production progress reports. Not all studio shooting is chronicled, only the location shooting followed by the episode in parentheses. "Bookends" are short segments designed to introduce and end episodes. (These were discarded for the most part when episodes were combined into video movies—see Filmography on page 252. "Connectors" are scenes designed to link episodes together. Gaps in dates indicate either weekends or travel days. Concurrent and overlapping dates mean that the crew was split up into smaller production units that worked simultaneously.

SERIES I
Movie of the Week (MOW): Egypt 1908, March 1916
Episode 1: London, England 1916
Episode 2: Paris, France 1908
Episode 3: Verdun, France 1916
Episode 4: Vienna, Austria 1908
Episode 5: Paris, France 1916
Episode 6: British East Africa (BEA) 1909
Episode 7: German East Africa (GEA) 1916
Episode 8: Congo 1917
Episode 9: Benares, India 1910
Episode 10: Barcelona, Spain 1917
Episode 11: China 1910
Episode 12: Vienna, Austria 1917
Episode 13: Petrograd, Russia 1917
Episode 14: The Somme, France 1916
Episode 15: Germany 1916

May 13–31, 1991: Shepperton Studios, London, England
June 2–17: London, England (London 1916)
June 25–29: Oxford, England (London 1916)
June 30–July 1: South Wales, England (China 1910)
July 1–6: Prague, Czechoslovakia (Spain 1917)
July 9–14: Egypt (Egypt MOW)
July 15–24: Barcelona, Spain (Spain 1917 and Mexico MOW)
July 27–30: Almeria, Spain (Egypt MOW)
July 31–August 14: Almeria (Mexico MOW)
August 20–September 9: Tana River, Kenya, Africa (Congo 1917/BEA 1909/GEA 1916)
September 12–October 12: Nairobi, Africa (Congo 1917/BEA 1909/GEA 1916)
October 21–November 7: Prague, Czechoslovakia (Verdun 1916)
Note: During all shoots in Prague, interiors were often shot at Barrandov Film Studios.
November 3–15: Shanghai & Beijing, China (China 1910)
November 11–December 3: Wilmington, North Carolina—Bookends Studio Shoot
November 25, 1991–March 20, 1992: Prague, Czechoslovakia (with interruptions, various Episodes)
January 25–26, 1992: Switzerland (Location shoot)
February 3–4: Stockholm, Sweden (Vienna 1908)
February 23–March 12: Benares, India (India 1910)
March 10: Germany (Somme 1916/Germany 1916)
March 14: Vienna, Austria (Vienna 1908)
March 15: Slovakia (Location shoot)
March 18–19: Paris, France (Paris 1908 & 1916)
March 21–22: St. Petersburg, Russia (Russia 1917)
March 21–25: Prague—Pick-ups for miscellaneous episodes

SERIES II
Movie of the Week II: New York City 1920
Episode 16: Princeton 1916
Episode 17: Chicage I 1920
Episode 18: Chicage II 1920
Episode 19: British East Africa early November 1916
Episode 20: German East Africa late November 1916
Episode 21: Northern Italy 1918
Episode 22: Ireland 1916
Episode 23: Beersheba 1917
Episode 24: Istanbul 1918
Episode 25: Berlin, Germany 1916
Episode 26: Paris 1919
Episode 27: Prague, Czechoslovakia 1917
Episode 28: Transylvania 1918
Episode 29: Florence 1908

May 13–August 27, 1992: Carolco Studios, Wilmington, North Carolina (location and studio shoot for bookends, Princeton 1916, Chicago 1920, New York MOW)
September 1–23: Dublin, Ireland (Ireland 1916 and miscellaneous episodes)
September 30–October 22: Tre Cime/Tomo/Feltre/Sospirolo, Italy (Northern Italy 1918)
October 25–29: Florence, Italy (Florence 1908)
October 29–30: Pisa, Italy (Florence 1908)
November 4–December 16: Taita Hills/Mambrui/Ngong Hills/Lukenya/Hopcraft Ranch, Kenya, Africa (BEA/GEA 1916)
December 19–20: Jackson Hole, Wyoming (Harrison Ford Bookends for Chicago 1920)
January 5–February 3, 1993: Istanbul, Turkey (Istanbul 1918)
February 4–21: Cesme/Manisa, Turkey (Beersheba 1917)
February 22–April 21: Prague & Brno, Czechoslovakia (location shoot for Transylvania 1918/Germany 1916/Paris 1919/Prague 1917/miscellaneous episodes)

SERIES III
*ABC sells the series to the Family channel, which wants ninety-minute movies, not fifty-minute episodes. Four double-length episodes are therefore filmed—*Hollywood Follies 1920, Treasure of the Peacock's Eye 1919, Attack of the Hawkmen 1917, *and* Travels with Father 1909*—between January and August, 1994. Incomplete records exist for this period.*

January 17–February 23, 1994: Ventura/Fillmore, California (Hollywood Follies)
March 1–April 3: Bangkok/Phuket Thailand (*Treasure of the Peacock's Eye*)
April 20–June 5: Prague, Czechoslovakia (*Attack of the Hawkmen* and *Travels with Father*)
June 4–17: Meteora/Delphi/Athens, Greece (*Travels with Father*)
June 11–December 20: Marin County, California; Huntsville, Alabama; Portland, Oregon; Esparta, California (aircraft and miniature work for *Attack of the Hawkmen*)
July 28–August 10: Wilmington, North Carolina (Pickups/Connectors)
May 18–June 4, 1995: London, England (Pick-ups/Connectors)
February 28–May 12, 1996: Morocco (Morocco/Tangiers connectors)
August 22, 1997: Tunisia, during location shoot for *Star Wars*: Episode I *The Phantom Menace* (Pick-up for Egypt video movie)

A Young Indy *partial travelogue: (clockwise from top left) Corey Carrier at the Great Wall of China; child Indy (Carrier) and Krishnamurti (Hemanth Rao) in India; Carrier and James Gammon (Theodore Roosevelt) in Kenya; in the snow in Jackson Hole, Wyoming; Young Indy (Sean Flanery) in Istanbul; extras in Germany; Flanery and Ronny Coutteure (Remy) in Thailand; and (center) Lucas with Terry Jones in Spain.*

NAME AND ADDRESS HERE
Břeclav
SOUTH GEORGIA
CHILE
POLICIA INTERNACIONAL
PUERTO
PUNTA ARENAS

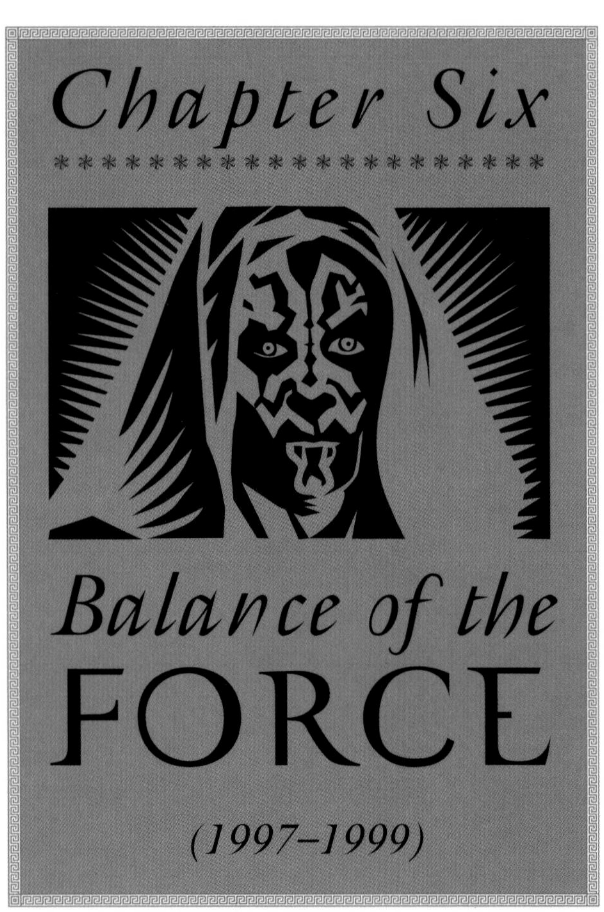
Chapter Six
Balance of the
FORCE
(1997–1999)

JEDI
ARRI
AVF-1
B

From 1995 to 1997, Lucas drafted five versions of his screenplay for Episode I. He let his imagination roam freely, creating an opulent underwater city, a marble kingdom of tranquil splendor, and a battle scene with thousands of extras. Most ambitious of all—he imagined new alien characters to play major roles throughout the story. The main narrative, a chronicle of Anakin Skywalker's earliest steps toward the dark side, was set against a backdrop of dense political intrigue. Both the images and the story would take those familiar with *Star Wars* into new, more demanding territory.

The inspiration for Episode I emerged from the back story for *The Star Wars* that Lucas had completed in the summer of 1973. He expanded the outline, weaving new characters and ideas into an epic set about thirty-two years before the events of *Star Wars*: Episode IV *A New Hope*. With meticulous forward planning, Lucas traced the story of Anakin Skywalker's tragic fall from grace. His first three films had all shown how characters imprisoned by their inhibitions had chosen a path to freedom. His next three would show that, without self-discipline, greed could force a character off the path to freedom . . .

Frustrated by the taxation of trade routes to outlying star systems, the greedy Trade Federation has blockaded the small planet Naboo. Headstrong Jedi Master Qui-Gon Jinn and his young "Padawan" apprentice, Obi-Wan Kenobi, are sent to negotiate with the Trade Federation on behalf of the Republic—but an attempt is made on their lives before the meeting begins. Qui-Gon and Obi-Wan discover an army of deadly battle droids and realize that the blockade is merely the first step in an invasion of Naboo.

They escape to the surface of the planet. As the Trade Federation begins deploying battle droids on the planet's surface, an accident-prone Gungan named Jar Jar Binks takes the Jedi to the underwater city of Otoh Gunga. Following a meeting with the Gungans' ruler, Boss Nass, Qui-Gon and Obi-Wan begin a perilous journey through the planet's watery core with Jar Jar as guide. Their submersible emerges in the kingdom of the Naboo.

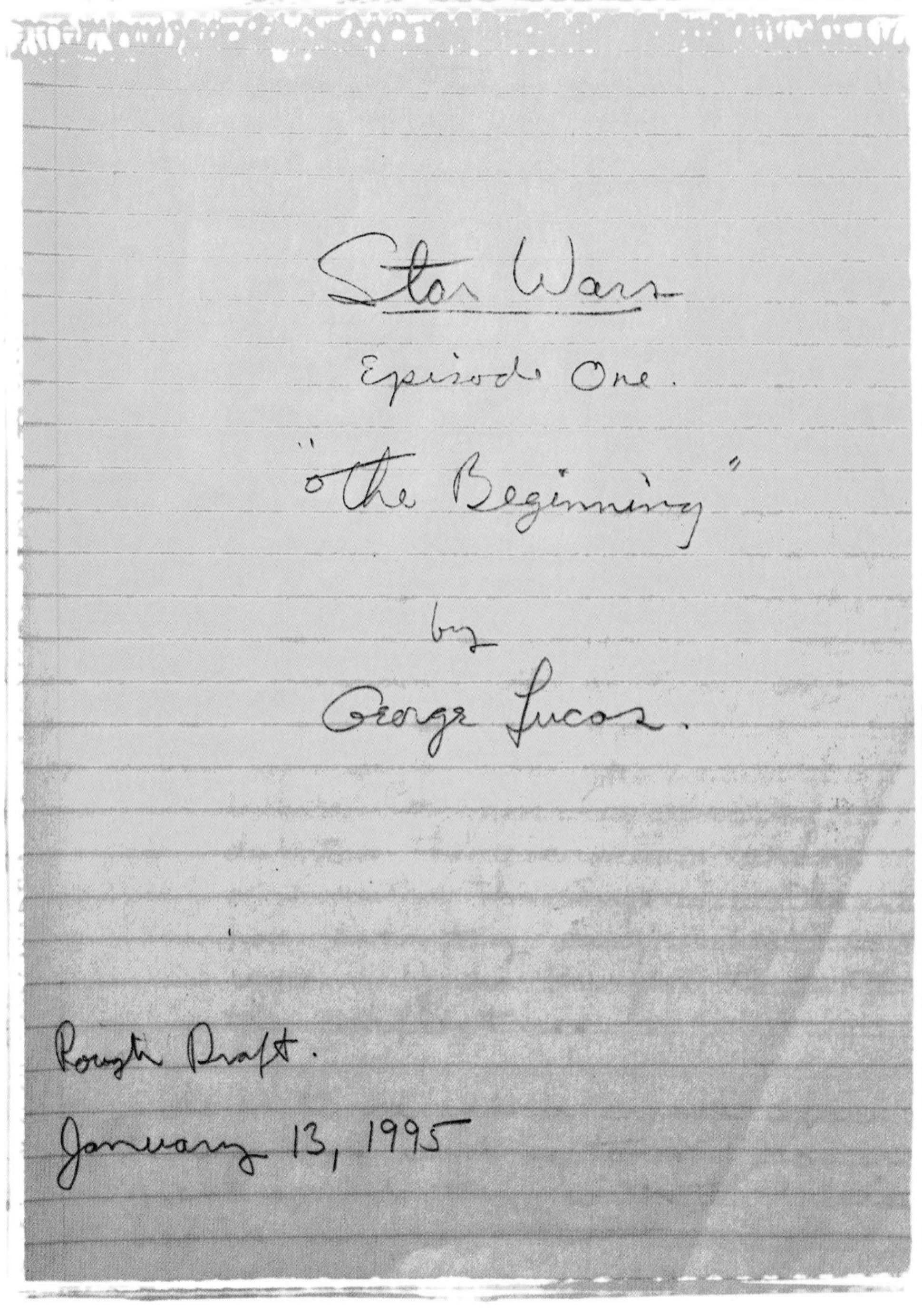

Star Wars

Episode One.

"The Beginning"

by

George Lucas.

Rough Draft.

January 13, 1995

Previous - *The return of the Jedi—Lucas on location in Tunisia for* Star Wars: *Episode I* The Phantom Menace.

Above - *Lucas's handwritten rough draft for Episode I was given the provisional title "The Beginning."*

Far left - *A proposed design for Sith assassin Darth Maul, by concept artist Iain McCaig.*

Middle - *Concept art for the opee sea killer by Doug Chiang.*

Left - *An early production painting of the swamp chase through Naboo by Tony Wright. The "trees" were designed to be the roots of one gigantic tree.*

Qui-Gon, Obi-Wan, and Jar Jar are taking Queen Amidala to Coruscant, when their ship is damaged. Although R2-D2 saves them from destruction, they are forced to land on the remote planet of Tatooine.

Qui-Gon, Jar Jar, R2-D2, and the Queen (disguised as a handmaiden) head for the township of Mos Espa to find parts to fix the ship. Junk dealer Watto has a hyperdrive generator but refuses to accept Republic credits as payment. As a sandstorm blows up, one of Watto's slaves, a small boy called Anakin Skywalker, takes Qui-Gon and his friends to the shelter of his home. Anakin shows his visitors the droid he is building to help his mother—an incomplete C-3PO.

Qui-Gon tests Anakin's blood and finds that it has the highest count of midi-chlorians ever recorded. Qui-Gon is determined to take Anakin back to Coruscant so he can be trained as a Jedi, and suggests a wager to Watto, who promises that Anakin can have his freedom if he wins a race. Despite some sabotage by rival Sebulba, Anakin pilots his Podracer around the treacherous course and wins. Anakin says a painful goodbye to his mother.

As Qui-Gon takes Anakin back to the ship, he narrowly survives a skirmish with a Sith named Darth Maul. On Coruscant, Amidala discovers that the Senate is mired in bureaucracy, and that there is little chance for her to bring about the end of her planet's invasion. She decides to take the offensive and return to Naboo.

Qui-Gon asks the Jedi High Council for its permission to train Anakin. It decides that Anakin is too old to be trained. They send Qui-Gon and Obi-Wan back to Naboo in an effort to discover more about the mysterious Darth Maul.

Amidala pleads with Boss Nass, asking that the Naboo and the Gungans unite to defend their planet. Nass agrees and Gungan troops are deployed to divert the battle droids away from the city so that Amidala and her friends can capture the Trade Federation viceroy.

As Qui-Gon, Obi-Wan, and Amidala lead the attack on the occupied royal palace, Anakin hides from the crossfire in the cockpit of a starfighter. Darth Maul appears, brandishing his twin-bladed lightsaber, and Qui-Gon and Obi-Wan step forward to meet him. An epic duel ensues, and Maul kills Qui-Gon. With R2-D2 as navigator, Anakin joins the battle in space. Meanwhile, a ferocious Obi-Wan attacks Darth Maul.

Anakin destroys the droid control ship orbiting Naboo, and all the droids on the planet's surface are deactivated. Obi-Wan slices Darth Maul in half. Qui-Gon's dying wish is that Obi-Wan should train Anakin—he believes the boy to be the Chosen One of Jedi prophecy.

The disgraced Nute Gunray is expelled. Yoda confers on Obi-Wan the status of Jedi Knight. He tells Obi-Wan that he perceives a danger in training Anakin, but the Jedi Council allows the boy to become Obi-Wan's Padawan. As the celebrations on Naboo begin, Chancellor Palpatine places a paternal hand on Anakin's shoulder. He looks down at the boy and says, "We will watch your career with great interest."

Lucas was aware that the complex narrative of the new film would surprise audiences almost as much as the ten-year-old hero. "I didn't want to do the craziness or, as someone once described it, the 'effervescent giddiness,' of the first film," he

Above - Concept art of a Podracer by John Bell.

Right - Concept art of the disguised Padmé Amidala by Iain McCaig.

Far right - A Doug Chiang production painting of the Queen's starship on Naboo, with a Gungan in the foreground.

says. "I knew the story eventually had to go to a dark place, so I purposely darkened it down. I realized early on that the original trilogy was a plot-driven story, a fable. The new trilogy is a history, a back story, a personal dossier on all these characters."

The thread running through Episodes I to III would shed light on Lucas's intended interpretation of Episodes IV to VI—all six *Star Wars* films would tell the story of Anakin Skywalker, from his childhood in slavery and his earnest struggle to become a Jedi to his tyrannical rule as Darth Vader and ultimate redemption by his own children.

"Nobody ever thinks of themselves as bad," says Lucas, using Anakin's rise and fall as a metaphor for the personal development of real-life despots. "They simply have different points of view, and that's something that's alluded to by Obi-Wan in Episode IV. Anakin has flaws, and those flaws ultimately do him in. Those flaws are hard to see in Episode I, but they are there."

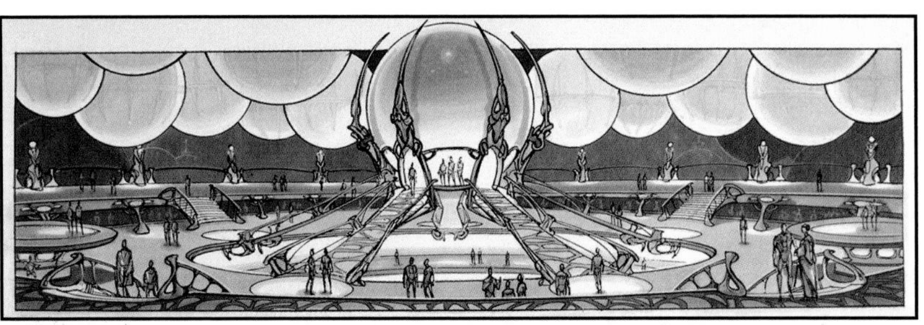

Above *- The opee sea killer attacks the bongo sub, in a production illustration by Doug Chiang.*

Far left *- A Theed power generator painting by Jay Shuster.*

Left *- The underwater world of Otoh Gunga by Marc Gabbana.*

In the midst of the innovative design and effects work, Lucas included a number of familiar motifs and scenarios in his script for Episode I. The race would be almost entirely computer generated, but it has much in common with the car chase in *THX 1138* and the head-to-head race at the climax of *American Graffiti.* The mastery of a high-powered vehicle—in this case Anakin's impossibly fast Podracer—becomes a rite of passage once again. Just as THX 1138 uses a stolen car to escape the underground city, Anakin's triumph earns him his freedom from slavery.

The scene in which Qui-Gon leads Anakin away from that life of slavery also has clear antecedents in Lucas's previous screenplays. When Anakin embarks on his uncertain life among the Jedi, he begins the same test of resolve that THX 1138 endures in the white limbo, the same path Curt follows when he boards the plane that will take him to college, and the same journey Luke begins when he agrees to accompany Ben Kenobi and learn the ways of the Force. Shmi tells her son: "The path has been placed before you. The choice is yours alone." When Anakin makes his decision, she tells him to "Be brave, and don't look back." This seemingly insignificant line of dialogue encapsulates not only this pivotal moment but also the underlying message in all of Lucas's screenplays.

It was decided that the look of Tatooine would remain faithful to the style established in *Star Wars.* The look for Coruscant was also inspired by illustrations created during the preproduction of *Return of the Jedi,* even though they were never realized at the time. "We went back and fleshed out those designs," says concept designer Doug Chiang. "Coruscant had been developed to a degree [under its original name Had Abbadon], but never shown."

Ralph McQuarrie, the artist who had painted the original illustrations of Tatooine and Had Abbadon, visited Chiang during preproduction of Episode I. "He was just the most gracious, gentle person," remembers Chiang. "George had said that we would need to design Tatooine and Coruscant, and those were the two places Ralph had already designed, so I deliberately didn't do any work on them in the hope that Ralph would want to do them. But he was

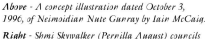

Above - *A concept illustration dated October 3, 1996, of Neimoidian Nute Gunray by Iain McCaig.*

Right - *Shmi Skywalker (Pernilla August) councils her fatherless son, Anakin Skywalker (Jake Lloyd).*

Far right - *In another Episode I pairing, Sith apprentice Darth Maul (Ray Park) stands behind Darth Sidious.*

very modest, and just said, 'You guys are doing a great job—just keep going.' I could respect that but I was kind of heartbroken."

The formal announcement that Lucas intended to direct Episode I came as a surprise to many who had assumed his directing career was over. He had, however, always intended to make his "comeback" with Episode I, and had spent a significant amount of time on the sets of Episodes V and especially VI. "As much as I wanted to hand over the last two films to other directors, I ended up being there all the time and I had to work as hard as if I were directing anyway," he said in 1999. "The other reason I wanted to direct Episode I was that we were going to be attempting new things; and, in truth, I didn't quite know how we were going to do them–nobody did. So I figured I needed to be there at all times."

Joining Lucas and producer Rick McCallum were production designer Gavin Bocquet, director of photography David Tattersall, and costume designer Trisha Biggar—all three veterans of *The Young Indiana Jones Chronicles.* Casting director Robin Gurland began looking for actors to recommend to Lucas in 1995, long before he had completed work on his script. She initially concentrated on the story's two youngest leads: ten-year-old Anakin Skywalker and fourteen-year-old Padmé Amidala. Gurland interviewed more than three thousand children for the role of Anakin, but George selected just three to attend a screen test at Skywalker Ranch in March 1997. Ultimately, Lucas chose Jake Lloyd, who was just five years old when Gurland had first met him two years earlier. Fortunately, Lucas's most recent revisions of the script had lowered Anakin's age to nine, meaning that Lloyd would be much closer to the right age when filming began.

The potential Anakins were screen-tested alongside Natalie Portman, whom Lucas had already cast as Padmé Amidala. The sixteen-year-old Portman had made an impressive film debut in Luc Besson's *The Professional* (1994).

Gurland next turned her attention to the Jedi team, Qui-Gon Jinn and Obi-Wan Kenobi. Lucas first saw Qui-Gon as being played by an American actor in his sixties, but changed his mind when he met Liam Neeson. The forty-three-year-old Irish actor had recently been nominated for an Academy Award and a Golden Globe for his performance as Oskar Schindler in Spielberg's 1993 film *Schindler's List.* "He was tall and very strong, with a powerful nature," said Lucas in 1999. "And, like Alec Guinness in the original movies, he was an actor that other members of the cast looked up

Above left *- Producer Rick McCallum raises the clapperboard for the first shot at Leavesden Studios on Thursday, June 26, 1997. Note that the director is listed as "Yoda."*

Above right *- Ewan McGregor was cast as young Obi-Wan Kenobi.*

Left *- Other key decisions cast Jake Lloyd as child Anakin Skywalker (far left) and Natalie Portman as Queen Amidala (middle). Anthony Daniels reprised his role as C-3PO.*

to." In preparing for the role, Neeson watched all three *Star Wars* films and Kurosawa's *The Seven Samurai.*

Thoughts of Sir Alec were never far from Lucas's mind as he considered the various options to play the young Obi-Wan Kenobi. Gurland's shortlist for the role comprised actors who bore a certain resemblance to Guinness during his time in the Ealing Studios comedies. Lucas was most impressed by twenty-five-year-old Ewan McGregor. Lucas was amused to learn that McGregor's uncle was actor Denis Lawson, who had appeared in the small role of Wedge Antilles in all three of the *Star Wars* films. McGregor was offered the part of Obi-Wan, and began voice lessons to help him reproduce Guinness's distinguished tones.

Swedish actress Pernilla August was cast as Shmi Skywalker, although Lucas had originally wanted an English actress. Pernilla had featured in the Northern Italy, June 1918, episode of *Young Indy*, but this had been a rare English-speaking role. "It's very hard to play in another language," she said during production. "George Lucas was so sweet the first time we met. I said, 'What about my accent? What should I do about it?' He said, 'Don't worry about it. She's coming from a Swedish galaxy.'"

Anthony Daniels returned to voice C-3PO, Kenny Baker climbed back inside R2-D2 for the shots not performed by the radio-controlled versions of the droid, and Frank Oz once again brought Yoda to life. Anakin's friend Wald, who resembled a junior version of the bounty hunter Greedo from Episode IV, was played by Warwick Davis. The only actor from the original trilogy to actually appear in any recognizable form was Ian McDiarmid. Since playing the Emperor in *Return of the Jedi*, McDiarmid had guest-starred in *The Young Indiana Jones Chronicles* and won acclaim as one of the artistic directors of London's Almeida Theatre.

"It's thrilling for me to be able to cast excellent actors such as Terence Stamp, who plays Chancellor Valorum, Ralph Brown as the Naboo pilot Ric Olie, Oliver Ford Davies as Sio Bibble, and Hugh Quarshie as Captain Panaka," said

Right *- Lucas with Ian McDiarmid, the only recognizable face from the original* Star Wars *trilogy, who returned to play Senator Palpatine.*

Far right *- Lucas chose Liam Neeson to play Qui-Gon Jinn. He and Lucas take shelter from the Tunisian sun, which sometimes raised the temperature to a sizzling 135 degrees Fahrenheit or more. Lucas wears a T-shirt sporting a critical definition of the words "Star Wars"—which everyone on the cast and crew received as a gift.*

Gurland in 1999. "These were smaller roles that, typically, they wouldn't do. But because they all wanted to work with George, everyone said, 'Absolutely! No question!'"

Even the more inconspicuous roles attracted some major talents: Brian Blessed voiced the blustering Boss Nass with characteristic gusto, and Andy Secombe delivered Watto's lines in a suitably sniveling fashion. The Trade Federation's devious viceroy, Nute Gunray, was played by Silas Carson, who voiced the character with a Transylvanian accent, thus emphasizing his corporate vampirism. Although Jar Jar Binks would be entirely computer generated in the finished movie, Lucas asked actor and dancer Ahmed Best to portray the character during filming. Best's carefully choreographed body movements would provide reference points for the digital artists at ILM, but Lucas was so impressed with the way Best spoke Jar Jar's patois-style lines that he asked him to voice the character as well. The creation of the accident-prone Jar Jar, the first entirely digital character to play a leading role in a *Star Wars* film, would prove to be ILM's greatest challenge to date.

Lucas was determined that Episode I would be produced without any studios breathing down his neck, but that independence came at a price. Lucas's original estimation that Episode I could be produced for between $60 and $70 million proved optimistic. The final cost would be closer to $115 million. The film would be offered to potential distributors only when it was finished. The project represented a financial investment as great—if not greater—than the risks Lucas had taken with making *The Empire Strikes Back* and building Skywalker Ranch.

"When you're making a $100 million movie and it's your own money—pretty much all the money you've got—there's a huge risk," says Lucas. "Studios can take that risk and then write it off onto something else. I didn't have anything else. If I didn't get my money back on Episode I, I wouldn't have been able to make Episode II, and so forth. I was gambling everything again."

Left - On location, the crew set up a shot of Mos Espa. 'A' camera operator Trevor Coop (on crane) looks down at key grip Peter Myslowski, both of whom are Young Indy *veterans.*

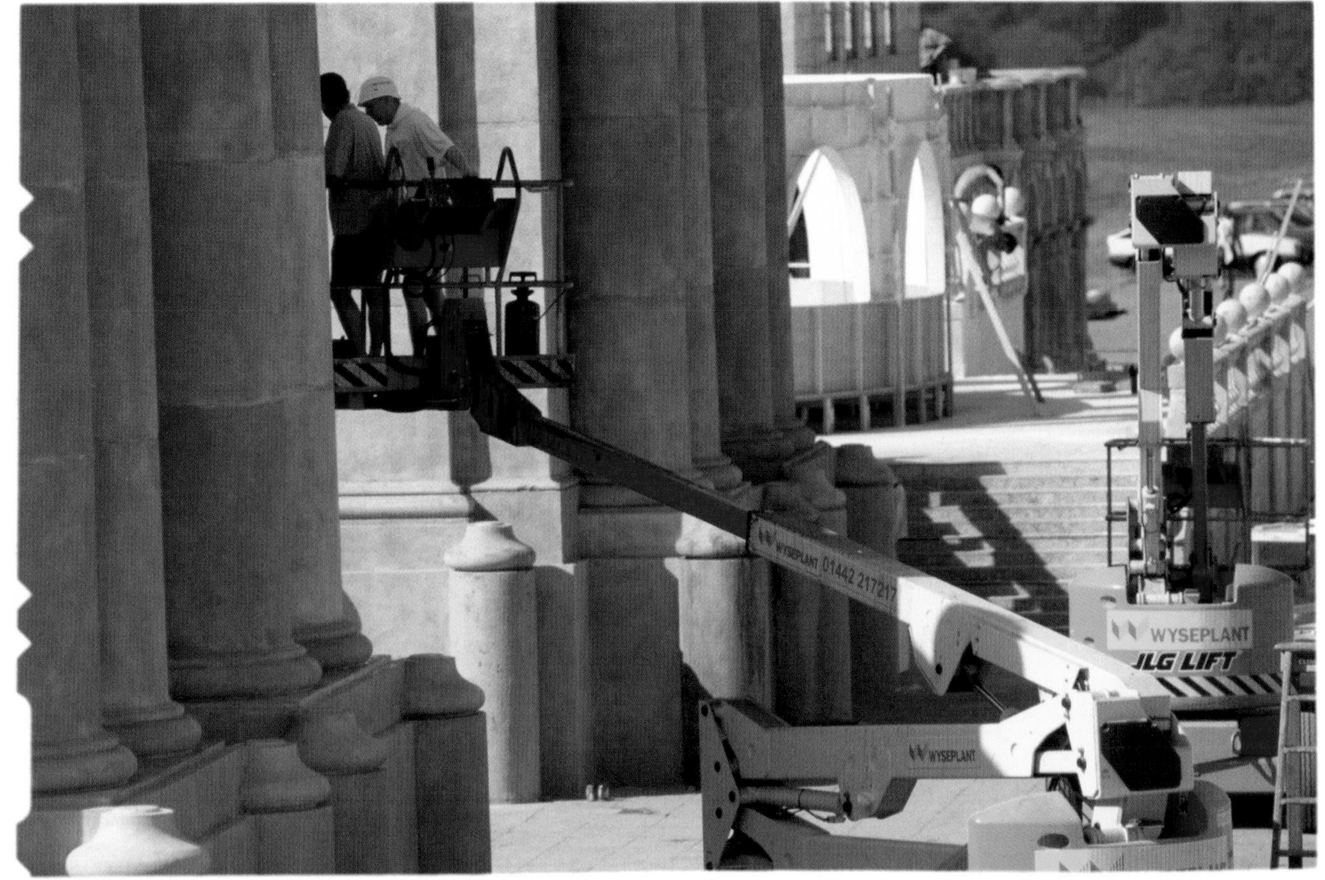

Producer Rick McCallum was entrusted with the budget and schedule for the most expensive independent film in history, and began preparing before Lucas even started work on his script. An exploratory visit to Elstree Studios confirmed suspicions that what was left of the facility was not big enough to accommodate Episode I. McCallum needed something five or six times as big, but he found a novel solution to the problem at a former Rolls-Royce factory twenty miles outside central London. The facility and a disused runway were situated on the 286-acre Leavesden Aerodrome. The factory had closed in 1993 and been converted for use as a studio the following year. The James Bond film *GoldenEye* (1995) was the first movie to occupy the specially built stages and 100-acre backlot.

Lucasfilm formed a new subsidiary to produce Episode I, and Lucas created its name from the first initials of his three children: Jett (whom Lucas adopted in 1993), Amanda, and Katie. JAK Productions Ltd. booked Leavesden for two-and-a-half years, beginning in summer 1996. The protracted lease would allow JAK to use the building as a preproduction base and enable Lucas to return to the standing sets for additional photography once the main shoot was over.

Bocquet's art department moved into Leavesden in August 1996 and was followed by the "Creatures Department," headed by Stuart Freeborn's erstwhile assistant, Nick Dudman. The Creatures Department would create the masks and prosthetics for the alien characters to be realized in the traditional way, such as Yoda and the Neimoidians. At around the same time, Biggar and her team started work on the first of more than one thousand costumes.

Set construction commenced in December 1996 with the interior of Anakin's home. Fifty-four sets would be built across eight sound stages in the 800,000 square feet available. Aware that many of these sets would be digitally augmented by ILM in post-production, Bocquet designed a number of walls that were only slightly higher than the tallest actors. Almost three-quarters of all the scenes would include at least a partial blue screen.

The script was still undergoing significant revisions in early 1997, some of which were due to some last-minute casting decisions. In December 1996, Samuel L. Jackson, famed for his appearances in such films as *Pulp Fiction* (1994) and *Die Hard: With a Vengeance* (1995), appeared on the British chat show *TFI Friday.* Aware that preparations were being made to film Episode I

Above - The Theed main plaza under construction at Leavesden Studios.

Left - Director of photography David Tattersall, another Young Indy *veteran, consults with Lucas, who returned to directing after an absence of twenty-one years.*

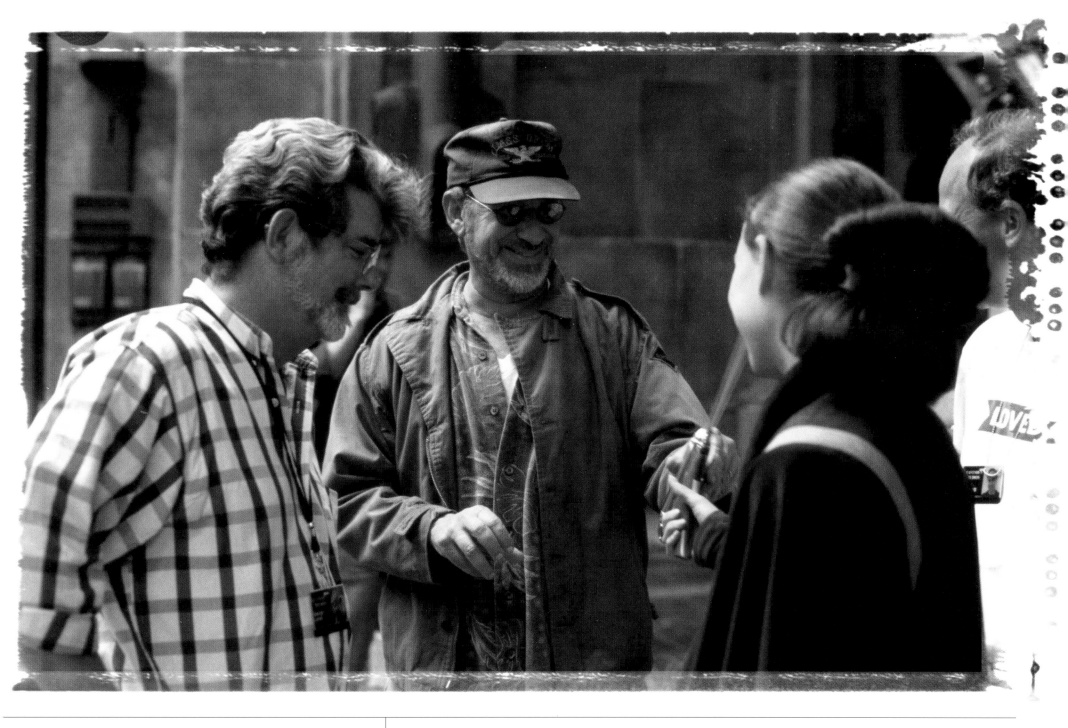

Above - *Spielberg shares a joke with Lucas and Natalie Portman (Queen Amidala) during a visit to Leavesden.*

Right - *Two modelers work on the interior of a Podracer at Leavesden.*

Far right - *At Leavesden, (from left) first assistant director Chris Newman, documentary logger Tim Clayton, Lucas, and special effects supervisor Peter Hutchinson watch a Flash speeder gun test.*

at Leavesden, Jackson told interviewer Chris Evans that he had been a *Star Wars* fan since 1977 and would love to appear in the new film. When Lucas heard about Jackson's on-air plea to be considered, he revived the character Mace Windu, who had first appeared in the early drafts for Episode IV, and offered it to the actor. The casting of stuntman and martial arts expert Ray Park as Darth Maul had a similarly profound effect, as Park's skill and dexterity prompted Lucas and stunt coordinator Nick Gillard to expand Maul's role, especially in the final duel with Qui-Gon and Obi-Wan. Park shaved his head in preparation for the striking red and black makeup that would make Maul an enduring icon.

Gillard rehearsed the complicated lightsaber movements with the actors, mindful of Lucas's instructions that the new trilogy would employ different fencing techniques from those seen in the original. "We'd never actually seen real Jedi at work," said Lucas. "We'd only seen old men and crippled half-droid half-men and young boys who learned from these people. So to see a Jedi fighting, in the prime of the Jedi, I wanted it to be a much more energetic and faster version of what we'd done before."

As preproduction continued, Lucas planned to make Episode I the first live-action feature shot without film. The difficulties of integrating the digital additions to the *Star Wars Special Edition* had strengthened his resolve to implement a new system for Episode I. Given the new film's proliferation of digital effects, Lucas wanted to make the whole movie using a digital medium. Episode I would not be filmed, but rather recorded directly to high-capacity hard discs. As usual, the developing technology struggled to keep pace with Lucas's imagination, and it proved impossible to develop satisfactory results for the widescreen format. Tests on the new system would, however, continue through 1997.

On June 26, 1997—almost exactly twenty years after principal photography on *A New Hope* ended—Lucas called "Action" on Episode I. The first scene in the can was Darth Sidious's briefing of Darth Maul on a balcony overlooking Coruscant. The call sheets carried the working title *Star Wars*: Episode I—*The Beginning*, and detailed a schedule that McCallum had pared to the bone. More than 3,700 camera setups would have to be completed in just sixty-five days. McCallum maintained a constant presence

Above *- Darth Maul (Ray Park) duels Qui-Gon Jinn (Liam Neeson, far left) and Obi-Wan Kenobi (Ewan McGregor, far right). McGregor trained throughout principal photography and was in tip-top form for his dueling scenes, which occurred at the end of the shoot.*

Far left *- An early Darth Maul character concept by Iain McCaig.*

Left *- Darth Maul (Ray Park) vents his frustration, a Sith characteristic.*

throughout the shooting, reminding everyone from the extras to the director of the importance of staying on schedule. "The great thing about Rick is that he never says 'no,'" says Lucas, describing how he granted shouting privileges to one of his own employees. "He will screw his face up into a painful look—that's when I know I've gone too far—and he will eventually come back to me having found a way it can be done. I know a lot of directors who don't have the luxury of hiring their own producers, and if you have a producer foisted upon you, it can undercut everything you're trying to do. The great thing about Rick is that he can do the impossible. If I say I don't want to shoot a particular scene tomorrow but that I want to do something else, he'll say OK. He'll then work all night and move it all around so we can get it done."

McCallum is frank about his relationship with Lucas during filming: "Often he can be stubborn and he will hold on to a position. He doesn't paint himself in a corner, he just believes it. If you're a good producer, I think that at the end of the day your job—your talent, if you have any—is to enable a director to achieve everything that he can within the confines of the schedule, money, and all the other compromises that you have to make. And, ultimately, you want him to have the best. You want him to win."

The reconnaissance trips McCallum had overseen began to pay off in July, when Lucas took the main unit from England to Italy to film at the Reggia Palace, Caserta, northeast of Naples. The marble palace, which doubled for Queen Amidala's royal palace at Theed, possessed an awe-inspiring splendor that would have been pointless to re-create digitally. Lucas made special virtues of the grandiose windows and 116-step staircase.

Natalie Portman sprained her ankle during the four days of filming in Italy, but this proved to be a minor inconvenience compared to the problems Lucas and McCallum faced when location filming moved to Tunisia. A construction crew had been sent in advance of the main unit to build six sets, including the smaller buildings of Mos Espa and segments of the Podrace arena (most of which would be created digitally by ILM). Fifty tons of materials,

Above *- In Tozeur, producer Rick McCallum (on walkie-talkie) managed to keep production on schedule despite a devastating sand storm that pulverized nearly all the sets and Podracers. The landing ramp of the Queen's ship survived in good enough shape to be filmed on while the production crew quickly repaired the other sets.*

Right *- Sebulba's Podracer engines before and (far right) after the storm hit. From left to right: second assistant director Roger Christian, Lucas, scenic artist James Gemmill, and financial controller Kathryn Ramos.*

including equipment, props, and costumes, had been flown to the desert location fifteen miles outside Tozeur in preparation for the anticipated two weeks of filming. As before, the weather proved to be one of Lucas's biggest obstacles: temperatures of between 130 and 145 degrees gave way to a devastating storm, which broke on July 29. Winds of 120 mph whipped up driving rain and sand, tearing through the wooden frames supporting the sets and destroying the tents housing costumes and props. "I had been through the same experience on the first *Star Wars*," said Lucas philosophically in 1999. "It was as if the storm had hidden away for twenty years, just waiting to come back. When we started to hear thunder, I asked Rick, 'What are we going to do tomorrow?' And he said, 'Don't worry—we'll shoot.' But he was being optimistic."

When it was safe to survey the damage, McCallum pronounced it to be "heartbreaking." Nevertheless, the director and producer rapidly reorganized filming to take place on the one surviving set, while McCallum looked for ways to rebuild the others. "In a perverse sense, the sandstorm was fun," he said in 1999. "The entire crew had to quickly pull together and improvise. The adrenaline was rushing through everybody's veins, and soon an almost military feeling overtook the set. Creature designers and cameramen worked to dig equipment out of the sand. Makeup artists and caterers worked to patch together shelter from the sun. And we didn't lose a day of shooting."

Things went more smoothly once the production returned to Leavesden, where Bocquet had used the main unit's absence to erect new sets. Following further location work at nearby Whippendell Wood, which doubled for the rural exterior of Naboo, the main unit returned to Leavesden, where principal photography wrapped on September 30.

ucas has always regarded the postproduction phase of his films to be the most gratifying. He would divide the editing of Episode I between Paul Martin

Left - The climactic space battle.

Right - Surveying a maquette of Mos Espa are, among others: Lucas (center), Tattersall (crossed arms), and another Young Indy *veteran, production designer Gavin Bocquet (second from right).*

Smith (another *Young Indy* veteran) and *Star Wars* luminary Ben Burtt when compiling various rough cuts over the next eighteen months (Burtt would also take on his traditional role as sound designer). Smith took responsibility for the dialogue-heavy scenes, while Burtt handled the action sequences. Episode I would have the most protracted postproduction period of any movie Lucas had ever directed in order to give ILM the time to complete its work. About 1,900 of the film's ultimate 2,200 shots would feature visual effects, so ILM designated the work to three visual-effects supervisors: John Knoll's team was given the responsibility for the Mos Espa Podrace and space battle sequences, Dennis Muren's team handled the underwater and ground battle sequences, and Scott Squires's team handled the energy beam, hologram, and lightsaber effects. The latter proved especially painstaking during the final duel, for which Squires and his digital artists expanded the small section of the generator room set built at Leavesden into a virtual room six hundred feet in length, complete with a pit to receive the sliced body of Darth Maul.

Muren was one of only a handful of Lucasfilm stalwarts who had worked on the production of the first *Star Wars.* "I was really surprised when George said he was going to do three more films, because I'd been hearing about it for years and years," he says. "I did a couple of big sequences and I had a really good time, but it was a lot different. Except for working with George, it wasn't much like working on *Star Wars.* The cast was all new, the creatures were all new, and the spaceships were all new, so it was really a different type of film. I know every little nook and cranny of the *Millennium Falcon* and the X-wings from working on those other shows, but Episode I had a whole new set of aesthetics. What was interesting was the enthusiasm of all the other ILMers who had grown up watching *Star Wars* and who were now working on Episode I. There was a constant buzz everywhere because people were so excited."

Above *- The reflective chrome surfaces of the Theed hangar recall Lucas's student film* Herbie.

Far left *- Dennis Muren supervised the ambitious computer-generated sequence that pitted thousands of Gungans against thousands of battle droids.*

Left *- Michael Lynch built and operated Episode I's skeletal C-3PO.*

DIGITAL CHARACTERS

* *

Robin Gurland saw actor Ahmed Best perform in the percussion-based theater show *Stomp* and recommended him to Lucas as someone with the dexterity and choreography skills necessary to act as the physical basis for Jar Jar Binks.

Live-action creature effects supervisor Nick Dudman and his team created a tight-fitting bodysuit for Best to wear during filming, and a hatlike headpiece that ensured the other actors in the production maintained the correct eye-line with Jar Jar. The bodysuit would provide ILM with lighting references from the set for when they came to replace Best with a computer-generated image.

Creating lifelike skin and muscular movements for Jar Jar was not the only challenge Lucas set for ILM. "George kept saying, 'We're not doing naked aliens in space,'" says animation director Rob Coleman. "The characters had to have clothes, leather props, swords, and other weapons."

"Jar Jar's constant presence in that film as an all-digital character was a real opportunity for us, both on an acting front and on a compositing front," says former ILM executive producer Patty Blau. "His interaction with the live-action characters and the other computer-graphics characters involved incredibly complex problem-solving. We were forced to accomplish all these things on Episode I and it was a very valuable experience."

Lucas is proud of the fact that Episode I effectively introduced digital characters to live-action filmmaking. "We made Jar Jar, Sebulba, and Watto believable characters who could act," he says. "And that opened the door for everybody else, whether it was *Lord of the Rings* or *Harry Potter*. Before *The Phantom Menace*, you couldn't create a character that was lifelike and have it do a performance. Pixar were the first to do it in a cartoon style, but even they hadn't attempted to do anything that was photorealistic."

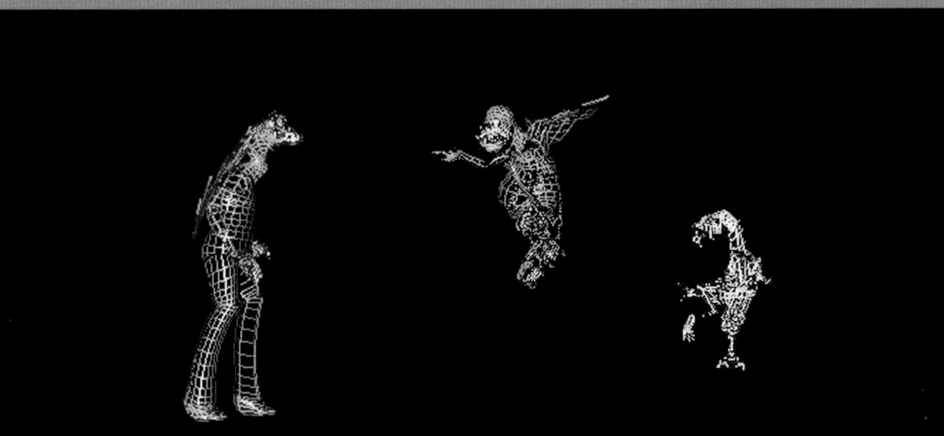

Four images show some of the steps to put digital character animation (Jar Jar, Watto, and Sebulba) into a live-action plate: (top left) a live-action plate; (bottom left) wire-frame figures are added; (top right) cloth simulation, skin, etc. is added; (bottom right) final frame.

Animation director Rob Coleman was responsible for the film's computer-generated characters, the most notable of which was the ubiquitous Jar Jar Binks. "From my point of view the biggest accomplishment on Episode I was the combination of realistic animation and live action," he says. "Having characters like Watto, Jar Jar, and Sebulba really interacting with the live actors. That was really important to me, and I know that was really important to George. He'd always wanted to be freed of the puppetry, animatronics, and cables. That was a wonderful experience, and I'm certainly glad to be sitting here having survived it."

The advancements made in digital filmmaking gave Lucas unprecedented flexibility during editing, as Burtt recalls. "It was common for George to look at a scene that had been cut together and say, 'I'd like to change the position of that actor—move him to here.' Or he would ask to modify the set in some way. Because of the technology we used to edit the film, we were able to manipulate everything in the frame. We could immediately interpret what George wanted to see."

In April of 1998, it was confirmed that Twentieth Century Fox would distribute the new trilogy in a deal reputed to earn Lucasfilm an unprecedented share of box-office proceeds. Expectations ran so high that Fox purchased the rights to the as-yet-untitled film sight unseen.

Lucas completed the first rough cut of Episode I the following month, and screened it for friends such as Joe Johnston and Lawrence Kasdan to gauge their opinions. Lucas had already returned to Leavesden for a round of pick-up shots and additional photography in March (which had been part of the original schedule and budget for the film); in August, he would return for another week of shooting based partly on issues he had identified from the rough cut. The second-unit pick-ups had special significance because they were Lucas's first opportunity to shoot material using a high-definition digital format. The prototype camera was used only for a few scenes, but the results were indistinguishable from film and integrated seamlessly with the existing footage. His confidence renewed, Lucas predicted that both Episodes II and III would be recorded digitally.

Above *- Digital camera matchmover Jack Haye holds camera reference material next to the Yoda puppet on the Jedi Council set.*

Far left *- A Yoda costume concept by McCaig.*

Left *- Yoda (voiced by Frank Oz) and Mace Windu (Samuel L. Jackson) during the cremation of Qui-Gon Jinn on Naboo.*

In September, Lucasfilm revealed that Episode I would be titled *The Phantom Menace*, in keeping with the *Star Wars* films, which had always carried melodramatic titles inspired by 1930s matinee serials. When the first trailer made its public debut seven days later, there were numerous reports of fans buying tickets to see the previews and leaving before the main program began. In London, Fox arranged a special screening of the trailer at the Leicester Square Odeon, and ended up running it twice to satisfy the packed house of applauding journalists. Delighted by the response, Lucas whetted the fans' appetites further by promising that Boba Fett would appear in Episode II. The second trailer made its debut on Lucasfilm's website, www.starwars.com, on March 11. There was a record 3.5 million downloads on the first day.

As ILM raced to meet its April 23, 1999, deadline, John Williams assembled the London Symphony Orchestra at EMI's Abbey Road Studios. The scoring sessions, which took place over eight days in late January, gave Lucas his first chance to hear Williams's completed score, which adopted the lyrical, leitmotif style familiar from the original films. Mindful that his contribution would be one of the crucial elements of consistency across the projected six-episode saga, Williams incorporated echoes of the themes he had composed for Episodes IV to VI. These included a brief reminder of his theme for Darth Vader in his new theme for Anakin.

Footage from the recording sessions was subsequently cut to a selection of clips from the film that accompanied "Duel of the Fates," the stirring theme that plays over the end credits. Williams's operatic combination of chorus and orchestra lent a quasi-religious feel to the climactic confrontation with Darth Maul, and served as an evocative promotional tool for the film on MTV.

Burtt completed the final sound mix in March, incorporating the thousand new sound effects he had created especially for the film, while ILM delivered the final visual effects on schedule in April. Chrissie England, ILM's visual-effects executive producer on Episode I, had seen progressively less of Lucas since her days at Parkway in the 1970s. "I would only see George at company parties and that sort of thing, so it was great to have him around on Episode I," she says. "After we did all the finals, George came over and gave me a big hug and said, 'You really did a great job, I'm really proud of you.' That was a special feeling."

The work that Lucas had begun in November 1994 culminated in a beautiful film. State-of-the-art visual effects brought his epic script to life with numerous scenes that evoked the film's retro influences. Queen Amidala's image appears on a circular screen before the leaders of the Trade Federation, its shimmering appearance and the accompanying sound effect representing the

Above - *Boss Nass (voiced by Brian Blessed) unites the Gungans and the Naboo in victory over the Trade Federation in the final scene of* The Phantom Menace.

Right - *Queen Amidala debates with the Neimoidians via a circular screen similar to those seen in the* Flash Gordon *serials.*

most explicit homage yet to the *Flash Gordon* serials. Aside from such homages, the technology was used to create incredible new vistas: the glowing hydrostatic bubbles of Otoh Gunga and the spires of Theed were among the more conspicuous effects, but the digital augmentation of Mos Espa was no less impressive. CGI was used to create diverse effects such as the flickering holograms of Darth Sidious (the "phantom menace" of the film's title) and the glowing energy shield that offers protection to the Gungans.

Following special charity screenings on May 16, 1999, *Star Wars*: Episode I *The Phantom Menace* went on general release in the United States on Wednesday, May 19. One employment agency predicted that about 2.2 million people would skip work to see the film on its opening day. The film's opening day gross of more than $28.5 million would set a new record, and box-office takings would hit $100 million in less than a week. Episode I would achieve an ultimate U.S. theatrical gross of more than $431 million, placing it fourth behind *Titanic* (1997), *Star Wars* (1977 and 1997), and *ET: The Extraterrestrial* (1982) on a non-inflation-adjusted chart of America's highest-grossing films. A worldwide gross of almost $926 million would place it second only to *Titanic* on a similar international chart.

Episode I polarized public and critical reaction like no other *Star Wars* film before it, leading Roger Ebert to make a fitting request for balance in the *Chicago Sun-Times*. "If it were the first *Star Wars* movie, *The Phantom Menace* would be hailed as a visionary breakthrough," he wrote on May 17. "How quickly do we grow accustomed to wonders. . . . There is a sense of discovery in scene after scene of *The Phantom Menace* as [Lucas] tries out new effects and ideas, and seamlessly integrates real characters and digital ones, real landscapes and imaginary places. . . . As surely as Anakin Skywalker points the way into the future of *Star Wars*, so does *The Phantom Menace* raise the curtain on this new freedom for filmmakers. And it's a lot of fun."

The writing of Episode II began in June 1999. It had taken more than twenty years, but Lucas's vision of fully fledged electronic filmmaking was about to become a reality.

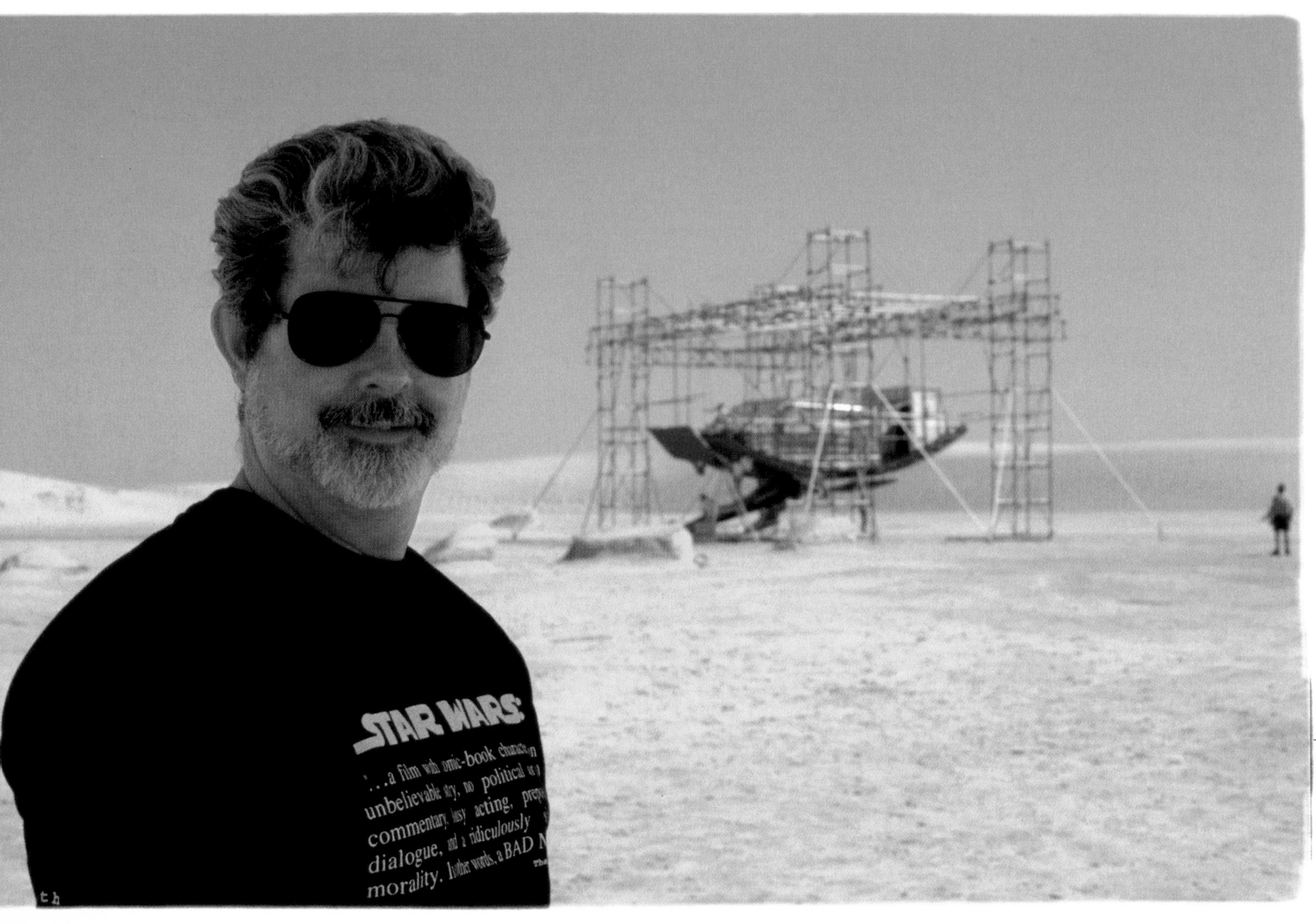

Left *- Lucas on location in Tunisia.*

Right *- The Episode I teaser poster.*

Far right *- The American one-sheet poster for* The Phantom Menace *featured artwork by Drew Struzan.*

STAR WARS
EPISODE I

EVERY SAGA HAS A BEGINNING
STAR WARS
EPISODE I
THE PHANTOM MENACE
STAR WARS EPISODE I THE PHANTOM MENACE
Starring LIAM NEESON EWAN McGREGOR NATALIE PORTMAN JAKE LLOYD IAN McDIARMID
Co-starring ANTHONY DANIELS KENNY BAKER PERNILLA AUGUST FRANK OZ
Music by JOHN WILLIAMS Produced by RICK McCALLUM
Written and Directed by
GEORGE LUCAS
LUCASFILM Ltd
Special Visual Effects and Animation by INDUSTRIAL LIGHT & MAGIC
A LUCASFILM LTD. Production – A TWENTIETH CENTURY FOX Release
Soundtrack Available on SONY CLASSICAL Read the Novel from DEL REY BOOKS
www.starwars.com
THX

Shooting Schedule

Star Wars: Episode I *The Phantom Menace*

* * * * * * * * * * * * * * * * * * *as shot* * * * * * * * * * * * * * * * * * *

Note: This information comes from the film's progress reports and call sheets. Not all scenes for each day are listed.

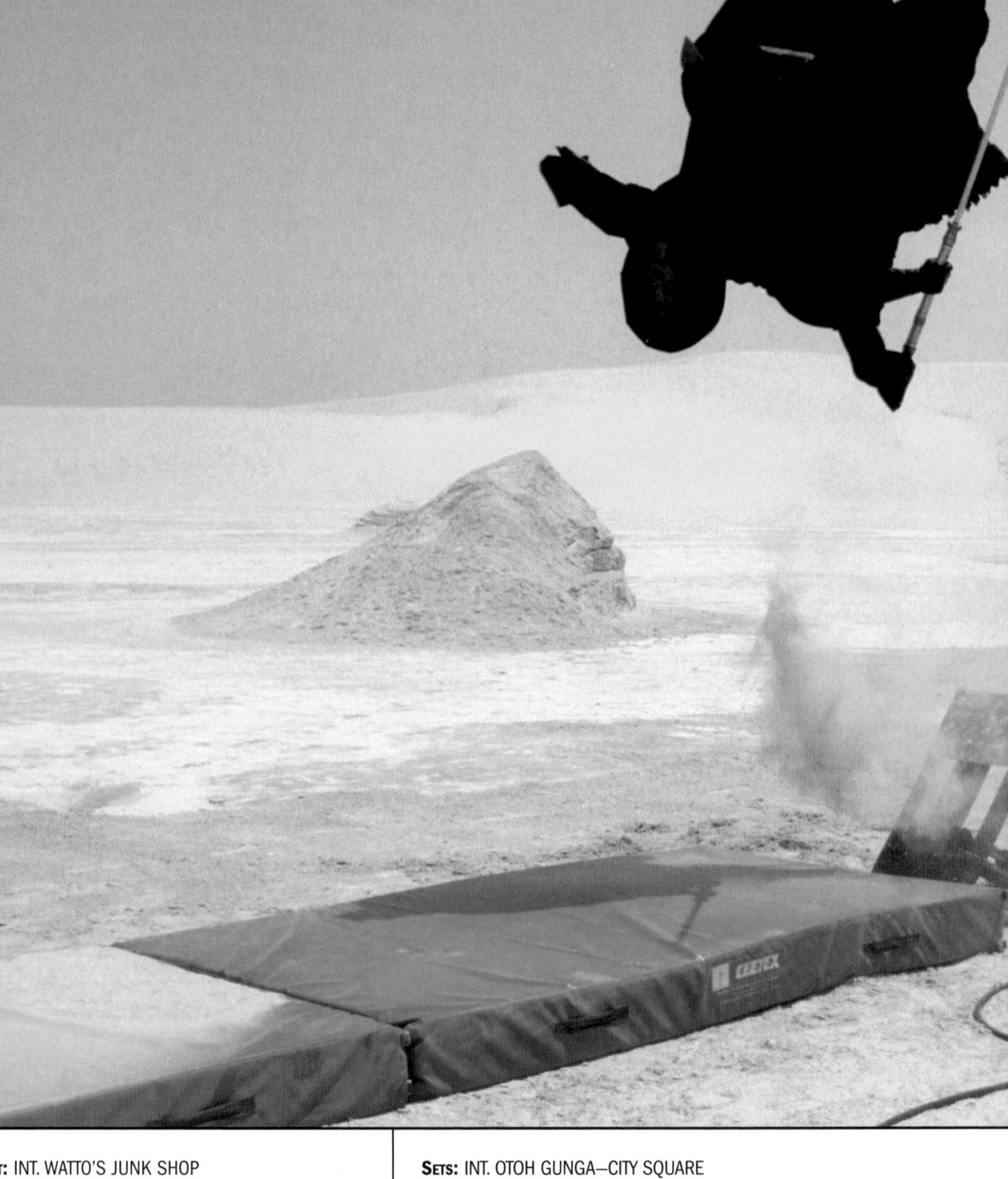

SHOOT DAYS SCHEDULED: 65

SHOOT DAY 1: THURSDAY, JUNE 26, 1997
Call On Set: 08.00 **Unit Dismissed:** 20.00
Location: MS2 STAGE LEAVESDEN [ENGLAND]
Sets: EXT. CORUSCANT–BALCONY
Sidious tells Maul to dispense with Queen & Jedi
INT. PALPATINE'S QUARTERS–LIVING AREA
Amidala confers with Palpatine
Pages: 7/8
Setups: 23

SHOOT DAY 2: FRIDAY, JUNE 27
Call On Set: 08.00 **Unit Dismissed:** 20.05
Location: MS2 STAGE LEAVESDEN
Sets: INT. PALPATINE'S QUARTERS
Palpatine nominated. Amidala to return to Theed
Pages: 0
Setups: 25
Catering Plate Count: 514

SHOOT DAY 3: MONDAY, JUNE 30
Call On Set: 08.00 **Unit Dismissed:** 20.35
Location: B STAGE
Sets: INT. ALDERAAN BOX–GALACTIC SENATE
Bail Organa seconds the motion
Pages: 0
Setups: 33

SHOOT DAY 4: TUESDAY, JULY 1
Call On Set: 08.00 **Unit Dismissed:** 19.15
Location: B STAGE
Sets: INT. CHANCELLOR'S POD–GALACTIC SENATE
Valorum is betrayed
INT. AKS MOE BOX–GALACTIC SENATE
Aks Moe concurs with Lott Dodd
Pages: 3 3/8
Setups: 20

SHOOT DAY 5: WEDNESDAY, JULY 2
Call On Set: 08.00 **Unit Dismissed:** 20.05
Location: FS1 STAGE
Sets: EXT. CORUSCANT SENATE–LANDING PLATFORM
Valorum & Palpatine meet group off Naboo craft
Pages: 1 3/8
Setups: 24
Notes: Crowd fittings for human and alien pod crews were held today at 14.00 HRS.

SHOOT DAY 6: THURSDAY, JULY 3
Call On Set: 08.00 **Unit Dismissed:** 20.09
Location: FS1 STAGE
Sets: EXT. CORUSCANT LANDING PLATFORM
Obi-Wan thinks Qui-Gon risks too much for the boy
Pages: 2
Setups: 23

SHOOT DAY 7: FRIDAY, JULY 4
Call On Set: 08.00 **Unit Dismissed:** 20.40
Location: A STAGE
Sets: INT. THEED–CENTRAL HANGAR HALLWAY
The Jedi and the Queen make their escape
Pages: 0
Setups: 22

SHOOT DAY 8: MONDAY JULY 7
Call On Set: 08.00 **Unit Dismissed:** 20.40
Location: A STAGE
Sets: INT. THEED–CENTRAL HANGAR HALLWAY
The Jedi and the Queen make their escape
Pages: 0
Setups: 22

SHOOT DAY 9: TUESDAY, JULY 8
Call On Set: 08.00 **Unit Dismissed:** 20.15
Location: B STAGE
Sets: INT. MOS ESPA ARENA–PIT HANGAR
Qui-Gon wipes blood off Anakin. Congratulations
Pages: 0
Setups: 29

SHOOT DAY 10: WEDNESDAY, JULY 9
Call On Set: 08.00 **Unit Dismissed:** 20.55
Location: D STAGE
Sets: INT. FED. BATTLESHIP–MAIN BAY VENT SHAFT
Jedi look on as droids load into landing craft
Pages: 3/8
Setups: 32
Notes: Prince Edward visited the set today.

SHOOT DAY 11: THURSDAY, JULY 10
Call On Set: 09.00 **Unit Dismissed:** 20.05
Location: D STAGE
Sets: INT. ANAKIN'S HOVEL–MAIN ROOM
They enter a small living space & meet Shmi.
Qui-Gon talks to Obi-Wan on comm link.
Pages: 1 1/8
Setups: 20

SHOOT DAY 12: FRIDAY, JULY 11
Call On Set: 08.00 **Unit Dismissed:** 20.00
Location: D STAGE
Set: INT. ANAKIN'S HOVEL–MAIN ROOM
Dinner. Talk of slavery and Podracing
Pages: 0
Setups: 27

SHOOT DAY 13: MONDAY, JULY 14
Call On Set: 08.00 **Unit Dismissed:** 20.02
Location: D STAGE
Set: INT. ANAKIN'S HOVEL–MAIN ROOM
Shmi tells Anakin it's time for him to let go
Pages: 2 4/8
Setups: 22
Props: Shmi's cleaning cloth, bag of coins, Qui-Gon's comm link

SHOOT DAY 14: TUESDAY, JULY 15
Call On Set: 08.00 **Unit Dismissed:** 20.00
Location: STAGE D
Set: INT. ANAKIN'S HOVEL–BEDROOM
Anakin shows off his droid; Anakin says goodbye to Threepio
Pages: 0
Setups: 27
Notes: Liam Neeson came in for a fight rehearsal.

SHOOT DAY 15: WEDNESDAY, JULY 16
Call On Set: 08.00 **Unit Dismissed:** 20.00
Location: C STAGE

Set: INT. WATTO'S JUNK SHOP
The group is greeted by Watto. They meet Anakin
Pages: 0
Setups: 34

SHOOT DAY 16: THURSDAY, JULY 17
Call On Set: 08.00 **Unit Dismissed:** 20.00
Location: C STAGE, A STAGE
Sets: EXT. MOS ESPA–JUNK DEALER PLAZA
Padme doesn't approve of Qui-Gon's plan
INT. WATTO'S JUNK SHOP
Watto and Qui-Gon make the deal
EXT. MOS ESPA–WATTO'S BOX
Qui-Gon holds Watto to the bet
Pages: 0
Setups: 22
Notes: A test was shot today on the animatronic Neimoidian heads.

SHOOT DAY 17: FRIDAY, JULY 18
Call On Set: 08.00 **Unit Dismissed:** 20.23
Location: MS1 STAGE
Sets: INT. OTOH GUNGA–CITY SQUARE
Gungan guards meet the dripping trio
Pages: 4/8
Setups: 30
Notes: Today was the last day of main unit U.K. shoot—phase 1. The main unit will now travel to Naples on Monday 21st July.

SHOOT DAY 18: TUESDAY, JULY 22
Call On Set: 13.30 **Unit Dismissed:** 00.07
Location: REGGIA PALACE–CASERTA, ITALY
Sets: INT. NABOO PALACE–THRONE ROOM–THEED
Queen & Bibble confer with Hologram of Palpatine
Pages: 2 5/8
Setups: 18
Notes: Please note that the script timings, page and scene counts have changed due to blue amendments to the script issued.

SHOOT DAY 19: WEDNESDAY, JULY 23
Call On Set: 11.30 **Unit Dismissed:** 00.31
Location: REGGIA PALACE–CASERTA

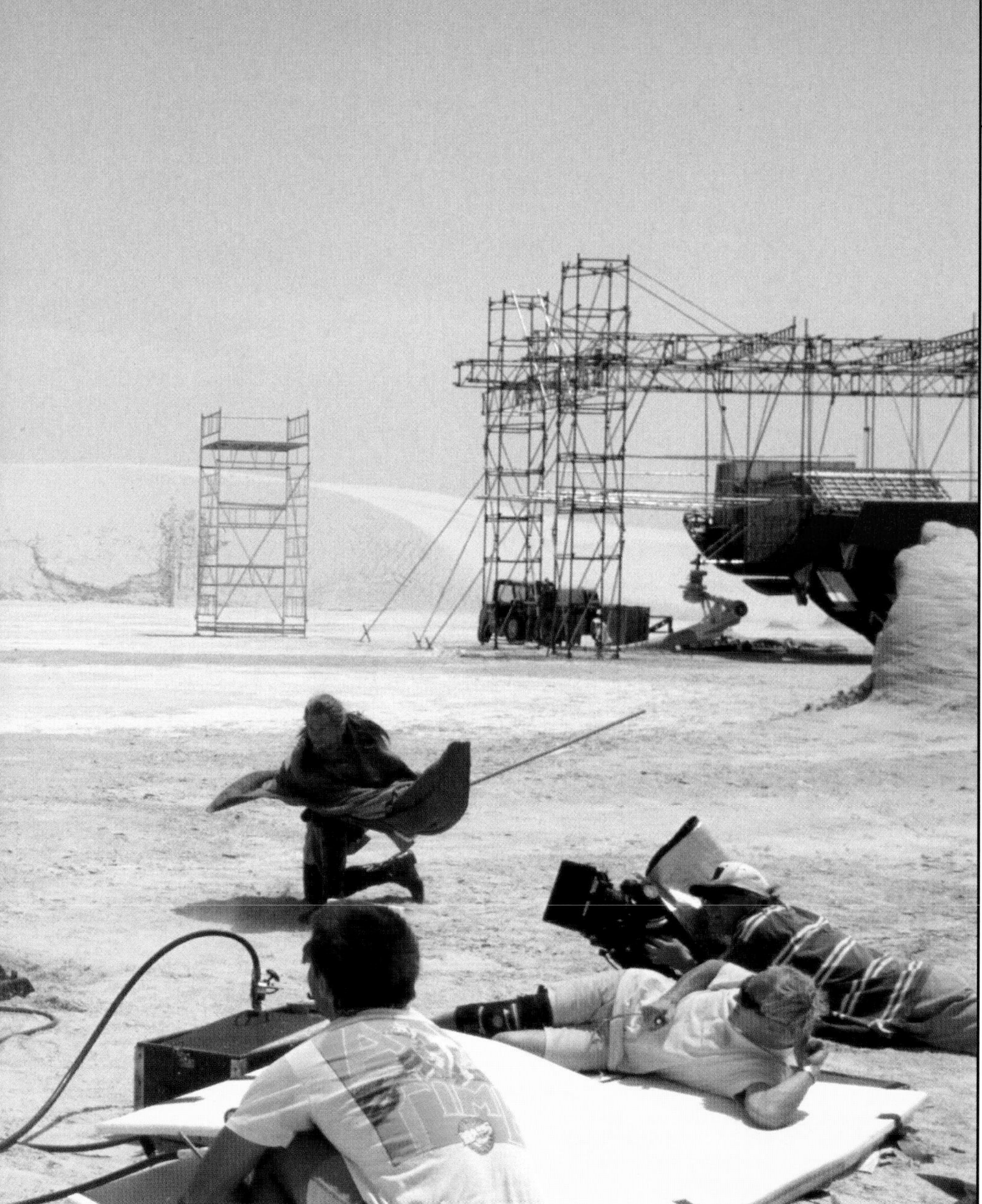

Sets: INT. NABOO PALACE—THRONE ROOM—THEED
Padme tricks Nute & Rune
Rune & Nute consult Hologram of Sidious
Pages: 8 7/8
Setups: 27
Notes: 2nd unit packed for traveling to Tunisia today.

SHOOT DAY 20: THURSDAY, JULY 24
Call On Set: 13.30 **Unit Dismissed:** 00.40
Location: REGGIA PALACE--CASERTA
Sets: INT. NABOO PALACE—THRONE ROOM—THEED
The Queen is captured and led away
Pages: 5/8
Setups: 21

SHOOT DAY 21: FRIDAY, JULY 25
Call On Set: 13.30 **Unit Dismissed:** 19.50
Location: REGGIA PALACE—CASERTA
Sets: INT. NABOO PALACE—THRONE ROOM—THEED
Wipe them out
Pages: 0
Setups: 18
Notes: The main unit travel [to] Tozeur from Naples on chartered aircraft on Saturday 26th July.

SHOOT DAY 22: MONDAY, JULY 28
Call On Set: 05.45 **Unit Dismissed:** 16.05
Location: CHOTT EL GHARSA, JAK HIGHWAY, NEAR TOZEUR, SOUTHERN TUNISIA
Sets: EXT. MOS ESPA STREET—FRUIT STAND
Anakin stops at Jira's fruit stand
EXT. MOS ESPA STREET—ALCOVE
They find a quiet spot & consider a solution
Pages: 0
Setups: 28

SHOOT DAY 23: TUESDAY, JULY 29
Call On Set: 05.45 **Unit Dismissed:** 16.35
Location: CHOTT EL GHARSA, TUNISIA
Sets: EXT. MOS ESPA STREET—MARKET
Sebulba confronts Jar Jar, Anakin steps in
Pages: 0
Setups: 21

SHOOT DAY 24: WEDNESDAY, JULY 30
Call On Set: 05.45 **Unit Dismissed:** 17.27
Location: CHOTT EL GHARSA, TOZEUR, TUNISIA
Sets: EXT. NABOO SPACECRAFT RAMP
Pages: 1
Setups: 29
Notes: SEVERE STORM DAMAGE TO LOCATION AND SET RESULTED IN A RESCHEDULE BRING FORWARD ON THE RAMP. DELAYS OCCURRED DURING THE DAY DUE TO REPAIR WORK NEEDED ON WIGS/COSTUMES/CREATURE COSTUMES, ETC. ADDENDUM TO PROGRESS REPORT NO: 24 30TH JULY 1997: AT APPROXIMATELY 20.00 ON THE NIGHT OF THE 29TH JULY A SEVERE DESERT STORM HIT THE TOZEUR AREA. THIS STORM CONSISTING OF THUNDER, LIGHTNING, RAIN, AND SAND WITH WINDS OF BETWEEN 70 AND 100 MPH . . . ON ARRIVAL AT THE LOCATION THE FOLLOWING SEVERE DAMAGE WAS DISCOVERED [PARTIAL LIST FOLLOWS]:

1. MOS ESPA STREET SET: 2 BUILDINGS COMPLETELY DESTROYED. LUKE'S SPEEDER MOVED SOME 50 METERS.

2. WATTO'S BACK YARD: ONE 2-TON SCRAP METAL THROWN 50 METERS.

8. ARENA GRID AND POD ENGINES AND COCKPITS: SEVERE DAMAGE . . . ANAKIN'S ENGINES SMASHED AND BROKEN IN TWO.

11. COSTUME: ALL COSTUMES STORED IN LARGE MARQUEES SOAKED AND COVERED IN SAND. CROWD CALLS IMPOSSIBLE WITHOUT MAJOR WORK TO DRY AND CLEAN COSTUMES.

ACTION UNDERTAKEN [PARTIAL LIST FOLLOWS]:

1. TUNISIA SHOOT RE-SCHEDULED TO ALLOW IMMEDIATE SHOOTING ON NABOO SPACECRAFT RAMP AND SUBSEQUENT DAYS SCHEDULED TO ALLOW REPAIR WORK TO BE UNDERTAKEN WHERE POSSIBLE . . . FULL IMPACT ON SHOOTING DESPITE RE-SCHEDULING STILL TO BE ASCERTAINED . . .

4. NEW FACILITIES SUCH AS TENTS AND CATERING EQUIPMENT, FRIDGES, ETC. HIRED IN FROM TUNISIA.

5. GOVERNOR OF TOZEUR PROVINCE CONTACTED AND VISITS SITE. MILITARY ASSISTANCE AND TENTS GIVEN BY TUNISIAN AUTHORITIES.

SHOOT DAY 25: THURSDAY, JULY 31
Call On Set: 06.15 **Unit Dismissed:** 14.07
Location: CHOTT EL GHARSA—TOZEUR
Sets: EXT. TATOOINE DESERT—NABOO SPACECRAFT
Darth Maul attacks on his speeder
Qui-Gon and Darth Maul continue their sword battle
Maul leaps up and falls back to the desert floor
Pages: 0
Setups: 33

SHOOT DAY 26: FRIDAY, AUGUST 1
Call On Set: 05.45 **Unit Dismissed:** 17.15
Location: CHOTT EL GHARSA
Sets: EXT. MOS ESPA—ARENA—PIT AREA
Artoo & Kitster in pit. R2 lets out a worried sigh
EXT. MOS ESPA—ARENA—VIEWING PLATFORM
Group prepare to watch race, Shmi looks nervously to Qui-Gon
Excitement, joy & smiles as Anakin wins
Pages: 4/8
Setups: 38
Notes: Annie Liebovitz and her crew were on the set today to photograph Liam Neeson, Natalie Portman, and Jake Lloyd.

SHOOT DAY 27: SATURDAY, AUGUST 2
Call On Set: 05.45 **Unit Dismissed:** 16.50
Location: CHOTT EL GHARSA—TOZEUR
Sets: EXT. MOS ESPA ST.—JUNK DEALER PLAZA
"We'll try one of the smaller dealers"
Pages: 2 4/8
Setups: 26

SHOOT DAY 28: MONDAY, AUGUST 4
Call On Set: 05.45 **Unit Dismissed:** 16.50
Location: CHOTT EL GHARSA—TOZEUR
Sets: EXT. MOS ESPA—SLAVE QUARTERS—BACK YARD
The pod rises, the engines ignite
Pages: 0
Setups: 25

SHOOT DAY 29: TUESDAY, AUGUST 5
Call On Set: 08.00 **Unit Dismissed:** 16.55
Location: CHOTT EL GHARSA
Sets: EXT. MOS ESPA—ARENA—STARTING GRID
The pilots bow to Jabba
Pages: 0
Setups: 28

SHOOT DAY 30: WEDNESDAY, AUGUST 6
Call On Set: 05.45 **Unit Dismissed:** 17.05
Location: CHOTT EL GHARSA
Sets: EXT. MOS ESPA ARENA—STARTING GRID
Pods shoot forward. Anakin's engines finally ignite
Pages: 0
Setups: 31

SHOOT DAY 31: THURSDAY, AUGUST 7
Call On Set: 09.00 **Unit Dismissed:** 19.30
Location: CHOTT EL GHARSA
Sets: EXT. WATTO'S JUNK YARD—BEHIND SHOP
They move thru the junkyard picking parts
Pages: 2 6/8
Setups: 25
Notes: MAIN UNIT COMPLETED CALLSHEET AS SCHEDULED. THE UNIT WILL NOW MOVE TO MEDININE AND TETOUNINE, SOUTHERN TUNISIA FOR REMAINDER OF TUNISIAN SHOOT. PLEASE BE CAREFUL OF WHAT YOU TOUCH IN WATTO'S. THERE ARE MANY PIECES OF REAL JUNK & JAGGED EDGES. PLEASE TAKE CARE IN THE SUN. DRINK PLENTY OF WATER AND RE-HYDRATE. WEAR A HAT, STAY IN THE SHADE.

SHOOT DAY 32: SATURDAY, AUGUST 9
Call On Set: 05.30 **Unit Dismissed:** 17.20
Location: THE KSAR—MEDININE, TUNISIA
Sets: EXT. MOS ESPA STREET—SLAVE QUARTERS
Anakin leaves Shmi and does not look back
Anakin fights with Seek
Probe droid searches
Pages: 1 7/8
Setups: 24

SHOOT DAY 33: SUNDAY, AUGUST 10
Call On Set: 04.30 **Unit Dismissed:** 11.45
Location: HOTEL KSAR, HADADA, TUNISIA
Sets: EXT. MOS ESPA—SLAVE QUARTER PORCH—BACK YARD
Qui-Gon and Shmi on porch discuss Anakin
Pages: 1 3/8
Setups: 29
Notes: The crew wrapped and packed up their equipment on camera wrap and traveled to Djerba. Monday 11th August will be a rest day. Shooting will resume at Leavesden on Wednesday 13th August.

Above - Stunt coordinator Nick Gillard (leaning on elbow) supervises a flip during the battle between Qui-Gon Jinn (stunt double Andrew Lawden) and Darth Maul (Ray Park) on location. Second-unit director of photography Giles Nuttgen (another Young Indy *veteran) and Andreas Petrides (Obi-Wan's stunt double) look on.*

SHOOT DAY 34: WEDNESDAY, AUGUST 13
CALL ON SET: 08.00 **UNIT DISMISSED:** 20.15
LOCATION: D STAGE—LEAVESDEN, ENGLAND
SETS: INT. NABOO SPACECRAFT—COCKPIT
Obi-Wan suggests Tatooine as a possible sanctuary . . .
PAGES: 4/8
SETUPS: 29

SHOOT DAY 35: THURSDAY, AUGUST 14
CALL ON SET: 08.00 **UNIT DISMISSED:** 19.55
LOCATION: FS2
SETS: INT. NABOO SPACECRAFT—MAIN AREA
The ship is asleep, Padme comforts Anakin
INT. NABOO SPACECRAFT—HALLWAY
Anakin & Obi-Wan find Qui-Gon collapsed on floor . . .
PAGES: 0
SETUPS: 27

SHOOT DAY 36: FRIDAY, AUGUST 15
CALL ON SET: 08.00 **UNIT DISMISSED:** 20.00
LOCATION: FS2 STAGE
SETS: INT. NABOO SPACECRAFT—HALLWAY
Anakin runs in to tell them they must take off
INT. NABOO SPACECRAFT—QUEEN CHAMBERS
R2-D2 congratulated.
PAGES: 3 1/8
SETUPS: 29

SHOOT DAY 37: MONDAY, AUGUST 18
CALL ON SET: 08.00 **UNIT DISMISSED:** 20.35
LOCATION: A STAGE
SETS: INT. THEED—CENTRAL HANGAR
They fight their way into the hangar
The pilots launch. Anakin hides
Panaka enters. Maul enters. Padme leaves for the palace. Anakin starts his fighter
PAGES: 0
SETUPS: 45

SHOOT DAY 38: TUESDAY, AUGUST 19
CALL ON SET: 08.00 **UNIT DISMISSED:** 19.45
LOCATION: A STAGE
SETS: INT. THEED—CENTRAL HANGAR
PAGES: 0
SETUPS: 52
NOTES: SHOOTING WAS STOPPED AT 19.45 HRS. DUE TO AN INCIDENT ON SET. A SQUIB SPARKED IN NATALIE PORTMAN'S FACE. JEANIE UDALL (UNIT NURSE) WASHED HER EYES AND REMOVED ALL VISIBLE PARTICLES OF THE SQUIB. NATALIE WAS THEN TAKEN TO A HARLEY STREET SPECIALIST, DR. PACKARD, WHO EXAMINED HER EYES AND REMOVED MORE PARTICLES UNDER A MICROSCOPE, THAT WERE NOT VISIBLE BY THE NAKED EYE [SIC]. HER EYESIGHT WAS NOT AFFECTED BY THE INCIDENT AND SHE WILL BE ABLE TO CONTINUE WORKING.

SHOOT DAY 39: WEDNESDAY, AUGUST 20
CALL ON SET: 08.00 **UNIT DISMISSED:** 18.35
LOCATION: BACKLOT—LEAVESDEN STUDIOS
SETS: EXT. THEED—CENTRAL PLAZA
Amidala is escorted by droids. Jedi ruin their day
PAGES: 0
SETUPS: 36
NOTES: NATALIE PORTMAN RETURNED TO SEE DR. PACKARD FOR A CHECK-UP TODAY. HE WAS HAPPY WITH THE RESULTS AND SHE WILL BE ABLE TO RETURN TO WORK.

SHOOT DAY 40: THURSDAY, AUGUST 21
CALL ON SET: 06.45 **UNIT DISMISSED:** 16.55
LOCATION: WHIPPENDELL WOODS, HERTFORDSHIRE, ENGLAND
SETS: EXT. NABOO SACRED TEMPLE RUINS
Padme reveals herself, asks Boss Nass to help
PAGES: 2
SETUPS: 50

SHOOT DAY 41: FRIDAY, AUGUST 22
CALL ON SET: 06.45 **UNIT DISMISSED:** 18.20
LOCATION: WHIPPENDELL WOODS
SETS: EXT. NABOO EDGE OF SWAMP/GRASS PLAINS
The plan is hatched. Resistance leaders join up
PAGES: 4 5/8
SETUPS: 29

SHOOT DAY 42: TUESDAY, AUGUST 26
CALL ON SET: 08.00 **UNIT DISMISSED:** 20.10
LOCATION: BACKLOT—LEAVESDEN STUDIOS
SETS: EXT. THEED—MAIN PLAZA
The patriots battle the droids and enter hangar
PAGES: 0
SETUPS: 35

SHOOT DAY 43: WEDNESDAY, AUGUST 27
CALL ON SET: 08.00 **UNIT DISMISSED:** 21.20
LOCATION: FS2 STAGE
SETS: INT. NABOO PALACE—HALLWAY
Padme and Panaka go out the window
PAGES: 2 6/8
SETUPS: 49

SHOOT DAY 44: THURSDAY, AUGUST 28
CALL ON SET: 08.00 **UNIT DISMISSED:** 20.07
LOCATION: B STAGE
SETS: INT. NABOO STARFIGHTER—COCKPIT
Anakin gets hang of controls. Heads for battle. Anakin is chased into Federation ship hangar . . .
PAGES: 0
SETUPS: 26

SHOOT DAY 45: FRIDAY, AUGUST 29
CALL ON SET: 08.00 **UNIT DISMISSED:** 20.10
LOCATION: BACKLOT
SETS: INT. THEED FUNERAL AMPHITHEATRE
Qui-Gon's funeral
EXT. THEED MAIN PLAZA
C/u Yoda, Mace & Jedi for Victory Parade
PAGES: 2 4/8
SETUPS: 37
NOTES: SFX—Jedi funeral pyre in flames, flame bars and Kenny's R2 unit were required.

SHOOT DAY 46: MONDAY, SEPTEMBER 1
CALL ON SET: 08.00 **UNIT DISMISSED:** 19.50
LOCATION: MS2 STAGE
SETS: INT. TEMPLE OF JEDI—COUNCIL CHAMBERS
Qui-Gon before council discuss Sith & Anakin
Anakin questioned by the Twelve Jedi
PAGES: 0
SETUPS: 42
NOTES: Underwater test at action underwater tank, Waltham Cross.

SHOOT DAY 47: TUESDAY, SEPTEMBER 2
CALL ON SET: 08.00 **UNIT DISMISSED:** 20.00
LOCATION: MS2 STAGE
SETS: INT. TEMPLE OF JEDI—COUNCIL CHAMBERS
Qui-Gon told Anakin is strong with the Force
PAGES: 0
SETUPS: 40

SHOOT DAY 48: WEDNESDAY, SEPTEMBER 3
CALL ON SET: 08.00 **UNIT DISMISSED:** 19.45
LOCATION: A STAGE
SETS: INT. THEED—CENTRAL HANGAR
Anakin returns with other pilots—Amazement
INT. NABOO STARFIGHTER—FED. HANGAR
Anakin lands in hangar as Droids surround. Droids attack the fighter. Anakin escapes
PAGES: 4/8
SETUPS: 26

SHOOT DAY 49: THURSDAY, SEPTEMBER 4
CALL ON SET: 08.00 **UNIT DISMISSED:** 20.20
LOCATION: BACKLOT
SETS: EXT. THEED—MAIN PLAZA
Victory! (for now)
PAGES: 1 1/8
SETUPS: 41

SHOOT DAY 50: FRIDAY, SEPTEMBER 5
CALL ON SET: 08.00 **UNIT DISMISSED:** 20.20
LOCATION: D STAGE
SETS: EXT. ANAKIN'S POD—MOS ESPA—RACETRACK
Int. Anakin's Pod—greenscreen work
PAGES: 5 6/8
SETUPS: 23

SHOOT DAY 51: MONDAY, SEPTEMBER 8
CALL ON SET: 08.00 **UNIT DISMISSED:** 19.56
LOCATION: D STAGE
SETS: INT. REPUBLIC CRUISER COCKPIT
The Ambassadors wish to board the battleship
Capt. & pilot see gun turret swing around
PAGES: 1 7/8
SETUPS: 29

SHOOT DAY 52: TUESDAY, SEPTEMBER 9
CALL ON SET: 07.00 **UNIT DISMISSED:** 19.05
LOCATION: OUTSIDE FS1, A STAGE
SET: EXT. NABOO SWAMP
Qui-Gon runs into Jar Jar
INT. THEED—CENTRAL HANGAR
Maul drives the Jedi into the Generator Room
PAGES: 0
SETUPS: 62
NOTES: Creatures—Jar Jar wet and muddy was required. Please remember to bring your Wellington boots for working in the swamp.

SHOOT DAY 53: WEDNESDAY, SEPTEMBER 10
CALL ON SET: 07.00 **UNIT DISMISSED:** 18.01
LOCATION: WHIPPENDELL WOOD
SET: EXT. NABOO SWAMP
Obi-Wan saved from the STAPS
PAGES: 0
SETUPS: 29

SHOOT DAY 54: THURSDAY, SEPTEMBER 11
CALL ON SET: 08.00 **UNIT DISMISSED:** 20.05
LOCATION: FS1B STAGE
SET: INT. FED. BATTLESHIP CONFERENCE ROOM
Jedi are led in. Obi-Wan has a bad feeling
"Is it in their nature to make us wait?"
Jedi leap to standing position. Gas!
PAGES: 7 4/8
SETUPS: 26
NOTES: Props/Art Dept.—Bird cage & birds, trays of food and Jedi lightsabers were required.

SHOOT DAY 55: FRIDAY, SEPTEMBER 12
CALL ON SET: 07.00 **UNIT DISMISSED:** 20.10
LOCATION: FS1B STAGE
SET: INT. FED. BATTLESHIP HALLWAY
Obi-Wan & Qui-Gon destroy Battle Droids . . .
Wheel droids roll down. Jedi make their escape
PAGES: 3 1/8
SETUPS: 50

SHOOT DAY 56: MONDAY, SEPTEMBER 15
CALL ON SET: 08.00 **UNIT DISMISSED:** 19.56
LOCATION: B STAGE
SET: INT. POWER GENERATOR PIT
Jedi and Sith fight
PAGES: 3/8
SETUPS: 47

SHOOT DAY 57: TUESDAY, SEPTEMBER 16
CALL ON SET: 08.00 **UNIT DISMISSED:** 20.45
LOCATION: B STAGE
SET: INT. POWER GENERATOR PIT
PAGES: 1/8
SETUPS: 60

SHOOT DAY 58: WEDNESDAY, SEPTEMBER 17
CALL ON SET: 08.00 **UNIT DISMISSED:** 20.00
LOCATION: FS1A STAGE
SET: INT. OTOH GUNGA—HIGH TOWER BOARD ROOM
Obi-Wan and Qui-Gon face Boss Nass
PAGES: 3 7/8
SETUPS: 21

SHOOT DAY 59: THURSDAY, SEPTEMBER 18
CALL ON SET: 08.00 **UNIT DISMISSED:** 20.34
LOCATION: B STAGE
SET: INT. SUB COCKPIT
The sub escapes the sea monsters
PAGES: 1 3/8
SETUPS: 27

SHOOT DAY 60: FRIDAY, SEPTEMBER 19
CALL ON SET: 08.00 **UNIT DISMISSED:** 19.55
LOCATION: FS1A STAGE
SET: INT. POWER GENERATOR ELECTRIC BEAM HALLWAY
Qui-Gon is Mauled
PAGES: 7/8
SETUPS: 26

SHOOT DAY 61: SATURDAY, SEPTEMBER 20
CALL ON SET: 08.00 **UNIT DISMISSED:** 17.50
LOCATION: ACTION UNDERWATER TANK ESAB INDUSTRIAL ESTATE, HERTFORD ROAD, WALTHAM CROSS, HERTS
SET: EXT. NABOO LAKE—UNDERWATER
Obi-Wan & Qui-Gon swim behind Jar Jar
PAGES: 0
SETUPS: 9

SHOOT DAY 62: MONDAY, SEPTEMBER 22
CALL ON SET: 08.00 **UNIT DISMISSED:** 20.56
LOCATION: LEAVESDEN STUDIOS—FS1A STAGE
SET: INT. POWER GENERATOR ELECTRIC BEAM HALLWAY
Qui-Gon dies
PAGES: 0
SETUPS: 49

SHOOT DAY 63: TUESDAY, SEPTEMBER 23
CALL ON SET: 08.00 **UNIT DISMISSED:** 20.15

Location: FS1A STAGE
Sets: INT. POWER GENERATOR ELECTRIC BEAM HALLWAY
Obi-Wan and Darth Maul fight
Pages: 1 1/8
Setups: 57

SHOOT DAY 64: WEDNESDAY, SEPTEMBER 24
Call On Set: 08.00 **Unit Dismissed:** 19.45
Location: OUTSIDE B STAGE, MS2 STAGE
Sets: INT. TEMPLE OF JEDI—BALCONY
Obi-Wan thinks boy will not pass the questioning
EXT. TATOOINE—NABOO SPACECRAFT RAMP
Qui-Gon knocks Maul off ramp onto desert floor
Pages: 7/8
Setups: 28

SHOOT DAY 65: THURSDAY, SEPTEMBER 25
Call On Set: 07.00 **Unit Dismissed:** 18.45
Location: PINEWOOD STUDIOS, PADDOCK TANK
Sets: EXT. THEED ESTUARY
The submarine and the rapids
EXT. NABOO SWAMP LAKE
Qui-Gon, Obi-Wan & Jar Jar walk into the lake
Pages: 3/8
Setups: 35

SHOOT DAY 66: FRIDAY, SEPTEMBER 26
Call On Set: 07.00 **Unit Dismissed:** 22.33
Location: LEAVESDEN STUDIOS—C STAGE
Sets: INT. FEDERATION BATTLESHIP BRIDGE
TC-3 reports the Ambassadors are Jedi; Nimoudians are ordered to kill Jedi
Pages: 9 6/8
Setups: 57
Notes: WRAP—TODAY WAS MAIN UNIT'S LAST DAY OF PRINCIPAL PHOTOGRAPHY. A FIGHT UNIT AND THE 2ND UNIT WILL CONTINUE TO SHOOT FOR ONE MORE WEEK.

Total Set-ups: 2,084
Total Pages: 121 1/8

2ND UNIT PROGRESS REPORT SUMMARY

SHOOT DAY 1 TO 69: THURSDAY, JUNE 26, 1997 TO FRIDAY, OCTOBER 3, 1997
Total Setups: 1,213
Notes: ADVANCE SCHEDULE—THAT'S ALL FOLKS!

FIGHT UNIT PROGRESS REPORT
SHOOT DAY 1: MONDAY, SEPTEMBER 29, 1997
Location: LEAVESDEN STUDIOS—FS2 STAGE, MS1 STAGE, MS2 STAGE
Sets: EXT. THEED PALACE CORRIDOR
Group leave & arrive on ledge of window.
INT. POWER GENERATOR PIT
Fight p/ups
EXT. NABOO SPACE CRAFT RAMP
Qui-Gon leaps onto ramp

SHOOT DAY 2: TUESDAY, SEPTEMBER 30
Location: MS2 STAGE, MS1 STAGE
Sets: EXT. TATOOINE—NABOO SPACE CRAFT RAMP
Qui-Gon about to collapse on ramp
INT. POWER GENERATOR PIT
Maul falls and Qui-Gon jumps after

SHOOT DAY 3: WEDNESDAY, OCTOBER 1
Location: LEAVESDEN STUDIOS—FS1 STAGE
Sets: INT. ELECTRIC BEAM HALLWAY/MELTING PIT
Obi-Wan cuts Maul's saber in two
INT. MELTING PIT
Looking down into blue as Maul falls into the pit

SHOOT DAY 4: THURSDAY, OCTOBER 2
Location: OUTSIDE FS1 STAGE, FS1 STAGE, A STAGE
Sets: Obi-Wan pulls up & out of the pit
INT. THEED HANGAR
Maul comes through the door and Obi-Wan flies over him

SHOOT DAY 5: FRIDAY, OCTOBER 3, 1997
Call On Set: 08.00 **Unit Dismissed:** 19.52
Location: A STAGE, B STAGE
Sets: INT. THEED HANGAR
Maul leaps to avoid Obi-Wan's lightsaber
INT. THEED POWER GENERATOR PIT
Maul snarls & jumps out of shot
Pages: 18 1/8
Setups: 18
Notes: TODAY WAS THE LAST DAY OF PHOTOGRAPHY FOR THE FIGHT UNIT.

NOVEMBER 1997 PICK-UPS

SHOOT DAY 1: THURSDAY, NOVEMBER 6, 1997
Call On Set: 08.00
Location: LEAVESDEN STUDIOS—A STAGE
Sets: EXT. NABOO EDGE OF SWAMP/GRASS PLAINS (Hologram from Fed. Battleship Bridge)

MARCH 1998 PICK-UPS

SHOOT DAY 1: MONDAY, MARCH 2, 1998
Call On Set: 08.00
Location: LEAVESDEN STUDIOS—BACKLOT, A STAGE, B STAGE
Sets: EXT. NABOO CENTRAL PLAZA
Panaka's ambush squad under arch
INT. THEED CENTRAL HANGAR
Jedi & Maul fight in bg while Queen fights droids
EXT. THEED ESTUARY—RIVER BANK & CASTLE
WS rear of Obi-Wan & Qui-Gon jump off sub

SHOOT DAY 2: TUESDAY, MARCH 3
Call On Set: 08.00
Location: B STAGE
Sets: EXT. TATOOINE DESERT—SHIP LANDING SITE
Maul running and leaping up
INT. THEED GENERATOR ROOM—WALKWAY
Jedi & Maul fight—Awesome Vista tiltdown

SHOOT DAY 3: WEDNESDAY, MARCH 4
Call On Set: 08.00
Location: B STAGE, FS1 STAGE
Sets: INT. NABOO SHIP DROID HOLD
R2 down elevator shaft smudged and scorched

SHOOT DAY 4: THURSDAY, MARCH 5
Call On Set: 08.00
Location: FS2 STAGE, B STAGE, D STAGE (2ND UNIT)
Sets: INT. THEED FUNERAL TEMPLE
High angle: Yoda against blue screen
EXT. TATOOINE DESERT MESA—MAUL'S SHIP
Maul walks down ramp
INT. ANAKIN'S HOVEL—ANAKIN'S BEDROOM
MS: R2-D2 in corner—"You really like him"

SHOOT DAY 5: FRIDAY, MARCH 6
Call On Set: 08.00
Location: C STAGE, D STAGE, FS1 STAGE
Sets: INT. NABOO SHIP COCKPIT
Ric Olie's new dialogue
INT. THEED GENERATOR—MELTING PIT
Top shot: cu Obi hanging on looking up at Maul

SHOOT DAY 6: SATURDAY, MARCH 7 (2ND UNIT)
Call On Set: 08.00 **Unit Dismissed:** 18.30
Location: LEAVESDEN STUDIOS, STAGES FS1, A STAGE, B STAGE
Sets: [FIGHT SCENES]
Total Pages: 9 2/8
Total Setups (1st and 2nd Units): 40

AUGUST 1998 PICK-UPS

SHOOT DAY 1: MONDAY, AUGUST 10, 1998
Call On Set: 07.00
Location: LEAVESDEN STUDIOS—FS1B; EXT FS1; FS1B; FS1A
Sets: INT. QUEEN'S QUARTERS CORUSCANT
Queen tells Anakin she has sent Padme on an errand
EXT. THEED MAIN PLAZA
Jedi Council arrive Nute & Rune taken away
INT. NABOO SPACECRAFT MAIN COMPARTMENT
Queen decoy in Gungan Battle dress

SHOOT DAY 2: TUESDAY, AUGUST 11
Call On Set: 07.00
Location: FS1A; EXT FS1; BACKLOT; WHIPPENDALE WOODS
Sets: EXT. MOS ESPA SLAVE QUARTERS-PORCH
Qui-Gon's not here to save slaves
EXT. PALACE THEED MAIN PLAZA
New scene Queen & entourage escorted by droids.
EXT. NABOO SWAMP
Helicopter shot

SHOOT DAY 3: WEDNESDAY, AUGUST 12
Call On Set: 08.00
Location: FS1B
Sets: INT. ANAKIN'S HOVEL MAIN ROOM
New scene: Qui-Gon, Anakin & Shmi talk

SHOOT DAY 4: THURSDAY, AUGUST 13
Call On Set: 08.00
Sets: INT. OTOH GUNGA HIGH TOWER BOARD ROOM
New scene: Qui-Gon walking R to L "We need a navigator"

SHOOT DAY 5: FRIDAY, AUGUST 14
Call On Set: 08.00
Location: WHIPPENDALE WOODS
Sets: EXT. NABOO SACRED TEMPLE RUINS
Plate for Gungans in background

MARCH 1999 PICK-UPS

SHOOT DAY 1: SATURDAY, MARCH 20, 1999
Breakfast: 7.30 **Unit Dismissed:** 12.55
Location: BLUE SCREEN UNDER COVERED WAY NEAR F STAGE—LEAVESDEN
Sets: EXT. THEED PLAZA
Palpatine greets Obi-Wan & Anakin
Setups: 6

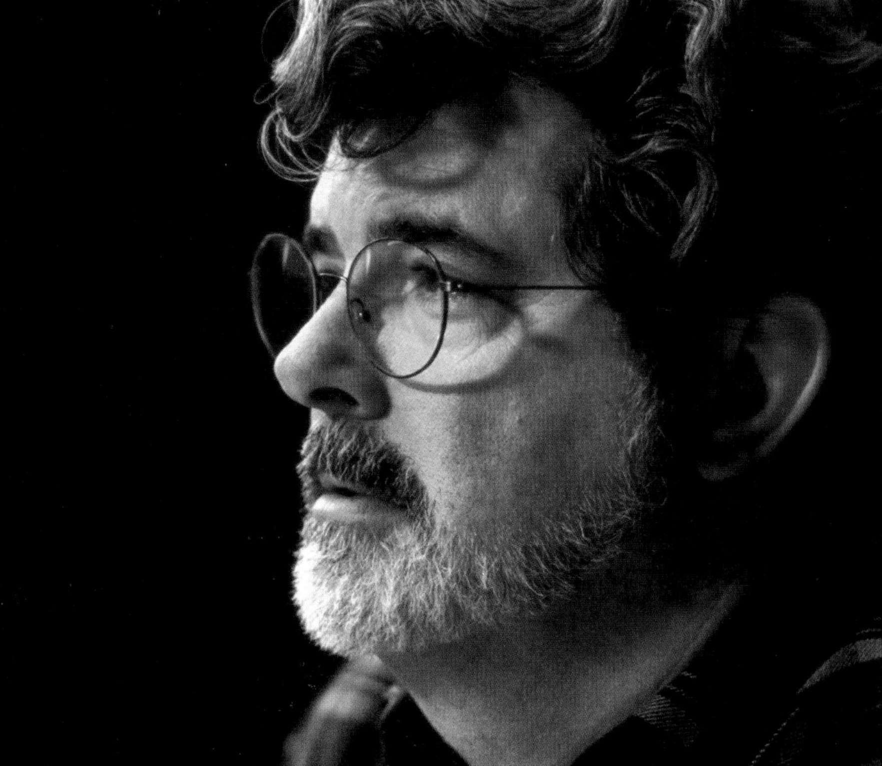

Above - Following the completion of Episode I, Lucas would have almost no downtime before work on Episode II would begin.

Chapter Seven

* *

HIGH Definition

(1999–2002)

The second script in the *Star Wars* prequel trilogy would resume the story ten years after the events of *The Phantom Menace.* Once he had written three drafts of the screenplay for Episode II, Lucas decided to hire a cowriter to help him rewrite some scenes while he was shooting the picture. He approached Jonathan Hales, with whom he had collaborated on *The Young Indiana Jones Chronicles* and *Radioland Murders*, and invited him back to Skywalker Ranch one week before shooting. "It kind of happened through osmosis," says Hales, who was more than happy to work with Lucas again. "Our first story conference lasted a day and a half, and I mainly listened. Then I went back to London and wrote the first draft. After George read it, he called me from the set in Australia and said, 'Some of this is brilliant, some of it is not so brilliant—we'll talk about what's not so brilliant.' We went on from there and I wrote another draft."

Lucas prepared the final draft of the screenplay himself, edging the story further toward the events of Episode IV, and throwing down a gauntlet to ILM by depicting the saga's first fully fledged "star war" . . .

Senator Padmé Amidala arrives on Coruscant to protest the creation of an army to assist the outnumbered Jedi against the growing Separatist movement. Her ship is sabotaged, however. Padmé thinks the Separatist leader, ex-Jedi Count Dooku, is behind the attack. Chancellor Palpatine assigns Obi-Wan Kenobi and Anakin to act as her bodyguards.

Mace Windu tells Anakin to accompany Padmé to the safety of Naboo, while Obi-Wan is assigned the task of discovering the identity of a mysterious assassin who has tried to kill her. Obi-Wan travels to waterlogged Kamino. The planet's prime minister shows him the army of clones created for Jedi Master Sifo-Dyas, and assumes that Obi-Wan has come to inspect the Jedi purchase.

On Naboo, Padmé initially resists Anakin's advances, but the two eventually kiss. They wrestle with their feelings, knowing that Jedi are forbidden to fall in love. Anakin agrees that living a lie "would destroy us."

Star Wars.

Episode two

Jar Jar's Great Adventure

By

George Lucas

March 13, ~~1999~~ 2000

Previous - *Lucas poses with Sony's revolutionary 24-P digital camera.*

Above - *Lucas's handwritten draft with a less-than-serious provisional title for "Episode Two."*

Left - *Skywalker Ranch continued to serve as home to the concept artists fashioning the new worlds of the prequel trilogy.*

On Kamino, Obi-Wan is introduced to bounty hunter Jango Fett, whose genetic blueprint is the basis of the clone army. Obi-Wan immediately recognizes Jango as the assassin. Jango resists Obi-Wan's attempts to capture him, and a fierce duel ensues. Jango and his son, Boba, eventually blast off in their spaceship, but not before Obi-Wan has attached a tracking device to its hull.

On Naboo, Anakin has continuing nightmares about his mother, and he decides to return to Tatooine to help her. Padmé and R2-D2 accompany him, and they return to Watto's junk shop. The destitute Watto explains that he sold Shmi to a moisture farmer called Lars, who had fallen in love with her and bought her freedom. At the Lars homestead, Anakin and Padmé are reunited with C-3PO and meet Cliegg Lars, his son Owen, and Owen's girlfriend, Beru. A despondent Cliegg explains that Shmi has been seized by Tusken Raiders.

Obi-Wan follows Jango's ship to the surface of the dusty red planet Geonosis. Obi-Wan discovers a vast subterranean droid foundry and spies on a meeting chaired by Count Dooku.

Anakin traces his mother to a Tusken camp. She dies in his arms. Blinded by his emotions, Anakin massacres all the men,

Above *- Senator Amidala's starship descends through the mist that shrouds Coruscant in the film's opening moments.*

Right *- Doug Chiang's concept illustration for the encounter between Jango Fett and Jedi Obi-Wan Kenobi, with the bounty hunter's spaceship* Slave I.

Far right *- An environment painting of Geonosis by Erik Tiemens.*

DIGITAL PROJECTION

* *

On June 18, 1999, *The Phantom Menace* became the first major full-length motion picture to be publicly screened using digital electronic projectors. Two venues in New York and two in Los Angeles were chosen for the experiment, which employed equipment devised by CineComm and Texas Instruments. The technology developed by Texas employed a system in which light from a projector was aimed at three Digital Micromirror Device units, each no bigger than a tea bag. Each of these units contained 1.3 million tiny mirrors, which could be switched on and off, thus creating the moving image on the screen.

Exhibitors paid close attention to the screenings, looking for the first signs that the days of traditional film projection were numbered. The industry had long regarded film duplication and distribution as costly and prone to piracy; digital projection from encrypted optical discs offered an economical solution to all these problems.

For Lucasfilm the major issue was, as ever, one of quality. "This is a milestone in cinematic history," said Rick McCallum in June 1999. "Why? Because, for the first time ever, a filmmaker can be certain that the audience will see and hear the film in the way the filmmaker intended it to be seen and heard. Like the introduction of sound and color, these digital screenings represent the beginning of a new era in film presentation. Digital projection guarantees a perfect print with each and every screening for the full life of the film and for every copy that is made."

When Episode II opened in May 2002, it was digitally projected in more than eighty venues around the world.

One of Episode II's digital images, featuring clone troopers and Yoda during the Clone Wars.

women, and children in the camp. Following Shmi's funeral, R2-D2 relays a message from Obi-Wan on Geonosis. Seeing that Obi-Wan is about to be captured, Anakin and Padmé go to his rescue. C-3PO joins them on the journey, getting to know R2-D2 along the way.

On Coruscant, a misguided Jar Jar Binks proposes that Chancellor Palpatine be granted emergency powers. Palpatine authorizes the creation of a grand army, comprising the clones that have already been commissioned.

Anakin and Padmé arrive on Geonosis, get caught up in the automated machinery of a droid factory, and are taken prisoner. Before they are to be executed, Padmé turns to Anakin and confesses that she loves him. In the execution arena, Anakin, Padmé, and Obi-Wan are faced with giant creatures. Padmé leads a resourceful defense as Count Dooku, Poggle the Lesser, Nute Gunray, and Jango Fett watch from the royal box.

Mace Windu appears behind Count Dooku, and numerous Jedi arrive. Violence erupts across the entire arena, and Boba witnesses Jango's decapitation at the hands of Windu. The Jedi are soon overwhelmed by super battle droids—but, just as Dooku gives the order for the captives to be executed, the sky fills with Republic gunships. Battalions of clone troopers take on the droids and Geonosians. Dooku prepares to escape, taking with him the Geonosian plan for "the ultimate weapon"—a huge battle station that resembles an armored moon.

Anakin and Obi-Wan catch up with Dooku in a secret hangar. Anakin rushes forward, only to be brushed aside with a seemingly effortless burst of blue lightning from Dooku. Obi-Wan fares little better. When Anakin rejoins the attack, Dooku severs Anakin's right hand with his lightsaber. Having injured both Obi-Wan and Anakin, Dooku prepares to leave—but is soon faced by a new opponent: Yoda. Yoda and Dooku embark on a furious and athletic duel. Unable to vanquish the Jedi Master, Dooku flees in his ship.

Dooku arrives at Coruscant, where Darth Sidious greets him. Dooku has good news for the Sith Lord—war has begun. On Coruscant, a troubled Yoda concludes, "The shroud of the dark side has fallen. Begun, this Clone War has!"

On Naboo, Anakin and Padmé make their vows in a secret ceremony witnessed by C-3PO and R2-D2. Anakin, now fitted with a robotic hand, kisses his bride, and the two turn to face an uncertain future.

In the earliest drafts of the script, Anakin and Padmé's secret wedding was more of a focal point and occurred earlier in the narrative. But Lucas decided that, like so many other aspects of Anakin's transformation, the relationship between the film's two lovers should be shown to develop at a gradual pace.

One of the key scenes shared between Anakin and Padmé took place in the dining room of their lake retreat on Naboo, which offered an alternate biblical interpretation of Anakin's path into temptation. As they sit down to eat, Anakin uses the Force to levitate a piece of fruit, and Padmé takes a bite. The parallels between the idyllic surroundings and the Garden of Eden are hard to ignore.

The Episode II screenplay also featured subtle resonances of Lucas's previous work. *Star Wars* enthusiasts would immediately pick up on a comment Obi-Wan makes to Anakin as they search a Coruscant gambling club for Amidala's assassin: "Why do I get the

Left *- Obi-Wan (a bearded Ewan McGregor) makes a Jedi "suggestion" to Elan Sleazebaggano (Matt Doran) in the Outlander gambling club.*

Above *- The dining room scene on Naboo. The Eden-like surroundings fit the couple's imminent fall from grace.*

Right *- A fantastic Naboo landscape.*

Far right *- After the dining room scene, the couple continues to flirt with disaster .*

feeling you're going to be the death of me?" The burial of Shmi outside the Lars homestead was a scene discarded from a 1975 draft of *The Star Wars*, which had Luke visiting his mother's grave.

The imagery suggested by the script would also maintain intriguing links with Lucas's previous films. Anakin steals an airspeeder in order to join Obi-Wan in the midair chase. In dialogue ultimately dropped from the final cut of the film, Obi-Wan asks Anakin why he took so long, and Anakin responds that he had to find an airspeeder with "a really gonzo color." That color happens to be bright yellow—as painted on Anakin's Podracer in *The Phantom Menace*, John Milner's hot-rod in *American Graffiti*, his dragster in *More American Graffiti*, and Pete Brock's racing car in Lucas's student film *1:42.08*.

The droid waitress in Dex's Diner glides from table to table on a central wheel, recalling the girls on roller skates who serve the patrons of Mel's Drive-in in *American Graffiti*, while the sterile white atmosphere of Kamino is inspired by *THX 1138*. The scene in

which Obi-Wan gazes out at the clones being cultivated in rows of jars is reminiscent of the poignant moment when THX discovers LUH's name assigned to a fetus in an artificial womb.

Lucas is reluctant to draw any kind of analogy between the *Star Wars* prequel trilogy and contemporary political events, explaining the demise of the Jedi in the context of a more general historical pattern. "One can only say that it's sad that we keep repeating ourselves," he said in 2002. "Everybody in the beginning [in 1977] was saying, 'Oh, it's about Vietnam, it's about World War II,' but it's closer to the Roman Empire than it is to anything else. When people look at something like *Star Wars*, I hope that they say, 'Well, what is all this based on?' and begin to look back through history and realize that it's based on certain mistakes that have been repeated over and over again. None of what's going on today is very new."

Many Episode I cast members, including Ewan McGregor, Natalie Portman, Samuel L. Jackson, and Ian McDiarmid, would reprise their roles in Episode II, but an older actor needed to be found to portray Anakin. Robin Gurland received more than 1,500 submissions for the role, and watched more than four hundred videotaped tests before selecting a short list of actors for Lucas to consider. He was most impressed with the relatively unknown Canadian actor Hayden Christensen. Born in Vancouver in 1981, Christensen had appeared in the daily soap opera *Family Passion* at the age of just twelve, and had subsequently appeared in the Fox Family Channel series *Higher Ground.* McCallum summed up Christensen's appeal: "I wouldn't say there is anything damaged about Hayden, but there is something about him that makes you think, 'Yeah, this guy could lose it.'"

Christensen was initially overwhelmed upon meeting Lucas. "It was a little daunting at first to create that actor-director relationship. But George makes it very easy once you get to know him," he said in 2002. "He was very aware that our relationship was going to be important to my portrayal of Anakin, so he did everything he needed in order to make me feel comfortable. That sense of linear development of character was very important. So I tried to take certain sensibilities from Jake Lloyd's performance, the naiveté and the immaturity that is just a part of being Anakin. And then there's only so much you can draw from a man beneath a mask, but I did try to instill the monotone aspect of the delivery of [James Earl Jones's] lines in my character as well."

Lucas had been impressed with Christopher Lee's performance in *Young Indy*, and called the actor at his London home to offer him the role of Count Dooku. Lee would soon follow Donald Pleasence and Peter Cushing as the third veteran of British horror films to appear in one of Lucas's films. Lucas is quick to point out that this does not betray a particular enthusiasm for the genre: "I like all film, but I was never very much into science-fiction films or horror films. For me, the essence of a whole film is in casting great actors. I picked those actors because they were, or are, great actors. I think a lot of people had disregarded or undervalued them because they had been in horror films."

Maori actor Temuera Morrison, notable for his appearance in *Once Were Warriors* (1994), was cast as grizzled bounty hunter Jango Fett, and Jimmy Smits, an Emmy Award-winner for his role in

Opposite above and below - The airspeeder with "a really gonzo color." Other yellow vehicles in Lucas's filmography include: 1) John Milner's hot-rod in American Graffiti*; 2) Milner's dragster in* More American Graffiti*; 3) Anakin's Podracer, and 4) the N1 starfighters from* The Phantom Menace*. (Not shown are Lucas's real-life yellow Fiat Bianchina and Brock's racer from Lucas's student film* 1:42.08.*)*

Above - Hayden Christensen was cast as the troubled Anakin Skywalker.

Right - Lucas chose Christopher Lee to play Count Dooku and (far right) Temuera Morrison to be Jango Fett, the progenitor of Boba Fett.

PROGRESSIVE FILMING

With the exception of just one scene—a shot of the Jedi Temple that was recycled from *The Phantom Menace* and used as a background image—Episode II was entirely shot using a digital high-definition format called 24-P. The HDC-F900 cameras used during the production of Episode II recorded twenty-four progressive frames per second, just like a film camera. A camera that could record progressive (i.e., distinct and separate) images of this kind represented a significant breakthrough, as electronic video cameras traditionally play back thirty frames per second, with frames that are often interlaced halfway between merged fields.

"We had to talk Sony into it, [but] they built the cameras and they tried really hard to make this work," says Lucas. "We also had to talk Panavision into committing a lot of money to build [the] lenses. Both companies really went out on a limb. This was a giant experiment for everybody." It was a gamble that paid off with spectacular results.

The high-definition supervisor on Episode II was Fred Meyers: "The benefits were clear even before we started the final, intensive, test," he says. "The system offered [director of photography] David Tattersall and his team the same tools they had before, with the added advantage of immediate feedback. We set up engineering stations on set and on location, and we saw the dailies with synchronized sound while we were shooting. It meant editing could begin immediately."

"We saved millions and millions of dollars shooting digitally," said Lucas in 2002. He went on to point out that, as with the innovations he had nurtured in the realm of visual effects, 24-P represented a means to an end. "Cinematography is not about technology; it's about art, it's about taste, it's about understanding your craft, it's about lighting and composition, and anyone who gets off on technological things is missing the point."

Digital cameras have met with some resistance from traditionalists, just as the digital editing systems developed by Lucasfilm were initially shunned. Digital editing is now standard in the filmmaking industry, however, and it seems likely that digital filming will become similarly prevalent. "I think it's inevitable," says Meyers.

Lucas checks a setup with Sony's 24-P digital camera. (Stand-by props Robert Moxham is in the foreground.)

NBC's *L.A. Law* (1986–91), was cast as Senator Bail Organa–the future adoptive father of Princess Leia.

Informal location scouting for Episode II had begun mere days after Episode I opened, and, by the end of 1999, Lucas was sufficiently advanced with the script to brief his various department heads. After visiting potential locations with McCallum and Bocquet, Lucas decided to shoot at Lake Como, Italy (doubling for the lakeside retreat in Naboo); the Plaza d'Espana in Seville, Spain (as the exterior of the royal palace in Theed); and Tunisia, once again, in order to film the Tatooine scenes.

Episode II would be the first *Star Wars* film to have its studio based outside the U.K. Bocquet, Biggar, Tattersall, and the other department heads established their offices at Fox Studios in Sydney, Australia. The sixty-acre site was opened by News Corporation, Twentieth Century Fox's parent company, in May 1998, and *Attack of the Clones* would be its first major film.

This time around, Lucas was confident enough to shoot an entire movie without using film. Following four months of intensive testing with Sony and Panavision's new 24-P high-definition digital camera, Lucas declared that the results were indistinguishable from film—even in a widescreen format. "I think that digital looks better actually," says Lucas now, "and we had fewer problems than we had with film cameras. We were learning how to use the new technology, and whenever you do something for the first time you always have to work a lot harder to figure things out. I think that was difficult for everybody, because the whole crew had to buy into this new way of working. But we were able to finish the film in a very short

Above - *Director of photography David Tattersall (in cap), producer Rick McCallum, and Lucas (center) join other crew in waiting for the rain to stop while on location at the Villa Balbianello in Italy (visual effects supervisor John Knoll is third from left).*

Right - *Costume designer Trisha Biggar, who began working with Lucas during the third season of* Young Indy.

Far right - *Lucas astride Owen Lars's speeder bike on location in Tunisia.*

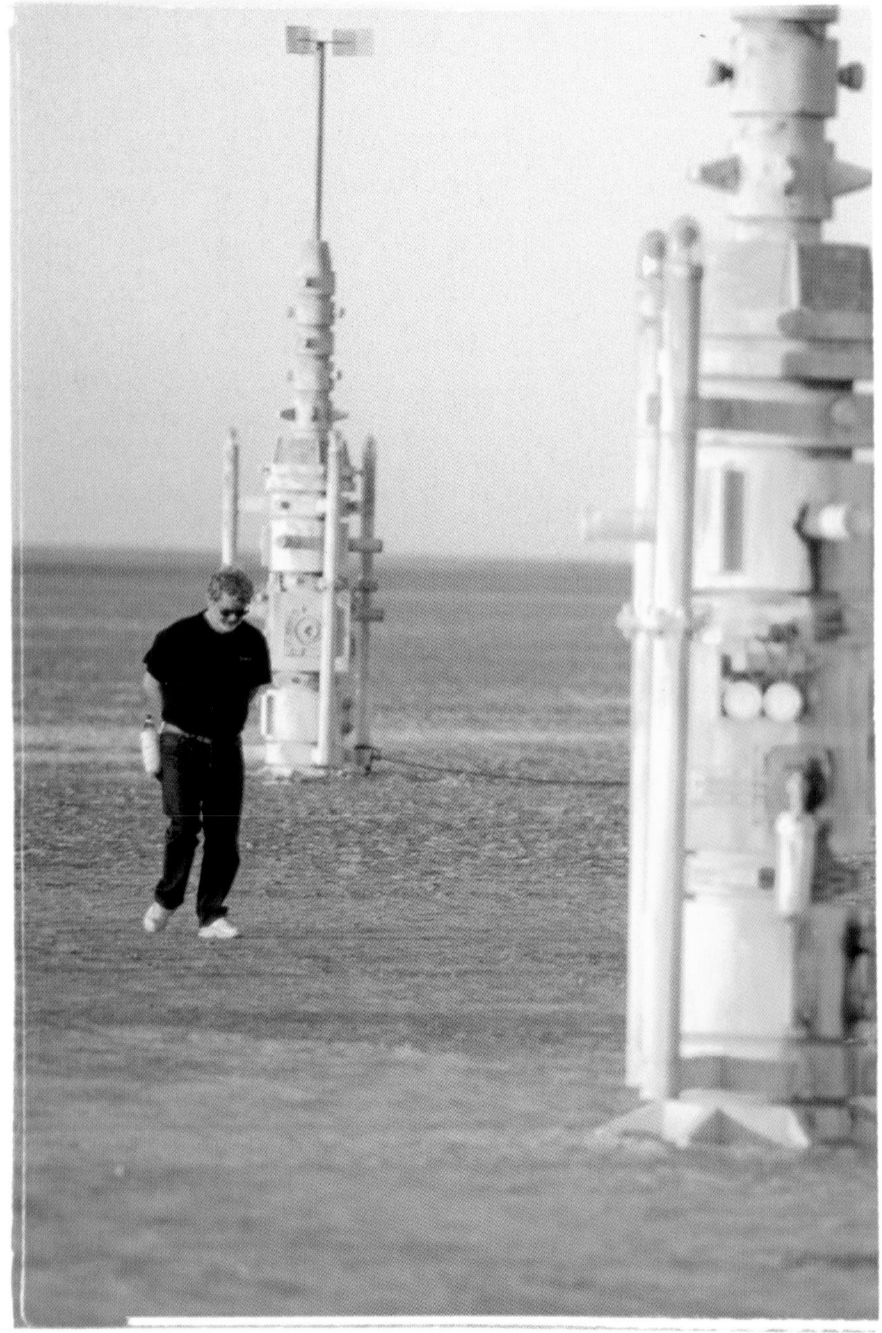

amount of time and I was able to get all the material I needed. So, in terms of production, it actually went better than *The Phantom Menace*."

The formal announcement that Episode II would be shot using digital cameras was made in April 2000 and led to intense speculation over the implications for the industry. "There is so much fear being projected all over by cameramen and studios," said McCallum at the time. "As far as we're concerned, we're not trying to convince the world that they need to go to a different way in making movies. It's the way we want to go. We're not trying to change their minds. If people like film, fine, let them shoot on film. For us, film is not as practical, because every single shot we do has a digital effect in it. There is no point in us shooting on film. It is just much easier and more economical to shoot it digitally—and the results are fabulous."

Following tests that showed the digital cameras were less forgiving in recording certain hard contrasts, director of photography David Tattersall elected to soften the lighting style he had used on Episode I. Tattersall also discovered that the new system offered advantages during shooting—unlike film cameras, which require frequent reloading, the digital cameras would run smoothly all day.

Bocquet and his team constructed sixty-seven sets across all six stages at Fox Studios, and in some surrounding warehouses. He relished the opportunity to design intimate rooms such as Padmé's apartment on Coruscant and the lodge at the lakeside retreat. "They're quite important for us, because you don't often get many personal environments in the *Star Wars* universe," he said during production. "There's a nice bit of characterization you can get in there, which you can't do so much when you're in the rather sterile environment of spacecraft and things like that."

The last draft of Lucas and Hales's shooting script was delivered to the crew at Fox Studios just three days before shooting began. In keeping with tradition, McCallum raised the clapperboard for the first morning of principal photography on June 26, 2000—three years to the day after shooting started on Episode I. One of the early visitors to the set was Francis Ford Coppola, whose

Above *- Seemingly lost in thought, Lucas paces between the vaporator props on location.*

Far left *- Rick McCallum once again does the honors, beginning Episode II's principal photography.*

Left *- Lucas's longtime friend Francis Ford Coppola (center) visits the set of* Attack of the Clones. *('A' camera operator Calum McFarlane is on Coppola's right.)*

Above and right *- Shooting the battle between Obi-Wan Kenobi (Ewan McGregor) and Jango Fett (Temuera Morrison) as they clash in the rain above the waves of Kamino.*

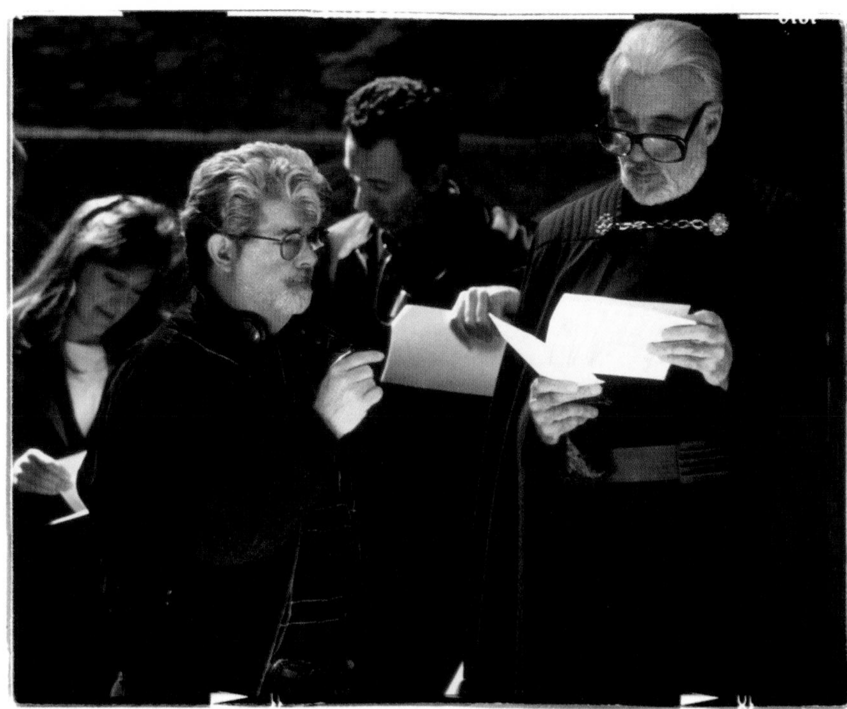

daughter Sofia had played one of Amidala's handmaidens in *The Phantom Menace.*

"It's great to be in *Star Wars,*" said Ewan McGregor in 2002. "Making them is a different story, because they're very, very difficult to make. It's a completely technical exercise to be completely surrounded by blue and to play to a character that's not there. It's a bit like playing chess and having to think seven steps ahead, and I'm not very good at chess. You do your reactions and you just hope that the computer-generating guy matches his actions to what you're doing. It's a weird process. You rely very heavily on your technique."

The seventy-eight-year-old Christopher Lee took the world of digital photography and blue-screen sets in his stride, even when performing close-ups for Dooku's lightsaber duel with Yoda, who for this movie would be digitally added in postproduction. Lee did, however, pause to consult Lucas over Count Dooku's character. "I didn't ask the dreaded question, 'What's my motivation?'" he says, "but I was intrigued by Dooku and told George that I didn't really know anything about the character's background. I asked him, 'What exactly are the Sith?' Filming was held up by a good thirty or forty-five minutes while George told me about the Sith, how many there were, and how I became one of the 'Lost 20' when I left the Jedi."

Lucas completed an impressive average of thirty-six setups per day at Fox, leaving Australia to begin location shooting in August. At one time, shooting locations at the end of a schedule would have been considered unusual. "Those days are long gone," said McCallum in 2000. "The reason you used to have to do your exteriors first was so that you knew what your lighting conditions would be like for the interiors. In the digital world, it doesn't matter. We can change the exterior to anything we want, to match the interior."

The scenes in which Anthony Daniels operated the life-size puppet of the skeletal C-3PO would give him his most active role in realizing the character since *Return of the Jedi.* While filming one scene outside the Lars homestead location in Tunisia, he experienced some emotional déjà vu. "I realized that George and I were the only people who had stood there before, twenty-five years ago. I was reflecting on this when Gavin Bocquet came up to me and asked me how I felt. I told him it was like I'd never been away."

In September 2000, Lucas shot a handful of scenes at Elstree Studios, marking the first time a Lucasfilm production had filmed at the diminished facility since *Indiana Jones and the Last Crusade,* twelve years before. After sixty-one days of shooting across five countries, principal photography came to an end on September 20.

Lucas's favorite part of the filmmaking process began soon after, when he spent several months working alongside Ben Burtt preparing a rough cut. Their

Above left *- Christopher Lee runs through his lines with Lucas at Fox Studios, Sydney, Australia. Between them is first assistant director James McTeigue; script supervisor Jayne-Ann Tenggren is on the left.*

Above right *- Lucas discusses a shot with visual effects supervisor John Knoll.*

Far left *- Anthony Daniels operates the skeletal C-3PO on location in Tunisia. Ultimately, it was decided to "clothe" the protocol droid, and the skeletal puppet was replaced by a gold-plated C-3PO.*

Middle *- Knoll and sound designer/editor Ben Burtt.*

Left *- Stunt coordinator/swordmaster Nick Gillard shows two Jedi younglings how to hold a lightsaber.*

first cut ran two-and-a-half hours. This time, responsibility for the visual effects on Episode II would be divided among four supervisors: John Knoll, Pablo Helman, Ben Snow, and Dennis Muren. Knoll's team created elements of the airspeeder chase in Coruscant, the asteroid-field dogfight, and the arena sequence. "There had been serious concerns during Episode I that we couldn't finish it in the amount of time that we had," admits Knoll. "On Episode II, we came into it with more confidence, but George and Rick, as they are wont to do, like to ratchet things up. I had suspected that the work would get a little harder, because at the end of Episode I, George had said to me, 'I held back in a few places because I wasn't sure you guys could do it. But now I know what you can do, I'm not so constrained.' That was a scary thing to hear."

When comparing Episode I to II, Dennis Muren draws a parallel with the original *Star Wars* trilogy. "I think the amazing thing about Episode II was how broad the work was, visually," he says. "It's very much like *Star Wars* was to *The Empire Strikes Back*. *Empire* had a much bigger palette than *Star Wars*, and I think Episode II is way beyond Episode I. Episode II looks like it was by far the most expensive movie ever made, and that's because it had 2,000 effects

Above - An army of clone troopers is drilled on Kamino.

Right *- Chief hairdresser Sue Love and costume stand-by Jamella Hassan prepare Natalie Portman (Senator Padmé), who is wearing her traveling dress as featured* ***(far right)*** *in a scene filmed on location in Seville, Spain.*

***Both pages** - In the most ambitious sequence in* Attack of the Clones, *after Obi-Wan and Anakin are defeated, a computer-generated Yoda (animated by Rob Coleman and his team) reluctantly tests his skills against the former-Jedi-turned-Sith Count Dooku (Christopher Lee).*

shots that look great. You've got night and day, interiors and exteriors, vastness and closeness, all sorts of speeds, quiet moments and complexities that are really aesthetically varied and pretty darn neat. All the folks working on it had the confidence to give George what he wanted. George guides the whole thing, and they were quick to understand what he was after and get to it faster."

Yoda's lightsaber duel with Count Dooku would prove the most challenging part of Episode II's final act. "I had a visual concept for the Yoda and Count Dooku fight in my mind for a

Above - *A concept painting ("Droid Factory Shot #690") by Ryan Church for a sequence added late in production and shot during pickups in England.*

Far left - *ILM animation director Rob Coleman.*

Left - *A final frame from the finished droid-factory sequence.*

long time before we did it," Lucas remembers. "It was one of those situations where we set ourselves an impossible task and then just hoped we could accomplish it." Lucas kept the stage directions in his screenplay brief:

> *YODA attacks! He flies forward. COUNT DOOKU is forced to retreat. Words are insufficient to describe the range and skill of Yoda's speed and swordplay. His lightsaber is a humming blur of light. Finally, their blades cross and the fighting slows.*

Lucas took special care with this confrontation, mindful that pitting Lee against the diminutive Yoda would provoke unintentional laughter if mishandled. "One of the longest conversations I had with George about this movie concerned that fight between Yoda and Count Dooku," animation director Rob Coleman recalls. "But until it evolved, it was difficult to visualize a fight between these two unlikely adversaries. I had a recollection of reading a 1983 interview where George said he had wanted to see Yoda walk or run—and I was now in the position to help realize that vision. So I took it very seriously. We put all our efforts into Yoda, and I was worried about the fight with Dooku right up to the very last day."

In September 2001, John Williams visited Skywalker Ranch to watch a rough cut of Episode II, by which time less than half the effects shots were complete. He began recording sessions with the London Symphony Orchestra at Abbey Road in

Above - Lucas joins composer and longtime collaborator John Williams at London's Abbey Road Studios.

EPISODE II IMAX

In fall 2002 ***Attack of the Clones*** **was converted for exhibition in IMAX theaters, on screens up to eight stories high with 12,000 watts of uncompressed sound. Rather than simply projecting the standard-size 35mm print, which would have magnified the film grain and any other imperfections, the image was remastered using a process called IMAX DMR.**

The IMAX DMR process scans, enhances, and enlarges a 35mm image to 70mm without compromising quality. IMAX projectors weigh over two tons and feature platters that spool film horizontally, rather than vertically. Weight restrictions on the platters mean that IMAX movies cannot run to more than 120 minutes, so the new version of ***Attack of the Clones*** **was edited to an acceptable length before the process began. The remastering took approximately fourteen weeks and was complete by September 2002. The print came in at the upper end of the IMAX limit, measuring fifty-eight inches in diameter and weighing 360 pounds.**

Attack of the Clones **opened in fifty-eight IMAX theaters across North America on Friday, November 1, 2002. The film earned an impressive $1,435,259 in its first weekend, and generally favorable comments from fans and critics about the editing, which accelerated the journey to the spectacular final act.**

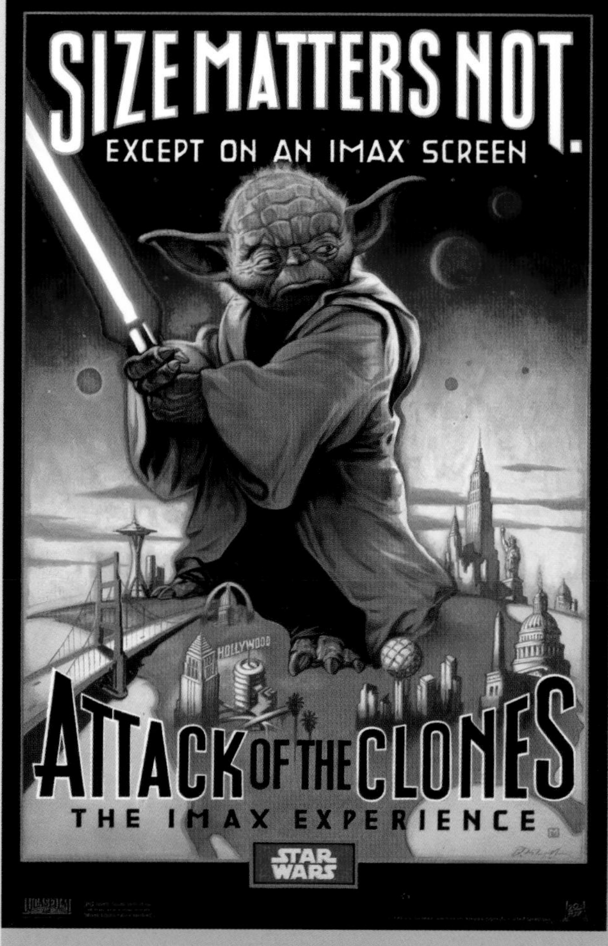

Yoda looms over several American architectural icons in the IMAX poster for Episode II.

January the following year. Williams introduced a wailing electric guitar to the airspeeder chase over Coruscant, and briefly reprised "Duel of the Fates" when Anakin searches Tatooine for his missing mother. When Anakin confesses to Padmé that he murdered the entire camp of Tusken Raiders, Williams's reprise of Darth Vader's theme would leave the audience in little doubt over the consequences of the young apprentice's actions. He also composed "Across the Stars," a love theme that swells with the fervent romance shared by Anakin and Padmé, and which subsequently plays over the end credits. Whether evoking the pitch and yaw of Kamino's stormy waves, or the fiery maelstrom of the Battle of Geonosis, Williams balances old and new while maintaining the musical texture familiar from the other films in the series.

Star Wars: Episode II *Attack of the Clones* was released on Thursday, May 16, 2002. During its first weekend in North American theaters it grossed more than $80 million, one of the highest figures ever recorded. The movie's total U.S. gross would top $302 million, its worldwide gross reaching more than $648 million.

"*Clones* is crammed with action, grand digital design and a dark side Lucas hasn't flaunted since 1980's *The Empire Strikes Back*," wrote Peter Travers in *Rolling Stone*. Writing in *Variety*, Todd McCarthy found plenty to admire on almost every level: "George Lucas has reached deep into the trove of his self-generated mythological world to produce a grand entertainment that offers a satisfying balance among the series' epic, narrative, technological, and emotional qualities. If *The Empire Strikes Back* represented an advance on the original *Star Wars*, *Clones* marks a big leap beyond *Menace*, while also holding out the promise of a climactic installment that could be even more dramatic."

"The first time I got to see the movie with a real audience, a non-ILM audience, I remember shrinking down in my seat before the Yoda/Dooku fight started," Rob Coleman remembers. "The

Above - *Computer-generated* vérité *during the Battle of Geonosis.*

Far left - *In another scene added late in production, Mace Windu (Samuel L. Jackson) gives orders to a clone trooper commander.*

Left - *In the final scene of* Attack of the Clones, *Anakin (Hayden Christensen) and Padmé (Natalie Portman) are secretly married by a holy man (Gaetano Gatti) on Naboo.*

Opposite - *The elegant teaser and final American one-sheets for* Attack of the Clones. *The latter features artwork by Drew Struzan.*

cheer that came out from the audience just relieved all the stress in my life. It was a great experience."

It is not just the technical excellence and exciting action of *Attack of the Clones* that impresses. Lucas never loses sight of the motivations, implications, and consequences that underlie both the intimate and the epic events in the movie. Moreover, Lucas's ideals have remained in many ways the same since he made *THX 1138.4EB*: the tools of his trade may have changed beyond all recognition, but the filmmaker behind the digital lens has stayed surprisingly consistent. When Senator Amidala's ship is sabotaged at the beginning of the film, Lucas momentarily shakes the camera, as though rocked by the force of the blast. During the ground battle at the end of the movie, there is a crash zoom onto the bridge of a Republic ship, and the camera judders once again as a stricken Trade Federation vessel is toppled in a huge explosion. These efforts to introduce a hand-held *vérité* feel to CG shots reveal that Lucas has not lost his passion for the documentary style that informed his student films many years ago.

In 2001, Lucas gave one of a number of interviews to discuss his tests with the new digital camera and his decision to make Episode II without film. "I think film will ultimately become a generic term," he told journalist Paula Parisi. "People will have forgotten what it means in the end."

Parisi wondered whether the whole process could still be referred to as "filmmaking." According to Lucas, the definition was academic: "It will be called cinema."

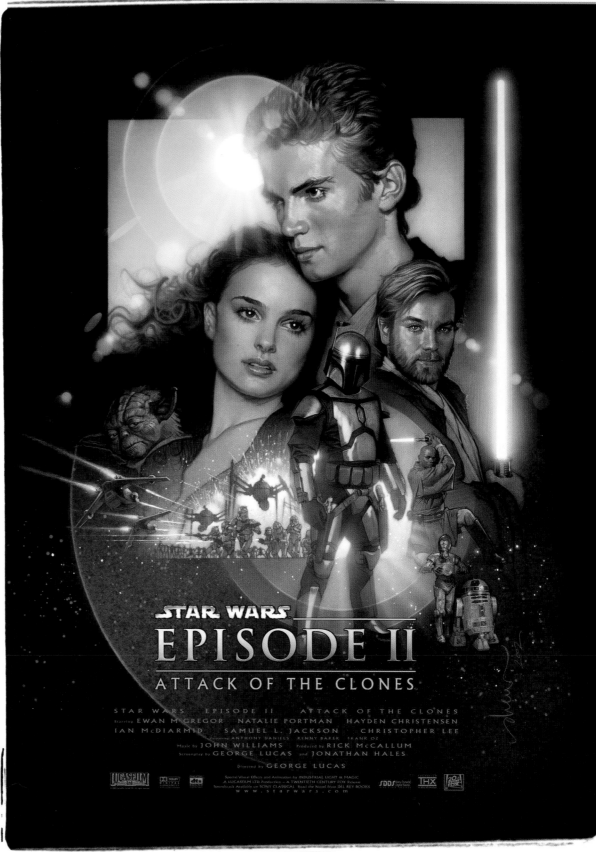

STAR WARS
EPISODE II
ATTACK OF THE CLONES

STAR WARS EPISODE II ATTACK OF THE CLONES
Starring EWAN McGREGOR NATALIE PORTMAN HAYDEN CHRISTENSEN
IAN McDIARMID SAMUEL L. JACKSON CHRISTOPHER LEE
Music by JOHN WILLIAMS Produced by RICK McCALLUM
Screenplay by GEORGE LUCAS and JONATHAN HALES
Directed by GEORGE LUCAS
www.starwars.com

Shooting Schedule

Star Wars: Episode II Attack of the Clones

* * * * * * * * * * * * * * * * * *as shot* * * * * * * * * * * * * * * * * *

SHOOT DAYS SCHEDULED: 59

SHOOT DAY 1: MONDAY, JUNE 26, 2000
Crew Call: 7.00 **Camera Wrap:** 19.05
Location: STAGE 6, FOX STUDIOS, SYDNEY, AUSTRALIA [FSA]
Sets: INT. CORUSCANT–SENATE
Palpatine speaks of the death of Senator Amidala; Jar Jar proposes Palpatine should be granted emergency power
Pages: 2
Setups: 36

SHOOT DAY 2: TUESDAY, JUNE 27
Crew Call: 7.00 **Camera Wrap:** 19.00
Location: STAGE 6
Sets: INT. CORUSCANT–SENATE
Amidala appears . . . in the Senate and other speeches
Pages: 2
Setups: 46
Notes: EWAN MCGREGOR CALLED FOR STUNT REHEARSALS TODAY.

SHOOT DAY 3: WEDNESDAY, JUNE 28
Crew Call: 7.00 **Camera Wrap:** 19.08
Location: STAGE 2
Sets: INT. NABOO STARFIGHTER COCKPIT
Amidala insists she and Anakin leave to help Obi-Wan . . .
Pages: 1 1/4
Setups: 32

SHOOT DAY 4: THURSDAY, JUNE 29
Crew Call: 7.00 **Camera Wrap:** 18.50
Location: STAGE 2 & STAGE 1
Sets: EXT. CORUSCANT-ALLEY OUTSIDE NIGHTCLUB
Obi-Wan starts to interrogate Zam
EXT. CORUSCANT–ENTRANCE TO NIGHTCLUB
Zam runs into the Nightclub
Pages: 7/8
Setups: 21
Notes: ALLEY DWELLERS X 5, NIGHTCLUB

SHOOT DAY 5: FRIDAY, JUNE 30
Crew Call: 7.00 **Camera Wrap:** 18.24
Location: ART DEPARTMENT BUILDING 48
Sets: EXT. CORUSCANT-SENATE LANDING PLATFORM
Pages: 1 4/8
Setups: 30

SHOOT DAY 6: MONDAY, JULY 3
Crew Call: 7.00 **Camera Wrap:** 19.45
Location: STAGE 1
Sets: INT. CORUSCANT–SENATE BUILDING–AMIDALA'S APARTMENT
Padme Amidala meets Obi-Wan, the Jedi are there to protect Amidala . . .
Pages: 3/4
Setups: 28

SHOOT DAY 7: TUESDAY, JULY 4
Crew Call: 7.00 **Camera Wrap:** 19.37
Location: STAGE 1
Sets: INT. COURSCANT–SENATE BUILDING
AMIDALA'S APARTMENT
Amidala packs her bags
Pages: 5 5/8
Setups: 30

SHOOT DAY 8: WEDNESDAY, JULY 5
Crew Call: 7.30 **Camera Wrap:** 20.30
Location: STAGE 1
Sets: INT. CORUSCANT–SENATE BUILDING
AMIDALA'S APARTMENT/BEDROOM
Anakin and Obi-Wan talk, Amidala is being used as bait . . .
Pages: 6-1/8
Setups: 16

SHOOT DAY 9: THURSDAY, JULY 6
Crew Call: 7.30 **Camera Wrap:** 19.12
Location: STAGE 2
Sets: EXT: CORUSCANT-SENATE BUILDING/CITYSCAPE (CHASE)
Anakin . . . grabs a speeder . . . Anakin tumbles from the speeder . . .
Pages: 1 2/8
Setups: 46
Notes: CATERING–BREAKFAST FOR SHOOTING CAST/CREW: FOR 270
LUNCH FOR SHOOTING CAST/CREW: FOR 400
AFTERNOON TEA IN THE HAND: FOR 370

SHOOT DAY 10: FRIDAY, JULY 7
Crew Call: 7.00 **Camera Wrap:** 19.00
Location: FODDER BUILDING 44A (MAIN)
Sets: INT. TATOOINE–HOMESTEAD GARAGE
Anakin tells Amidala he did a terrible thing
Pages: 2 7/8
Setups: 26
Notes: EXTRAS CASTING CALL FOR "YOUNG JEDI'S" [SIC] HELD TODAY FOR APPROXIMATELY 60 CHILDREN FROM 1600

SHOOT DAY 11: MONDAY, JULY 10
Crew Call: 7.00 **Camera Wrap:** 19.40
Location: FODDER STAGE (BLDG 44A), ART DEPARTMENT BLDG 48
Sets: INT. TATOOINE–HOMESTEAD GARAGE
C-3PO is happy with his new skin
INT/EXT. JEDI TEMPLE, EXT. LANDING PLATFORM
Obi-Wan says goodbye to Mace Windu
Pages: 1 4/8
Setups: 39

SHOOT DAY 12: TUESDAY, JULY 11
Crew Call: 7.00 **Camera Wrap:** 19.40
Location: ART DEPT. BLDG 48, STAGE 6
Sets: INT. TIPOCA CITY–PRIME MINISTER'S OFFICE
Obi-Wan learns of the Clone army and that Jango Fett was the host . . .
Pages: 4 4/8
Setups: 46
Notes: COMPANY STAGE MOVE FROM ART DEPARTMENT, BUILDING 48 TO STAGE 6 @ 11.00. ASSISTED BY 5 STAGEHANDS

SHOOT DAY 13: Thursday, July 13
Crew Call: 7.00 **Camera Wrap:** 19.45
Location: STAGE 1

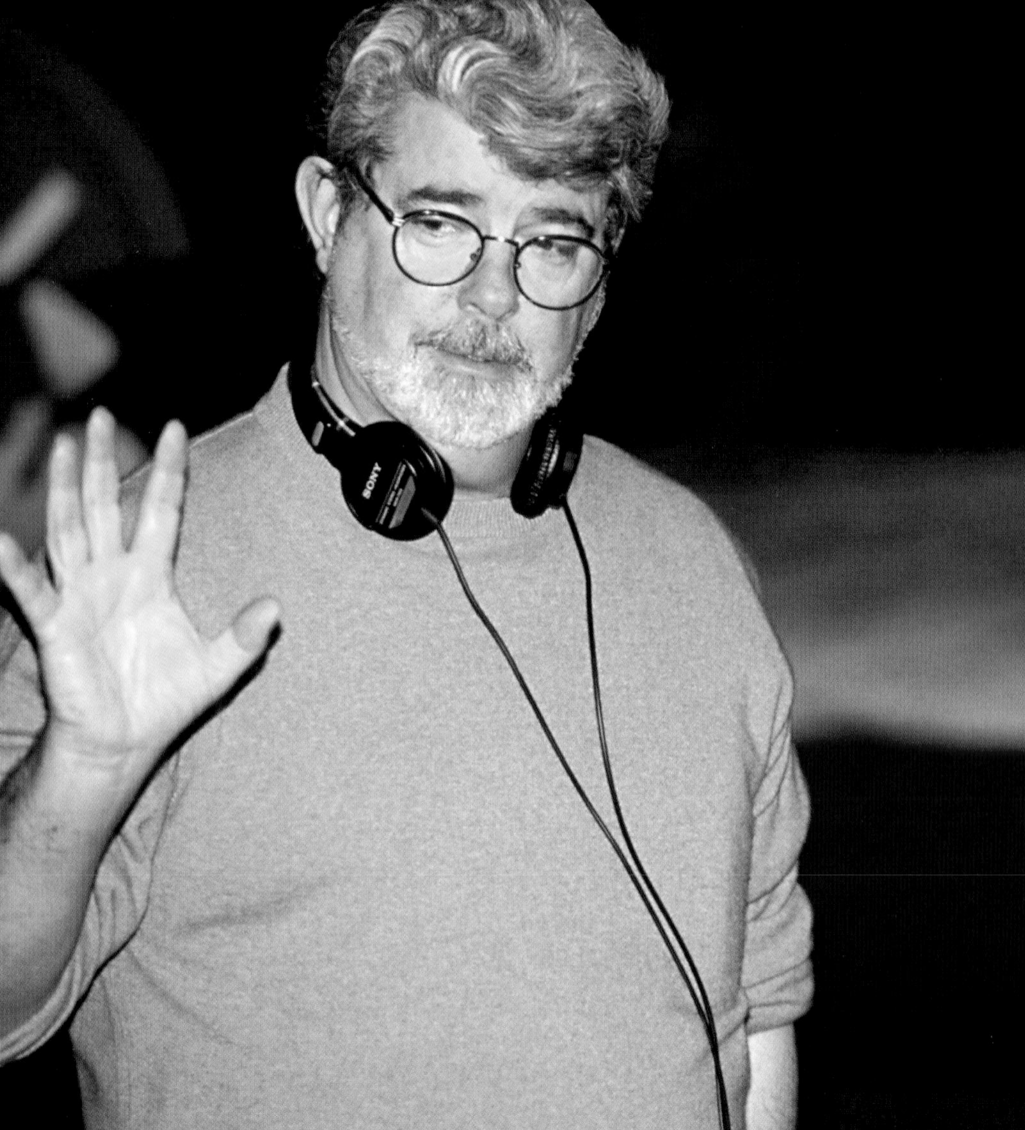

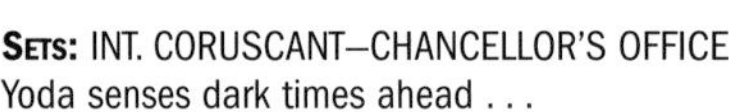

Sets: INT. CORUSCANT–CHANCELLOR'S OFFICE
Yoda senses dark times ahead . . .
Pages: 0
Setups: 34

SHOOT DAY 14: THURSDAY, JULY 13
Crew Call: 7.00 **Camera Wrap:** 20.55
Location: STAGE 1
Sets: EXT. CORUSCANT–MILITARY STAGING AREA
They watch as thousands of Clone troops . . . make ready for war (The End)
Pages: 2/8
Setups: 42

SHOOT DAY 15: FRIDAY, JULY 14
Crew Call: 7.00 **Camera Wrap:** 18.45
Location: DEPOT–BLDG 48, ART DEPT-BLDG 48, STAGE 5
Sets: INT. TATOOINE HOMESTEAD KITCHEN
Amidala and Beru prepare food for Anakin
Pages: 3 3/8
Setups: 40
Notes: NEW SCENE 117A ADDED TODAY

SHOOT DAY 16: MONDAY, JULY 17
Crew Call: 6.30 **Camera Wrap:** 19.00
Location: STAGE 3, STAGE 2
Sets: INT. CORUSCANT–NIGHTCLUB
Obi-Wan slices off Zam's arm
Pages: 1 4/8
Setups: 23

SHOOT DAY 17: TUESDAY, JULY 18
Crew Call: 8.00 **Camera Wrap:** 19.35
Location: DEPOT–BUILDING 48
Sets: INT. STARSHIP FREIGHTER HOLD
Anakin is having a nightmare
Pages: 1 7/8
Setups: 23

SHOOT DAY 18: WEDNESDAY, JULY 19
Crew Call: 7.30 **Camera Wrap:** 20.00

Location: STAGE 4
Sets: INT. NABOO LAKE RETREAT DINING ROOM/FIRE-PLACE ALCOVE
Anakin is in love with Amidala . . . but do they want to live a lie?
Pages: 2
Setups: 20

SHOOT DAY 19: THURSDAY, JULY 20
Crew Call: 7.30 **Camera Wrap:** 19.36
Location: STAGE 5
Sets: INT. JEDI TEMPLE—TRAINING VERANDAH
Obi-Wan visits Yoda and the 4 yr old trainees
Pages: 1 4/8
Setups: 18
Notes: JEDI CHILDREN EXTRAS ON FOUR-HOUR CALLS, COMPLETED WORK AS SCHEDULED, HOWEVER REQUIRED SOME CAJOLING TO REMOVE COSTUMES . . .

SHOOT DAY 20: FRIDAY, JULY 21
Crew Call: 7.00 **Camera Wrap:** 19.10
Location: STAGE 2
Sets: INT./EXT. CORUSCANT—CITYSCAPE (ANAKIN'S SPEEDER)
Anakin and Obi-Wan give chase (Obi-Wan clears flag from speeder)
Pages: 0
Setups: 22

SHOOT DAY 21: MONDAY, JULY 24
Crew Call: 7.00 **Camera Wrap:** 19.25
Location: STAGE 2
Sets: INT/EXT.: CORUSCANT—CITYSCAPE
Zam sees the droid and takes off, shooting at it
Pages: 0
Setups: 34

SHOOT DAY 22: TUESDAY, JULY 25
Crew Call: 7.00 **Camera Wrap:** 19.10
Location: STAGE 2
Sets: INT. TIPOCA CITY—FETT APARTMENT/CORRIDOR
Obi-Wan and Jango size each other up
Pages: 0
Setups: 30

SHOOT DAY 23: WEDNESDAY, JULY 26
Crew Call: 7.00 **Camera Wrap:** 19.45
Location: STAGE 2
Sets: INT. TIPOCA CITY—FETT APARTMENT/CORRIDOR
Taun We and Obi-Wan arrive at the Fett's apartment
INT/EXT. LOW MODE GIMBLE BLUESCREEN SET
Anakin leaves on Owen's speeder bike
Pages: 3 2/8
Setups: 47
Notes: NUMBER OF MAIN SHOOT DAYS HAS BEEN REVISED TO 60 DAYS.

SHOOT DAY 24: THURSDAY, JULY 27
Crew Call: 7.00 **Camera Wrap:** 19.45
Location: STAGE 2, ART DEPARTMENT—BLDG 28, DEPOT—BUILDING 48
Sets: EXT. NABOO SPEEDER BUS
Amidala and Dorme have a tearful farewell . . .
EXT. THEED RESIDENTIAL SIDE STREET
Amidala takes Anakin to her parents' house
Pages: 2 4/8
Setups: 27

SHOOT DAY 25: FRIDAY, JULY 28
Crew Call: 7.00 **Camera Wrap:** 19.09
Location: STAGE 2
Sets: EXT. CORUSCANT CITYSCAPE, ZAM'S SPEEDER
Anakin fights with Zam
Pages: 0
Setups: 26

SHOOT DAY 26: MONDAY, JULY 31
Crew Call: 7.00 **Camera Wrap:** 19.06
Location: STAGE 2
Sets: INT. JEDI STARFIGHTER—COCKPIT (ASTEROID)
Obi-Wan appears to smash into an asteroid . . .
INT. TIPOCA CITY—FETT COCKPIT (LANDING PLATFORM)
Young Boba Fett fires at Obi-Wan
Pages: 2 3/8
Setups: 28

SHOOT DAY 27: TUESDAY, AUGUST 1
Crew Call: 7.00 **Camera Wrap:** 19.45
Location: STAGE 1
Sets: INT. JEDI TEMPLE, ARCHIVE LIBRARY, MAIN HALLWAY (STAIRS)
Obi-Wan and Madame Jocasta Nu discuss Count Dooku
Pages: 2 6/8
Setups: 25

SHOOT DAY 28: WEDNESDAY, AUGUST 2
Crew Call: 7.00 **Camera Wrap:** 19.20
Location: STAGE 3
Sets: TATOOINE DESERT—TUSKEN TORTURE HUT
Anakin enters the tent to find the tortured Shmi
Pages: 1 3/8
Setups: 32

SHOOT DAY 29: THURSDAY, AUGUST 3
Crew Call: 7.00 **Camera Wrap:** 19.45
Location: STAGE 3, STAGE 2
Sets: EXT. GEONOSIS LANDING AREA
Obi-Wan sends a message to Yoda—send all available Jedi . . .
INT. TUNNEL UNDER THE ARENA
Anakin and Amidala say, "I love you"
Pages: 6/8
Setups: 38

SHOOT DAY 30: FRIDAY, AUGUST 4
Crew Call: 7.00 **Camera Wrap:** 19.00
Location: STAGE 5, STAGE 2
Sets: INT. JEDI TEMPLE, ANALYSIS CUBICLES
The droid doesn't know where the dart comes from
INT. GEONOSIS EXECUTION AREA (ARENA)
Anakin rides and fights the Reek
Pages: 1 6/8
Setups: 40

SHOOT DAY 31: MONDAY, AUGUST 7
Crew Call: 7.00 **Camera Wrap:** 19.30
Location: STAGE 6, STAGE 1
Sets: EXT. CORUSCANT, DOWNTOWN BACKSTREET (CAFÉ)
Obi-Wan enters
INT. DEXTER JETTSTER CAFÉ
Dexter Jettster explains to Obi-Wan that he has a Kamino Cyberdart
Pages: 2 4/8
Setups: 24

SHOOT DAY 32: TUESDAY, AUGUST 8
Crew Call: 7.00 **Camera Wrap:** 19.01
Location: STAGE 1
Sets: EXT. TIPOCA CITY—LANDING PLATFORM/FETT SHIP
The Obi-Wan/Jango Fett landing platform fight
Pages: 1 4/8
Setups: 18

SHOOT DAY 33: WEDNESDAY, AUGUST 9
Crew Call: 7.00 **Camera Wrap:** 20.05
Location: STAGE 1
Sets: EXT. TIPOCA CITY—LANDING PLATFORM/FETT SHIP
The Fetts unhitch lines and Boba climbs in
Pages: 0
Setups: 46

SHOOT DAY 34: THURSDAY, AUGUST 10
Crew Call: 7.30 **Camera Wrap:** 19.30
Location: STAGE 1
Sets: EXT. GEONOSIS, EXECUTION AREA
Anakin picks up Padme . . . they ride toward Obi-Wan
Pages: 0
Setups: 28
Notes: SHOOTING SUSPENDED FOR 45 MINS AFTER BULB IN SPACE LIGHT EXPLODED ABOVE SET AND DAMAGED BLUE SCREEN AND SILK

SHOOT DAY 35: FRIDAY, AUGUST 11
Crew Call: 7.00 **Camera Wrap:** 18.30
Location: STAGE 1, STAGE 3
Sets: EXT. GEONOSIS—EXECUTION AREA (PADME'S POLE)
Amidala climbs the pole to escape the Nexu
EXT. DOOKU'S SPEEDER
Dooku rides his speeder to the secret hangar

Above - Lucas and Ian McDiarmid (Supreme Chancellor Palpatine) on the set.

Pages: 0
Setups: 41

SHOOT DAY 36: SATURDAY, AUGUST 12
Crew Call: 6.30 **Camera Wrap:** 16.30
Location: STAGE 3
Sets: EXT. GEONOSIS–EXECUTION AREA
Padme falls from the Orray . . . she hides with Anakin in the cart . . .
Pages: 0
Setups: 48

SHOOT DAY 37: MONDAY, AUGUST 14
Crew Call: 7.00 **Camera Wrap:** 19.00
Location: STAGE 3
Sets: EXT. GEONOSIS–EXECUTION ARENA
Jango Fett and Mace Windu fight fiercely
Pages: 0
Setups: 54
SHOOT DAY 38: TUESDAY, AUGUST 15
Crew Call: 7.00 **Camera Wrap:** 19.10
Location: STAGE 3
Sets: EXT. GEONOSIS–EXECUTION ARENA
Jango falls to the dirt and Mace is the victor
Pages: 0
Setups: 71

SHOOT DAY 39: WEDNESDAY, AUGUST 16
Crew Call: 7.00 **Camera Wrap:** 19.10
Location: STAGE 5
Sets: EXT. GEONOSIS–EXECUTION ARENA (DOOKU'S BOX)
Dooku orders in the destroyers . . .
Pages: 0
Setups: 54

SHOOT DAY 40: THURSDAY, AUGUST 17
Crew Call: 7.00 **Camera Wrap:** 19.27
Location: STAGE 4
Sets: INT. GEONOSIS HOVERCRAFT
The Jedi go after the escaping Count Dooku
EXT. TERRAIN OUTSIDE THE ARENA
Amidala falls to the ground
Pages: 0
Setups: 48

SHOOT DAY 41: FRIDAY, AUGUST 18
Crew Call: 7.00 **Camera Wrap:** 19.00
Location: STAGE 1
Sets: INT. GEONOSIS CONFERENCE ROOM
Count Dooku and his conspirators hammer out a deal . . .
Pages: 3 3/8
Setups: 42

SHOOT DAY 42: SATURDAY, AUGUST 19
Crew Call: 6.30 **Camera Wrap:** 16.30
236 **Location:** STAGE 6
Sets: EXT. GEONOSIS CORRIDORS/CENTRAL SQUARE
Anakin and Amidala enter the empty tower . . .
Pages: 2 5/8
Setups: 44

SHOOT DAY 43: MONDAY, AUGUST 21
Crew Call: 7.00 **Camera Wrap:** 19.30
Location: STAGE 2
Sets: INT. GEONOSIS–SECRET HANGAR (DOOKU'S SHIP)
The Hovership arrives at the secret hangar . . .
Pages: 0
Setups: 22

SHOOT DAY 44: TUESDAY, AUGUST 22
Crew Call: 7.00 **Camera Wrap:** 19.00
Location: STAGE 2
Sets: INT. GEONOSIS–SECRET HANGAR (DOOKU'S SHIP)
The Jedi are toast . . .
Pages: 0
Setups: 56

SHOOT DAY 45: WEDNESDAY, AUGUST 23
Crew Call: 7.00 **Camera Wrap:** 19.20
Location: STAGE 2
Sets: INT. GEONOSIS–SECRET HANGAR (DOOKU'S SHIP)
Enter Yoda . . .
Pages: 3 6/8
Setups: 47

SHOOT DAY 46: THURSDAY, AUGUST 24
Crew Call: 7.00 **Camera Wrap:** 19.00
Location: STAGE 2, ART DEPOT
Sets: INT. CORUSCANT–SECRET LANDING PLATFORM (DOOKU'S SHIP)/CONFERENCE ROOM ALCOVE/STAIRS/CORRIDORS
Count Dooku and Darth Sidious meet on the dark side of Coruscant . . . it's War!
INT. GEONOSIS–THRONE ROOM/AUDIENCE CHAMBER
Anakin and Amidala are tried for espionage.
EXT. THEED RESIDENTIAL STREET, BLUESCREEN
CU Anakin outside Parents' house
Pages: 1
Setups: 34
Notes: UNSCHEDULED SCENE 149PT (BOBA FETT AT EXECUTION ARENA) ALSO SHOT

SHOOT DAY 47: FRIDAY, AUGUST 25
Crew Call: 7.00 **Camera Wrap:** 16.47
Location: ART DEPARTMENT DEPOT
Sets: INT. THEED, AMIDALA'S PARENTS' HOUSE
They tease Amidala about Anakin . . .
Pages: 2 4/8
Setups: 29
Notes: FINAL DAY OF PRINCIPAL PHOTOGRAPHY IN SYDNEY FOR MAIN UNIT. MAIN UNIT TO RESUME FILMING IN LAKE COMO ITALY ON WED 3RD AUGUST 00

SHOOT DAY 48: WEDNESDAY, AUGUST 30
Crew Call: 10.00 **Camera Wrap:** 14.30
Location: VILLA BALBANIELLO, LAKE COMO, ITALY
Sets: EXT. NABOO LAKE RETREAT–GARDEN
Anakin kisses Amidala . . .
Pages: 0
Setups: 1

SHOOT DAY 49: THURSDAY, AUGUST 31
Crew Call: 6.45 **Camera Wrap:** 20.15
Location: MAYER STEPS, TREMEZZO, LAKE COMO
Sets: EXT. NABOO LAKE GONDOLA SPEEDER/SPACECRAFT
Anakin and Amidala step off the Speeder
EXT. NABOO LAKE RETREAT BALCONY
Anakin is meditating
Pages: 1
Setups: 29
Notes: LONG DELAYS DUE TO BAD WEATHER CONDITIONS; VANITY FAIR STILLS SHOOT TEAM ON SET TODAY WITH ANNIE LEIBOVITZ

SHOOT DAY 50: FRIDAY, SEPTEMBER 1
Crew Call: 6.30 **Camera Wrap:** 19.40
Location: VILLA BALBANIELLO, LAKE COMO
Sets: INT. THEED AMIDALA'S PARENTS' HOUSE (AMIDALA'S ROOM)
Pages: 3 1/8
Setups: 44

SHOOT DAY 51: SATURDAY, SEPTEMBER 2
Crew Call: 7.00 **Camera Wrap:** 16.20
Location: STRADA S. MARTINO, LENNO, LAKE COMO
Sets: EXT. NABOO LAKE RETREAT–ROLLING HILLS
Anakin and Amidala picnic in Eden . . .
Pages: 2 3/8
Setups: 38
Notes: COMPANY WRAPPED LOCATION EARLY AND WRAPPED VILLA TO TRAVEL ON TO CASERTA.

SHOOT DAY 52: TUESDAY, SEPTEMBER 5
Crew Call: 12.00 **Camera Wrap:** 20.50
Location: REGGIA DI CASERTA, ITALY
Sets: INT. NABOO THRONE PALACE–THRONE ROOM
The Queen recognizes Anakin's infatuation . . .
Pages: 0
Setups: 26
Notes: TRAVEL & PREP DAY MONDAY 4TH SEPTEMBER AT REGGIA DI CASERTA.

SHOOT DAY 53: THURSDAY, SEPTEMBER 7
Crew Call: 13.45 **#1 Camera Wrap:** 17.15
#2 Camera Wrap: 19.00
Location: CHOTT EL JERRID, TOZEUR, TUNISIA
Sets: EXT. TATOOINE–HOMESTEAD–DUNE SEA/CAMPFIRE
Anakin finds the bodies of the search party . . .
EXT. TATOOINE–DESERT; EXT. TATOOINE–JAWAS CAMP
Anakin talks to the Jawas . . .
Pages: 3/8
Setups: 22

SHOOT DAY 54: SATURDAY, SEPTEMBER 9
Crew Call: 5.30 **Camera Wrap:** 18.40
Location: CHOTT EL JERRID, TOZEUR, TUNISIA
Sets: EXT. TATOOINE–HOMESTEAD MOISTURE FARM
Anakin takes off on Owen's speeder bike
EXT. TATOOINE–HOMESTEAD GRAVESITE
The funeral of Shmi
Pages: 2
Setups: 62

SHOOT DAY 55: SUNDAY, SEPTEMBER 10
Crew Call: 6.00 **Camera Wrap:** 15.45
(Location Wrap: 21.30)
Location: TOZEUR, TUNISIA
Sets: EXT. MOS ESPA/WATTO'S SHOP
Pages: 1 7/8
Setups: 23
Notes: ON WRAP AT MOS ESPA, CAST AND CREW RELOCATED IN CONVOY TO MATMATA FOR SHOOT DAY NO. 56. JOURNEY TIME APPROX. 2 HRS 30 MINS

SHOOT DAY 56: MONDAY, SEPTEMBER 11
Crew Call: 6.45 **Camera Wrap:** 19.05
Location: SIDI DRISS HOTEL, MATMATA, TUNISIA
Sets: EXT. TATOOINE–HOMESTEAD COURTYARD
Anakin meets the Lars family
Pages: 1 7/8
Setups: 40
Notes: ON WRAP, CAST AND CREW RE-LOCATED TO DJERBA FOR OFFICIAL REST DAY BEFORE CATCHING CHARTER PLANE TO SEVILLE ON WED. 13TH SEPT

SHOOT DAY 57: WEDNESDAY, SEPTEMBER 13
Crew Call: 5.45 **Camera Wrap:** 18.40
Location: PLAZA D'ESPANA, SEVILLE, SPAIN
Sets: EXT. NABOO PALACE–GRAND COURTYARD
They cross the great piazza on the way to the throne room
Pages: 1 5/8
Setups: 19
Notes: COMPANY MOVE SCHEDULED FOR THURSDAY 14TH SEPT–SEVILLE-LONDON

SHOOT DAY 58: FRIDAY, SEPTEMBER 15
Crew Call: 7.00 **Camera Wrap:** 18.50
Location: ELSTREE FILM STUDIOS, LONDON, UK
Sets: INT. GEONOSIS/DROID CONTROL SHIP
Ki-Adi-Mundi leads the raid onto the Droid Control Ship . . . they fight their way inside
Pages: 4 4/8
Setups: 54
Notes: BE AWARE THAT DUE TO THE PETROL CRISIS TRANSPORT WILL BE LIMITED. PLEASE BE PATIENT.

SHOOT DAY 59: MONDAY, SEPTEMBER 18
Crew Call: 7.00 **Camera Wrap:** 19.10
Location: ELSTREE
Sets: INT. GEONOSIS/DROID CONTROL SHIP–R2-D2 BLUESCREEN
Ki-Adi-Mundi and the surviving Jedi make their way through the command ship
EXT. GEONOSIS EXECUTION ARENA
Obi-Wan fights the acklay (refer storyboards)
Pages: 2 4/8
Setups: 50

SHOOT DAY 60: TUESDAY, SEPTEMBER 19
Crew Call: 7.00 **Camera Wrap:** 19.12
Location: ELSTREE
Sets: INT. GEONOSIS EXECUTION ARENA
The Picador challenges Obi-Wan . . .
Pages: 4 7/8
Setups: 70

SHOOT DAY 61: WEDNESDAY, SEPTEMBER 20
Crew Call: 7.30 **Camera Wrap:** 13.30
Location: ELSTREE
Sets: EXT. CORUSCANT SENATE BUILDING & CITYSCAPE
Obi-Wan disconnects a wire . . . bad move . . .
Pages: 9 3/8
Setups: 24
Notes: WORK COMPLETED AS SCHEDULED. END OF PRINCIPAL PHOTOGRAPHY.

TOTAL PAGES: 104 5/8
TOTAL SETUPS: 2,175
TOTAL SCENES: 137
TOTAL DAYS (INC. TRAVEL/PREP): 70

MARCH 2001 PICK-UPS

SHOOT DAY 1: MONDAY, MARCH 26, 2001
CREW CALL: 7.30 **UNIT DISMISSED:** 19.40
LOCATION: EALING STUDIOS, LONDON, UK–STAGE NO. 2 & 3
SETS: NABOO STARSHIP PADME
Reaction to Obi-Wan getting jumped by Geonosians
PAGES: 1 4/8
SETUPS: 46

SHOOT DAY 2: TUESDAY, MARCH 27
CREW CALL: 7.30 **UNIT DISMISSED:** 19.50
LOCATION: STAGE NO. 3, 3A, 2
SETS: NABOO PALACE
Wide shot of Padme and Anakin
PAGES: 1 4/8
SETUPS: 46

SHOOT DAY 3: WEDNESDAY, MARCH 28
CREW CALL: 7.30 **UNIT DISMISSED:** 20.10
LOCATION: STAGE NO. 2 & 3A
SETS: GEONOSIS CITY PADME
[fight in droid factory]
PAGES: 7/8
SETUPS: 63
NOTES: ADR WAS RECORDED TODAY WITH THE FOLLOWING ARTISTS: HAYDEN CHRISTENSEN & ANTHONY DANIELS

SHOOT DAY 4: THURSDAY, MARCH 29
CREW CALL: 7.30 **UNIT DISMISSED:** 19.35
LOCATION: STAGE NO. 2 & 3A, 3B
SETS: GEONOSIS CITY PADME
PAGES: 6/8
SETUPS: 39

SHOOT DAY 5: FRIDAY, MARCH 30
CREW CALL: 7.30 **UNIT DISMISSED:** 19.45
LOCATION: STAGE NO. 3B, 3A
SETS: CORUSCANT BALCONY
Close shot Zam morphs into girl
TATOOINE RAIDER SEARCH
Reshoot Anakin riding on speeder on Tatooine
PAGES: 1 3/8
SETUPS: 38

SHOOT DAY 6: SATURDAY, MARCH 31
CREW CALL: 7.30 **UNIT DISMISSED:** 18.40
LOCATION: STAGE NO. 2
SETS: GEONOSIS JEDI BATTLE
Mace, Anakin, & Padme meet up at overturned cart & wonder why Ki-Adi hasn't shut downt the droids
JEDI TEMPLE OFFICE
Shoot new dialogue for Mace & Yoda
PAGES: 1 2/8
SETUPS: 36
NOTES: ADR WILL TAKE PLACE TOMORROW AT THE STUDIO INVOLVING GWL, RICK MCCALLUM, MATT WOOD, KEVIN SELLERS, MARK GILBERT, FRANK OZ, DAVID GANT, RAAD RAWI, PHIL ALLCHIN, GARRY CLARK, PAUL VENEZIA

SHOOT DAY 7: MONDAY, APRIL 2
CREW CALL: 7.30 **UNIT DISMISSED:** 19.17
LOCATION: STAGE NO. 2 & 1
SETS: JEDI TEMPLE COUNCIL
New scene: Anakin & Obi-Wan receive their assignments from Mace & Yoda
JEDI LANDING PLATFORM
New scene–Obi-Wan & Mace head to the landing platform
PAGES: 4/8
SETUPS: 37
NOTES: PLEASE NOTE THAT SAMUEL L. JACKSON (4. MACE WINDU) WAS PART COMPLETE TODAY.

SHOOT DAY 8: TUESDAY, APRIL 3
CREW CALL: 7.30 **UNIT DISMISSED:** 19.23
LOCATION: STAGE NO. 2
SETS: PADME APPARTMENT ATTACK
New Obi-Wan reaction to droid
PAGES: 1 4/8
SETUPS: 30

SHOOT DAY 9: WEDNESDAY, APRIL 4
CREW CALL: 7.30 **UNIT DISMISSED:** 18.50
LOCATION: STAGE NO. 2 & 1
SETS: CITY PROBE DROID
Close shot of Obi-Wan hanging from droid, reacting to his feet running
PAGES: 0
SETUPS: 34

SHOOT DAY 10: THURSDAY, APRIL 5
CREW CALL: 7.30 **UNIT DISMISSED:** 19.24
LOCATION: STAGE NO. 3A, 3B, 2
SETS: CITY SPEEDER CHASE
Obi-Wan & Anakin in speeder cockpit–new dialogue
TATOOINE ANAKIN MOM
Tighter shot of Anakin on bluff overlooking Tusken camp
DOOKU JEDI BATTLE
Obi-Wan & Anakin arrive on gunship and go into hangar
PAGES: 2 4/8
SETUPS: 22

SHOOT DAY 11: FRIDAY, APRIL 6
CREW CALL: 7.30 **UNIT DISMISSED:** 19.56
LOCATION: STAGE NO. 3A, 3B, 2
SETS: DOOKU JEDI BATTLE
Dooku fights Yoda
GEONOSIS JEDI BATTLE
C-3PO firing weapon
PAGES: 1/8
SETUPS: 66

SHOOT DAY 12: SATURDAY, APRIL 7
CREW CALL: 7.30 **UNIT DISMISSED:** 19.04
LOCATION: STAGE NO. 3A, 3B, 2
SETS: NABOO PALACE
Add Sio Bibble into wide shot
DOOKU JEDI BATTLE
Anakin is flung backward by the force of Dooku
NABOO RETREAT WEDDING
C-3PO and R2-D2
PAGES: 6/8
SETUPS: 57

NOVEMBER 2001 PICK-UPS

SHOOT DAY 1: THURSDAY, NOVEMBER 1, 2001
CREW CALL: 7.30 **UNIT DISMISSED:** 19.40
LOCATION: EALING STUDIOS, STAGE NO. 3A
SETS: TUSKEN RAIDER HUT
Medium shot–Shmi tied up
DOOKU JEDI BATTLE
Wide: new shot of Dooku in force duel with Yoda: "You have interfered . . ."
PAGES: 1 4/8
SETUPS: 45

SHOOT DAY 2: FRIDAY, NOVEMBER 2
CREW CALL: 7.30 **UNIT DISMISSED:** 19.35
LOCATION: STAGE NO. 3A
SETS: PALPATINE OFFICE ANAKIN
Wide: "I will talk with her"
PAGES: 1 2/8
SETUPS: 37

SHOOT DAY 3: SUNDAY, NOVEMBER 4
CREW CALL: 7.30 **UNIT DISMISSED:** 19.02
LOCATION: STAGE NO. 3A
SETS: JEDI YODA MEDITATION
C/up Mace: "Something terrible . . ."
PAGES: 5/8
SETUPS: 28

SHOOT DAY 4: MONDAY, NOVEMBER 5
CREW CALL: 7.30 **UNIT DISMISSED:** 19.27
LOCATION: STAGE NO. 3A
SETS: GEONOSIS CLONE WAR
"Aim right above the fuel tanks . . ."
CITY FOOT CHASE
"Patience. Use the Force Anakin. Think"
PADME APARTMENT MEET AND GREET
"I haven't seen you this nervous . . ."
PAGES: 1 5/8
SETUPS: 28

SHOOT DAY 5: TUESDAY, NOVEMBER 6
CREW CALL: 7.30 **UNIT DISMISSED:** 12.30
LOCATION: STAGE NO. 3A
SETS: PADME APARTMENT MEET AND GREET
"You fell into that nightmare . . ."
CITY SPEEDER CHASE
"I hate it when he does that . . ."
PAGES: 7/8
SETUPS: 12

JANUARY/FEBRUARY 2002 PICK-UPS

SHOOT DAY 1: TUESDAY, JANUARY 15, 2002
CREW CALL: 7.30 **UNIT DISMISSED:** 17.10
LOCATION: ELSTREE FILM STUDIOS
SETS: DOOKU JEDI BATTLE/GEONOSIS CLONE WAR
PAGES: 5/8
SETUPS: 34
CATERING: ACTUAL HEADCOUNT–60

SHOOT DAY 2: FRIDAY, FEBRUARY 1
CREW CALL: 8.00 **UNIT DISMISSED:** 16.43
LOCATION: ELSTREE FILM STUDIOS
SETS: GEONOSIS CLONE WAR, DOOKU JEDI BATTLE, GEONOSIS JEDI BATTLE
PAGES: 1 3/8
SETUPS: 24

Above - A gunship strafes battle droids in the Geonosian arena.

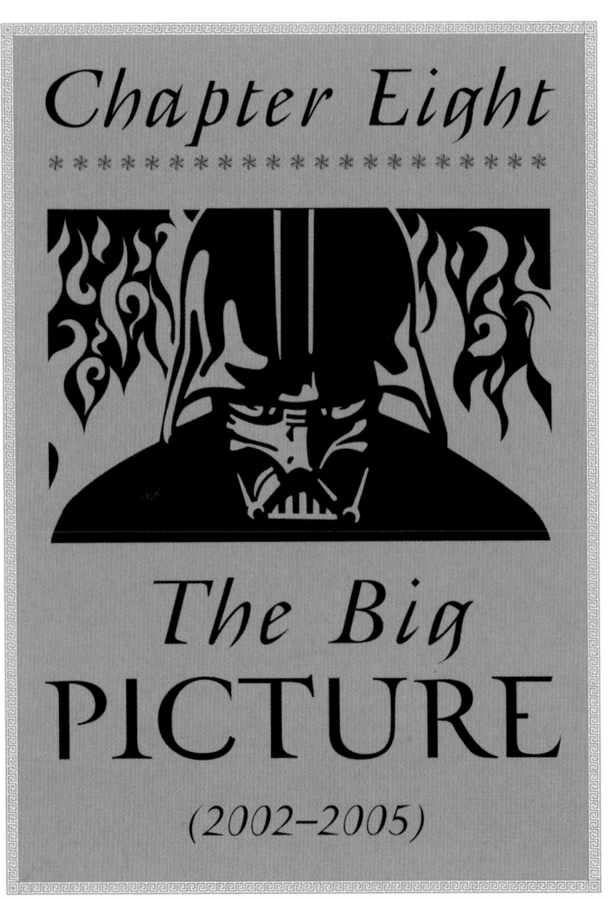
Chapter Eight
The Big PICTURE
(2002–2005)

In August 2002, thirty years after he began work on what would become *Star Wars* Episode IV, Lucas began writing the screenplay for his final *Star Wars* film. As the third installment in the prequel trilogy, Episode III presented a unique writing challenge.

"The issue is that I've painted myself into a corner," says Lucas, drawing a line in mid-air to illustrate the gap between the prequel trilogy and the classic trilogy. "I have to get from there to here, and I have to connect these two things in a very precise way. When I started this I thought it was going to be the easiest one, but there were so many things to balance that I soon found it locked me in. Writing involves a lot of puzzle-solving, and there's more than usual in Episode III." Lucas was also aware that audiences may be surprised by a plot where the villains win, establishing a Galactic Empire by crushing the democratic Republic.

A few weeks after Lucas finished the final draft of *Star Wars*: Episode III *Revenge of the Sith*, principal photography took place at Sydney's Fox Studios between June 30 and September 17, 2003. Lucas directed once again, using improved digital cameras but retaining many of the essential production team and cast from *Attack of the Clones*. Notable additions to the latter included Peter Mayhew, reprising his role as Chewbacca; Genevieve O'Reilly, playing Mon Mothma (a character last played by Caroline Blakiston in *Return of the Jedi*); and Gary Oldman, who added the voice of Separatist General Grievous in postproduction. Fans had already been introduced to Grievous in the Cartoon Network animation series *Star Wars: Clone Wars*, which bridged the gap between Episodes II and III. (Series creator Genndy Tartakovsky was entrusted with the first original *Star Wars* programming since the 1980s.)

Editing of Episode III continued throughout 2004, with Lucas pausing to visit Shepperton Studios for two weeks of additional shooting from August 23 to September 3. As postproduction neared its end, Lucas remained adamant that the new *Star Wars* film would be the last. "Somebody once asked me in an interview if I would be making sequels to the original trilogy," he recalls. "I said that it might be fun to come back and do sequels with all the characters in their eighties, and to ask Mark [Hamill]

Previous - *The general's quarters set from* Star Wars*: Episode III* Revenge of the Sith.

Left - *For the last* Star Wars *film, producer Rick McCallum continues the tradition of initiating the first shot.*

Right - *Concept art of General Grievous by Warren Fu.*

Above *- A volcano planet painting by Ryan Church.*

Right *- On April 20–21, 2002, Lucas was joined at Skywalker Ranch by Steven Spielberg and (middle) Francis Ford Coppola and (far right) Ron Howard for a Digital Conference. Among the others invited to these demonstrations of (and consciousness raising for) digital cinema were: Michael Bay, Frank Darabont, Roland Emmerich, Ron Fricke, Joe Johnston, Phil Kaufman, John Lasseter, Michael Mann, Robert Rodriguez, Martin Scorsese, Bryan Singer, Oliver Stone, Saul Zaentz, and Robert Zemeckis.*

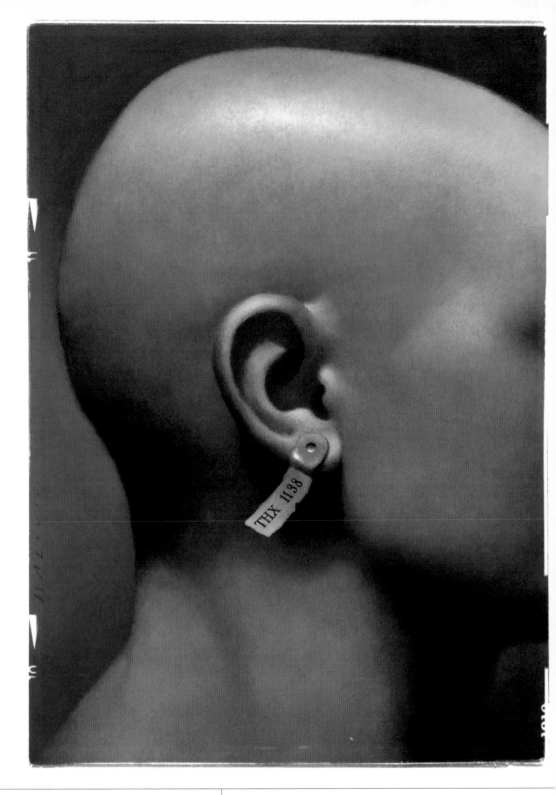

to come back when he's eighty. What I forgot, or didn't realize at the time, was that I'd be eighty too! So, no, I'm not about to make another *Star Wars* film at eighty."

Although Lucas prioritized the writing and production of Episode III during 2003 and 2004, two other projects vied for his attention. The long-awaited fourth *Indiana Jones* film moved a step closer when Lucas, Spielberg, and Harrison Ford finally coordinated space in their respective schedules, but progress stalled in summer 2003. Lucas chose to focus his attention on Episode III, promising to return to the *Indiana Jones* sequel when production of the new *Star Wars* film was complete.

Another project close to Lucas's heart was the restoration of *THX 1138.* Lucasfilm worked with Lowry Digital Images to restore and remaster the picture (founder John Lowry has been restoring film since 1971 and numbers the *Adventures of Indiana Jones* DVD box set among the company's numerous commissions). *THX 1138: The George Lucas Director's Cut* was theatrically released on September 10, 2004, making its DVD debut four days later. A similarly restored version of the original *Star Wars* trilogy was finally released on DVD later that month. The most highly anticipated DVD release in the medium's history, the box set went on to record-breaking sales.

Above left *- A poster for the Emmy Award–winning* Star Wars: Clone Wars *cartoon series.*

Above right *- The striking American one-sheet for* THX 1138: The George Lucas Director's Cut, *prepared for the re-release of the film on DVD and in a limited theatrical run.*

Left *- Scenes from the acclaimed animated series* Star Wars: Clone Wars: *(**far left**) Anakin Skywalker, (**middle**) General Grievous, and (**left**) alien bounty hunter Durge (based on concept designs by Robert E. Barnes).*

RESTORATIONS

"George said he wanted to release *THX 1138* on DVD," says Lucasfilm post-production supervisor Mike Blanchard. "Which meant that the film would have to be transferred to a digital format and restored. So I went to George's vault and pulled out his print—and that was quite a shock. There was a lot of damage to the negative, and the white 'prison' set was particularly problematic because of the level of dirt and grain in the picture. So we started gathering elements—what Warner Bros. had and what Lucasfilm archives had—and it was all in pretty bad condition. We scanned the original negative, which was in Techniscope, and started a traditional film-cutting room at the Ranch with our editor, Jett Sally. The first step was to restore it in-house at Skywalker Ranch and at ILM, which we did thanks to Paul Hill and his team. ILM completely painted out all the dirt and scratches, digitally repaired the negative, and color graded the movie. After that, the finishing touches were done at Lowry Digital Images. They enhanced some of the detail to give it additional punch and removed the grain. We also had George go through and color correct the entire movie, so it would look like he'd always wanted it to. We're all pretty proud of this."

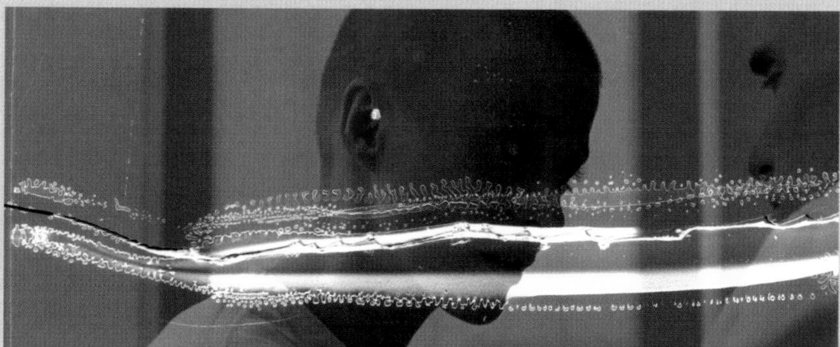

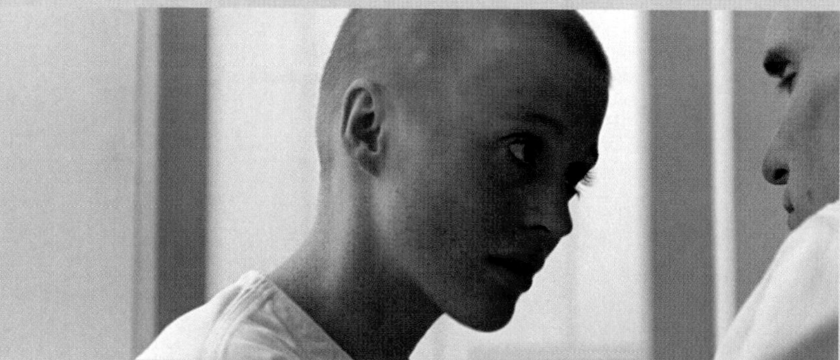

The frame above illustrates the kind of severe damage discovered when old prints of *THX 1138* were taken out of storage. The frame below illustrates the miraculous powers of the restorers.

Coming close on the heels of the *THX* restoration was the much larger and more anticipated *Star Wars Trilogy* job. "The great thing about the *THX* experience is that it actually made our *Trilogy* DVD better. After *THX* we had fine-tuned our pipeline with Lowry. We knew how to proceed with them in order to give the film as much sharpness and punch as possible—we knew at that point how to get the most out of their great work. And because of that, they were then able to take their work to a higher level."

"There were sandstorms of dirt on the film," says John Lowry, CEO and founder of Lowry Digital Images. "In the desert scenes alone, we probably removed more than a million pieces of dirt." In many ways, the films of the *Star Wars Trilogy* suffered from success. "Generally, the more successful a film, the worse condition it's in," Lowry adds.

Although some of those issues were addressed with the 1997 reissue of the films, which was accompanied by a restoration, Lowry says his company was unprepared for the state in which they actually found the films. Armed with a bank of 600 Power Mac G5 computers—each of which holds four gigabytes of RAM—Lowry's staff took on nearly thirty years of handling and storage. Prior to being sent to Lowry, the original negatives had been transferred to high-definition video (in a 10-bit 4:4:4 RGB format) through the telecine process, then sent to ILM, where technicians worked with Lucas to digitally "color time" the movies.

Two before-and-after frames show how, in particular, the Tatooine scenes were cleaned up for *Star Wars* transfer to a digital format. On September 22, 2004, it was reported that first-day sales of the boxed set made it one of the best-selling film collections ever released on DVD.

"When you're shooting a movie, things are shot at different times, on different days, under different lighting conditions," explains Blanchard. "Then the film gets sent to a lab to be developed, and the chemical bath is always slightly different, which results in inconsistencies in the film. Color timing is the process by which you smooth everything out." Prior to the advent of digital technology, color timing was hit or miss. "It was really hard to get right," Blanchard says. "But in the digital environment, there's a lot more control. We were able to retime the movie to make it look the way George originally wanted it to be."

Rick McCallum, producer of the *Star Wars* prequel trilogy as well as the 1997 *Special Edition*, says Lowry Digital's restoration and the work of ILM surpassed expectations. "This is probably one of the most extensive restoration projects in movie history, but we needed to spend the time and effort to deliver a phenomenal final product. These movies have been rescued and restored, and will look their best forever."

With all of his previous films now in a form he was happier with, and the production of Episode III drawing to a conclusion, Lucas was finally free to consider new projects. These included *Red Tails*, a drama about a squadron of African-American fighter pilots that had been on Lucasfilm's preproduction roster since the early 1990s. Lucas also considers that many of his future productions may be made for television. "The feature side of things is too restrictive," he says.

The revenue from the *Star Wars* prequel trilogy helped fund an expansion of Lucasfilm's headquarters, beginning with the construction of Big Rock Ranch, an office complex near Skywalker Ranch. The striking building was inspired by Frank Lloyd Wright's 1901 Ward Willits House in Highland Park, Illinois, and its corridors are decorated with carefully preserved film posters

Left *- On the set of* Revenge of the Sith *at Fox Studios, Sydney. During the shooting of underwater footage, Lucas and crew look on: first assistant director Colin Fletcher (standing on the left, next to the monitors), matchmove supervisor Jason Snell (seated on box at left), and (moving right) visual effects supervisor John Knoll, Lucas, script supervisor Jayne-Ann Tenggren, and Chris Neil.*

Above *- The 130,000-square-foot main building of Big Rock Ranch is just down the road from Skywalker Ranch. Lucas restored and created wetlands around the offices, seen here reflected in the 7.2-acre lake.*

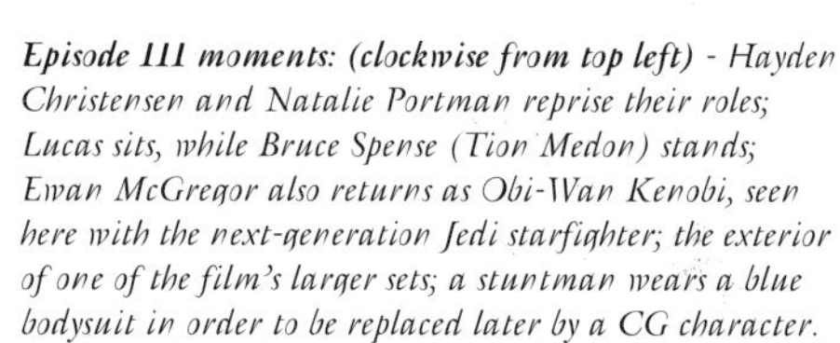

Episode III moments: (clockwise from top left) *- Hayden Christensen and Natalie Portman reprise their roles; Lucas sits, while Bruce Spense (Tion Medon) stands; Ewan McGregor also returns as Obi-Wan Kenobi, seen here with the next-generation Jedi starfighter; the exterior of one of the film's larger sets; a stuntman wears a blue bodysuit in order to be replaced later by a CG character.*

STAR WARS EP. III
13 05 58 06
A65
V77A
2

Above - *Anakin (Hayden Christensen) and Mas Amedda (David Bowers) are followed by four Red Guards.*

Left - *At the ground-breaking ceremony for the Letterman Digital Arts Center: (from left) chairman of the Presidio board of directors Toby Rosenblatt, congressional minority leader Nancy Pelosi, Lucas, and then-San Francisco Mayor Willie Brown.*

Far left - *An aerial view of the building site.*

from Lucas's extensive collection. "Skywalker Ranch was really designed to be a like a large ranch that had been converted into a film facility, but with Big Rock I wanted to build a real office building," says Lucas. "I took what was basically a residential concept and turned it into a large-scale version of a Frank Lloyd Wright Prairie-style house. It was challenging in terms of the design, but in the end it worked out pretty well." Big Rock Ranch, named after the large boulder that sits on its perimeter, opened for business in August 2002.

An even more ambitious venture will see LucasArts, Industrial Light & Magic, and the business divisions of Lucasfilm relocate to purpose-built premises in San Francisco's Presidio national park. "It should be easier to function out of there, and all of the companies will be in one place instead of spread out all over Marin the way they are now," says Lucas, who ensured that the design of the new premises—the Letterman Digital Arts Center—was in keeping with the other buildings in the Presidio. "I wanted it to look like something that was built by the military in 1900," he says. "And once I did that I kind of stepped away from it. I didn't go to the level of detail that I had on these other buildings [Skywalker and Big Rock], which I became more personally involved in. Ultimately the Digital Center will be the center of business, and out here at Big Rock and Skywalker, we'll be focused mostly on the concept side of things." Construction of the Digital Center is scheduled for completion in summer 2005.

"You only have to accomplish one thing in life, and that is to make your parents proud of you," said Lucas in 1999. "If you're healthy, you can take care of yourself, and [if] you're a good person—you contribute to society and not take away—that's all your parents want in the end."

The current expansion of Lucasfilm would doubtless have made George Sr. proud of his son's achievements. But this expansion is just one facet of the restless determination that has been pushing the boundaries of filmmaking for over forty years. "George has been keeping a lot of plates spinning for twenty,

Above - Stunt performers are used because of the explosive squibs.

Right *- A Yoda statue sits atop a pedestal in this painting by Erik Tiemens. Ultimately, a statue of Yoda was created for the courtyard of Big Rock Ranch.*

Far right *- Another painting by Tiemens depicts Lucas's Digital Arts Center, under construction in San Francisco's Presidio.*

Above, clockwise from top left *- Peter Mayhew returns as Chewbacca; Nick Gillard (kneeling) watches part of the climactic duel between Anakin (Hayden Christensen) and Obi-Wan (Ewan McGregor); two handmaidens in Padmé's apartment; stunt doubles traverse a pipe.*

Left *- The crew props up part of a set.*

twenty-five years," says Rick McCallum. "And the payback is that all the companies can survive on their own. All this is paid for. And now he's got enough to be able to go off and make twenty, thirty movies—and if nobody wants to see them, it doesn't matter. You don't have to release them. That's the true nature of independence."

McCallum adds, "He's got a very loyal following here [at Skywalker Ranch] and in England because he's a decent guy. There's no hidden agenda. He's very straight, very relaxed. He's got qualities you would not normally associate with the film business. He's a good guy."

When asked to evaluate his own career, Lucas smiles and modestly suggests, "I'll probably be forgotten completely. I hope I'll be remembered as one of the pioneers of digital cinema. In the long run, that's probably all it will come down to."

And what of the *Star Wars* saga, some of the best-loved and most successful films in history? "They might remember me as the maker of some of those esoteric twentieth-century science-fiction movies," he suggests. "The ones that are always on back order at the local dot.com video store."

Considering the remarkable scale of George Lucas's achievements and influence, it seems unlikely that history will be so harsh.

Right *- What will Lucas do next? The opening of Lucasfilm Animation Singapore, announced in August 2004, may be an indication of things to come. . . .*

Filmography

Student Films and Documentaries

Look at Life (1965)
Freiheit (1965)
Herbie (1966)
1:42.08 (1966)
THX 1138 4EB (1967)
(*Note*: The words "Electronic Labyrinth" were subsequently added to the title of this student film in 1969.)
anyone lived in a pretty [how] town (1967)
The Emperor (1967)
6.18.67 (1967)
filmmaker (1968)

Feature Films

THX 1138 (released on March 11, 1971)
Director, co-screenwriter, editor

American Graffiti (March 1, 1973)
Director, co-screenwriter

Star Wars: Episode IV *A New Hope* (May 25, 1977)
Director, writer

Star Wars: Episode I *The Phantom Menace* (May 19, 1999)
Director, writer, executive producer

Star Wars: Episode II *Attack of the Clones* (May 16, 2002)
Director, co-screenwriter, story, executive producer

Star Wars: Episode III *Revenge of the Sith* (May 19, 2005)
Director, writer, executive producer

Other Feature Films

More American Graffiti (August 3, 1979)
Executive producer

Star Wars: Episode V *The Empire Strikes Back* (May 21, 1980)
Executive producer, story

Kagemusha (*The Shadow Warrior*) (October 6, 1980)
Co-executive producer of the international version

Raiders of the Lost Ark (June 12, 1981)
Co-executive producer, co-story

Body Heat (August 28, 1981)
Executive producer (uncredited)

Star Wars: Episode VI: *Return of the Jedi* (May 25, 1983)
Executive producer, co-screenwriter, story

Twice Upon a Time (August 5, 1983)
Executive producer

Indiana Jones and the Temple of Doom (May 23, 1984)
Co-executive producer, story

Return to Oz (June 21, 1985)
Special thanks

Mishima: A Life in Four Chapters (October 4, 1985)
Co-executive producer

Latino (February, 1986)
A Lucasfilm Ltd. presentation

Labyrinth (June 27, 1986)
Executive producer

Howard the Duck (August 1, 1986)
Executive producer

Captain Eo (a short film released at Disneyland on September 13, 1986)
Executive producer

Willow (May 20, 1986)
Executive producer, story

Powaqqatsi (April 1988)
A Francis Coppola and George Lucas presentation

Tucker: The Man and His Dream (August 12, 1988)
Executive producer

The Land Before Time (November 18, 1988)
Co-executive producer

Indiana Jones and the Last Crusade (May 24, 1989)
Co-executive producer, co-story

Television Films

The Ewok Adventure: Caravan of Courage (broadcast on ABC November 25, 1984)
Executive producer, story

Ewoks: The Battle for Endor (ABC, November 24, 1985)
Executive producer, story

The Great Heep (ABC, June 7, 1986)
Produced in association with Lucasfilm Ltd., based on characters created by Lucas

Maniac Mansion (Family Channel, September 14, 1990)
Produced in association with Lucasfilm Ltd. Television

Television Series

Ewok and Droids Adventure Hour (ABC, September 7, 1985)
Co-production of Lucasfilm Ltd.

Ewoks (second season, ABC, November 1, 1986)
Produced in association with Lucasfilm Ltd.

The Young Indiana Jones Chronicles (ABC, March 4, 1992)
Executive producer

For release on home video the episodes and movies-of-the-week (MOW) were combined, renamed, and reordered into the following movies:

Chapter 1: My First Adventure
(combination of: Egypt 1908 MOW and Tangier connectors)

Chapter 2: Passion for Life
(Ep. 2 Paris 1908 & Ep. 6 British East Africa 1909)

Chapter 3: The Perils of Cupid
(Ep. 4 Vienna 1908 & Ep. 29 Florence 1908)

Chapter 4: Travels with Father
(originally shot as double episode: Greece/Russia 1910)

Chapter 5: Journey of Radiance
(Ep. 9 Benares, India 1910 & Ep. 11 China 1910)

Chapter 6: Spring Break Adventure
(Ep. 16 Princeton 1916 & Mexico 1916 MOW)

Chapter 7: Love's Sweet Song
(Ep. 22 Ireland 1916 & Ep. 1 London 1916)

Chapter 8: The Trenches of Hell
(Ep. 14 The Somme 1916 & Ep. 15 Germany 1916)

Chapter 9: Demons of Deception
(Ep. 3 Verdun 1916 & Ep. 5 Paris 1916)

Chapter 10: The Phantom Train of Doom
(Eps. 19 & 20 British & German East Africa 1916)

Chapter 11: Oganga: The Giver and Taker of Life
(Ep. 7 German East Africa 1916 & Congo 1917)

Chapter 12: Attack of the Hawkmen
(double episode, Austria 1917)

Chapter 13: Adventures in the Secret Service
(Ep. 12 Austria 1917 & Ep. 13 Russia 1917)

Chapter 14: Espionage Escapades
(Ep. 10 Spain 1917 & Ep. 27 Prague 1917)

Chapter 15: Daredevils of the Desert
(Ep. 23 Beersheba 1917 & connectors)

Chapter 16: Tales of Innocence
(Ep. 21 Northern Italy 1917 & Morocco connectors)

Chapter 17: Masks of Evil
(Ep. 24 Istanbul 1918 & Ep. 28 Transylvania 1918)

Chapter 18: Treasure of the Peacock's Eye (double episode, South Pacific 1919)

Chapter 19: The Winds of Change (Ep. 26 Paris 1919 & Princeton connectors)

Chapter 20: Mystery of the Blues (Eps. 17 & 18 Chicago 1920)

Chapter 21: Scandal of 1920
(MOW New York City 1920)

Chapter 22: Hollywood Follies
(double episode, Hollywood 1920)

Note: For complete lists of cast & crew, go to www.starwars.com, www.lucasfilm.com, www.thx1138movie.com, and www.indianajones.com.

*An early costume concept design (**right**) and the final design (**far right**) for George Lucas's cameo as Baron Notluwiski in* Star Wars: *Episode III* Revenge of the Sith. *Both designs are by Sang Jun Lee.*

Notes

During the course of my research for this book I conducted new interviews with Jane Bay, Patty Blau, Ryan Church, Anthony Daniels, Peter Diamond (shortly before his death in March 2004), Chrissie England, Jonathan Hales, Willard Huyck and Gloria Katz, Joe Johnston, Randal Kleiser, Christopher Lee, Fred Meyers, Dennis Muren, Howard Roffman, Erik Tiemens, Lucy Autrey Wilson, and, of course, George Lucas.

Additional new quotes from Lucas are taken from interviews conducted by James Erskine, Jonathan Rinzler, and Paul Scanlon between 2002 and 2003. Extracts from these appear in print here for the first time.

The Lucasfilm Research Library made available numerous archive interviews, almost all of which were previously unseen and unpublished. Many of these interviews were filmed by BBC Scotland for inclusion in the 1997 television documentary *Omnibus Special Edition: George Lucas—Flying Solo*. The program, which was produced by Richard Downes and directed by James Erskine, used only a fraction of the material compiled during its preparation. I was grateful for the opportunity to draw upon the rest.

Two major sources of new archival interviews were: those conducted by producer Pamela Glintenkamp for the Lucasfilm History Project, and those conducted by Gary Leva for inclusion as supplemental material on the DVD release of *THX 1138: The George Lucas Director's Cut*. The majority of these interviews took place in the years 2002–03. Extracts from these appear in print here for the first time.

Key to regularly cited sources:

AMPAS = Discussion following a screening of *American Graffiti* hosted by the Academy of Motion Picture Arts and Sciences, 1998.

Chutkow = Paul Chutkow, "The Lucas Chronicles," *The San Francisco Examiner*, Mar. 21, 1993.

Glintenkamp = Previously unpublished interview with Pamela Glintenkamp for the Lucasfilm History Project, 2002–03.

Harrison = Interview for radio documentary *The Making of American Graffiti*, written and produced by Mike Harrison for Lucasfilm, 1978.

Leva = Interview conducted in 2002–03 by Gary Leva for supplemental material on the DVD of *THX 1138: The George Lucas Director's Cut*.

Lucasfilm = Previously unpublished and uncredited interview on audio tape from the Lucasfilm Research Library.

Moyers = Interview by Bill Moyers for the PBS television documentary *The Mythology of Star Wars*, 1999.

Omnibus = Interview from *Omnibus Special Edition: George Lucas—Flying Solo*, BBC Scotland, 1997.

Prometheus = Interview conducted by Prometheus Entertainment for the DVD documentary *Empire of Dreams: The Story of the Star Wars Trilogy*, for the DVD collection of the *Star Wars Trilogy*, transcribed April 17, 2004.

Radioland = "*Radioland Murders* Production Information," Universal Pictures, 1994.

Scanlon = Previously unpublished interview with Paul Scanlon, 2002–03.

Chapter One: A Hard Road (1944–1971)

John Calley, Ron Colby, Robert Dalva, Willard Huyck, John Milius, Matthew Robbins, and Mona Skager are quoted from Leva.

Eleanor Coppola, Francis Ford Coppola, John Korty, Steven Spielberg, and Haskell Wexler are quoted from *Omnibus*.

Additional quotes from George Lucas are from Ahmed Best interview (previously unpublished), July 2000; Chutkow; Carrie Fisher interview for the Oxygen television show *Conversations from the Edge*, 2002; Moyers; Kerry O'Quinn, "The George Lucas Saga," *Starlog*, July 1981; *Radioland*; Uncredited interview for the supplemental material on the DVD of *The Hidden Fortress*, Jan. 2001; Gene Youngblood interview for the PBS television documentary *George Lucas: Maker of Films*, 1971.

Chapter Two: Some Enchanted Evening (1971–1973)

Champlin, Charles, "A New Generation Looks Back in *Graffiti*," *Los Angeles Times*, July 29, 1973.

Francis Ford Coppola, John Milius, Matthew Robbins, and Walter Murch are quoted from Leva.

Richard Dreyfuss and Wolfman Jack are quoted from Harrison.

Ron Howard is quoted from *Omnibus*.

Gloria Katz is quoted from Harrison; AMPAS.

Gary Kurtz is quoted from AMPAS; Ken Plume interview for the website http://filmforce.ign.com, Nov. 11, 2002.

Additional quotes from George Lucas are from AMPAS; Paul Gardner, "'Graffiti' Reflects Its Director's Youth," *New York Times*, Sept. 19, 1973, p. 40; Stephen Zito, "George Lucas Goes Far Out," *American Film*, Apr. 1977.

Fred Roos is quoted from Ann Martin and Regis Philbin interview for *Eyewitness News*, May 31, 1978; *Omnibus*.

Charles Martin Smith is quoted from *The Making of American Graffiti*, written, produced, and directed by Laurent Bouzereau for the DVD of *American Graffiti*.

Haskell Wexler is quoted from "An American Film Institute Seminar with Haskell Wexler, ASC," *American Cinematographer*, July 1977; *Omnibus*.

Chapter Three: A Galaxy Far, Far Away (1973–1977)

Bunny Alsup is quoted from Glintenkamp, Dec. 6, 2002.

Carroll Ballard is quoted from Scanlon, Dec. 2002.

Hal Barwood is quoted from Glintenkamp, June 21, 2002.

Ben Burtt is quoted from Scanlon, March 31, 2003.

Richard Chew is quoted from Laurent Bouzereau, ed., *Star Wars: The Annotated Screenplays*, 1997.

Robert Dalva and John Milius are quoted from Leva.

John Dykstra is quoted from "Behind the Scenes of *Star Wars*," *American Cinematographer*, July 1977.

Carrie Fisher is quoted from Lucasfilm, Jan. 4, 1977.

Harrison Ford and John Williams are quoted from Charles Champlin, *The Creative Impulse*, rev. ed., 1997.

Sir Alec Guinness is quoted from Philip Oakes, "World Enough and Time," *The Sunday Times*, May 2, 1976.

Mark Hamill is quoted from James Van Hise interview, Sept. 1976, published in the fanzine *Rocket's Blast Comicollector*, Oct. 1977; Prometheus, Apr. 17, 2004.

Paul Huston is quoted from Glintenkamp, June 19, 2002.

Gary Kurtz is quoted from Philip Strick, "In the Picture," *Sight and Sound*, summer 1976.

Alan Ladd Jr. is quoted from Lucasfilm, Sept. 21, 1977.

Additional quotes from George Lucas are from Claire Clouzot, "The Morning of the Magician: George Lucas and *Star Wars*," *Ecran*, Sept. 15, 1977; Moyers; Paul Scanlon, "The Force Behind George Lucas," *Rolling Stone*, Aug. 25, 1977.

Peter Mayhew is quoted from Joe Nazzaro, "Roowarragh!" *Star Wars: The Official Magazine*, Dec. 1997.

Ralph McQuarrie is quoted from Lucasfilm, July 5, 1977.

Tom Pollock, Fred Roos, Steven Spielberg, and Gareth Wigan are quoted from *Omnibus*.

Gil Taylor is quoted from Jamie Painter and Chris Gardner, "Taylor-Made," *Star Wars: The Official Magazine*, Feb.–Mar. 1997.

Chapter Four: Cliffhanging (1977–1989)

Jim Bloom, Carrie Fisher, and Mark Hamill are quoted from Prometheus.

Mik Clark, "*Willow*: Delightful Kid Stuff," *USA Today*, May 20, 1988.

Francis Ford Coppola, Kathleen Kennedy, John Korty, and Rick McCallum are quoted from *Omnibus*.

Caleb Deschanel is quoted from Leva.

Harrison Ford is quoted from John Phillip Peecher, *The Making of Return of the Jedi*, 1983; Michael Sragow, "*Raiders of the Lost Ark*: The Ultimate Saturday Matinee," *Rolling Stone*, June 25, 1981.

Howard Kazanjian is quoted from Glintenkamp, Jan. 30, 2003.

Irvin Kershner is quoted from Rex McGee, "*Star Wars* Strikes Again! Or the Revenge of Darth Vader," *American Film*, May 1980; Prometheus.

Akira Kurosawa is quoted from Tony Rayns, "Shadow Warrior," *Time Out*, Nov. 14–20, 1980.

Additional quotes from George Lucas are from Alan Arnold, *Once Upon a Galaxy: A Journal of the Making of The Empire Strikes Back*, 1980; Kearney, "The Road Warrior," *American Film*, June 1988; Dan Madsen, "George Lucas: The Force Behind Lucasfilm," *Lucasfilm Fan Club*, winter 1989; Paul Scanlon, "George Lucas Wants to Play Guitar," *Rolling Stone*, July 21–Aug. 4, 1983; David Sheff, "George Lucas," *Rolling Stone*, Nov. 6–Dec. 10, 1987.

Richard Marquand is quoted from Lee Goldberg, "Richard Marquand: Director of the *Jedi*," *Starlog*, June 1983. Peecher, *The Making of Return of the Jedi*.

Frank Marshall is quoted from Glintenkamp, Mar. 19, 2003.

Dennis Muren is quoted from the documentary *From MORF to Morphing: The Dawn of Digital Filmmaking*, produced by Ian T. Haufrect for the DVD of *Willow*.

Arnold Schulman is quoted from Michael Schumacher, *Francis Ford Coppola: A Filmmaker's Life*, 1999.

Gene Siskel, "*Return of the Jedi*: Another Quality Toy in *Star Wars* Line," *Chicago Tribune*, May 25, 1983.

Douglas Slocombe is quoted from David Heuring, "*Indiana Jones and the Last Crusade*," *American Cinematographer*, June 1989.

Steven Spielberg is quoted from Adam Eisenberg, "Father, Son and the Holy Grail," *Cinefex*, Nov. 1989; Murray Elkins, "Steven Spielberg on *Indiana Jones and the Temple of Doom*," *American Cinematographer*, July 1984; Sragow; Derek Taylor, *The Making of Raiders of the Lost Ark*, 1981.

Haskell Wexler is quoted from Gloria Emerson, "Haskell Wexler Zooms in on Nicaragua," *Mother Jones*, Aug./Sept. 1985; *Omnibus.*

Chapter Five: Immaculate Reality (1989–1997)

Gavin Bocquet is quoted from a previously unpublished interview conducted in April 2003 by Jonathan Rinzler for the forthcoming *The Making of Star Wars Episode III Revenge of the Sith.*

Ben Burtt is quoted from Scanlon, Mar. 31, 2003.

Frank Darabont is quoted from *Omnibus.*

Additional quotes from George Lucas are from Denise Abbott, "George Lucas: His First Love is Editing," *American Cinemeditor*, spring 1991; Chutkow; Thomas R. King, "Lucasvision," *Wall Street Journal*, Mar. 21, 1994; KQED radio interview, Mar. 10, 1992; "Lucas Works Magic on *Radioland* Bottom Line," *Hollywood Reporter*, Oct. 21, 1994; Madsen.

Rick McCallum is quoted from *Omnibus*; Radioland; Scanlon, Dec. 2002.

Chapter Six: Balance of the Force (1997–1999)

Pernilla August is quoted from *Star Wars*: Episode I—*The Phantom Menace Collectors' Souvenir Edition*, 1999.

Ben Burtt and Robin Gurland are quoted from Laurent Bouzereau and Jody Duncan, *The Making of Episode I: The Phantom Menace*, 1999.

Doug Chiang is quoted from Glintenkamp, May 15, 2003.

Rob Coleman is quoted from Glintenkamp, Oct. 28, 2002.

Roger Ebert, "*Star Wars: Episode I—The Phantom Menace*," *Chicago Sun-Times*, May 17, 1999.

Additional quotes from George Lucas are from Bouzereau and Duncan; *Fights*, featurette from the DVD of *Star Wars: Episode I—The Phantom Menace.*

Rick McCallum is quoted from *Star Wars: Episode I—The Phantom Menace Collectors' Souvenir Edition*; Scanlon, Dec. 2002.

Dennis Muren is quoted from Glintenkamp, Feb. 18, 2003.

Chapter Seven: High Definition (1999–2002)

Gavin Bocquet is quoted from Marcus Hearn, *Star Wars: Attack of the Clones—The Illustrated Companion*, 2002.

Hayden Christensen is quoted from David Welch, "The Cast and Crew of the Latest *Star Wars* Flick Aren't Cloning Around," *Science Fiction Weekly*, issue 265, 2002, www.scifi.com.

Rob Coleman is quoted from Glintenkamp, Oct. 28, 2002.

John Knoll is quoted from Glintenkamp, Aug. 2, 2002.

Additional quotes from George Lucas are from David Kamp, "Love in a Distant Galaxy," *Vanity Fair*, Mar. 2002; Ron Magid, "Exploring a New Universe," *American Cinematographer*, Sept. 2002; Paula Parisi, "Prime Mover," *The Hollywood Reporter*, Mar. 30–Apr. 1, 2001.

Rick McCallum is quoted from "Episode I Digital Screening," www.starwars.com, June 3, 1999; Hearn; Scanlon, Dec. 2002.

Todd McCarthy, "This Lucas Clone is a Force Majeure," *Variety*, May 13, 2002.

Ewan McGregor is quoted from Mark Kermode interview for FilmFour television, Apr. 2002.

Pete Travers, "*Star Wars: Episode II—Attack of the Clones*," *Rolling Stone*, June 6, 2002.

Chapter Eight: The Big Picture (2002–2005)

Additional quote from George Lucas is from Moyers.

Rick McCallum is quoted from Scanlon, Dec. 2002.

Selected Bibliography

Arnold, Alan. *Once Upon a Galaxy: A Journal of the Making of Star Wars: The Empire Strikes Back.* Del Rey, 1980.

Bouzereau, Laurent, ed. *Star Wars: The Annotated Screenplays.* Del Rey, 1997.

__________, and Jody Duncan. *Star Wars: The Making of* Episode I *The Phantom Menace.* Del Rey, 1999.

Bresman, Jonathan. *The Art of Star Wars:* Episode I *The Phantom Menace.* Del Rey, 1999.

Champlin, Charles. *George Lucas: The Creative Impulse.* Harry N. Abrams, 1992, 1997.

Corman, Roger, with Jim Jerome. *How I Made a Hundred Movies in Hollywood and Never Lost a Dime.* Muller, 1990.

Duncan, Jody. *Star Wars: Mythmaking—Behind the Scenes of Attack of the Clones.* Del Rey, 2002.

Finler, Joel W. *The Hollywood Story.* Octopus, 1988; Mandarin, 1992.

Hearn, Marcus. *Star Wars: Attack of the Clones—The Illustrated Companion.* Ebury Press, 2002.

__________, and Alan Barnes. *The Hammer Story.* Titan, 1997.

Henderson, Mary. *Star Wars: The Magic of Myth.* Spectra, 1997.

Kline, Sally, ed. *George Lucas Interviews.* University Press of Mississippi, 1999.

Lucas, George. *Star Wars:* Episode I *The The Phantom Menace—The Illustrated Screenplay.* Del Rey, 1999.

Ondaatje, Michael. *The Conversations: Walter Murch and the Art of Editing Film.* Alfred A. Knopf, 2002.

Peecher, John Phillip, ed. *The Making of Star Wars: Return of the Jedi.* Del Rey, 1983.

Pirie, David, ed. *Anatomy of the Movies.* Windward, 1981.

Rigby, Jonathan. *Christopher Lee: The Authorised Screen History.* Reynolds & Hearn, 2001, 2003.

Schumacher, Michael. *Francis Ford Coppola: A Filmmaker's Life.* Crown, 1999.

Taylor, Derek. *The Making of Raiders of the Lost Ark.* Ballantine, 1981.

Vaz, Mark Cotta. *The Art of Star Wars:* Episode II *Attack of the Clones.* Del Rey, 2002.

__________, and Patricia Rose Duignan. *Industrial Light & Magic: Into the Digital Realm.* Del Rey, 1996.

Warren, Patricia. *British Film Studios: An Illustrated History.* B. T. Batsford, 1995.

__________. *Elstree: The British Hollywood.* Elm Tree, 1983.

INDEX

Page numbers in *italics* refer to illustrations.

Photo Credits

Lucasfilm Rights & Clearances: Christopher Holm, Sarah Garcia

Sue Adler, 221 (bottom right), 223 (bottom left), 224 (bottom left), 226 (top right, bottom right), 234; Forest Anderson, 172 (bottom left), 187 (top left); Blaine, 220 (bottom, second from left); Jim Bridges, 181 (bottom left); Ben Burtt, 80 (top), 81, 83 (bottom right), 90 (top), 94 (bottom), 95 (top, bottom left); Peggy Burtt, 90 (bottom), 108 (bottom left), 110 (bottom left); Frank Connor, 138 (top right); Tobi Corney, 231; Jonathan Fisher, 198 (top), 200 (bottom right); Tom Forster, 216, 241 (bottom left, middle, right); Cathy Frazier, 248 (bottom right); Keith Hamshere, 153 (top), 154 (bottom left), 155 (top), 157 (top), 167, 168, 171 (bottom), 172 (middle left, center of triptych & bottom right), 173 (top, bottom left), 175 (top left and right, bottom right), 178 (Al Capone, Patton, Hemingway, Pancho Villa, Halide Edib, Sidney Bechet, Kemal Atatürk), 180, 181 (top, bottom right), 187 (right corner), 189, 194 (top left, bottom left, middle, right), 195 (top, bottom), 199 (top), 200 (top left, right), 201 (bottom left), 206 (top), 208, 213, back cover flap; Pablo Hidalgo, 246 (bottom left); Mark Hundley, 248 (bottom left); Karan Kapoor, 187 (top middle); Gloria Katz and Willard Huyck, 79 (box), 83 (top), 89 (top right); Giles Keyte, 194 (middle right), 196, 198 (bottom), 199 (bottom left, right), 201 (bottom right), 203 (bottom), 204 (bottom right), 210; Jaromir Komarek, 176 (bottom left), 179 (top), 187 (bottom middle); Halina Krukowski, 256 (top); Gary Kurtz, 125 (top); Barbara Lakin, 148 (bottom right); Susan Meiselas, 150 (bottom middle, right); Tina Mills, 114 (bottom left), 156 (bottom left, right), 169 (bottom left, right); Merrick Morton, 240 (bottom), 246 (top left), 248 (top), 250 (top right, top left); Ralph Nelson Jr., 158, 159 (bottom right), 176 (top right), 187 (right middle), 238, 244, 246 (top right), 247, 249 (top), 250 (top middle, middle); Kerry Nordquist, 154 (top), 155 (bottom left); David Owen, 230 (bottom left); Barry Peake, 149 (top left); Brent Petersen, 172 (middle right of triptych); Matthew Porter, 156 (bottom middle), 245 (middle); Josef Rezac, 176 (top left, bottom right), 178 (Dracula), 187 (right bottom); Georgina Ritchie, 59; Robbie Robinson, 151 (bottom right); Paul Ryan, 54 (bottom left, right), 55 (bottom left), 56 (bottom left, right), 60 (box), 67 (bottom), 71 (bottom middle, right), 220 (bottom left); Robin Ryan, 148 (top); Pera Silva, 174 (middle), 187 (middle); Michael Sullivan, 83 (bottom left), 84 (bottom right), 87 (bottom); Paul Tiller, 224 (top), 226 (top left), 246 (bottom right), 250 (triptych); Lisa Tomasetti, 221 (bottom left), 222, 223 (top, bottom right), 224 (bottom right), 225 (all), 226 (bottom left), 227 (bottom left); Minsei Tominaga, 171 (box); Bengt Wanseling, 171 (middle); Giles Westley, 226 (bottom middle); and George Whitear, 122, 124, 125 (bottom right), 126, 127 (bottom left).

Photos on pages 83 (bottom left), 84 (bottom right), and 87 (bottom) are copyright Edward Summer. All Rights Reserved. A scene from "The Men Who Made the Comics," a film by Edward Summer supported by the National Endowment for the Arts, a Federal Agency in Washington, D.C.

Thanks to the following for providing photos from their collections: American Zoetrope, Peggy and Ben Burtt, Gloria Katz and Willard Huyck, John Korty, George Lucas, the city of Modesto, Walter and Aggie Murch, Matthew Robbins, Mona Skager, Edward Summer, University of Southern California.

American Graffiti © 1973 Universal City Studios, Inc. Courtesy of Universal Studios Licensing LLLP.

Body Heat © 1981 The Ladd Company. All Rights Reserved.

Captain EO © Disney Enterprises, Inc. Used by permission from Disney Enterprises, Inc.

The Hidden Fortress (aka *Kakushitoride No San-Akunin*) © 1958 Toho Co., Ltd. All Rights Reserved. Used Courtesy of Toho Co., Ltd.

Howard the Duck © 1986 Universal City Studios, Inc. Courtesy of Universal Studios Licensing LLLP.

Kagemusha © 1980 Toho Co., Ltd. All Rights Reserved. Used Courtesy of Toho. Co., Ltd.

Labyrinth ™ & © 2004 The Jim Henson Company/Lucasfilm Ltd.

Land Before Time © 1988 Universal City Studios, Inc. Courtesy of Universal Studios Licensing LLLP.

Photograph of George Lucas accepting Irving G. Thalberg Award at the 64th Academy Awards Ceremony in 1991: Copyright © Academy of Motion Picture Arts and Sciences

Mishima: A Life in Four Chapters © 1985 The M Film Company. All Rights Reserved; © 1985 by American Zoetrope. All Rights Reserved. (License commences after Warner Bros. expires)

More American Graffiti © 1979 Universal City Studios, Inc. Courtesy of Universal Studios Licensing LLLP.

POWAQQATSI Copyright © Institute for Regional Education

Radioland Murders © 1994 Universal City Studios, Inc. Courtesy of Universal Studios Licensing LLLP.

Return to Oz © Disney Enterprises, Inc. Used by permission from Disney Enterprises, Inc.

Star Tours image © Disney Enterprises, Inc. Used by permission from Disney Enterprises, Inc.

THX 1138 © 1970 Warner Bros. Inc. All Rights Reserved.

Twice Upon A Time © 1983 The Ladd Company. All Rights Reserved.

Zoetrope brochure and founders photographs Courtesy of American Zoetrope. All Rights Reserved.

Zoetrope roof photograph © Douglas Kirkland/CORBIS

*The sand dunes of Tatooine—after years of celluloid wear-and-tear (**far left**) and after painstaking digital restoration (**left**).*

Acknowledgments

Lucasfilm Ltd.

Senior Editor Jonathan W. Rinzler
Art Director Iain R. Morris
Image Archives Project Coordinator Michelle Jouan

Harry N. Abrams, Inc.

Editor Elisa Urbanelli
Art Director Michael Walsh
Designer Scott A. Erwert

Lucasfilm and Abrams would like to give a special thanks to: Jane Bay and Anne Merrifield for their help in finding original scripts, notes, progress reports, and call sheets; Michael Blanchard for his insights into the restoration processes involving the *Star Wars Trilogy* and *THX 1138: The George Lucas Director's Cut;* Ben Burtt for his photos and his recollections, which are a never-ending source of invaluable information and fun; Anthony Daniels for his fond memories; Jo Donaldson and Robyn Stanley at the Lucasfilm Research library, who tracked down many hard-to-find films, audio tapes, newspaper articles, and books; Scott Erwert, whose design creativity drove this book home; Amy Gary and Howard Roffman, whose ambassadorial acumen is always essential; Pamela Glintenkamp, producer of the Lucasfilm History Project, for her thousands of pages of interview transcripts, which form much of the archival bedrock of this book (and thanks to Cindy Russell who kept those transcripts flowing); Lynne Hale and Karen Rose at Lucasfilm public relations for timely and key help; Eric Himmel, editor-in-chief at Harry N. Abrams, Inc., whose patience and kindness made this book possible; Chris Holm and Sarah Garcia for their considerable skill with image clearances; Ron Howard for his warm recollections and time, and Louisa Velis for shepherding the foreword along; Michelle Jouan in Image Archives, who, under the supervision of Tina Mills, and with the help of Scott Carter, tirelessly kept track of and supplied all the book's photos—more than once!; Gloria Katz and Willard Huyck for sharing their unique photos; Gary Leva for sharing the interviews he conducted for the documentaries included on *THX 1138: The George Lucas Director's Cut* DVD; the city of Modesto; Rick McCallum for his time and great interviews (if only we could print them in unexpurgated form); Iain Morris, for his bold and exciting vision for the book's design; Kathryn Ramos for, among other invaluable help, wading through countless boxes in the Lucasfilm archives in search of *Young Indy*; Jonathan Rinzler, for his expertise, diligence, and editorial acumen; Matthew Robbins, for supplying the original treatment for Breakout; Paul Scanlon and James Erskine for their interview transcripts; Valarie Schwan at the University of Southern California; Erik Tiemens, who donated his time and exceptional talent to creating paintings of both Skywalker Ranch and the Letterman Digital Arts Center; Elisa Urbanelli, whose counsel, good sense, and editorial skills were an integral constant; Michael Walsh, creative director at Harry N. Abrams, Inc., for his advice and support; Lucy Autrey Wilson, who started the ball rolling; and of course to George Lucas, who volunteered his input, corrections, guiding spirit, and time away from work on the last chapter of *Star Wars.*

From the Author: Much of the research for this book was made possible by Jonathan Rinzler, my editor at Lucasfilm, who put me in contact with numerous interviewees and reproduced the shooting schedules that appear between chapters.

Other Lucasfilm staff who helped me during my happy visits to Skywalker Ranch and Big Rock Ranch included Lynne Hale, Iain Morris, Steve Sansweet, and Robyn Stanley. Lucasfilm's Lucy Autrey Wilson and Amy Gary have been similarly supportive. I am indebted to Pamela Glintenkamp, the producer of the Lucasfilm History Project—whose parallel research I have drawn upon throughout the book—and to former Lucasfilm staffers Chris Cerasi, Halina Krukowski, and Brian Lew.

A full list of interviewees appears in the "Notes" on page 254. I would like to thank them all for sharing their thoughts and memories of working with George Lucas.

I am grateful to Herb Farmer, Professor Emeritus at the USC School of Cinema-Television Archives, who provided background material for chapter one. The staff of the British Film Institute National Library facilitated my research into the establishment of American Zoetrope and many other parts of the book that were not directly related to Lucasfilm and its subsidiaries. Jonathan Clements helped provide an insight into Lucas's Japanese influences and Lisa Drury transcribed many of my interviews. Andrew Darling, James King, and Iain Lowson plugged the gaps in my knowledge of the *Star Wars* saga, and Joel Finler loaned me background material that was similarly useful for chapter two. Eric Himmel and Elisa Urbanelli oversaw the project at Harry N. Abrams, and David O'Leary helped to grease the wheels. Samantha put up with it all, as patient and understanding as ever.

My final thanks go to George Lucas for answering my questions, commenting on the manuscript, and giving me clues to follow.

For Alan

S T A R   W A R S
Preview Questionnaire

1 Male______________ Female______________ Profession___________________________

2 Age: Under 10______ 11 to 15______ 16 to 20______ 21 to 25______
26 to 35______ 36 to 45______ 46 to 55______ 56 & over______

3 How many times per month do you attend a movie? Less than once____ One____
Two____ Three____ Four____ Five____ Six ____ Seven____ More____

4 What are your all time favorite films? ________________/________________________

5 Which of the following films have you seen?

Wizards_____	King Kong_____
Demon Seed_____	Three Women_____
Cousin Cousine_____	Welcome to LA_____
Drive-In_____	Silver Streak_____
The Late Show_____	Black Sunday_____
Raggedy Ann and Andy_____	Audrey Rose_____
Annie Hall_____	American Graffiti_____
Network_____	Slap Shot_____
The Valley_____	Airport 77_____
THX 1138_____	Carrie_____
The Eagle Has Landed_____	Fun With Dick and Jane_____
In The Realm of the Senses_____	Island in the Stream_____
Harlan County, U.S.A._____	The Pink Panther Strikes Again_____
The Domino Principal_____	Les Zozos_____
Aloise_____	Rocky_____

6 How would you rate this film? Excellent____ Good____ Fair____ Poor____

7 Would you recommend it to your friends?____

8 In what order did you like the characters? (1-6)
Luke Skywalker_____
Ben Kenobi_____
Han Solo_____
Princess Leia Organa_____
Governor Moff Tarkin_____
Darth Vader_____

9 In what order did you like the non-human characters? (1-3)
Artoo-Detoo (R2-D2)
See Threepio (C-3PO)
Chewbacca the Wookie_____

10 Which other characters did you like?____

11 Which character did you like best?____

12 Which scene did you like the best?
Jawas kidnap Artoo-Detoo and sell the robots._____
Luke in the spaceport cantina bar._____
Freeing the princess in the Death Star detention area._____
Garbage/trashmasher room._____
Luke and the princess swing across the metal canyon._____
Darth Vader-Ben Kenobi light saber fight._____
Escape from the Death Star air battle._____
End space battle over Death Star._____

13 Which other scenes did you like?____

14 What, if anything, didn't you like about the film?________________________________

15 Is there any place where the plot was confusing?_________________________________

16 Which "team" did you like best?
R2-D2 and C-3PO_____
Han Solo and Chewbacca_____
Ben Kenobi and Darth Vader_____
Luke and the Princess_____

17 Had you heard about STAR WARS before the screening?

Teaser Trailer____	SF or Comic Fanzines_____	Radio_____
Comic Book_____	Magazines_____	Television_____
Novel_____	Newspapers_____	SF or Comic Conventions_____

18 Further comments on back of questionnaire.

The original "preview questionnaire" given to attendees of the Northpoint Theatre screening of Star Wars *on Sunday, May 1, 1977.*